Complete Guide to Financial Management
for Small and Medium-Sized Companies

Complete Guide to

for Small

Prentice-Hall Inc.

Financial Management
and Medium-Sized
Companies

Donald S. Brightly and the
Prentice-Hall Editorial Staff

Englewood Cliffs, N.J.

*Complete Guide to Financial Management
for Small and Medium-Sized Companies
by Donald S. Brightly and the
Prentice-Hall Editorial Staff*

PRENTICE-HALL INTERNATIONAL, INC., *London*
PRENTICE-HALL OF AUSTRALIA, PTY. LTD., *Sydney*
PRENTICE-HALL OF CANADA, LTD., *Toronto*
PRENTICE-HALL OF INDIA PRIVATE LTD., *New Delhi*
PRENTICE-HALL OF JAPAN, INC., *Tokyo*

LIBRARY OF CONGRESS
CATALOG CARD NUMBER: 74–140095

PRINTED IN THE UNITED STATES OF AMERICA
ISBN-0-13-160184-9
ENCYCLOPEDIA

HOW TO USE THIS READY REFERENCE

As financial manager you bear direct responsibility for the financial performance of your firm. It rests with you to take the initiative in solving problems and making improvements in the financial sector. The pressure of time and diversity of duties can make the unsolved problems *seem* insoluble. Ultimately these unresolved issues will persist until the financial manager takes direct action. Business suffers more from decisions not made and improvements not attempted than poor decisions. This book seeks to motivate the financial manager to take action and to guide him to the best course of action. The book spells out specific workable plans and methods which will solve these problems. Many of the methods can be applied directly. Others may require modification.

The book has been developed for use by busy managers. Each chapter is independent of the others and can be studied without referring to previous chapters. For instance, in the case of credit policy and techniques the reader need only turn to the chapter on receivables and quickly find the answers to his questions.

The busy manager has little time to master the many specialized skills within finance. Topics such as taxes and insurance could each become a manager's full-time project. In small and medium-sized companies the financial manager must be his own expert in all areas, and for this reason the Guide covers all major areas of finance. It provides the important concepts and techniques. Within a topical format it lays out step-by-step ways to improve the financial operation of the firm. These detailed methods are the major substance of the book.

The financial manager who wants to take a fresh look at his department or try a new approach can use this book. Systems and the reports they produce start to decay soon after they are installed. Minor changes are made. Personnel change jobs and more alterations take place. Eventually the original purpose is forgotten. The modified system may be carried on for years with no review of its effectiveness. Newer systems make obsolete parts of older systems and further distort their purpose. The man with an overview of this process is the financial manager. The book helps him review the important systems required for financial control.

The readership of this book should include financial managers and people interested in financial management. Such people understand the basic principle of finance. Many of them are interested in applying these principles to their jobs. They can be found in companies of all sizes under a variety of job titles. These titles include president, financial vice president, treasurer, controller and accountant. Although profit improvement is emphasized, the management of non-profit organizations would find this book very helpful. Because of its comprehensive nature it will prove an invaluable aid to the newly-appointed financial manager.

860

CONTENTS

Complete Guide to Financial Management
for Small and Medium-Sized Companies

1

The Financial Manager's Job

1

The Financial Manager's Job

The treasurer is the financial executive who serves as custodian of a corporation's funds, retaining them in trust for the benefit of the corporation, and disbursing them when authorized. The controller is the financial executive who serves as chief accountant, exercising control through accounting, auditing, and budget planning.

Though these duties represent the basic activities of the treasurer and controller, as we will observe when we describe their functions in detail later, the finance officer today shoulders a growing array of new challenges and responsibilities.

Gone are the days when the finance officer was nothing more than a guardian of assets. He is now a leader and planner whose council is heard before important decisions are made. In addition to financial matters, his influence penetrates all areas of business activity—research, marketing, production, statistics, computers, office systems, personnel. Business surveys show that financial executives are playing an increasing role in overall corporate management. Many more are getting there on the wings of a technological revolution called electronic data processing.

THE FINANCE OFFICER AND THE COMPUTER

It was just two decades ago that an electronic computer first solved a data processing problem. Now there are over 60,000 EDP systems in operation. These systems are undergoing extensive exploitation as business seeks not merely a faster way for doing routine operations, but a more profitable tool for solving management problems.

Since the accounting department of a firm generally receives and produces the most data, it is not surprising that computers first move into the office of the chief accountant. The preparation of payrolls, financial statements, and budgets are among the first to be handed over to a computer. In determining the impact of new systems on a firm, management must rely substantially on the finance officer's judgment.

3

EDP places the financial man on the ground floor of a technical change. Whether he rides this change to the heights of "EDP director" depends very much on his talents and adaptability, on whether he not only grasps what is new today, but also foresees the trends of tomorrow.

Of the 30,000 EDP systems in operation, more than 50 percent have already become obsolete. Equipment for replacements and new installations provide for more sophisticated uses.

The most important advances are taking place in integrated management-information systems for decision making and control. This is a business intelligence system that goes far beyond the gathering of typical accounting information. It processes a broad range of data—from production to marketing to finance to plant layout—in order to make all kinds of information available for "total management." Firms that most successfully link problem solving with their accounting and finance system will stand the best chance of competing in the years ahead.

THE FINANCE OFFICER AND PUBLIC POLICY

The modern breed of finance officer has an imaginative and searching viewpoint and recognizes the value of new methods; he also possesses another quality that is equally important; he is assertive.

Until fairly recently, the average treasurer and controller was the trusted employee who rather passively accepted established routines in husbanding his firm's resources. Now, however, many of his colleagues are making their views known outside their companies as well as within.

For example, they speak before the Accounting Principles Board of the American Institute of Public Accountants to help insure the establishment of proper accounting principles. And when Congress studies new tax legislation, such as the abolition of an excise tax or the accelerated depreciation of an asset, they give their views to the legislators in an effort to help make the final legislation stand the test of time.

In such ways as these, the finance officer has emerged from internal company management and has extended his influence beyond his immediate company, joining with college professors and government economists in making public policy. This development augurs well for everyone—the finance officer himself, his company, and society in general, for the greatest advances are most often made when theory and practice become fused.

The dynamic forces in financial management are enabling the finance officer to become a catalyst for bringing new concepts and procedures into practical use. His basic authority flows from the duties specifically assigned to him, usually by the corporate bylaws. Since he could not play a major part in management without this authority, we will now examine the functions typically designed for treasurers and controllers, noting their relationship to other members of the corporate hierarchy. Then, by learning how controllers spend their time, we will see how formally prescribed duties become translated into action.

FUNCTIONS OF THE TREASURER

The treasurer in a business corporation is the financial executive who is essentially responsible for all the functions which are classified under the general heading of "money management." As we have noted, this means that the treasurer serves chiefly as the custodian of a corporation's funds. He retains the corporate funds in trust for the benefit of the corporation and disburses funds only when authorized.

In many companies, the treasurer serves in other corporate capacities, such as a director, or as a vice president of finance. In smaller companies he also serves as a controller. The position of controller exists primarily among larger companies. The two positions are closely related; the treasurer is responsible for money management activities, the controller serves as chief accountant and financial planner.

Duties Assigned to Treasurer by Bylaws

An examination of the bylaws of many corporations shows a wide variety of functions delegated to the treasurer. This is due to the differences in the general organization of many corporations. The following are the duties usually assigned to the treasurer by the bylaws. This list is comprehensive; in many corporations, some of the powers listed here may be delegated to the controller, secretary, or auditor, rather than to the treasurer.

1. Supervising, having custody of, and assuming responsibility for all funds and securities of the corporation.
2. Maintaining bank accounts in designated banks.
3. Making books and records available to any of the directors during business hours.
4. Preparing statements on the company's financial condition for all regular meetings of the directors, and a complete report at the annual meeting of stockholders.
5. Receiving monies due to the corporation.
6. Maintaining records giving a full account of monies personally received and paid for by the corporation.
7. Signing certificates of shares in the capital stock of the company (together with the president or vice president).
8. Signing all checks, bills of exchange, and promissory notes, with such other officer as the board of directors may designate.
9. Advising the corporation on financial matters.
10. Maintaining custody of the stock book, and preparing dividend payments.
11. Preparing and submitting tax reports.
12. Performing all other duties connected with the office, and any duties that the board of directors may assign.

Duties Assigned to Treasurer by Directors, Committees, and Officers

Bylaw provisions are often brief, and many of the treasurer's duties are delegated to him by special action of the board of directors or of its committees, and by direction of higher executive officers, such as the president and the chairman of the board. These duties are either of a temporary character, usually terminating in a report to the board, or are of a general nature, representing permanently assigned functions.

Typical functions delegated by special authorization and assignment are investigation for the development of pension plans and group insurance plans; examination of companies in which the corporation contemplates purchasing an interest; arranging for listing the company's securities on the stock exchange; and investigation of the feasibility of stock offerings.

THE TREASURER'S MAJOR AREAS OF RESPONSIBILITY

1. *Provision of Capital.* Establishing and executing programs for providing capital need by the business, including procurement of capital and maintaining required financial arrangements.

2. *Investor Relations.* Establishing and maintaining an adequate market for the company's securities and maintaining liaison with investment bankers, financial analysts and shareholders.

3. *Short-Term Financing.* Maintaining adequate sources for the company's current borrowing from commercial banks and other lending institutions.

4. *Banking and Custody.* Maintaining banking arrangements for receiving, holding and disbursing the company's monies and securities, plus responsibility for the financial aspects of real estate transactions.

5. *Credits and Collections.* Directing credit granting and collection of accounts and supervising arrangements for financing sales, as through time payment and leasing plans.

6. *Investments.* Investing the company's funds as required and establishing and coordinating policies to govern investment in pension funds and similar trusts.

7. *Insurance.* Providing coverage as required.

Duties Assigned by Treasurer to Staff

Many treasurers delegate most of the details of their work to members of their staff, giving their attention to the supervision, study, and adoption of procedure consistent with the policies of the corporation.

If a treasurer is in charge of stock books and dividend payments, most of the actual work is performed by the staff. The treasurer, however, ascertains personally whether liquid funds will be available at dividend dates to meet the obligation.

Similarly, when the treasurer is in charge of the interchange of bonds, his staff does the actual work of handling registration and coupon payments. If the treasurer's department is in charge of group insurance plans and employees' saving and profit-sharing funds, the staff, under the direction of the treasurer, keeps the necessary records. And upon the adoption of an employee stock ownership plan, the staff performs the actual detailed work of recording installment payments and stock deliveries.

The extension of credit is usually handled by the credit manager, who has considerable responsibility, but is subject to the authority of the treasurer. In such cases only special matters are brought to the treasurer's attention. In regard to receipts and disbursements, the responsibility is often placed on the cashier, who refers special cases to the treasurer. In many instances, the treasurer issues reports prepared by assistants under his direction.

Assistant Treasurer

The assistant treasurer is the officer of a corporation who assists the treasurer in the care, custody, receipt and disbursement of company funds.

The bylaws of large corporations sometimes provide for one or more assistant treasurers authorized to perform, in the order of their rank, all of the duties of the treasurer in the latter's absence or inability to act. Assistant treasurers perform any duties assigned to them by the treasurer or by the board of directors, and assist the treasurer at all times.

Some treasurers departments follow the policy of assigning as much work as possible to assistants without getting out of touch with the general trend of affairs. This prevents the treasurer from becoming so burdened with detail that he loses sight of more important matters. Assistant treasurers may be delegated nearly all the details of the work of the treasurer's office to enable the treasurer to give most of his attention to outside matters.

If a growing company is financing its expansion through new issues of stocks and bonds, the treasurer's tasks may be confined to the handling of security issues, while the other duties of the office are carried out by an assistant treasurer.

In some cases, specific duties are assigned to the assistant treasurer. For example, the assistant treasurer of a parent company, with subsidiaries in many states, may be required to devote his entire time to tax matters. His full-time job will be to keep constantly informed of the tax status of all subsidiaries and branches and to follow closely all changes in the tax laws of various states. He will also keep a calendar of report dates, and see that taxes are paid within the periods prescribed by law.

In some large corporations, especially where the treasurer performs the function of controller, an assistant treasurer heads up the accounting department.

FUNCTIONS OF THE CONTROLLER

The controller is the financial executive of a large or medium-sized corporation who combines the responsibilities for accounting, auditing, budgeting, profit planning, performance reporting, tax control, and other corporate activities.

The control that controllers exert is based on the word "control" in the indirect sense of making decisions and controlling action toward enabling the company to make profits.

The purest example of the controllership principle in common practice is in budgetary control, which includes all kinds of appraisal and measurement.

The Office of Controller

Although relatively new in American corporations, the office of controller, so described earlier, continues to increase in importance. Legal statutes recognize the existence of the office of controller. The Securities Act of 1933 provides that the registration statement filed with the Securities and Exchange Commission must be signed by the controller of the issuing corporation or by its principal accounting officer, as well as by its other principal officers.

In some corporations, the office of controller is not an elective one; the controller is employed like any other department head. In other corporations, the board of directors elects the controller, and his duties are outlined in the corporate bylaws. In still other corporations, the office of controller is established by act of the executive committee, and the powers and duties are prescribed by resolution of the committee. Some organizations specify the controller's duties in an order signed by the president.

Duties Assigned to Controller

The controller's duties, as assigned to him by the bylaws, by resolution, or by executive order, usually require him to:

1. Serve as the chief accounting officer in charge of the company's accounting books, accounting records, and forms.
2. Audit all payrolls and vouchers and have them properly certified.
3. Prepare the company's balance sheet, income accounts, and other financial statements and reports, and give the president a complete report covering results of the company's operations during the past quarter and fiscal year to date.
4. Supervise the preparation, compilation, and filing of all reports, statements, statistics, and other data that the law requires or that the company president requests.
5. Receive all reports from agents and company departments that are needed for recording the company's general operations or for directing or supervising its accounts.
6. Maintain general control over the accounting practices of all subsidiary companies.
7. Supervise the enforcement and maintenance of the classification of accounts and any other accounting rules and regulations that any regulatory body prescribes.
8. Endorse for the company any checks or promissory notes for deposit, collector, or transfer.
9. Countersign all checks that the treasurer draws against funds of the company or its subsidiaries, except as otherwise provided by the board.

10. Approve the payment of all vouchers, drafts, and other accounts payable, when required by the president or any other persons he designates.
11. Countersign all warrants that the treasurer draws for the deposit of securities in the company's safe deposit boxes or withdrawal therefrom.
12. Appoint the auditor and his staff and set their salaries.
13. Compose a budget showing the company's future requirements as shown by its accounts and the requisitions of the general manager and other officers.
14. Supervise all records and clerical and office procedures for departments of the company and its subsidiaries.
15. Perform any other duties and have any other powers that the board of directors may occasionally prescribe and that the president may assign.

Other Responsibilities Placed on Controllers

The controller's office is often responsible for tax matters, insurance of corporate property, leases, and office management. In some companies, the controller has charge of all service departments such as telephone, messenger service, janitors, filing, mailing, and similar matters.

The controller frequently serves on various committees, such as the finance committee, investments committee, pension board, budget committee, insurance committee, and special committees of various kinds.

The functions of the controller cover a broad field and relate to the activities of all departments, including the treasurer's department. Primarily the controller wields a check on disbursements and receipts of the treasurer. He may approve vouchers before payment, and frequently prescribes the methods for keeping accounts in the treasurer's office.

The controller performs a quasi-official duty in supplying the president or the treasurer with statistical data drawn from the accounting records and from other sources, as a basis for current or future financing of the corporation. Included also as controllership activities are the application of electronic data processing to accounting systems and procedures, and the installation and coordination of paperwork flow.

The controller sometimes acts in an advisory capacity, with his recommendations carried out by the executives in charge of the departments concerned. The controller may recommend accounting procedures for various branches, with implementation left to each branch manager. He frequently cooperates with the sales manager in compiling data for the production budget. He usually works with the factory superintendent or sales executive, as appropriate, to see that purchases remain as low as possible, consistent with production or sales requirements.

Assistant Controller

The assistant controller is charged with assisting the controller in special areas. His qualifications should supplement those of the controller. If a controller's chief training is in accounting, his assistant should be qualified in cost standards, statistics, budgets, or other areas requiring special experience.

Many companies have more than one assistant controller. A company with two assistant controllers may put one in charge of general accounts and budgetary procedures, and the other in charge of cost accounting. A company with three assistant controllers may delegate accounts and accounting methods to one, standards and statistics to another, and budgeting and forecasting to the third.

An assistant controller, in turn, delegates responsibility to supervisors for a certain amount of the routine work. The aim is to relieve the controller of as much detail as possible by apportioning much of the work among subordinates. This leaves the controller free to concentrate on procedures and policy matters.

FITTING THE TREASURER AND CONTROLLER ON THE ORGANIZATION CHART

The treasurer and controller may each report to a member of top management, such as the president (Figure 1-1), or to a financial vice president, if the size and complexity of the corporation are great enough to warrant the additional level of supervision.

Another possibility is illustrated in Figure 1-2, where the controller reports to the treasurer.

Although not shown on these organization charts, the tax department may be a separate organization reporting to the controller or the treasurer.

HOW CONTROLLERS SPEND THEIR TIME

A controller's activities and the extent of his authority depend in part on his technical competence, on the persuasiveness of his personality, and the makeup of the company's executive team. To get a clearer picture of how individual controllers spend their time, the following administrative processes are defined:

1. Planning (setting goals or objectives and determining courses of action);
2. Organizing (identifying areas of jurisdiction and establishing relationship);
3. Staffing (procuring, developing, and maintaining personnel and other resources);
4. Directing (activating or getting things done through others);
5. Controlling (reviewing, evaluating, and improving performance). Directing, or getting things done through others, consumes more time than any other single activity, followed by controlling and planning. Organizing is fourth in time consumption and staffing is fifth. As the size of the company increases the controlling and planning functions consume more time.

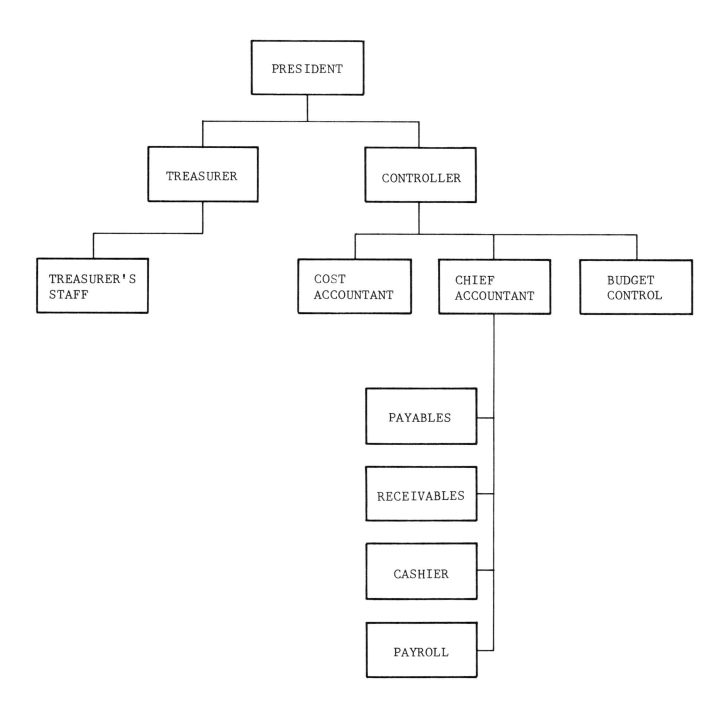

Figure 1-1
Typical Organization Chart

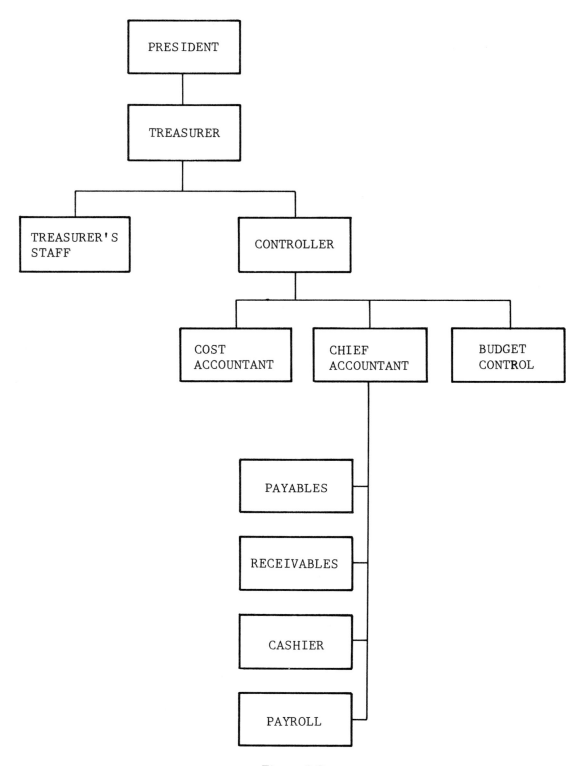

Figure 1-2
Alternate Organization Chart

2

Handling Cash and Making It Work

2

Handling Cash and Making It Work

||||||||||||||||||||||||||||||||||||||||||||||||||||||||||||||||||||||||||||||||||||||||||||||||||||||||||||||||||||||||||||||||||||||||||||||||||||||||||||||||||||||||

CASH—ITS FUNCTION AND IDEAL LEVEL

Cash balances are the credentials which make a company an accepted part of the business community. Corporations have been formed which have no machinery, no airplanes, no contracts and even no employees. But no corporation can exist without cash. The absence of cash to settle liabilities is insolvency. Insolvency for any extended period of time leads to bankruptcy. Protecting the company from a cash shortage is a fundamental responsibility of the financial officer. High cash balances can be as damaging as cash shortages. Cash on hand is a non-productive asset and, as such, earns no return for the stockholder.

The optimum level of cash provides enough security but no more. To determine this a financial manager must decide two things, a basic safety amount and a variable amount. The basic safety amount would, in theory, never be used. The variable amount would be set at seven days' average cash receipts, for example. This variable amount would allow for unforeseen variations in the normal billing, collection, and disbursement cycle. Having decided on an optimum cash level a financial manager would set out to maintain that level.

YOUR CASH—KEEP ALL OF IT WORKING ALL OF THE TIME

Begin with a Cash Budget

Businesses used to keep large amounts of cash on hand at all times—just in case they needed it. Scientific management techniques now make it possible to manage a business prudently while retaining minimum amounts of cash. One of these techniques is cash

15

budgeting—a procedure that helps to control the flow of cash by projecting receipts and disbursements over the budget period.

Some cash budgets, however, fall short of their promise. The accuracy of a cash budget depends on the accuracy of other budgets—sales budget, production budget, labor budget, etc. (See Chapter 8). It also depends on answers to questions such as these:

1. What is the turnover of accounts receivable?
2. How fast do inventories turn over?
3. How much cash should be kept in the bank to discount suppliers' bills and to provide working capital margin? Does the firm's bank require a compensating balance?

Two Key Items

Since the cash budget describes the cash income estimate and the cash disbursements estimate for a stated period, sharp forecasting is essential. This is critically true in the two areas of collections and material purchases.

Collections. A firm's cash income depends very much on the collection of accounts receivable—one of the most important phases of the business. Establishing a sound method for estimating collections is simple for some firms, complicated for others. In either case, the basic method remains the same because estimates must be based on past sales and collection experience.

To project collections, calculate these four experiences over a three-year period:

1. The average sales figure for each month.
2. The average increase in sales.
3. The collection pattern—the proportion of billings for which payment is received the first month, the second month, and the third month.
4. The proportion of uncollectible accounts.

Figure 2-1 illustrates a forecast of monthly collections, based on the above four experiences. The sales figures for each month reflect averages for the past three years, after adding 5 percent for the average annual increase in sales. Collections have formed this pattern: 60 percent of a month's sales is received the first following month, 30 percent the second following month, and 5 percent the third following month. Collections from slow-paying accounts (3 percent) appear in the miscellaneous column. The remaining 2 percent is charged off.

> EXAMPLE: The collections for October, November and December in the current
> year, which must be carried over to January, February, and March of the following
> year, reflect the 5 percent lower sales for the current year.

Some firms sell on discount, others offer 90-day credit, still others sell to prime accounts who almost invariably remit payment within 30 days. Although every business requires a slightly different approach, collections can be forecast with reasonable accuracy, *provided* they are constantly revised to reflect changes as they occur.

Sales	Jan.	Feb.	Mar.	Apr.	May	June	July	Aug.	Sept.	Oct.	Nov.	Dec.	Misc.
Jan. $200,000	(Oct.) 15,200	120,000	60,000	10,000									
Feb. 180,000	(Nov.) 114,000	(Nov.) 19,000	108,000	54,000	9,000								
Mar. 300,000	(Dec.) 239,400	(Dec.) 119,700	(Dec.) 18,850	180,000	90,000	1,500							
Apr. 400,000					240,000	120,000	20,000						
May 350,000						210,000	105,000	17,500					
June 290,000							174,000	87,000	14,500				
July 240,000								144,000	72,000	12,000			
Aug. 220,000									112,000	66,000	11,000		
Sept. 280,000										168,000	84,000	14,000	
Oct. 320,000											192,000	96,000	
Nov. 400,000												240,000	
Dec. 410,000													
Total 3,600,000	368,600	258,700	187,850	244,000	339,000	345,000	299,000	248,550	218,500	246,000	287,000	350,000	108,000

Figure 2-1
Forecast of Monthly Collections

Material purchases. A manager can estimate such items as payroll, taxes, and insurance with a close degree of accuracy. Purchases, however, may pose a nettlesome problem. For a more accurate estimate of material purchases, study your sales forecast in conjunction with the production schedule. Determine material needs on the basis of both production plans and delivery dates. Then, outline projected purchases and due dates for payments, while keeping in mind these variables: (1) revisions in production schedules; (2) failure of suppliers to deliver material; (3) price changes in major items; (4) extra buying because of strikes; unexpected shortages, or announced price increases. The cash outlay for materials must also include an appropriate provision for scrap, damage, or other losses. Be sure to add the amount of these variances to the total standard cost of materials budgeted. Otherwise, the budget will fail to reflect the actual costs you may expect to incur.

The Budget Period and a Common Pitfall

Budget estimates will be most effective if limited to a one-year period. Cash projections become even more useful if you break the annual budget down to show quarterly and monthly subtotals. Some financial managers go a step further and calculate their firm's probable cash position on a weekly basis, or even daily totals. If totals are run monthly, beware of the "Tenth of the month phenomena." The practice of mailing checks on the tenth of the month can lead to a cash shortage between the first and the tenth.

Which method of cash budgeting works best? Financial officers use two methods for preparing cash budgets: (1) the receipts and disbursements method, and (2) the adjusted income method.

In using the *receipts and disbursements method,* the first step consists of listing all sources of cash receipts for the budget period—1 year, for example. Then, break these amounts down into monthly totals. Follow the same procedure for cash payments. The resulting budget will then indicate the cash income and outlay on a monthly basis, and the cash deficit or surplus.

In using the *adjusted income method,* the income statement is adjusted by taking into account non-cash charges and receipts. This means adding depreciation, other non-cash charges, and estimated earnings to cash on hand at the beginning of the period. Principal cash outlays are for fixed assets, retirement of liabilities, payment of dividends, and the like. The resulting balance gives the amount of cash available for non-operating expenses or for investment. It also gives the cash on hand for the beginning of the next budget period.

The adjusted income method works well for spotlighting working capital needs, but it doesn't offer as much control over cash as does the receipts and disbursements method, especially in companies with inconsistent sales and earnings. Most financial officers prefer the receipts and disbursements method (Figure 2-2). This method traces the movement of cash through each item of income and expense, simplifying comparisons of budgeted and actual figures. If cash projections are a particular problem, both methods can be used and the results compared.

		January	
Cash receipts	*Budget*	*Actual*	*Difference*
Opening balance	$121,400	$121,400	$ 0
Cash sales	36,000	35,600	(400)
Charge sales	160,800	159,000	(1,800)
Sales of fixed assets	20,000	19,000	(1,000)
Interest, dividend income	0	0	0
Bank loans	0	0	0
Total cash available	$338,200	$335,000	($3,200)
Cash disbursements			
Wages	25,600	25,800	(200)
Taxes	7,400	7,500	(100)
Insurance	25,200	25,100	100
Material purchases	48,000	49,700	(1,700)
Operating expenses	120,000	121,000	(1,000)
Rent	1,600	1,560	40
Interest expense	2,700	2,900	(200)
Repayment of bank loans	0	0	0
Capital expenditures	20,000	18,000	2,000
Dividends	4,000	4,000	0
Total cash required	$254,500	$255,560	($1,060)
Cash excess	$ 83,700	$ 79,440	($4,260)
or			
Additional cash needed	0	0	0

Figure 2-2
**Typical Cash Budget for One Month — Receipts
and Disbursements Method**

Follow-up with Cash Control Reports

During the cash budget period, the company's cash position must be checked against that envisaged in the cash budget. This information is considered so important that many financial officers require cash reports on a daily basis.

Cash budgets are not set up on a daily basis. Cash receipts and disbursements in any one day are rarely very significant. However, daily reports over a period of several days do indicate whether the rate of flow is proceeding as expected. A daily cash report is normally a simple document (see Figure 2-3). It shows the previous day's cash balance, cash flows for the day, and the day's closing balance.

Despite the importance of cash reports, the finance manager must remember that they give him only a part of the financial picture. For a sound assessment of a firm's cash position at a particular time, he must also know the amounts of accounts receivable and payable, the inventory position, and the accrued payroll. To accomplish this a

August 15, 197___

Balance August 14, 197___	$100,000
Receipts:	
Cash Sales	28,000
Accounts Receivable (collections)	25,000
Other Income	13,000
TOTAL RECEIPTS	$ 66,000
Expenditures:	
Supplies and materials	$ 10,000
Payroll	54,600
Taxes	8,800
Accounts Payable (reduction)	27,000
Other Expenses	4,200
TOTAL EXPENDITURES	$104,600
Balance August 15, 197___	$ 61,400
Balance July 31, 197___	$ 45,300
Forecast Balance for August 15, 197___	60,000
Anticipated Receipts for August 16, 197___	50,000
Anticipated Expenditures for August 16, 197___	100,000

Figure 2-3
Daily Cash Report

Daily Financial Position Report is more meaningful to many financial managers than a simple cash report.

DAILY FINANCIAL POSITION REPORT

This daily report, Figure 2-4, is a management tool and not an accounting record. Quick comparative data is more important than auditor type precision. The report starts with a computation of cash and three comparative figures—Last Month's Budget, Last Month's Actual, and Next Month's Budget. If weekly budgets are kept these comparative figures would be weekly. Next are listed the major cash demands in the next ten days as a reminder and planning guide for the manager. The figures should be a rough estimate based on the number of people on the payroll. The receivables and payables sections are similar to the cash section. The figures entered are control totals from bookkeeping runs—either on machine, accounting systems or manual systems. If cash receipts are posted only twice a week, the cash receipts would be subtracted only twice a week. In that case the comparative data would only be applicable to receivables twice a week when the balances were accurate. The inventory section has two plus quantities—Purchases and Man-Hours. In manufacturing firms the addition to inventory is the sum of purchases and man-hours times a labor and overhead rate. Cost of Sales can be computed as a percentage of Invoices Sent or actually costed out on an item-for-item basis.

Receivables

      Bal. Fwd.   _____ . __

      ADD Daily Billing   + _____ . __

      SUBTRACT credits issued   − _____ . __

      SUBTRACT paid via cash rec. − _____ . __

      ADD Adjustments   + _____ . __

      SUBTRACT Adjustments   − _____ . __

        New Balance

Payables

      Bal Fwd.   _____ . __

      ADD Invoices posted   + _____ . __

      SUBTRACT debits issued   − _____ . __

      SUBTRACT bills paid   − _____ . __

      ADD Adjustments   + _____ . __

      SUBTRACT Adjustments   − _____ . __

        New Balance

Cash

      Bal. Fwd.   _____ . __

      ADD Cash rec'd   + _____ . __

      SUBTRACT Cash disb'd   − _____ . __

        New Balance

Figure 2-4
Daily Financial Position Report

MAJOR PITFALLS OF THE DAILY FINANCIAL POSITION REPORT

The report can be a useful management tool if properly used as a simple quick guide. It is not uncommon for one or both of the following faults to show up.

1. The manager may demand more accuracy than is necessary and subordinates will comply by spending large amounts of time generating each day's flash report.

2. Subordinates may be afraid to estimate and will, without informing the manager, spend and go to great lengths to make the report accurate. Left to their own discretion bookkeepers will try to make the balances on this report equal the general ledger to the penny.

Both situations are to be avoided since they make timely information hard to get and very expensive.

Weekly Cash Meetings Help to Spot Variances

Study each week's activity with top financial personnel and other concerned executives. Seek explanations for variances in the cash budget and probe their influences on future planning. The meeting should result in a decision on the action required to bring results back in line.

Action decisions may be such as these:

1. To change forecasts because of new facts or previous misinterpretations of facts.
2. To change the amount to borrow or pay back next week under your bank loan arrangement.
3. To exert extra effort in a particular area to speed cash flow.
4. To add or remove contingent items.
5. To alter dates for paying major items, when flexibility permits.
6. To determine whether collection trends justify the accounts receivable turnover rate used in calculating income from sales.

Use Monthly Meetings to Appraise Longer-Range Developments

At monthly meetings broader trends and their effects on the monthly, quarterly, semi-annual and annual budgets can be assessed. Items to review at these meetings include financing policies, types of accounts with banks, and timing of new acquisitions and types of funds required. These discussions should include other executives from key areas. The marketing executive can supply data for that all-important area—sales and billings. The purchasing officer can project the receipt of materials based on the orders he has placed. Other division officers can give profitability estimates for their areas of responsibility. These meetings will provide the interchange of information that is so essential for spotlighting slippages in the budget that, if left undetected, could seriously jeopardize anticipated cash flows.

HOW TO MAKE CASH AVAILABLE FASTER

Any company may face occasional cash shortages despite good earnings. They may stem from faulty operating procedures that prolong the interval between the time the firm makes a sale and the time the bank converts the customer's check into usable funds.

This conversion rate directly determines how often a dollar becomes cash during the budget period. The more often a firm turns over its cash supply, the more funds will be available when needed, and the less money will be borrowed. Here are some suggestions for accelerating the availability of funds.

1. Improve the billing procedures. A customer will rarely remit payment before he receives a billing. The longer the delay sending him an invoice, the longer the wait for payment. The objective is to get payment as quickly as possible; you must expedite the transmittal of invoices. A delay of even one day is costly. Example A—If a firm has a daily billing of $60,000, a delay of one day in converting invoices into usable funds, at five and one-half percent, costs $3,300 on an annual basis.

2. Centralize the cash functions. The longer a check is in motion from one processing point to another, the longer it remains unavailable as cash. Centralizing the cash function avoids the "float" that results from a decentralized system.

3. Step up collection procedures. Slow payers use cash while they force others to get along without it. The more funds that are tied up in receivables, the more borrowing must be done. A well-managed collection system quickly reconverts goods sold back into cash, See Chapter 3.

4. Streamline banking arrangements. An important method for making cash more readily available consists of shortening the time lag between payments of funds by customers and the deposit of those funds to a firm's bank account. The banking industry offers several ways to do this.

A. *The "pouch loose" system.* In this procedure, checks from all companies in one city, such as Chicago, drawn on banks in a distant city, such as New York, are sent by air mail to that city in a specially designed and marked pouch. Upon its arrival at the airport, the pouch is taken to the Clearing House where messengers at scheduled times deliver the checks to the various banks. This procedure may save anywhere from seven hours to two days, depending on closeness to weekends or holidays that the checks are mailed.

B. *The "area concentration" system.* Many companies with a great number of distribution centers find it both practical and profitable to regionalize their market areas to speed cash turnover. The company divides its market area into geographic regions, based on the volume of business activity, and selects a depository bank within each region. It then instructs customers to send their checks to a regional company office, which deposits the checks in the regional bank.

This arrangement speeds collections because checks received inside a region and deposited with the regional bank have in the main been drawn on banks within the region. Arrangements are made with the regional bank to keep funds on deposit to meet regional office expenses, and these funds can be drawn by using wire transfers until the account reaches a prearranged minimum.

C. *The "lock box" system.* The lock box system is a refinement of the area concentration system. When using the lock box system, a company regionalizes its market areas as with the area concentration system, but asks its customers to send payment to a post office box instead of a regional company office. The regional bank picks up the checks at the post office box and sends them to the banks on which they are drawn for payment.

Concurrently, the regional bank sends the accounting office a list of the checks, and a photographic reproduction of each check. The accounting or billing department processes these lists and photocopies while the original checks go on their way to being cashed. The checks are often cashed before the accounting process is completed.

The lock box system offers several advantages: it hastens cash availability by one to three or more days; it may eliminate some clerical expenses when volume is heavy; it helps ensure that checks will not be returned for lack of funds.

But it can also be expensive. It costs as much to process a $5.00 check as a $10,000 check. In most cases the lock box system justifies its cost only when a company has a heavy volume of checks of large amounts. The economics involved, however, frequently differ from company to company. A banker can study each situation to determine if this service warrants the cost. When consulting with your banker to determine cost, have this information ready—estimate of how many checks you expect to process annually; estimate of the average check amount; type of check reproduction required; listings desired, etc.

D. *The "bank wire" system.* Another technique for improving cash turnover is the bank wire procedure, which provides for a quick transfer of cash to the point where it is needed. Banks that are members of the bank wire system are connected by telegraph or telephone into a wire network. Each bank has its own special code word, and prefaces its messages with this code word to authenticate a transaction. Within minutes a money transfer of any size is completed. Any bank that is not a member of a wire network can take advantage of these services through a member bank with which it corresponds.

OTHER WAYS TO MAKE FULL USE OF CASH

Take advantage of cash discounts. Cash discounts may be viewed as bonuses offered to customers for advance payment. Cash discounts are typically stated as:

(1) 2/10, net 30
(2) 3/10, E.O.M.

The first set of terms means that the seller will reduce the customer's bill by 2 percent for submitting payment within 10 days. Otherwise, he pays the full amount in 30 days. The second set of terms permits the purchaser to deduct 3 percent for payment by the 10th of the month following the invoice date, with the full amount payable by the end of the month.

These discounts offer significant savings. On a $1,000 order, terms of "2/10, net 30" permit a savings of $20. Another way of recognizing the value of this arrangement is to consider the loss incurred by *not* taking the discount. By paying the full amount in 30 days, the buyer pays 2 percent interest for using $1,000 for only 20 days. In this example, he would pay $1 interest per day for holding onto his money. In terms of yearly interest rates—the only true basis for measuring money costs—this equals $365 a year, or 36.5 percent on $1,000. As a corollary of the rule to take advantage of cash discounts, there is also the rule that where no discount is available, the payment should be made at the last possible date, consistent with the maintenance of good credit standing. Thus, with a net 30 day account, payment should be made at the end of the 30 days.

Manufacturers and wholesalers offer a variety of credit terms free of interest charge. In many industries, payment terms up to 90 days are common, and even longer in seasonal lines. Taking advantage of these terms can help stretch your cash supply.

Lease Instead of Buy

Numerous industries now make available a wide variety of leasing plans that avoid the large initial cash outlay required in making a purchase. Tax-deductibility is an added fillip. Each finance officer must review his own case in detail. Short-range advantages may not always outweigh long-range drawbacks, but as an immediate means of preserving working capital, leasing has great appeal.

WORK IDLE CASH HARDER

Almost every company occasionally has more cash than it needs for the immediate future—the next four to six months or longer. When cash is available to meet near-term obligations and when no benefit, such as a discount, can be gained by making advance payment, that idle cash can be put to work in income-producing investments.

Of paramount concern is the safety of the investment, because surplus funds are not intended for investment purposes, but are merely in excess supply for a short period. They will soon be needed to meet upcoming obligations. Fortunately, there are ways for idle cash to earn income and incur virtually no risk.

Bank Time Deposits

Many companies transfer surplus funds from their checking accounts (demand deposit) to savings accounts, or time deposits. The investment manager restricts time deposits to those banks that are insured by the Federal Deposit Insurance Corporation. This government agency insures accounts up to $15,000 in all insured banks. Firms wanting to deposit more than this amount must open accounts with additional banks.

Interest rates on time deposits are regulated either by the Federal Reserve System or by the Federal Deposit Insurance Corporation. Both of these Federal Agencies set their rates at the same levels. This rate varies, depending on economic conditions. Typical rates are 3.5 percent per annum on deposits of less than a year, and 4 percent on deposits of a year or longer.

Savings and Loan Associations

These associations acquire funds by selling shares for the purpose of lending the proceeds for the construction, repair, and purchase of residential property. They are chartered by both Federal and State governments, and deposits of most associations are insured up to $25,000 by the Federal Savings and Loan Insurance Corporation.

An advantage of buying shares in a savings and loan association is that dividends on shares generally amount to more than interest on a time deposit in a commercial bank. A disadvantage is that savings and loan associations are not required to meet withdrawal demands if money is not available. However, they must use substantial proportions of amounts collected on loans to meet outstanding withdrawal requests. In practice, investments are as accessible and safe in insured savings and loan associations as they are in commercial banks.

Treasury Bills

Treasury bills are short-term obligations of the United States Government. The maturity period does not exceed one year, and is generally for three or six months. The

Treasury Department issues these bills in denominations of $1,000, $5,000, $10,000, $100,000, $500,000 and $1,000,000. Two batches of bills are sold every week on a discount basis in the open market. Income from a Treasury bill is represented by the difference between the purchase price and the maturity value. This return varies, but it has been above 3.5 percent on an annual basis.

Business corporations comprise the largest group of Treasury bill holders, with total corporate holdings estimated at more than $25 billion dollars. Since an issue matures every week, Treasury bills offer an ideal media for investing idle funds that will not be needed for three to six months.

Treasury Certificates

Treasury certificates have maturities ranging from six months to one year. They are issued as the Government's need for cash arises, and not weekly, as are bills. It is generally possible, however, to buy any amount of outstanding certificates through banks and other brokers in government securities. The certificates have a coupon attached providing for the payment of principal and interest at maturity.

Negotiable Time Certificate's Deposit

Banks introduced negotiable time certificates of deposit in 1960 to lure back corporate funds that had been disappearing into other short-term securities that we describe in this section. The "CDs," as they are called, have become phenomenally popular. They now represent the second most important money-market instrument, surpassed in volume only by Treasury bills. Corporate holdings now amount to over $11 billion.

What is a CD? A CD is a bank time deposit, but unlike other time deposits, the CD draws interest and is negotiable. Under the provisions of the CD, the bank provides as evidence of the time deposit a negotiable certificate of deposit, payable to the order of the named depositor or to bearer. The corporate treasurer can select any maturity ranging from 3 months to 1 year.

Interest. The interest rate on CDs is calculated on a 360-day basis and depends on conditions in the money market, but it has invariably been above the Treasury bill rate by amounts ranging from 0.15 percent to 0.40 percent, depending on fluctuations in the bill rate. However, CDs with a popular maturity date (as just before a tax date) often trade at a spread as low as 10 basis points (1/10 of 1 percent) above the rate on similarly dated Treasury bills. Although CDs compete with all short-term instruments for corporate funds, financial officers see them competing most directly with commercial finance paper. When the rates of these two instruments differ by as much as ⅛ of 1 percent, there is a noticeable flow of funds from the lower to the higher paying investment.

The CD gives the corporate investor the benefits of the time deposit (interest) while avoiding the time deposit's disadvantage (poor liquidity). Banks generally require a notice of 30 days before releasing time deposit funds, but the negotiable form of the CD gives it high liquidity, since the principal and interest are guaranteed by the depository bank.

Bankers' Acceptances

Bankers' acceptances, sometimes called "time drafts," are time bills of exchange, drawn on and accepted by a bank or trust company. Companies use bankers' acceptance to finance the sale of manufactured goods or raw goods in large quantity, either through export-import channels or in domestic transactions.

How they originate. Suppose that Walters, in New York, wants to purchase a large shipment of goods from LeBlanc, in Paris. To finance the purchase, Walters asks his bank to issue a commercial letter of credit in favor of LeBlanc. This letter permits LeBlanc to draw a time draft on Walters' American bank, which LeBlanc discounts with his local bank in Paris so as to have immediate use of the funds. The Paris bank then forwards the draft with the appropriate documents to the American bank, which, if everything is in order, "accepts" the draft, and thereby substitutes its credit for that of Walters'.

There is a broad market for the purchase and sale of bankers' acceptances, with about $4 billion worth outstanding. They offer liquidity, safety, and usually a higher rate of return than Treasury bills and commercial paper. A local bank, or its correspondent, has probably created a number of acceptances. If a bank cannot offer an acceptance from its own supply, it can enter the market and bid for a prime acceptance on a customer's behalf.

Commercial Paper

Commercial paper is unsecured promissory notes issued by industrial and finance companies with excellent credit ratings to raise short-term funds. These notes are usually sold payable to bearer on a discount basis, although interest-bearing notes are also available. Some companies issue 3-day paper, but for the most part, maturities range from 5 to 270 days for prime finance paper (notes issued by leading finance companies), and from 30 to 120 days for prime industrial paper (notes issued by leading industrial firms). Denominations range from $1,000 to $5,000,000. An investor in commercial paper can usually select the day the note is to be issued and select the maturity date. This gives the advantage of having funds become available on a predetermined date to match specific commitments.

Federal agency issues. Securities issued by various U.S. Government agencies enjoy wide acceptance by corporate finance officers because of their investment merits and favorable yields. Their popularity in the public market is reflected by a growing similarity in yields between them and Treasury obligations, but securities of government agencies still offer a higher yield. The agency is solely responsible for its obligation. The Federal government assumes no liability, but it does maintain an interest in these obligations through supervision and, in many cases, through capital ownership.

There are six Federal agencies whose securities make excellent short-term investments:

1. Federal Home Loan Bank. The Federal Home Loan Bank System consists of 11 government-supervised banks, organized to stabilize the home financing field. These banks issue consolidated notes and bonds, having maturities up to 1 year, backed by all 11 banks.

2. Federal Land Banks. There are 12 Federal Land Banks that offer long-term mortgage credit to farmers. Loans may not exceed 65 percent of the appraised value of the property offered as security. Their consolidated bonds, with maturities up to 1 year, are secured joint-and-several obligations of the 12 banks.

3. Federal Intermediate Credit Bank. There are 12 of these banks, established to provide seasonal credits for the production and marketing needs of farmers and stockmen. The banks raise their lending funds chiefly by selling short-term consolidated collateral trust debentures, having a maturity of 9 months or less.

4. Federal National Mortgage Association (Fannie Mae). This Association buys and sells mortgages insured by the Federal Housing Administration or guaranteed by the Veterans Administration. Its borrowings from the public provide it with funds to repay the Treasury for previous advances.

5. Banks for Cooperatives. A Central Bank for Cooperatives and 12 District Banks were created by the Farm Credit Act of 1933 to make credit available to eligible cooperative associations owned or controlled by farmers. Banks for Cooperatives sell to the public collateral trust debentures, with maturities up to 1 year, that are the joint-and-several obligations of the 13 banks.

6. Tennessee Valley Authority. TVA is a corporate agency of the Federal government, established to develop the Tennessee River and other resources of the Tennessee Valley. TVA sells bonds and notes, with maturities up to 1 year, to finance its power program and to refund such bonds.

Five of the six Federal agency issues have the same tax status as Treasury obligations —interest earned is subject to Federal taxes, but exempt from state and local taxes. Securities of the Federal National Mortgage Association are taxed by all three levels of government: Federal, state and local. To avoid sacrificing income for unneeded liquidity, consider investing some of excess cash in high-grade, short-term, tax-free securities.

Tax-Free Securities

The first step is to segregate surplus cash into two categories: a reserve for unpredictable needs, and money set aside to meet planned disbursements, such as tax or dividend payments, progress money on contracts, and the like. The excess cash set apart for unpredictable needs to securities must have the greatest liquidity, such as Treasury obligations and Federal agency issues. Less than maximum liquidity is needed for planned disbursements. So why pay for maximum liquidity? An investor gets an extra ⅛ to ½ or 1 percent in tax-free basis points by holding the following securities to maturity.

1. Public Housing Authority temporary notes. Local agencies of the Public Housing

Authority, organized under local state laws, develop and administer low-rent housing projects. Obligations issued by these agencies prior to permanent bond financing are called "temporary notes." These notes are unconditionally secured by the Public Housing Administration.

2. Housing and Home Finance Agency preliminary loan notes. Local public housing and development agencies issue "preliminary loan notes" to finance slum clearance and urban redevelopment projects. These notes are secured by the local agency and the United States of America acting by and through the administrator of the Housing and Home Finance Agency.

3. State and local housing obligations. These either are direct obligations of the state concerned or are guaranteed by it, and are treated as "full faith and credit" instruments. Major issuers of this type are Connecticut, Massachusetts and New York State.

4. Other notes of states and municipalities. Another broad category of short-term securities arises from borrowing by states and municipalities, either in anticipation of taxes or other revenue, or in anticipation of longer-term bond financing.

A word of warning is appropriate with respect to the use of tax-free securities, when the corporation has debt outstanding. For many years there has been a rule that for Federal income tax purposes, the interest deduction would be disallowed with respect to interest on money borrowed to carry tax-exempt securities. The courts seem now to be accepting the interpretation that the funds need not be traced specifically to the tax-exempt security. Thus, if a corporation purchases a tax-exempt security, rather than paying off the interest-bearing debt, interest on an equivalent amount of interest-bearing debt may be disallowed. As a result of these rulings, some corporate treasurers consider it safest to avoid the use of exempt securities altogether.

Select the maturity that fits the investment planning. Corporations don't have to hold tax-exempt securities to maturity, but it's to their advantage to do so. The originators of these securities try to make it easy to find a security that meets each investment schedule by tailoring maturities to the requirements of most corporate investors. For example, the largest obligor—the Public Housing Authority—schedules most of its short-term financing to mature on quarterly tax and dividend dates. Securities that mature on quarterly dates are of greater value to most corporations than securities that mature on intermediate dates and command a better price. If the exact maturity can not be found, it will usually be advantageous to take a nearby shorter date and fill in the unexpired investment period with other short-term obligations.

A REFERENCE TABLE FOR CASH INVESTMENT

The use of the table in Figure 2-5 is a quick reference guide for help in selecting the best investment for your surplus cash.

BE SURE TO MAINTAIN A MINIMUM CASH BALANCE

The finance manager must maintain adequate working capital to maintain the flow of capital from cash to inventories to receivables and back to cash. This means that it is important not only to maintain an adequate margin of current assets over current lia-

	Obligation	Marketability	Maturities	Denominations	Basis
United States Treasury bills	U.S. Government obligation. U.S. Treasury auctions 3- and 6-mos. bills weekly. Also offers, through special auctions, one-year maturities and tax anticipation bills.	Excellent secondary market.	Up to 1 year.	1M to 1MM	Discounted. Actual days on a 360-day year.
Prime sales finance paper	Promissory notes of finance companies placed directly with the investor.	No secondary market. Companies under certain conditions will usually buy back paper prior to maturity. Most companies will adjust rate.	Issued to mature on any day from 30 to 270 days.	1M to 5MM	Discounted or interest bearing. Actual days on a 360-day year.
Dealer paper I. Finance	Promissory notes of finance companies sold through commercial paper dealers.	No secondary market. Buy-back arrangement can usually be negotiated through the dealer	Issued to mature on any day from 30 to 270 days.	5M to 5MM	Discounted or interest bearing. Actual days on a 360-day year.
Dealer paper II. Industrial	Promissory notes of leading industrial firms sold through commercial paper dealers.	No secondary market.	Usually available on certain dates between 60 & 180 days.	5M to 5MM	Discounted. Actual days on a 360-day year.
Prime bankers' acceptances	Time draft drawn on and accepted by a banking institution, which in effect substitutes its credit for that of the importer or holder of merchandise.	Good secondary market. Bid usually 1/8th of 1% higher than offered side of market.	Up to 6 months.	25M to 1MM	Discounted. Actual days on a 360-day year.
Negotiable time certificates of deposit	Certificate of a time deposit at a commercial bank.	Good secondary market.	Unlimited.	500M to 1MM	Yield basis. Actual days on a 360-day year. Interest at maturity.
Short-term tax-exempts I. Temporary & preliminary notes of local public housing agencies	Notes of local agencies secured by a contract with Federal agencies. Also pledge of "full faith & credit" of U.S.	Good secondary market.	Up to 1 year.	1M to 1MM	Yield basis. Thirty-day month on a 360-day year. Interest at maturity.
Short-term tax-exempts II. Tax & bond anticipation notes	Notes of States, municipalities or political subdivisions.	Good secondary market.	Various, usually 3 mos. to 1 year from issue.	1MM to 1MM	Yield basis. Usually 30 days on a 360-day year. Interest at maturity.

Figure 2-5
Guide to Money-Market Investments

bilities, but that it is also important to see that cash represents an appropriate proportion of the total current assets. Both trade creditors and banks give first attention to a corporation's cash account.

Trade Suppliers' View of Cash Holdings

Suppliers do not sell on account to every company that asks for this service. They base their decision on an assessment of whether the prospective buyer will be able to pay within the credit period. This means that they concentrate their attention on the buyer's cash holdings, along with his entire working capital position. Consider the different cash positions of these two corporations having identical total current assets.

CORPORATION X

Current Assets		Current Liabilities	
Cash	$6,000	Accounts payable	$48,000
Accounts receivable	72,000	Accrued wages	6,000
Inventories	90,000	Notes payable	18,000
Total Current Assets	$168,000	Total Current Liabilities	$72,000

CORPORATION Y

Current Assets		Current Liabilities	
Cash	$28,000	Accounts payable	$48,000
Accounts receivable	48,000	Accrued wages	6,000
Inventories	92,000	Notes payable	18,000
Total Current Assets	$168,000	Total Current Liabilities	$72,000

At first glance, it appears that both corporations offer a supplier equal security for a credit sale, but a closer look reveals marked differences. Although the dollar amounts of their working capital are equal ($96,000), a credit manager would notice that Corporation X has only about one-fifth as much cash as Corporation Y. Corporation X could pay off less than 8 percent of its current liabilities out of its cash holdings, whereas Corporation Y could pay off almost 40 percent of its current liabilities.

If some of the inventory became difficult to sell, or if many of the accounts receivable became uncollectible, Corporation X would be hurt much more than Corporation Y. Though a credit manager might not reject Corporation X's credit application, he would grant Corporation Y's application much more readily, all other considerations being equal.

Financial managers must never succumb to the temptation to lower their standards for minimum cash balances when money is in short supply. It is at these times that trade suppliers can be particularly selective, causing a firm to exhaust its cash balance and to find no one willing to lend it—the very situation that the minimum cash balance is designed to prevent.

A bank may require a compensating balance. The lending capacity of commercial banks stems largely from deposits left with them by their customers, rather than from the proceeds of the sale of stock to stockholders. Therefore, when considering an application for a loan, bankers give preference to those who strengthen this lending capacity by leaving substantial balances with them. Especially is this true during times of tight money—when loan applications exceed money supply. During such times, bankers may not be willing to make even a small loan to a firm that doesn't have a qualifying minimum balance.

In addition, commercial banks often stipulate that borrowers must maintain a balance equal to a stated percentage of the loan, usually about 10 or 15 percent. These are called compensating balances; they not only expand the bank's lending capacity, they also give it a higher rate of interest than that stated in the loan contract. This arrangement places a certain burden on the borrowing firm, but partially offsetting this disadvantage are the reduced service charges that most banks offer their best customers, such as the free processing of checks drawn on the account, and notes taken for collection.

Counteract the Compensating Balance with Link Financing. From the borrower's viewpoint, a compensating balance has the drawback of raising the interest rate on his bank loan. For example: The Smith Company borrows $2,000,000 from its bank at 5 percent interest or $100,000 a year. But if the company must keep a 20 percent compensating balance with the bank, its effective interest cost rises to 6.25 percent, since it is paying $100,000 for the use of $1,600,000.

How Link Financing Works

Under link financing, a firm can make full use of a bank loan by having an insurance company (or mutual or pension fund) replace the compensating balance at prevailing interest rates. Here's how the arrangement works.

1. After first getting the bank's approval for a substitution deposit, the insurance company is given the requirements and other information.
2. The insurance company deposits with the bank an amount equal to the required compensating balance, usually in the form of a Certificate of Deposit that carries a specified maturity date.
3. If the deposit must be made for longer than 1 year—the normal maximum period—the firm can ordinarily renew the deposit without renegotiation.
4. Upon retirement of the bank loan the substitute deposit is returned to the insurance company, along with interest, usually at the rate of 5 percent.

Chief advantages of link financing. Two chief advantages accrue from using link financing to replace compensating balances.

1. *The total interest rate declines.* As noted earlier, 5 percent on a $2,000,000 loan is nominally $100,000 but the effective rate is 6.25 percent, only $1,600,000 is actually available. When paying 5 percent for link financing $400,000 for a year, the total interest for the bank loan plus the substitution deposit comes to $120,000, or 6 percent. Thus, .25 percent less interest is paid when a firm maintains its own compensating balance.

2. *The compensating balance is now available for full use.* If the freed capital generally brings a return of 10 percent, the gain is 4 percent, or a dollar-profit increase of $16,000 (4 percent × $400,000).

These advantages apply to companies that need all the money they can get—a situation typical of firms that must build up inventories to deliver products during seasonal peaks. But the value of these advantages diminishes to the extent that a borrower needs a day-to-day working balance that approaches the required compensating balance.

Fees as a Substitute for Compensating Balances

Historically, banks have insisted on compensating balances, not only in connection with certain loans, but also in connection with a number of other services which the bank performed. As banks have become more sophisticated and competition among them has become more intense, there has been a willingness to negotiate with important customers as to the value of the services performed. It is then possible to pay a cash fee to the bank in lieu of maintaining an additional compensating balance. This sort of negotiation merely recognizes that the funds may have a greater value to the customer than to the bank, so that a cash fee can provide the bank with the profit it had hoped for, without depriving the customer of an equivalent value.

3

Streamlining Credit and
Collection Management

3

Streamlining Credit and Collection Management

||||||||||||||||||||||||||||||||||||||||||||||||||||||||||||||||||||||||||||||||||||||||||||||||||||||||||||||||||||||||||||||||||||||||||||||||||||||||||||||||||||||||||||||||||||||||||||||

RESPONSIBILITY FOR CREDIT MANAGEMENT

Because of the need to maintain a steady flow of cash into a firm's treasury, credit management is generally the responsibility of the treasurer or controller, usually the treasurer. Many companies have a credit manager who is responsible to the treasurer. This arrangement is popular when there is enough credit work to require the full-time services of at least one man.

Among companies not having enough credit and accounts receivable work to keep a credit manager busy, the treasurer usually performs these duties in addition to his other responsibilities. Occasionally the credit department is under the chief sales executive, who may be called the sales manager, vice president of sales, or vice president of marketing.

WHERE TO FIND CREDIT INFORMATION

An informed decision on the granting of credit must be based on information about the customer's three C's: his character, his capacity, and his capital. The more complete the information, the more reliable the judgement. Fortunately, the credit manager can turn to a variety of sources for aid in making a sound decision.

Mercantile Agency Reports

Mercantile agencies are organizations formed to supply credit information on virtually all business concerns in the United States and Canada. There are two types of mercantile agencies: general and special.

General mercantile agency. The general mercantile agencies—among which Dun & Bradstreet, Inc., is by far the largest—report and analyze the credit of every business in almost every field. Few credit men can have access to complete and current credit information without a subscription to the service of Dun & Bradstreet or of some other agency. The *Dun & Bradstreet Reference Book,* for example, is published every two months, and gives credit ratings for more than 3,000,000 firms. In addition, the subscription rate usually entitles the credit department to a certain number of comprehensive reports on individual companies. An example of such a report is shown in Figure 3-1.

Figure 3-1
Dun & Bradstreet Report

Special mercantile agency. In addition to the general agency, there are special mercantile agencies that limit their credit analyses to a particular field. Examples are the Jewelers Board of Trade, the Electrical Wholesale Credit Bureau, and the Lyon Furniture Mercantile Agency. Although a credit manager must avail himself of these services if he is to do his job properly, he must not forget that these sources of information merely guide his decision. Information from mercantile agencies must be analyzed and considered in light of information received from other sources.

Credit Interchange Among Suppliers

Complete credit information on prospective buyers is so essential to profitable operations that business firms find it to their advantage to freely exchange credit information about their customers. This practice—called the interchange of ledger information—consists of credit men exchanging the following standard items of information about a customer:

1. *Period of experience with the account and date of last sale.* A supplier's credit experience with an account over a long period clearly reveals the customer's paying habits.
2. *Highest recent credit.* This figure shows the maximum amount of credit the supplier extended to the customer during the past twelve months. (This figure does not necessarily represent the customer's credit limit.)
3. *Amount owing.* This is the account's present balance taken from the ledger.
4. *Amount past due.* The customer may be a poor risk if several suppliers report that he is behind on payments.
5. *Credit terms.* The customer's ability to pay is open to question if the terms are shorter than those normally extended.
6. *Payment record.* This information tells whether the customer pays promptly or is "slow pay."

The Bank Can Help

The information that a bank releases about an account is sometimes very helpful to the credit man, who may want to get a general idea of the applicant's balance. However, banks rarely release specific information, unless authorized by the depositor. Information the bank will not ordinarily release includes:

1. Information relating to the depositor's financial statement.
2. Information on depositor's outstanding loans.
3. Information on the exact amount in the depositor's account.

Such terms as "high three-figure balance" or "low five-figure balance" are generally used. When facing a particularly difficult decision, the credit man can sometimes get information from the customer's bank through his own bank. Banks can quickly obtain desired information through their own credit-exchange system. The success of this method depends very much on the reputation of the credit manager and his working relationship with his bank's officers. If the relationship is weak, the financial manager should work to strengthen it. The bank officers will think more of a client which aggressively seeks credit information than one that rarely asks for it.

Salesmen Can Get Special Kinds of Information

Salesmen don't like to collect typical credit information. They feel that questions about a customer's financial condition damage the chance for a sale. But there are special kinds of valuable information that a firm's salesman can glean unobtrusively:

1. *Is the customer an able business man?* A glance at the stock—its quality, style, and price—indicates whether the customer buys wisely and sets competitive prices.
2. *Is the customer's business in a thriving location?* The character of the streets and whether business is moving away from or into the customer's section of town augur well or ill for his business.
3. *Is the community prospering?* Local conditions sometimes affect an entire community. The salesman on the scene knows whether a major industry is shutting down or a new one opening up.
4. *Does the customer enjoy a good reputation among his creditors?* An alert salesman can quickly appraise the customer's local reputation. More important, from direct observation the salesman often can give his credit department names of other creditors.

The Customer Can Also Supply Valuable Information

As a matter of routine, the seller asks the customer to supply trade and bank references. The customer has a natural tendency to list only those creditors that will give him a favorable report, but information learned from these sources helps to fill out the applicant's total credit picture.

The most important item to obtain directly from the customer is his financial statement. A creditor can easily get a financial statement from a credit agency, but there are advantages to getting one directly from the customer. A financial statement in an agency report is sometimes out of date, and it may contain information completed by the agency reporter instead of the customer. In the second place, it is a good practice to ask for financial statements at regular intervals directly from the customer. This procedure encourages him to keep his business in good shape so as to be able to supply a favorable statement.

WHAT TO LOOK FOR IN FINANCIAL STATEMENTS

If a certified public accountant's unqualified report accompanies a financial statement, the credit executive can accept the figures at face value. Without such a report, the creditor must study the statement closely and probe the figures to learn what they really represent. Here are some vital areas where investigation can mean the difference between taking on a profitable account and an uncollectible one.

Cash

Does the cash figure represent the amount of cash on hand and in the bank? Before accepting the amount reported as correct, the credit man must satisfy himself that:
1. Post-dated checks or I.O.U.'s are not included in the cash balance.
2. Outstanding checks have been deducted from the bank balance.
3. The balance is not inflated by inclusion of amounts received after close of balance period.
4. The balance does not include amounts set aside for sinking funds and the like.

Accounts Receivable

This item represents one of the most important assets. The credit executive looks to the total of accounts receivable and cash in determining ability of debtors to meet short-term obligations. Here are some things to look for:
1. Do the accounts receivable include advances to salesmen, loans to officers, or goods shipped on consignment? If so, the statement should segregate these receivables from accounts receivable for merchandise. They have no place in computing the current ratio or the sales-receivables turnover.
2. Is a large part of the accounts receivable due from only a very few customers? If so, do these accounts carry credit insurance?
3. Are the accounts current or past due? It may be necessary to age the receivable to determine their liquidity. In some industries, it is acceptable trade practice to include installment receivables due many years after the balance sheet date.
4. Is the reserve for bad debts adequate? The credit man must use current conditions and trends, previous experience, and the comparison of the average of accounts outstanding with the average terms of credit as guides to the adequacy of bad debt reserves.
5. Is the turnover ratio inflated by inclusion of cash sales with credit sales? Cash sales are often insignificant, but they *can* also be sizable.
6. Are the receivables pledged? Assigned or pledged accounts should be disclosed in the financial statement.

Notes Receivable

Is this account "dressed up" by including notes from partners, officers, stockholders, employees, subsidiaries, or any other similar notes? Only negotiable promissory notes from customers in payment of goods sold and delivered belong in this account.

Trade Acceptances Receivable

In placing a valuation on trade acceptances, the credit manager must seek answers to these questions:

1. Was the acceptance received at the time of the sale? Trade acceptances should originate with the transaction, not as a settlement for a past-due account. Legitimate trade acceptances are generally considered more reliable than open accounts receivable, but improper use of the acceptance lowers its debt-paying value.
2. Does the credit applicant follow the practice of taking acceptances only from doubtful risks? Clearly, acceptances arising from transactions with less reliable customers have questionable credit value.

Inventories

The most dangerous item in a balance sheet is inventory. It can be used to hide operating losses for one, two and even three years. It can easily hide losses due to changes in market price, product obsolescence, and a host of other problems facing businesses. The safest course of action is to ignore inventory. This approach leads to three questions which the credit manager must answer:

1. What would profit have been if inventory were constant for the last two years? If the answer is "No Profit," then the profit exists only in inventory. This is a sure danger signal.
2. What would the trend of gross margin be if inventory were held constant for the past two years? The answer should be slightly less but not drastically reduced. A big drop indicates a company in a price squeeze.
3. What would the liquidity be if inventory were zero valued? This is called the "Acid Test Ratio" and is cash plus receivables divided by current liabilities. Most manufacturing concerns should have an acid test ratio of 1.00 or better. Retailers selling for cash can have a much lower ratio however and still be solvent.

A Quick Inventory Checklist

Besides these factors the questions on the following checklist are useful in analyzing inventory:

1. What part is finished goods? _____
2. What part is work-in-process? _____
3. What part is raw material? _____
4. What part is supplies? _____
5. Are the finished goods saleable? _____
6. What is the value based on:
   physical count? _____

look inventory? _____

estimate? _____

7. Is any inventory pledged as security? _____

SETTING CREDIT LIMITS

After considering all factors, the credit man sets a credit limit for a new customer. A common practice consists of granting an arbitrary amount of credit—$100, $500, or $2,000—for a short trial period of about six months. At the end of the test period, this amount is raised, lowered, or continued, depending on the customer's payment record.

Agency Recommendations

Some special mercantile agencies recommend credit limits for customers of their clients. The recommendations are intended only as a guide, but credit managers generally find the recommendation reliable, and use it as the credit limit for the new customer. Sometimes the credit recommendation is not specific, but is suggested in such terms as "Reasonable trade needs," or "Excellent risk for requirements."

Net Worth Limit

Sellers frequently determine the credit limit of small buyers by selecting a certain percentage of the customer's net worth—5, 10, or 15 percent. Another practice consists of dividing the applicant's net worth by the number of his suppliers. Net working capital also serves as the basis for making calculations. These methods are easy to apply, but credit limits established in this manner do not always indicate actual capacity to pay debts, and are later adjusted to conform with experience. The most effective way to determine a credit limit is by conducting an extensive credit investigation. This investigation uses all the methods we have previously discussed for determining credit limits, and when properly conducted, should lead to an objective study of the credit applicant's financial condition and the determination of an appropriate credit limit.

HOW TO SPOT AN APPROACHING BANKRUPTCY

Buyer's financial conditions continually change. Some thrive and expand their capacity for handling indebtedness; others encounter difficulties and become starved for working capital. A bankrupt tips his hand long before he goes under. An alert treasurer can spot the telltale signs and take steps to help prevent his firm from getting caught with other creditors.

Excuses Signal the First Sign

A debtor that is going bad begins by making excuses for slow payment. These excuses take one or more of these forms:

1. His company is expanding. Any financial officer knows how risky it is for a business to try to expand on meager capital. A customer that frequently offers this excuse is simply saying that he is undercapitalized. Unless corrected, this situation will soon jeopardize the customer's solvency. A seller doing business with an undercapitalized buyer should actively consider reducing or withdrawing the buyer's credit.

2. His bookkeeper made a mistake. When given rarely, this excuse may be valid (though he had better hire a new bookkeeper). When cited repeatedly, however, this excuse may be translated as a stall for time. The creditor is probably paying some customers one month; others the next.

3. He's engulfed in the rush season. If this statement is true, the buyer is confessing that he's a very poor businessman. More than likely, he simply hasn't got the cash. Either way, if the debtor offers this excuse a second time, he is conforming to a dangerous pattern. The credit manager should consider asking for immediate payment.

Other Danger Signs

A potential bankrupt may reveal his plight to an alert credit man in a number of other ways. If the customer cannot offer an acceptable explanation for any of the following situations, the seller must suspect fraud and stop shipments immediately:

1. The financial statement is substantially false.
2. Pertinent records and accounts are withheld from the seller.
3. Salaries and expense accounts are excessively high.
4. Inventory has been sharply reduced for no apparent reason.
5. Inventory has been increased out of proportion to sales.
6. Loans have been suddenly paid off.

FILING A PETITION IN BANKRUPTCY AGAINST A BAD ACCOUNT

To file an involuntary petition in bankruptcy against an insolvent debtor, creditors must prove that the debtor committed one or more of the six acts of bankruptcy within the previous four months. Mere insolvency, no matter how serious, does not give creditors the right to force a debtor into bankruptcy—a status that permits the court to take charge of the debtor's property for the protection of the creditors.

An alleged bankrupt commits an act of bankruptcy when he:

1. Conveys, transfers, conceals, or removes any part of his property, with the intent to hinder, delay or defraud his creditors.
2. Transfers, while insolvent, any portion of his property to a creditor, with intent to prefer such creditor over his other creditors.
3. Permits, while insolvent, any creditor to obtain a lien upon any of his property through legal proceedings, and fails to vacate or discharge such lien within thirty days from that date or at least five days before the date set for any sale or other disposition of the property.
4. Makes a general assignment for the benefit of creditors.
5. Permits, either voluntarily or involuntarily, the appointment of a receiver

or trustee to take charge of his property, while insolvent or unable to pay his debts as they mature.

6. Admits in writing his inability to pay his debts and his willingness to be adjudged a bankrupt.

In an ordinary involuntary petition, where the alleged bankrupt has twelve or more creditors, at least three creditors must sign the petition. Where there are less than twelve creditors, one or more creditors must sign. In either case, the total amount of the petitioning creditors' unsecured claims must be $500 or more.

WHEN TO START LEGAL ACTION

If a client does not respond to normal collection requests, one of two things is happening. Either, the customer wants to negotiate an adjustment in his bill or the customer can't pay. The first case can be solved by a letter from a lawyer and legal action if necessary. This type of account can also be handled by a collection agency. These firms act as arbitrators and can often settle matters which the disputants alone can not agree upon. Before going to a collection agency or a lawyer, the sales department should be notified. If a customer is to be lost in the collection process, the sales department should be told. This does not mean that their permission is required, however.

If the debtor is short of funds and in danger of insolvency, a collection agency will have the same problem collecting which the credit manager has. That problem revolves around the debtor's use of what cash he has available. The debtor will set up a priority list of uses of cash as follows:

1. A minimum reserve held in the bank.
2. Payroll money.
3. Funds to pay payroll taxes.
4. Funds to prevent outsiders from forcing bankruptcy.
5. C.O.D. and other payments to suppliers whose material is essential to continued sales volume.
6. Funds to pay all overdue bills.

When collection letters and stopped shipments do not get results, the credit manager can conclude the following:

1. Funds will not be allocated to obtain more shipments (#5 above).
2. The credit manager must get his firm on the fourth level of priority.
3. To do this he must take legal actions.

The Advantages of Legal Action

By establishing a legal claim against the debtor, the credit manager can improve his legal standing in the following ways:

1. If a reorganization is the outcome, a claim established in court in advance of the reorganization often has preference. As such a larger part, possibly total amount due, can be salvaged.

2. If arrangements are made under the Bulk Sales Act, a prior claim can, depending on the timing, become a preferential claim.

3. In some cases firms which continue under the bankruptcy law can be forced to recognize the oldest court established claims as preferential.

Another major advantage of legal action is that a debtor may fear that one law suit will bring on many more and force bankruptcy. To forestall this possibility he is likely to pay up and prevent the first lawsuit.

The disadvantages of legal action are as follows:

1. The cost of using a lawyer. Depending on the debtor's situation, legal action is not justified on claims less than $500 to $1,000.

2. The time delay involved in processing a claim through the court.

Choice of a Lawyer

The right lawyer given the proper information and instructions can collect from a debtor. The right lawyer is a man in the county or municipality where the suit will be filed. He knows the court, the state laws involved, the debtor's lawyer, and probably the debtor. There are two ways to find a reputable local lawyer—through the corporation's law firm via reference or by recommendation of the local legal association. The local legal association will for ethical reasons supply a list of several lawyers who handle such matters. The instructions to the lawyer must be specific. If he is to start with a threatening letter, a time limit must be set and held to. If immediate legal action is required, the court, the nature of the legal action, and the particulars of the complaint must be laid out. Follow-up contact with the lawyer is required to make sure that the case is receiving proper attention.

A BUSINESS CAN PROTECT ITSELF WITH CREDIT INSURANCE

Any business that sells on credit will have some bad accounts. Credit insurance protects a company against some of the risks that credit management cannot control. It is issued to manufacturers, distributors, and some service companies, especially advertising agencies. It is not available to retailers.

Types of Policies

A company may arrange to have credit insurance apply to accounts that are current at the inception of the policy, and to cover losses occurring within the policy term (the back coverage policy). It also may have the insurance apply to losses stemming from sales made during the policy term (the forward coverage policy). A company may also purchase insurance to cover individual debtors (individual account form) or all debtors as a group (general coverage form). Most credit insurance is written on a back coverage and general coverage form.

How the Deductible Provision Works

The policyholder's cost of commercial credit insurance is less if he assumes part of the risk through two deductible provisions: the primary loss deductible and the coinsurance deductible.

The primary loss deductible specifies an amount that approximates normally expected losses from bad debts, based on the type of business. Normal bad debt losses are not insurable because they are a *certain* loss which both the policyholder and the underwriter would find prohibitively costly to cover.

The coinsurance deductible requires the policyholder to sustain a percentage of credit losses that exceeds the primary loss. This deductible usually amounts to about 10 percent of the insured amount.

The following example illustrates how deductibles work:

Annual sales	$1,000,000
Expected primary bad debt loss of ¼ of 1 percent (varies with type of business)	2,500
Bad debts during year	20,000
Less primary loss deductible	2,500
Less 10 percent coinsurance deductible	1,750
Net to policyholder	$ 15,750

If the insuring company later collects a delinquent account, the policyholder receives an additional sum. Collections are divided between the insurer and policyholder in proportion to the loss each has suffered.

Cost of Credit Insurance

The premium varies with the kind and amount of coverage and the sales volume of the policyholder. Recently, the premium has averaged 91 cents for each $1,000 of goods sold. The premiums paid by most policyholders range between 1/20th and 1/5th of 1 percent of the total sales volume of the insured.

How Credit Insurance Can Help a Company

Credit insurance offers several advantages to the management of a business:
1. It gives a guaranteed value to accounts receivable.
2. It places the collection of overdue accounts with an efficient, reliable agency.
3. It provides a sound basis for bank financing of accounts receivable, since banks can be made collateral beneficiaries of the policy.

4. It reinforces the credit rating of the policyholder.
5. It speeds capital turnover.

Its Disadvantages

As with all types of insurance, the policyholder pays for protection he may never use, and the cost of this protection must be included in a company's prices. Many financial managers feel that a good credit man's long-run losses will be less than the cost of credit insurance. Another matter to consider is that the compulsory collection feature of some credit insurance policies can mar relations with good but slow paying accounts.

Many firms may not need credit insurance. These include companies that (1) factor their receivables, (2) sell to Federal, state, and local governments, (3) use conditional sales contracts or other liens rather than sell on open account, (4) sell on a cash or C.O.D. basis. For further information about commercial credit insurance, it can be obtained with the help of the firm's insurance broker.

MAINTAINING A SUCCESSFUL COLLECTING SYSTEM

One of the treasurer's responsibilities is to see that his credit manager maintains a system for collecting accounts promptly. Since slow collections deny a firm the use of its own capital, prompt collections are vital to the success of any business. Most debtors respect a business that is attentive to its accounts and requires prompt payment.

Keeping Tabs on Accounts Receivable

A successful collection system includes a method of classifying receivables according to the length of time they have been outstanding. This is called "aging accounts."

Importance of aging accounts. The credit manager ages his accounts receivable on a regular basis to pinpoint trouble early and to take the necessary steps to prevent the situation from developing into serious proportions. Firms that are lax in this area of credit management frequently end up with a considerable amount of dead wood on their books.

The credit department usually prepares the aging statement once a month, when it takes the accounts receivable trial balance. The statement gives each account's name and address, his credit limit, total balance, and balance broken down by age: current, 30 days past due, 60 days past due, 90 days past due, and over 90 days past due (see Figure 3-2).

A report such as this enables the credit analyst to compare the current month with other periods and to discern trends. If more and more accounts are becoming past due for longer periods, the treasurer or controller has a basis for tightening up the firm's credit policy. This report also serves many other purposes:

1. It shows how soon and how much cash can be brought in from receivables.
2. It enables the accountant to determine the amount of reserve to set aside for bad debts.

Name	Address	Credit Limit	Date Assigned	Total Balance of Acct.	Current	Due 30 Days	Due 60 Days	Due 90 Days	Due Over 90 Days
Lester W. Brown	Medford, Mass.	2,500	9/24/70	240.00	36.48	203.52			
Butler Company	Berlin, N. H.	5,000	3/26/62	1,117.96	1,079.86		38.10		
Evans & Co.	Newark, N. J.	2,500	12/9/66	3,009.81	1,686.26	214.45	411.25	697.85	
Fuller & Smith	Hawthorne, N. Y.	1,000	8/25/66	1,389.06		1,389.06			
R & H Engineering Co.	Boston, Mass.	2,500	5/28/63	853.56	612.83	240.73			
Halsey Lumber Co.	Groton, N. Y.	5,000	12/13/68	5,166.65	2,709.11	2,457.54			
Hingham Company	Jersey City, N. J.	2,500	9/7/69	1,015.26	247.26		768.00		
Laurence R. Landreth	Warwick, R. I.	10,000	8/18/67	3,100.78		3,100.78			
Morristown Heating Co.	Morristown, N. Y.	1,500	3/9/70	2,770.77	1,827.46		251.74	691.57	
Orville Company	Elizabeth, N. J.	1,000	9/19/69	1,165.26	582.85	254.87	327.54		

Figure 3-2

Accounts Receivable Aging Report.

3. It supplies banks and commercial finance companies with information they need for financing accounts receivables.
4. It demonstrates to trade creditors the liquidity of the debtor's receivables.

APPLYING DATA PROCESSING TO RECEIVABLE AGING

Accounts receivable is readily adaptable to automation. Financial managements are able to automate even when the transaction volume is relatively low because of the need for accurate and detailed information on balances due. From a cost standpoint, hand-typed hand-posted line-items of billing cost about $1.00. Thus with as few as 10,000 line-items per year, automation becomes feasible.

What Part Should Be Automated

Depending on the system and machines employed it may be possible to convert only part of the billing cycle to automated procedures. This is the safer approach to data processing. There are systems, however, which require the entire system be changed. For example, if the open balance file is put on magnetic tape, the old hand-posting method of applying cash receipts must also be changed.

An ideal piecemeal application of data processing is to the aging report. Cards are punched at month-end which represent each invoice and credit memo and contain a customer number. As cash is received against these open items the cards are pulled from the open file. The cards remaining are the unpaid invoices. If these are sorted into order by invoice date and customer number, an aging report can be produced (see Figure 3-3).

A More Complicated System

The system described in Figure 3-3 is quite simple and adaptable to any business. Figure 3-4 describes a bigger more involved system involving magnetic tape files. The input could come from any of several sources. These sources capture the invoice information as a by-product of producing the invoice. The cash receipts information is also a by-product of the cash holding procedure and is fed directly onto a magnetic tape. The customer balances are kept on a magnetic tape along with detailed data on each open item. The cash receipts transaction must accurately identify which invoice (or part of an invoice) a customer is paying. Since the machine will do the matching, a special report listing unmatched items is produced. Items in such a list would include:

1. Invoice number not as shown in master file.
2. Invoice numbers match but amounts do not and cash receipt was not coded as a partial payment.
3. If applied as designated, transaction would cause an overpayment.
4. No such customer number.

A report is printed showing all exceptions which were not matched against the master file. This report is gone over and a disposition is made of all items. These are then

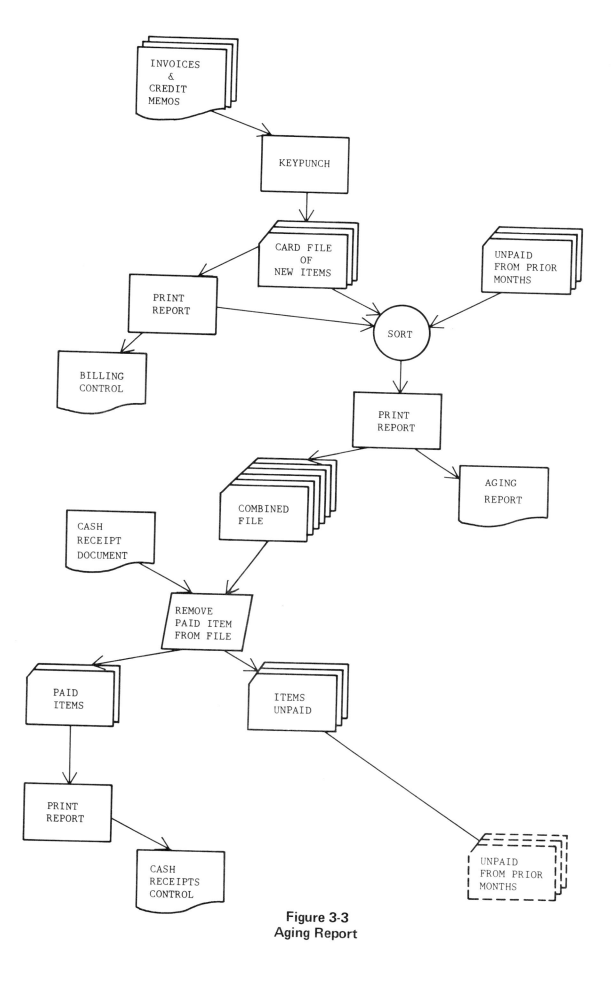

Figure 3-3
Aging Report

processed possibly with the next cash receipts run. It is important to note that managerial attention must be given to exception routine. Without positive action to match or adjust the exceptions the master file would be out of balance. Quality of accounting records in an automated environment requires the same careful management attention as that found with good hand-posted records.

THE THREE STAGES OF COLLECTION

The aging report invariably reveals accounts that need attention. Since the customer has ignored a monthly statement or an invoice describing his purchase, it is now necessary to remind him that the due date has passed without payment.

The Reminder Stage

Most companies let several days pass between the due date and the date of the reminder. A first reminder is mild and may consist simply of a duplicate invoice, a courteous form letter or a printed card. A statement giving the date of purchase for the overdue balance is more effective than showing the number of days or months the account is past due. A customer receiving a statement in August with a May balance is more likely to remit payment than if he receives a notice describing the balance as 90 days old.

The Follow-Up Stage

If the reminder produces no results, the account requires follow-up treatment. This consists of taking a series of actions until the customer makes payment. The techniques available to the credit manager are numerous:

1. Follow-up letters. Most firms base their follow-up method on a series of letters. The first letter resembles the earlier reminder letter. It is often a letter of inquiry to determine whether the customer is stalling or is genuinely unable to pay. Subsequent letters become more demanding and appeal to the customer's pride, self-interest, and sense of fair play. Many collection letters never get read. Too often they arrive in look-alike envelopes. The customer spots the letter and tosses it in the wastebasket unopened.

Varying the shapes and colors of envelopes will make each letter look different. Use of a different return address and printed "reply requested" on the envelope is also recommended.

2. Follow-up telephone call. A company may run through its cycle of form letters and still not hear from some accounts. Additional letters will simply result in pushing up collection costs. At this point the collection manager uses the telephone. The customer can't ignore a telephone call. The caller always gives his own name, never the firm's name. He may be gentle or forceful, as the situation requires.

Some credit men use the telephone even for reminders. Regardless of when the telephone is used in the collection process, it is necessary to set a minimum debt for making

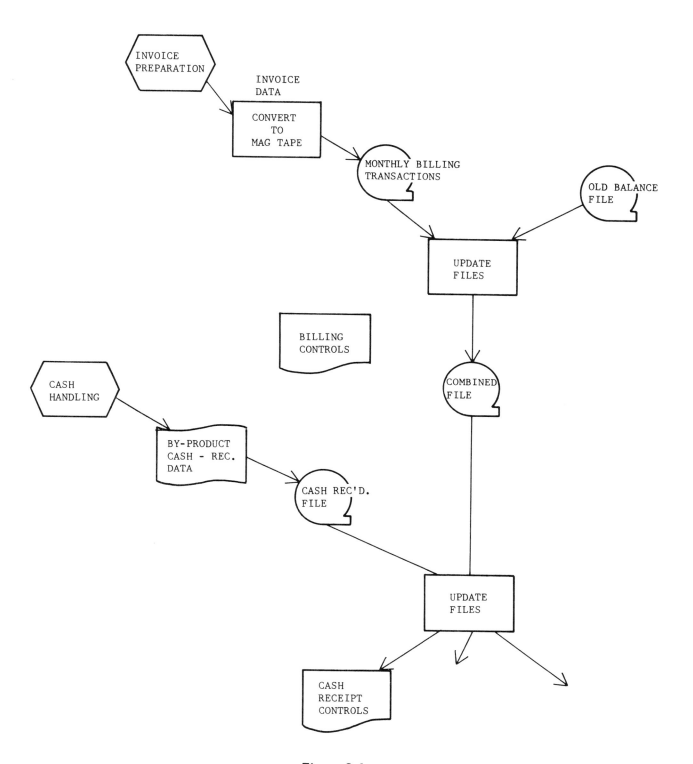

Figure 3-4

long-distance calls. The prevailing policy limits phone calls to bills that run over $100. Callers are asked to keep the cost of the call within 1 percent of the amount of the bill. The cost of a call about a bill for $500 should not exceed $5. If a firm doesn't have the manpower to make its own phone calls, it should check with local collection agencies to see if they offer this type of service.

3. Follow-up telegram. Collection telegrams often "get the money." A businessman attributes a greater urgency to a telegram than to a letter or even a phone call. A note of caution: telegrams are "published" documents not limited to the sender and addressee. They may therefore easily run afoul of the law of libel. To avoid this possibility, the credit manager should consider using a form collection telegram prepared by the Western Union Telegraph Company, as shown in Figure 3-5.

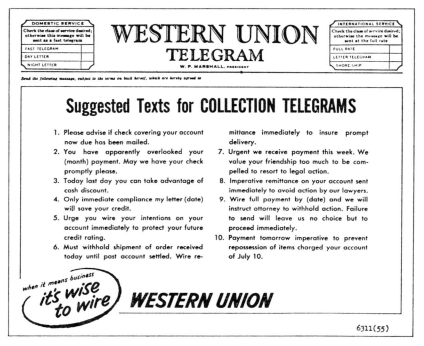

Figure 3-5
Suggested Collection Telegrams

4. Follow-up registered letter. As with the telephone call and telegram, the registered letter demands the creditor's attention and suggests urgency. A certified letter serves the same purpose and is less expensive.

5. Follow-up personal call. When the methods tried thus far prove ineffective, a personal call on the debtor by a collector may show striking results. Even the most obstinate debtors abhor the collector—the collector always calls at an embarrassing moment. From the practical standpoint, the collector is a creditor's only recourse when the account is too small to warrant legal action.

The Drastic Stage

At this stage the collection manager realizes that collection by moderate methods is impossible and he considers it fruitless to attempt to maintain a profitable relationship with the customer. He has two remaining recourses: collection by draft, or collection through an agency or attorney.

1. Collection by draft. A collection draft is an order drawn by the creditor on the debtor directing him to pay the stated amount. The creditor sends the draft to the debtor's bank; for a slight fee, the bank presents the draft to the debtor. The draft has no more legal compulsion than a collection letter. What prompts payment is not the draft itself, but a warning letter that precedes the draft by a week or two. Most debtors will try their best to make payment so as to prevent the bank from learning of their delinquency.

2. Collection by an agency. Collection agencies are an important means of collecting overdue accounts. Disputed claims are one specialty of a collection agency. Often the buyer and seller become "locked in" in contradictory positions and cannot negotiate a settlement. The collection agency can act as a mediator and arrange a settlement. The fee charged is a percentage of the amount collected which assures that the agency will attempt to get the largest possible settlement. Collection agencies are also useful if a large number of small balances due require attention. The fee charged is a larger percentage on small amounts. However, the techniques which they employ are quite effective against the petty chiseler who, in effect, dares you to sue him for $50.

3. Collection by lawyer and lawsuit. The most expensive but powerful tool is the lawyer. As previously explained under "When to Start Legal Action" a lawyer is most effective if given the case early. The size of the claim must be large enough to justify the legal fee. Lawyers generally start with a threatening letter on their letterhead. If the debtor does not respond, legal action must be started promptly. If this is not done, the debtor comes to believe that the creditor and his lawyer are bluffing.

HOW TO APPROACH TERMS OF SALE

When to Use No Discounts

Many companies offer a cash discount to customers who pay their bills early. The typical arrangement is stated as "2/10/30" or "2/10/net 30," meaning that the seller will grant a cash discount of 2 percent if he receives payment within 10 days from the invoice date. Otherwise, the full amount is payable 30 days after the invoice date. The discount does speed collections, as intended, but Figure 3-4 showed that the typical company still finds that more than 15 percent of its receivables are past due. Hence, many financial officers are reviewing the merits of the discount.

Credit men who are critical of the discount maintain that it creates ill will among customers who expect two percent off the net price, even though they pay after the ten-day period. Not allowing the discount may alienate the customer; giving in to him defeats the purpose of prompt payment. They also maintain that the discount is expensive—the equivalent of borrowing at 36 percent on an annual basis 2 percent $\times$ 360 $\div$ (30–10).

As alternatives, some firms cut prices to volume customers rather than give discounts indiscriminately. Some others charge the customer interest if he doesn't pay within 30 days.

The feasibility of dropping the cash discount depends very much on the condition a firm's cash account would be in if most of its customers paid in 30 days rather than in 10 days. If a firm needs speedy collections to pay suppliers, it must retain the discount, even though the discount may pose certain disadvantages.

When to Offer Cash Discounts

To improve the collection period means more cash on hand. Several moves can be made to speed up collections. Tighter credit rules and tougher collection procedures are major steps and run the risk of lowering sales. Offering cash discounts will, if anything, attract new sales. The drawback is the cost of offering a cash discount. The cost to go from Net 30 to 1%, 10 days would be computed as follows:
1. With $100,000 outstanding and a 50 day collection period, the sales per day would be $100,000 $\div$ 50 or $2,000 per day.
2. If, 1%, 10 days were offered, and the collection period became 20 days, the receivable then becomes 20 $\times$ $2,000 or $40,000. This means increased cash of $100,000 — $40,000 or $60,000.
3. The cost per year, if all sales were discounted, would be 365 $\times$ 2,000 01. or $7,300.
4. The percentage cost of the $60,000 would be $7,300 — $60,000 or 12.2%.

At first glance a financial manager might discard the idea as too expensive. First he must consider:
a. He has increased his cash on hand which would immediately be used to pay off a 6% loan and, thereby, further improve his current ratio (explained below) and acid test ratio.
b. The improved current ratio is lower and may allow him to get new long term debt to finance capital projects which would otherwise have been turned down.
c. The discount terms may attract more customers and offset the financial cost with greater sales.

FACTORING SERVICES OBVIATE NEED FOR COLLECTION SYSTEM

A factoring firm is a financial institution that renders the specialized service of buying accounts receivable from sellers of goods. In return for a fee, the factor purchases all accounts receivable for cash, maintains the ledgers, and performs all accounting duties relating to the accounts receivable. He also collects the accounts receivable, assumes all credit losses, and offers advisory services, such as management counseling and marketing surveys.

The Factoring Contract

The contract between the factor and the client describes the agreement of the parties in very general terms, and permits either party to withdraw from the arrangement sixty days after submitting written notice. The duration of the contract, therefore, depends on the client's satisfaction with the factor's services, rather than on any contractual agreement.

Factoring in Action

A client telephones his factor for approval before filing a new order above a certain amount, usually $100. The factor's staff of credit and collections men refers to detailed credit files before deciding whether to approve the credit sale. When making shipment, the client furnishes his factor with a copy of the invoice showing the date payment is due. He also notifies the customer to remit payment directly to the factor.

The client receives payment from the factor either immediately, or on the due date, depending on the arrangement agreed upon. The client always receives payment no later than the due date, regardless of when—or whether—the factor collects from the client's customer.

Some factors offer a non-notification plan. Under this plan, you collect directly from your customer and forward payment to the factor. Credit men who prefer this method believe that it helps them to maintain a closer relationship with the customer.

Factoring Fees

Factoring fees are relatively high. They range from three-fourths of 1 percent to 2 percent of sales, depending on trade terms, the average size of invoices, volume, and the credit standing of the client's customers. If the client draws cash on invoices before they come due, he pays interest at the rate of about 7 percent a year on the money used.

Is Factoring the Answer?

Factoring offers attractive advantages: it eliminates the need for a credit accounting and collection department, and it accelerates the reinvestment of working capital. Whether the merits of this service warrant the cost depends on each company's situation. Although more and more companies elect to sell their receivables to factors, the great majority still handle their own credit and collection operations.

In general, factoring offers the greatest benefits to companies faced with one or more of the following situations:

1. The volume of credit work requires a credit specialist, but the expense of a full-time, top notch credit manager is not warranted.
2. The credit extended to customers is disproportionate to total working capital.
3. The problems of credit and collection are taking up an unprofitable amount of management's time.
4. The business is highly seasonal.

For some types of businesses, the cost of factoring outweighs the value of the services obtained. A factoring arrangement is rarely worthwhile for a company that:

1. Makes credit sales against confirmed or irrevocable letters of credit, or some other form of security.
2. Sells its entire output to a few customers of unquestioned credit responsibility.
3. Accumulates ample cash resources, or has access to unlimited bank credit.

4

Controlling Inventory

4

Controlling Inventory

DETERMINE THE RIGHT QUANTITY TO BUY

The financial officer is not directly responsible for purchasing, inventory, and distribution, but as the watchful guardian against waste, he is responsible for proper utilization of the dollars invested in inventory. The objective is to invest enough dollars in the right items to prevent shortages without carrying excess stock.

Sound purchasing procedures are essential to profitable operations. Scarce or overabundant stocks, lost sales, and rush orders are a few of the profit-draining consequences of faulty purchasing. Finding the right quantity to buy involves reaching a compromise between two opposing considerations—the cost of acquiring inventory and the cost of carrying it. When these two factors are in balance, we have an optimum cost of inventory (Figure 4-1):

A Practical Example

Suppose that a firm forecasts an annual sale of 50,000 units of a particular item at $5 each, and that the acquisition cost for each order is $10. At first glance it appears that the easiest thing to do is to order the entire 50,000 units at one time and avoid further acquisition costs. But this would obviously thrust up inventory carrying costs by tying up an average of $125,000 in this one item throughout the year ($5 times average inventory of 25,000).

If carrying costs average 22 percent, the cost of maintaining the inventory would reach about $27,500 per year. What is needed is a method for finding the order size at which the sum of the inventory carrying cost and acquisition cost is at the lowest point. This point is called the *economic order quantity* (EOQ).

61

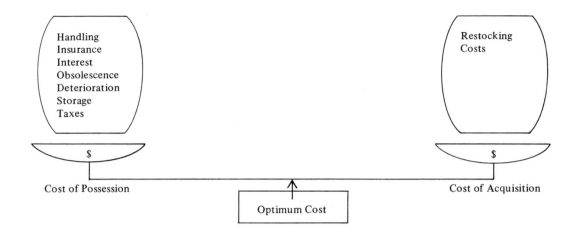

Figure 4-1
Cost of Possession Versus Cost of Acquisition
(Adapted by permission from "General Information Manual, Inventory Control
and Material Accounting." International Business
Machines Corporation.)

Using an Economic Order Quantity Formula

For every inventory item, there is an economic order quantity that balances minimum restocking costs against minimum inventory maintenance costs. A common formula for calculating the economic order quantity states:

$$EOQ = \sqrt{\frac{2RS}{KC}}$$

Substituting in the formula,
  R = Annual requirements (50,000 units)
  S = Restocking costs ($10)
  C = Unit cost ($5)
  K = Carrying charge (22 percent)

$$EOQ = \sqrt{\frac{2 \times 50,000 \times \$10}{.22 \times 5}} = \sqrt{909,091} = 953$$

The most economical number of items to order at one time is 953. A weekly order of 953 items will almost provide the 50,000 units required during the year. Average inventory on hand will amount to 476 (953 ÷ 2), for an average inventory investment of $2,380 (476 × $5). The cost of maintaining the inventory will be $523.60 (22% × $2,380), and restocking costs will be $520 ($10 × 52).

The cost of acquiring and maintaining this inventory will amount to the total of the carrying costs ($523.60) and restocking costs ($520), or $1,043.60—drastically less than the $27,510 it would cost to acquire and maintain the average inventory if the entire 50,000 units were ordered at one time.

Don't Rely on a Strict Mathematical Approach

In the example, several assumptions are made which tend to oversimplify the problem. For example, it is assumed that the usage rate will be fairly constant so that the average inventory level equals one-half the amount ordered. It is also assumed that the storage space poses no limitations that may affect certain EOQ's. If, when applied to bulky items, the formula indicated a lot size of several thousand pieces, it might nevertheless be necessary to handle a smaller number at one time.

Optimum quantity figures produced by the formula are valid only as long as there is no change in annual usage, unit costs, carrying costs, or restocking costs. A change in unit costs obviously affects the dollar value of annual usage, thereby changing the economic order quantity. The only way to compensate is to make a new calculation using the revised values in the formula.

These variables have been traditionally applied manually, either by desk calculator, slide rule, or nomograph. Since these methods are tedious and inefficient (a variable may change as soon as a new order quantity is "optimized"), data processing systems are taking over their functions in purchasing and inventory control.

A DATA PROCESSING APPROACH TO INVENTORY LEVEL

Shown in Figures 4-2, 4-3, and 4-4 are three systems for computing the Economic Order Quantity. In each case the files shown and the input data (withdrawals and receipts) are arranged in Item Number order. This means each item in inventory must be assigned a unique number to identify it. The item numbers can be arranged by type of item, type of end product, physical nature or any other logical system. Listed below are the systems with an explanation of the processing steps involved.

Processing Step #1 (Figure 4-2)—The first withdrawal is matched against the master file account with the same Item Number. The quantity withdraw is subtracted from the balance on hand which results in the updated on-hand file. All items of the same number (or type) are summarized and printed out on a consumption report for cost accounting purposes.

Processing Step #2—The receipts are matched against the on-hand file and added to the balance. The dollar amount of receipts is recapped by item number (or type) which can be used as a control figure for postings to accounts payable.

Processing Step #3—The balance-on-hand file is printed out showing each item and the current balance in stock. Reorders are determined from this listing.

Processing Step #1 (Figure 4-3)—Receipts and withdrawals are coded and combined into one input stream. They are matched against the on-hand file and added and subtracted from the balance on hand. The same written reports are generated as in Figure 4-2. A Master Order Quantity and Level file is maintained including the following information:

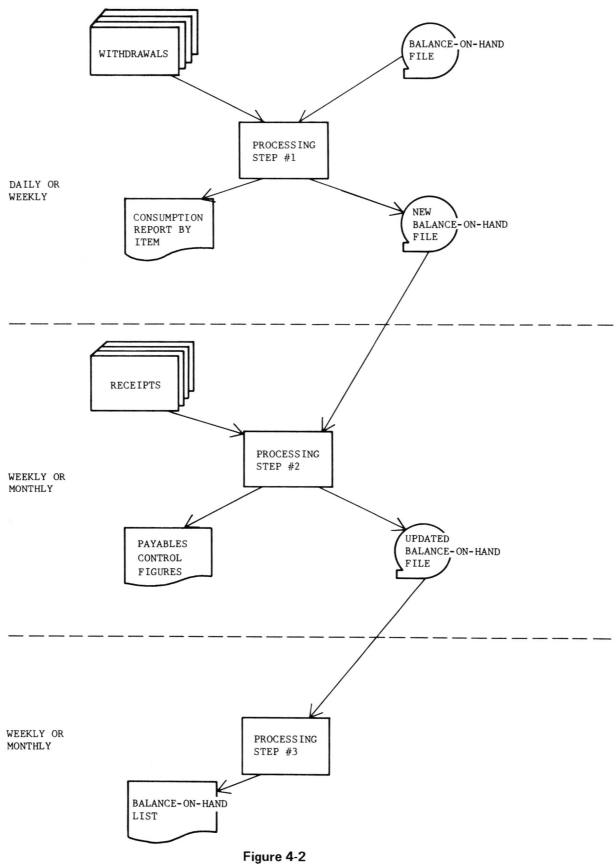

**Figure 4-2
Processing Step #1**

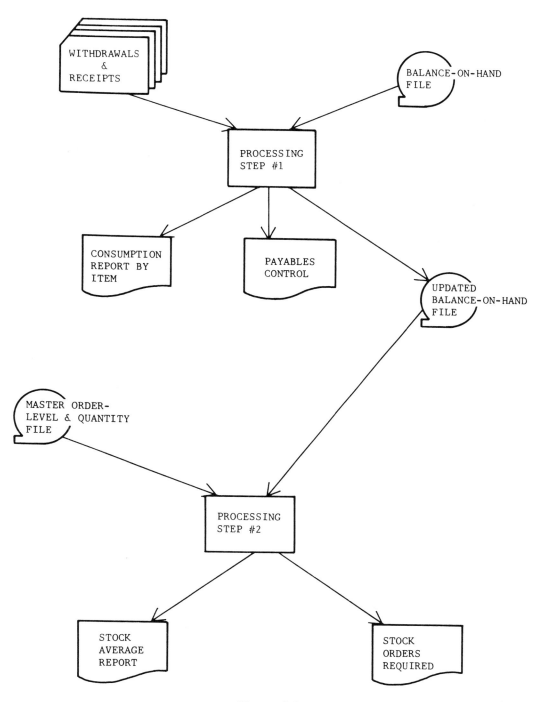

Figure 4-3
Processing Step #1

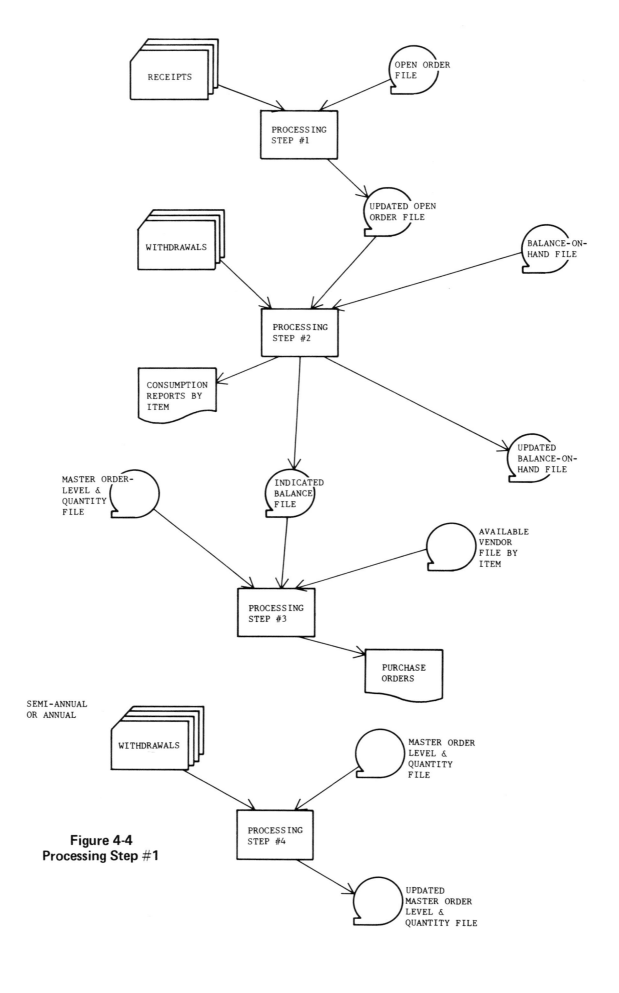

Figure 4-4
Processing Step #1

1. R—Annual requirements—estimated
2. S—Restocking Costs
3. C—Unit Costs—based on past history
4. K—Carrying Cost Factor
5. Maximum Inventory Level
6. Minimum Inventory Level (Reorder Point)
7. EOQ—Economic Order Quantity

The balance on-hand is compared to the Minimum Inventory Level. If reorder is indicated, the item is printed out on the Order Indicated Report (Figure 4-5). Estimated annual usage is shown and compared to actual rate of usage to point out items whose usage is increasing drastically. A second report shows stock levels above the maximum inventory level which should be investigated.

Item No.	Description	Bal. on Hand	Min. Quant.	Actual Rate of Consumption	Estimated Rate of Consumption	Indicated Order Quantity

Figure 4-5
Indicated Reorder Report

Processing Step #1 (Figure 4-4)—A file of unfilled purchased orders is processed against receipts. This subtraction gives the net quantity on order but not received.

Processing Step #2—The net open items file is added to the balance on-hand while withdrawals are subtracted from the balance on-hand to give the Indicated Balance File. The withdrawals are recapped into a report for cost accounting purposes.

Processing Step #3—The Indicated Balance File (not the balance-on-hand-file) is used to decide the items and quantities to be ordered. The Master Order Level and Quantity File is the same as that described in Figure 4-3. The Vendor File cross references Item Number with vendor numbers which enables the computer to print purchase orders or purchase requisitions.

Processing Step #4—The withdrawal recaps are arranged in Item Number sequence and are used to compute actual rates of consumption. These replace the estimated rates on the Master Order Level and Quantity File. Mathematical techniques can also be used to optimize the minimum stock level and the maximum stock level. The revised levels can be put on the updated Master Order Level and Quantity File.

BASE PURCHASING ON AN ACCURATE INVENTORY COUNT

How certain can one be that the firm's physical inventory count is accurate? A figure that is significantly above or below the actual total affects the purchase and cash budgets, distorts profits and taxes, and jeopardizes production schedules. Many companies labor under inaccurate totals because they fail to observe essential principles in taking their inventory on raw materials, work-in-process, and finished goods.

Preparatory Steps

Accuracy depends on preparation. Follow these proven ground rules before beginning the actual count.

1. Devise overhead factors for use in pricing raw materials, work-in process, and finished goods.
2. Set a deadline date for stopping production, not only to speed the inventory-taking but to ensure against a duplicate count as well.
3. Decide what will be excluded from the final count, such as construction materials, consignments, supplies, and items held for repair.
4. Decide what property not on hand will be included in the inventory count. This category includes inventories in public warehouses, at branch or sales offices, or at contractors.
5. See that purchase and sales invoices and receiving records are numbered consecutively to prevent the inclusion of items after the cutoff date.
6. Have department heads make sure that all mechanical counting, weighing, and measuring equipment is working properly. See that they prepare written instructions and work out details for the actual counting. They should specify what units they are going to use, such as feet, meters, pounds, grams, and so on.
7. See that arrangements have been made for the department head or his subordinate to supervise the actual count in each department.
8. Prohibit the use of nonstandard abbreviations. Too often only their originators know what they mean.
9. During inventory-taking preparations, see that the personnel who will participate are told of their specific duties well in advance. Some companies find it helpful to hold an inventory-taking rehearsal to better acquaint supervisors and counters with sample situations and with methods for meeting them. The time element is critical since inventory must be done in no more than a day or two. This requires a careful calculation of available man-hours and a detailed plan of every step.

The Use of Prenumbered Stub Tags

This aid can be employed by issuing to every department head a block of prenumbered tags, and entering the numbers in a tag-issue record. These tags may vary considerably in design, depending on the method used for counting, verifying, and reporting, but they are always composed of two sections so that a portion of the tag can remain with the stock to assure that all piles are counted. A member of the inventory team places one of these serial-numbered tags on every pile, bin, shelf, carton, or container. The person actually making the count then writes in the quantity and tears off the tag at its perforation. When he finishes his count, he tabulates and signs the tags.

Secure All Necessary Data

Since a physical inventory is a major undertaking, you want to secure all data pertinent to evaluating the inventory. The information to be recorded varies with each company's particular needs. Here are some typical useful items:

Part number	Location
Part name	Condition
Kind or class of material	Old or slow moving
Lot number or batch number	Unit cost for labor, material, overhead
Quantity	Unit selling price
Unit of measure	Unit profit
Account number	

Much of this information should be acquired from stock records either before or after the counting operation. The inventory taker should be responsible for only a minimum of information—the count, the condition, and, in some cases, the location of the item. Be sure to keep accurate processing cost records to avoid the problem of setting prices for partly finished products and subassemblies. These records will enable you to know true labor and material costs, once you determine the manufacturing stage.

Some Methods for Speeding the Count

Time spent in inventory-taking adds to inventory-maintenance costs. Here are some devices department heads may be able to use to shorten the time spent in taking physical inventory.

1. Ratio scales. When counting a product of many and small parts, ratio scales save time by balancing a predetermined multiple against the weight of one component. These scales are geared in various ratios—1 to 10, 1 to 100, 1 to 1,000, and so on, speeding the count accordingly.

2. Mark-sensing cards. These cards are widely used in data processing systems of inventory control. As the counters make their rounds, they need only sense-mark with magnetic lead the appropriate date, and initial the card. This information is then

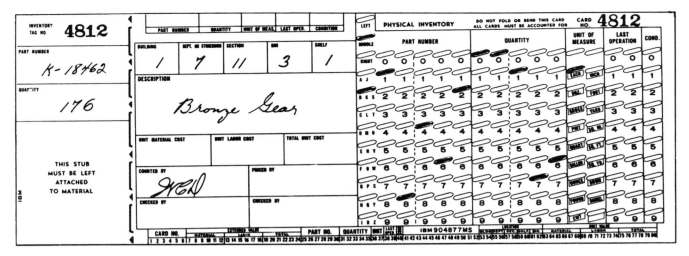

Figure 4-6
Mark Sensing Saves Time
(Reprinted by permission from "General Information Manual,
Inventory Control and Material Accounting." International
Business Machines Corporation.)

automatically mark-sense-punched at high speed. Figure 4-6 illustrates a mark-sensing card.

3. Two-way radio. If your plant has narrow aisles, high shelves, or other hard-to-get-at places, a two-way radio facilitates inventory taking by enabling the counter to relay his count to the writer sitting at his desk some distance away.

4. Portable tape recorder. A tape recorder eliminates the need for a writer to accompany the counter in the tedious task of checking goods. Observe, however, these "musts" in recording:

    A. Number consecutively each reel of tape.

    B. Mark the location of the inventories material on the reel.

    C. Be sure to inventory every item, no matter how unimportant its use or how low its price.

Verifying the Count

The department head should conduct a spot check to verify the count, and note discrepancies with inventory records. He must seek an explanation for a substantial difference between the supply on hand and the book quantity. He also notes items that are in excess or in short supply, and items that are obsolete or deteriorated. Since 20 percent of the total stock items may account for 80 percent of the inventory value, the verifier should be guided in his audit accordingly.

TRY THIS SIMPLE SYSTEM FOR COMPLETING BACK ORDERS

With even the best inventory control system, a firm is likely to have occasional stock-outs and orders waiting to be filled. To prevent this from ever happening would require an inordinate investment in every item of inventory. Since the manager cannot entirely eliminate back orders, he must set up a simple system for maintaining positive control over them. Customers who have to wait too long for their orders become dissatisfied and switch their business elsewhere.

Traditional Practice

Typically, when a firm gets an order for a stockout item, a clerk places in a special file a copy of the invoice showing the item or items on back order. As new inventory comes in, the clerk scans the invoices in the back order file to learn the need for shipping the back-order items just received. If an invoice in the back-order file contains more than one item, the clerk refiles it and refers to it again when more inventory comes in. Two disadvantages of this method are that it is time-consuming, and, more important, back-order items which are currently available for shipment are often overlooked.

The Simple, Fool-Proof Way

The following system avoids the drawbacks of the conventional back-order system.

Step 1. From the invoice containing a back-order item, a clerk posts the following information on a 3″ × 5″ cross-indexed file card (Figure 4-7) merchandise stock number, merchandise description, invoice number, and quantity ordered.

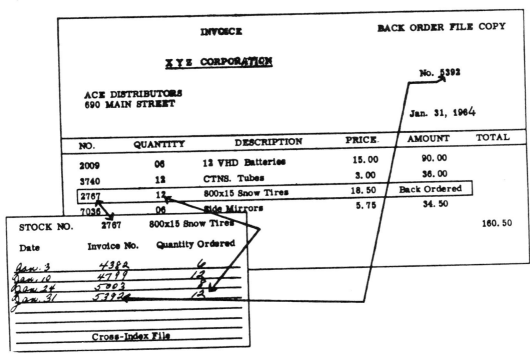

Figure 4-7
Posting from Invoice to Cross Index File

Step 2. The clerk files the invoice copy in a back-order file in numerical order by invoice number. He then places the file card in a box-type file in stock-number sequence.

Step 3. When inventory arrives at the warehouse, a receiving report is prepared and sent to the office. Working from each line of the receiving report, the back-order clerk removes from the file box the 3″ × 5″ cross-index card having the same stock number listed on the receiving report. (Figure 4-7).

Step 4. Referring to the numbered invoices on the cross-index card, the clerk removes the proper invoice-file copies. He then uses a back order form to initiate usual shipping and invoicing practices, just as though a new order had been received.

This system corrects the weaknesses of traditional back-order methods by (1) relieving the back-order clerk from repeatedly checking each back-order file copy against goods received at the warehouse, (2) reducing the chances for overlooking an item by pinpointing back-ordered goods, (3) enabling the file cards to serve as a summary of all unfilled orders, (4) indicating which items should be carried in greater amount, as reflected in the quantity of invoice numbers on the cross-index cards.

The manager can also quickly check the duration of back orders by periodically changing the color of the cards.

INVENTORY MEASUREMENT & APPRAISAL

The Financial Approach to Inventory

The complexities of inventory control as practiced in industry come about for very definite reasons. Inventory is the linkage between production and sales. If inventory control were left to production personnel, it would be kept all in its raw form or as work in process. It is these components which feed the production lines and provide insurance against out-of-stock which results in lost production. If left to sales personnel, inventory would be 100% finished goods. Sales can't be made without plenty of ready-to-ship merchandise available. The financial manager is a third party who is interested in inventory. His aim is to keep the dollar investment in inventory to an absolute minimum. Satisfying these three conflicting demands is the essence of inventory control. The objective of inventory control is to have on hand at all times enough physical stock to satisfy all or most demands without carrying excess stock.

The financial manager can improve a company's inventory position by taking these three steps:

1. Analyze inventory performance for weak spots.
2. Institute control procedures to improve the situation.
3. Follow through with control and review procedures which assure the improvements are permanent.

The best technique for discovering weak spots is the calculation of inventory turnover.

How to Put Inventory Turnover to Use

The number of times per year that the inventory "turns over" is measured by dividing the Cost of Goods Sold by the Average Inventory. The greater number of times indicates a greater physical velocity of merchandise through a factory or store. An increase in this ratio indicates greater financial efficiency since a greater volume of sales is being made with the same amount of capital.

Gathering Accurate Data

A retail store would use its total inventory valued at acquisition cost and its cost of sales. A factory would use an inventory valued so as to contain the same proportion of overhead as the cost of goods sold. If direct costs were used to value the inventory, the same direct costs should be used to compute costs of goods sold.

Find the Slowest Moving Items to Speed Up the Inventory Turnover

If the total inventory can be broken down into several smaller inventories, some important facts will come to light. Take the example of a clothing store—

	Last Year	This Year	Average	CGS	Turnover
Men's Wear	25,000	35,000	30,000	48,000	1.6
Women's Wear	48,000	52,000	50,000	144,000	2.9
Children's Wear	24,000	18,000	21,000	78,000	3.7
Total Inventory	97,000	105,000	101,000	270,000	2.7

This shows clearly the variation in turnover when an inventory is broken down into components. In view of the low turnover in the men's wear, the manager would do well to—
1. Expand only in children's and women's clothes.
2. Promote the men's wear in some new way.
3. Buy only the most popular sizes and styles in men's clothes.

Keep Looking for Slow Moving Items

Suppose the same inventory and cost of goods sold are broken down into different categories as follows:

	Old Inventory	New Inventory	Average	Cost of Sales	Inventory Turnover
Nationally Advertised Brands	44,000	34,000	49,000	152,000	3.1
Unbranded	34,000	30,000	32,000	79,000	2.5
Private Label	19,000	21,000	20,000	39,000	1.9
Total	97,000	105,000	101,000	270,000	2.7

Thus, the same inventory shows a second weakspot—Private Label. The same decision process on how to improve inventory turnover applies to Private Labels that applies to men's wear.

How to Handle Common Raw Materials

Factories having a common raw material or components inventory still can use this method as follows:

1. Segregate the total inventory into two sub-inventories—common and product line.
2. Subdivide the product line inventory into each of several product lines.
3. Add to each product line inventory its proportional share of the common inventory.
4. Proceed as in other cases.

Keep Track of Inventory Turnover Item by Item

Data processing is the key to the successful use of inventory turnover. If inventory can be categorized in two or more ways, data processing can generate useful management information. Figure 4-8 shows several methods of categorizing inventory. The rule for devising categories is: The set of sub-categories derived must be mutually-exclusive and all-inclusive. Applying this rule to Line 1 of Figure 4-8 would mean that:

1. That no item can be in two product lines at once (housewares and furniture). The sub-categories are then called mutually exclusive.
2. All items must fall into one of the sub-categories (housewares, furniture or hardware). They are thus all-inclusive.

Categories	*Examples*
1. Product Line	Housewares, furniture, hardware
2. Type of Customer	Distributor, OEM, Direct User Sales
3. Brand	Private Label, Advertised Brand
4. Location	Warehouse No. 1, etc.
5. Raw Material Type	Petroleum-base, Water-base
6. Packaging Method	Bulk packed, Drums, Cartons

Figure 4-8
Different Methods to Categorize Inventory

Coding System

The decision as to how many and what inventory categories will be used leads to the code design needed. Assume a two way breakdown (by product line and brand) is

INVOICES

KEYPUNCH DATA
FROM INVOICE
ONE CARD PER
LINE ITEM

LIST AND
TOTAL ALL
LINE ITEMS

SALES
REGISTER

MASTER
FILE

LINE ITEM
CARDS

CHECK
CONTROL
TOTALS

MATCH ON
ITEM CODE

EDIT FOR
MISSING
ITEMS

MATCHED
SETS

UNMATCHED
MASTERS

COMPUTE
COST OF
GOODS
SOLD

FILE

SEPARATE
MASTER
AND LINE
ITEM CARDS

MASTERS

LINE ITEM
CARDS CONTAINING
COST OF GOODS
SOLD DATA

FILE

1

Figure 4-9
Flowchart for Cost of Goods Sold Report or Inventory
Analysis by Type of Item

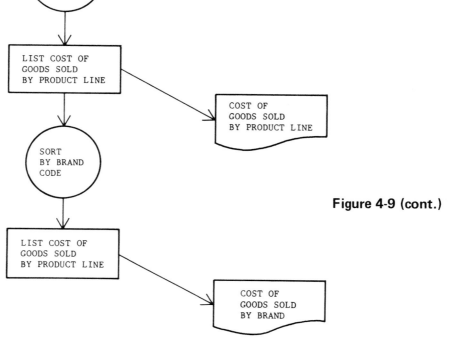

Figure 4-9 (cont.)

decided on. Each item sold is assigned a code number such as 12-1-8884. The 12 means product line number 12 and the 1 means brand number 1. The 8884 or any other letters or numbers can be used to designate size, style, color, etc. In order to arrive at cost of goods sold figures, all invoice line items would have to be coded in the same way. Standard costs which were computed for that particular item would be contained in a master file which could be a deck of tab cards, reel of magnetic tape, or magnetic disk. Assuming a card system is in use, the flow chart would look like Figure 4-9. One final report would show total sales for cash product line with its cost of goods sold. The other would show the total sales and cost of goods sold for each brand. By substituting inventory item cards for invoice item cards, the same flow chart would value the finished goods inventory. The reports would show inventory broken down by product line and also by brand.

Keep Track of Out-of-Stock

Inventory turnover is not the only yardstick of inventory performance. It is possible that inventory turnover is *too fast* and causes out-of-stock with its accompanying loss of sales or production. The financial manager must be as systematic about this problem as he is about low inventory turnover. To accomplish this requires reports on the frequency and nature of out-of-stock occurrences. Figure 4-10 shows such a report. The responsibility for making such a report should be carefully delegated within the organization. The person responsible should be one of the following job titles, depending on the situation encountered:

Date_____   No.
Item

Max. Stock Level _____
Min. Stock Level _____
Date of Last Replenishment _____
Quantity Ordered _____

Cause of Shortage_____
_____
_____

Date of Restock

Quantity Rec'd.

Cost Computation
   Tangible_____
   _____

Overhead or Lost Margin _____
_____

Potential _____
_____

                                         Signature_____

                              Figure 4-10
                    Report of Out-of-Stock Condition

                    1. Production Control Manager
                    2. Storeroom Supervisor
                    3. Shipping Supervisor
                    4. Traffic Manager
                    5. Production Manager
                    6. Purchasing Manager
                    7. Order Department
Assessment of the cost of out-of-stock conditions is difficult and may involve some
arbitrary assumptions. Cost computations can take any of the following forms:
   1. Special freight or handling costs involved in replacing missing stock.
   2. Overtime or extra costs incurred in replacing short stock.
   3. Lost gross margin on sales lost.
   4. Lost overhead not absorbed because productive machines couldn't run.

The cost computation is often made difficult by the many alternatives available to management once a stock shortage occurs. Sometimes finished goods not available for shipment can be back-ordered thereby preventing lost revenue. When one raw material is out of stock, production schedules can be altered to avoid loss of production. Cost computations in such situations are difficult. Such items should be classified as Potential Costs. Figure 4-11 shows a tabulation of "Out-of-Stocks" which can be of aid in spotting problem areas.

Date	Report No.	Item	Type	Cash Cost	Overhead or Lost Sales	Potential Cost
7/1	1122					
7/4	1123					
7/4	1124					
7/8	1125					
7/9	1126					
7/11	1127					
7/14	1128					
7/17	1129					
7/28	1130					
7/28	1131					
7/28	1132					
7/31	1133					

Figure 4-11
Tabulation of Out-of-Stocks

5

Planning the Financial Future

5

Planning the Financial Future

PLANNING PROFITS FOR FUTURE YEARS

What Is Financial Planning?

Financial planning is subdivided into two types—short-term and long range. Short-Term financial planning is covered in a later chapter on financial analysis and is concerned with plans over the next twelve months. Long range planning generally covers a span of about five years, although some companies do long range planning over a greater period, and a few use a shorter period. Financial long range planning seeks to state in specific terms the goals which the company has and the effect these goals will have on the future financial posture of the company, if they are successfully implemented.

Since long range planning deals with the future, it is an estimating process. Many estimates are required to spell out where the firm expects to be three or five years hence.

What Is Gained From Long Range Planning?

Several important advantages accrue to the manager who uses long range planning. A few such advantages are:
1. To give management enough lead time to aid it in reaching its goals.
2. To unify and coordinate company-wide efforts toward reaching the goals.
3. To make the goals as high as can reasonably be achieved.
4. To motivate managers to achieve clearly defined goals.
5. To provide a basic supporting document upon which to base the annual budget.

6. To highlight the assumptions which underlie management's expectations for profit.

Besides the advantages which accrue to the manager who develops long range plans, there are the following trends in business which make such plans essential:

1. The diversity of end products sold by a single corporation.
2. The increasing size and organizational complexity of the business enterprise.
3. The increasing length of time required to develop new technology and end products.

Who Performs Long Range Planning?

With the development of sophisticated long range planning procedures, many organizations have set up separate planning departments. These departments are given the responsibility for the long range planning function. In other corporations and smaller business organizations, the chief financial officer will commonly be given the responsibility for long range planning. In either instance, an important part of the responsibility for the financial portion of the long range plan rests with the financial officer. Basically, the preparation of long range financial plans involves an extension of the skills which the financial officer utilizes on a day to day basis.

FORECASTING THE ENVIRONMENT

Before it is possible to engage in meaningful long range planning, it is necessary to assess the environment in which the company will be operating over the next several years. This business environment consists of the entire business climate in which the company will be operating.

Forecasting the Economic Environment

The forecast of the economic environment must be considered in general terms (those things which affect all industries), and in specific terms (those things which affect only our industry).

The general economic factors to be forecast are such things as growth in gross national product (GNP), level of tax rates, interest rates, and inflation in costs, particularly labor costs. Forecasts of this sort are routinely made by various agencies of the government, as well as by various private organizations. Where a company's interest in a particular factor is great enough to justify internal staff work on the subject, this work will be performed by a staff of economists.

The specific factors affecting the particular industry of interest will present a more difficult forecasting problem. These environmental factors really involve the total activity of the companies operating in the industry. Some of the industry information on sales levels and historical growth rates may be available from published sources. Also, there may be outside agencies (governmental and private) who forecast some of the key factors for specific industries. Trade associations sometimes do a good job in assembling historical information and making forecasts based on this information.

Important specific factors on which forecasts will be made are such things as the demand for key products, the capacity which the industry will have to supply such products, and important cost trends. Forecasts of labor rate escalation will be important. If there is industry oversupply, price weakness may well be indicated; this will be a vital factor in planning expansion of future productive capacity. The inflation in labor costs will be an important factor in assessing profitability, and also in judging whether new equipment can be justified to save labor.

Preparing these specific environmental forecasts really involves an estimate of what competitors will do, as a group. (We shall be discussing specific competitors' activities in the next section.) At the outset, this forecasting task would seem a formidable one. However, by making judicious use of information prepared by outside agencies, as well as the knowledge which the operating management will have about the industry, surprisingly good forecasts of major trends can be made. One can never expect to make an accurate long range forecast which will comprehend more than the important trends. There may be good and sufficient reasons why the industry is operating above or below these trends at any particular time; this is not the fault of the environmental forecaster. The important thing is to foresee major trends.

Forecasting Specific Competitive Activity

We are now in a position to go to the next step of the general planning cycle. The next important forecast is the forecast of specific competitive activity, as distinguished from the forecasts of total industry activity. Some companies do not make this separate forecast, as a specific part of their planning cycle. But if they are to plan successfully, they all must have considered the elements of a forecast of competitor activity in the preparation of long range plans.

The forecast of individual competitors' activities can be vital to the consideration of the company's own long range plans. We noted earlier that conditions of industry oversupply could have a softening effect on prices for the industry's products. The same effect can result from situations in which an important competitor has large unused manufacturing capacity. But it can also result from a situation in which a major competitor (or worse still, several major competitors) has lower costs than we can achieve on a particular product or at a particular manufacturing location. In this case, the competitor will be able to price at a lower level and still realize an adequate margin over costs. It will not always be possible to spot these anomalies of cost or excess capacity from gross industry statistics; only a careful analysis of major competitors' operations will reveal them.

It may seem foolish at the outset for us to suppose that we are competent to forecast actions which the competitor will take when we do not have access to his decision making process and we do not even have access to the books of account which reflect his actual historical results. The undertaking is not so formidable as it sounds. We are not interested in reconstructing the balance sheet and income statement of the competitor in every detail. Instead, we are interested in detecting those important factors which distinguish the competitor in an economic sense.

For example, we may discover that a competitor's plant is located in such a place as to give him a significant advantage in transportation costs. This important fact must be borne in mind when we are assessing our own expansion capabilities.

Or it may be that the competitor has a very antiquated manufacturing facility, and therefore, is incurring costs which are higher than ours. However, if we have also noted that the competitor has considerable opportunity for modernization, which would result in significantly reduced costs, we must be wary in taking actions which ignore this possibility. We cannot always safely plan future growth on a cost base which is competitive with the current cost levels in the industry. Some competitor may well have the ability to reduce costs significantly and thereby have a margin for pricing which will permit much more aggressive selling activity than is possible for our company.

Obtaining the necessary information to do a good job in forecasting competitive activity is of course always a difficult matter. The amount of information which is gathered must be weighed against the value which is expected from such information. As we implied from the above examples, the following are some of the types of information about competitors which will likely be of value to our long range planning effort:

> —*Manpower levels, by primary location.* This information will be available only from people (generally operating people) who have sufficient knowledge of the competitor's activity and the type of operation to be able to estimate the size of the work force.
>
> —*Present and forecast capacity of major facilities.* This information may be available in trade journals. Plans for expansion or for new facilities can be obtained from trade publications, or from general industry contacts.
>
> —*Key factors in operating costs.* Here we are concerned with such things as transportation cost differentials, major differences in operating efficiency which characterize the competitor, etc.
>
> —*Sales and production levels.* This information may be published or it may have to be estimated with the help of knowledgeable operating or sales management.
>
> —*Major contractual commitments.* Long term contracts for purchases, sales, or other important matters may provide key intelligence as to likely future activity of the competitor. The existence of these commitments will be known principally from trade journals or other industry sources, and their terms may be difficult to determine; rarely will the contract itself be seen.

PREPARING THE COMPANY'S GOALS AND OBJECTIVES

Before it is possible for the company to estimate future growth and future financial results, it is first necessary to decide what the major goals and objectives of the company are—or ought to be.

General Goals

Clearly, it is not possible to set these broad objectives without knowing what is a feasible level of activity. By the same token, we also want objectives that represent a challenge to the company. The first set of objectives for the company may be largely arbitrary and they will have to be improved after experience is gained in dealing with them.

Initially, some general rules of thumb can appropriately be used in describing the objectives of the company. In the first place, if the company has shareholders, these shareholders must have an expectation with respect to the future growth in earnings. Unless there are only a few shareholders, it will not be possible to ask them what their expectation is. We must therefore infer this expectation from other information.

We cannot quantify all of the factors which motivate a shareholder to acquire a company's stock, or to continue to hold it. Nevertheless, it seems fair to state that growth in earnings per share is a factor which is reflected over time in shareholders' attitudes toward the security. This is particularly so if the company responds to growth in earnings per share with regular increases in dividend payout.

Another factor which probably influences shareholders is the return on shareholders' equity. Of course the return on equity can be fairly sensitive to the amount of debt which a company has, so that this criterion may not be a true reflection of the inherent profitability of investments. Nevertheless, some rate of return criterion will likely be desirable as a corporate objective.

There may well be other specific objectives which can be derived from looking at the industry. Initially it will not be desirable to select a large number of objectives, and care will have to be exercised in setting any quantitative objectives so that on the one hand they do not stifle growth that might otherwise be desirable, and on the other hand that they present an adequate challenge to the organization.

Once the broad goals and objectives have been formulated (e.g., an average profit growth rate), it is time to express these broad goals in more specific terms.

Profit Objectives Needed?

At first glance the financial manager would be inclined to set no limit of profits. There is no such thing as too much profit. There is such a thing as setting the sights too high. The higher the goal is the higher the risk involved. As the risk increases the danger of making even less and less profit also increases. This is an example of the principle of leverage. Figure 5-1 shows the leverage principle applied to this problem. Added fixed costs causes the following two beneficial effects:

1. The volume potential is increased.
2. Variable costs are lowered.

This is shown on the lower graph as a lower angle on the cost line and the higher volume. The higher fixed costs make higher profits possible (Success) but open the door to lower profits (Failure).

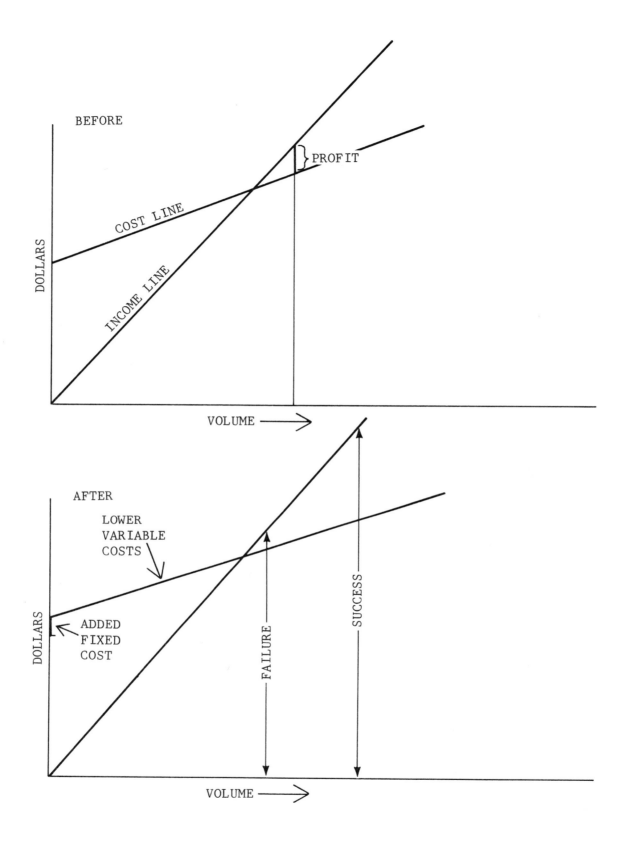

Figure 5-1

Setting Long Range Profit Objectives

There are several factors which must be taken into account in setting profit objectives. They are as follows:

       1. The profit after taxes.
       2. The plowed-back earnings required to increase the equity base.
       3. The dividend payout to stockholders.
       4. The debt to equity ratio.

For example a company in the petrochemical field may find itself faced with the following facts:

      Product demand rate of growth . . . 4% per year

      Profit rate on equity . . . 10%

      Rate of Increase of "Invested Assets per unit of Product" . . . 2% per year

With these facts the dividend yield can be computed as follows:

       1. If product demand is growing at a 4% rate, the total assets must grow at a 4% rate in order that the company maintain its share of the market.
       2. If technology is causing more investment per unit of product, an additional 2% must be added to the 4% to give a total growth rate of assets of 6%.
       3. If the current debt-to-equity ratio is to be maintained, then equity must grow at the annual rate of 6%.
       4. If no stock issues or debt-to-stock conversions are planned, then 6% of the 10% return on equity must be retained earnings.
       5. This leaves 4% on equity as the dividend payout. A publicly owned company would probably sell at a premium over book value, thus the yield based on market-price would be lower.

The same approach might yield an entirely different set of answers to a company such as the following:

      Return on Equity 10%

      Rate of Growth of Demand 10%

      Rate of Increase of "Invested Assets per Unit of Product" 5%

Additional Requirement: The company desires to go from 20% share of market to 25% in five years. The procedure for computing dividend payout would be:

       1. Assets would have to grow at the rate of 10% (for demand) plus 5% (for increased investment) which is a total of 15% before allowing for change in market share.
       2. To go from 20% of market means $\frac{25}{20}$ or 25% growth in 5 years (which is approximately a 4% annual rate compounded). This 4% added to the 15% gives a total growth of assets of 19%.
       3. The equity demand would, therefore, rise 19% per year. With a return on equity of 10%, there is a shortage of 9% of the equity each year.
       4. Possible alternate approaches could be considered such as:
          A. Increasing the debt-to-equity ratio and replacing the needed funds with debt.

B. Issuing stock each year in the amount of 9% of the outstanding stock.

C. Modify the plans for increasing the market share.

Other Factors to Consider

The model described above is simplified. In some situations it is necessary to consider other factors such as:

1. Changing price levels.
2. Changing profit margins.
3. Extra capital required for special projects such as acquisitions.
4. Changing debt-to-equity ratio.
5. Penetrating new markets.

The development of the plan should result in a clear statement of objectives and financial approach to attain the objectives. The financial dimensions of this statement should include all or most of the following:

1. Annual profit targets.
2. Debt-to-equity ratios.
3. Capital budgets.
4. Sales and rate of profit targets.

Figure 5-2 shows a flowchart which depicts the planning process. Once the broad goals and policies and the more specific profit objectives are set, the next important step requires the cooperation of operating managers. The financial plan must be expanded into a set of interlocking operational plans. Major plans required are:

1. Sales and product development plan
2. Production facilities and technology plan
3. Manpower plan.

The responsibility for the data shown in each plan rests with the appropriate line manager. The plans are written analyses of what will be accomplished in future years. Standard formats do not exist. However, the line manager should describe his plans in terms of entire programs, rather than isolated projects.

What Is a Program?

A program may involve the introduction and commercialization of a product through all the phases from pilot plant operation to the final commercial sales program. It is important when planning to introduce a new product that we consider the entire program at that time. The sponsoring organization should not be permitted to propose a pilot plant operation without a forecast of the probable additional commitments that would be involved in the event that the pilot plant operation is successful. The commitment can take the form of manufacturing facilities as well as advertising and research activity to back up successful product development. These forecasts may be hard to develop because there is great uncertainty in the early stages of product development and it is not easy to forecast likely levels of future financial and other commitments. But it is essential that those people who have the most intimate knowledge of the subject be

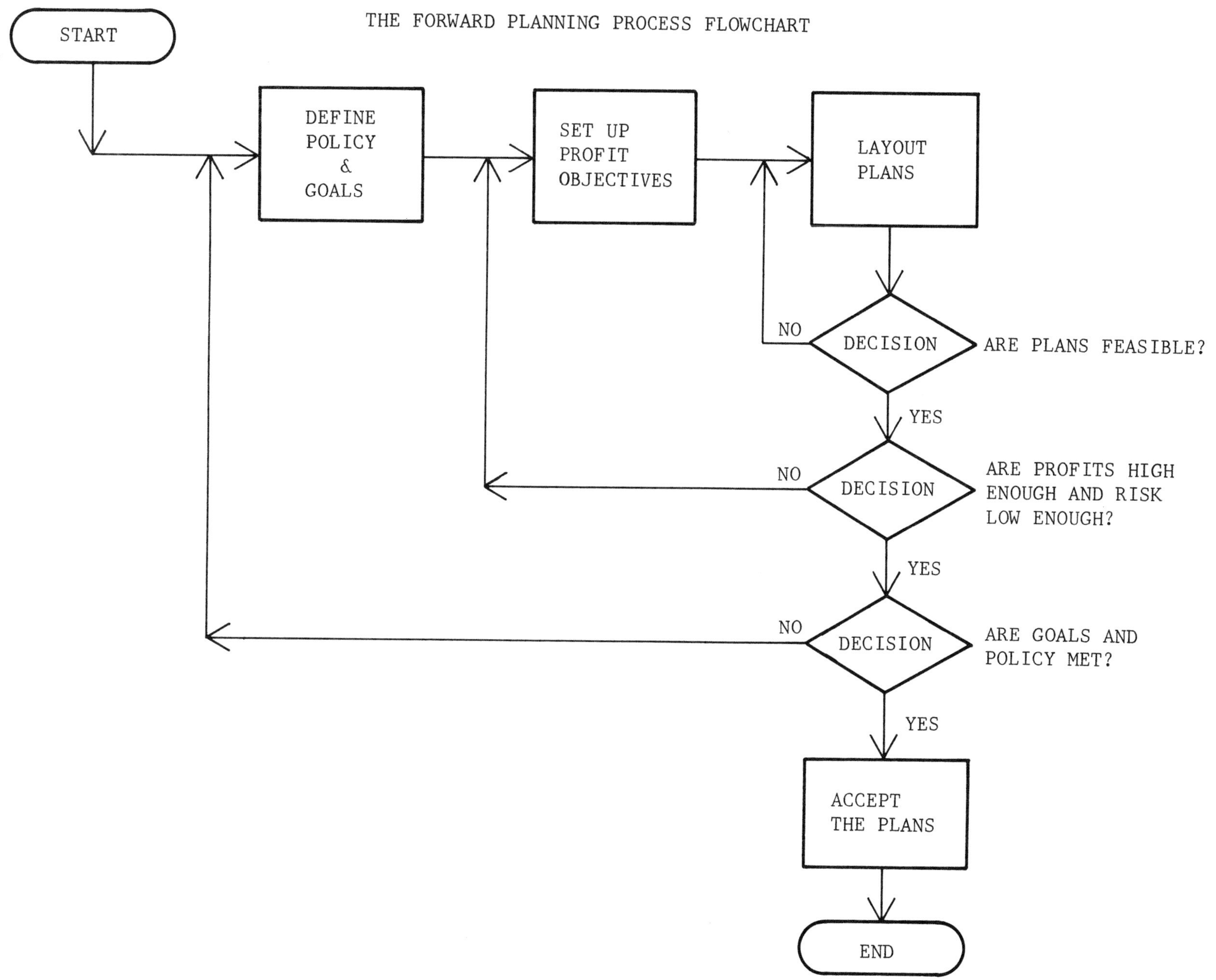

THE FORWARD PLANNING PROCESS FLOWCHART

START → DEFINE POLICY & GOALS → SET UP PROFIT OBJECTIVES → LAYOUT PLANS → DECISION (ARE PLANS FEASIBLE?)

- NO → LAYOUT PLANS
- YES → DECISION (ARE PROFITS HIGH ENOUGH AND RISK LOW ENOUGH?)
  - NO → SET UP PROFIT OBJECTIVES
  - YES → DECISION (ARE GOALS AND POLICY MET?)
    - NO → DEFINE POLICY & GOALS
    - YES → ACCEPT THE PLANS → END

Figure 5-2
The Forward Planning Process Flowchart

asked to hazard their best guess as to the financial consequences of undertaking a pilot operation. Failing to do this the company may well find that it has an invention in hand which appears to be technically successful, but which will involve too much additional money to commercialize it.

Another type of program might involve the construction of manufacturing facilities to provide supplies of the company's products. These facilities will last 15 or 20 years or even longer and their justification must be expressed in financial terms.

Contents of a Sales Plan

Below is a suggested table of contents for a sales plan. Major programs should be separately described in each case.
1. Projection of sales volume by product line—annually for five years.
2. Price and gross margin projection by product line—annually for five years.
3. Market share by product line—annually for five years.
4. Total market potential by product line—annually for five years.
5. Projected changes in capital required for marketing operations—by year of occurrence. (Examples would be a new fleet of delivery trucks, purchase of warehouses, or a new plan of dealer financing.)
6. Any major changes planned in the marketing operation.
7. Sales projection by new product line—annually for five years.
8. Gross margin projection by new product line—annually for five years.
9. New capital investment in support of new products by product line—annually for five years.

It is important to note that this plan projects the marketing operation only. If new products require new production facilities, then capital spending for such facilities is shown in the production plan, but will be identified with the relevant marketing programs.

The Production Plan

A table of contents for such a plan would include the following:
1. Replacement plan listing major and minor capital projects to replace existing plant—annually for five years
2. New plant and equipment for existing production—annually for five years
3. New plant and equipment for new products (as specified in Marketing Sales Plan)—annually for five years
4. Production cost trends by production plant or by product line—annually for five years
5. New processes and techniques with approximate date of installation and effect on cost

The new projects detailed in this plan should be coordinated with the new products detailed in the sales plan. The new developments should make reference to engineering feasibility studies where they exist. Care should be taken to avoid rough guesses whenever possible. Projecting five years in the future is understandably difficult. However, the plan loses its value as a management tool if the financial manager resorts to "rough estimates".

Since we are dealing with somewhat uncertain forecasts, it is important that the substance of the major programs be described as fully as possible, at least in the supporting text of the report, if quantification is not feasible. Where new facilities are recommended, the justification must be stated, both in absolute terms (i.e., versus doing nothing), and in terms of alternate courses of action which are available.

Some other questions that may be relevant are:

—Why were the facilities not leased?

—What are the possible dangers of premature obsolescence?

—Is the proposed technology commercially reliable?

—Have start-up difficulties been estimated at appropriate levels?

The Manpower Plan

The rapid change of technology requires careful planning of new talents and types of experts required in future years, as well as the normal requirements for more ordinary skills. For example, data processing experts, biochemists, or astrophysicists may be needed within five years. Companies often find that a nationwide shortage exists in certain fields and most plan to develop whole departments and staff groups from within the firm. The objectives of this plan should be carefully coordinated with the sales and production plans.

THE FIVE-YEAR FINANCIAL PLAN

The Pay-off to Management

As the marketing production and manpower plans take shape, the major document, the financial plan, will take form along with them. It should be a condensed projection of three major items shown below:

1. The operating statement
2. The balance sheet
3. The capital budget

The results of careful planning will be an accurate picture of the future trends and prospects for the company. Three examples of the results of forward financial planning illustrate these benefits:

1. A computer manufacturer found that its marketing plan was so encouraging that its growth over the next five years was limited only by the capital required to match the rapidly growing sales. The financial manager recognized that the company's stock was well-received by the public and carried a high price-earnings ratio. Since the sales growth was highly predictable, the risks were considered reasonable in spite of the high growth

rate shown in the sales plan. The decision was made to conduct regular stock issues in future years to provide the growth capital required.

2. An airframe and airplane engine manufacturer was faced with a declining market as the military converted to missiles and rockets. The financial projection showed large quantities of cash being generated in future years as production facilities were phased out. However, the manpower plan indicated substantial risks if the firm tried to convert rapidly to the new technologies. This technical expertise was becoming obsolete. The decision was made to use the cash to buy small technically oriented firms to help make the transition.

3. A consumer goods manufacturer found that its market would continue to grow at a steady rate. Its production plan showed the sales increase could be handled readily and that manpower and plant facilities would in fact outstrip the sales growth. The financial picture looked stable and secure. The decision was made to make a major effort at new product development and new market development for existing products. A heavy market research and product planning effort was required, plus the development of an international division for sale of existing products.

The Components of the Financial Plan

The techniques of developing balance sheets, operating statements and capital budgets are described in the next chapter. The same methods apply to the five year plan as to the one and two year plan. However, the five year plan does not contain so much detailed information. The formats of these reports are shown in Figures 5-3, 5-4 and 5-5. In the balance sheet and operating statements, comparative data of recent actual performance is included. The capital budget (Figure 5-5) shows a breakdown into three major groups. The replacement and volume expansion portions deal with existing product lines, with new products shown as the third category.

PUTTING THE LONG RANGE PLANS TO WORK

Once the plans are put down on paper they should become a management tool, rather than a file filler. They are first submitted to the executive committee for suggested alteration. They then go to the Board of Directors. Once approved, they become the basis for implementation by the line departments.

Linkage to the Annual Budgets and Profit Plans

The five year financial plan will be developed in less detail than the annual capital budget and profit plans. This does not mean that the two are unrelated. Rather, it will be necessary to establish a definite link between the first year of the financial plan and the capital budget and profit plan which is subsequently prepared covering that year. To establish this linkage without at the same time creating an inordinate burden in the

	Comparative Data		*Projected Years*				
	Two Years Ago	Last Year	1st	2nd	3rd	4th	5th

Sales
Product Line I
Product Line II
Product Line III

Direct Costs
Material
Labor
Variable Selling
Variable Overhead

Fixed Overhead
Wages & Salaries
Depreciations
Other

Corporate S & A
Salaries
Other

Profit Before Taxes

Other Income
Other Expenses

Income Taxes

Profit After Tax

Figure 5-3
Projected Operating Statement

planning process is a matter of some skill. However, it is an absolute necessity if we are to be certain that the same general concepts and objectives are present in the two sets of forecasts. Unless the two systems are consistent, there is no basis on which to approve the year's capital budget and profit plan, since there is no certainty that they are consistent with the long range financial plan for the company. In order to avoid the creation of unnecessary detail, it is desirable to have the operating departments comment in an affirmative fashion that their budgets and profit plans are in fact consistent with the approved long range financial plan for their activity.

	Comparative Data		*Projected Data*				
	Two Years Ago	Last Year	1st yr.	2nd yr.	3rd yr.	4th yr.	5th yr.

Cash
Receivables External
Receivables Internal
Inventories
Other Current Assets

Internal Dept & Equity

Fixed Asset Old
Fixed Assets
Future Purchases
Less Depres. Res.

Other Assets

Payable-External
Payable-Internal
Accruals

L.T. Debt-External
L.T. Debt-Internal

Reserves
Net Worth-Bal. Forward
Plus Earnings
Less Dividends

Plus New Capital
Stock

Figure 5-4
Projected Balance Sheet

Post Audit

Once the long range planning system has been installed, it is necessary to establish an orderly method of recording the "track record" against this planning system. This is desirable to provide a means of revising the company's goals and objectives, and to provide insights into better means of forecasting.

It is also necessary to evaluate the performance of the various managers who are responsible for the forecasts that are built into the plan. Some managers are characteristically "target" forecasters; that is, they make a forecast which does not provide for

	1st. Yr.	2nd Yr.	3rd Yr.	4th Yr.	5th Yr.
Replacement Program					
Machinery					
Land & Building					
Automotive					
Marketing					
Other					
Volume Expansion					
Machinery					
Land & Building					
Automotive					
Marketing					
Other					
New Product					
Machinery					
Land & Building					
Automotive					
Marketing					
Other					

Figure 5-5
Projected Capital Budget

the possibility of a normal amount of "bad luck". Consequently, their forecasts are achievable only under optimum circumstances. At the other extreme are managers who retain a "cushion" which will permit them to offset unfavorable performance. A post audit will help to expose both types of forecasting.

The post audit must be timed so as to provide a useful measure of actual performance and still be early enough to give information that can be utilized in the preparation of new plans. The post audit will rarely be of value in correcting deficiencies in the particular project under audit, because the post audit cannot really be undertaken until some reliable experience has been obtained from the project. By the time this experience is available, the project will generally have been so fully committed as to be irreversible. When dealing with construction projects or the purchase of equipment, the post audit can usually take place once the facility is operating under so-called "normal" conditions. When dealing with the introduction of a new product, the post audit can begin once sales have reached normal commercial levels. This may mean in general that the post audit might take place at the end of the first third or quarter of the project's estimated life.

6

Analyzing Financial Performance

6

Analyzing Financial Performance

Financial facts and data cannot be used in their raw form. There must be interpretation and analysis of these data—and this interpretation and analysis is an important function of the financial department. By analyzing data, the financial officer can assist management in:

1. Understanding historical results
2. Highlighting current trends
3. Forecasting the financial future

Since the data are not usable in their raw form, there must be some basis for comparison. Basically, these comparisons can take two forms. The first, and most general of these comparisons, is a comparison of the company's operations with industry generally, or with specific competitors. These are external comparisons. The second type of comparison is a comparison with goals and objectives which the company set for itself; these are internal comparisons.

External comparisons can be made with specific companies (e.g., competitors), or with statistics for entire industries or groups of companies. Particularly in the latter case these comparisons can be made by means of financial ratios.

FINANCIAL RATIOS

The ratio is one quantity (a numerator) divided by another (the denominator). The ratios fall into several categories as shown in Figure 6-1.

The ratio is an indicator which is used to find weak spots in the financial structure. To use this indicator norms must be available to measure against. For example, to say that the ratio of debt to equity is .650 is meaningless unless some means of evaluating .650 is available. Dun & Bradstreet publishes every year complete tables of ratios for 72 types of businesses. Figure 6-2 shows a sample of these ratios. Many trade associations publish financial ratios for their particular industries. These reports are produced

99

Type	Name of Ratio	Numerator	Denominator	Notes
Liquidity	Current Ratio	Current Assets	Current Liabilities	
	Acid Test Ratio	Cash & Securities & Receivables	Current Liabilities	
	Collection Period	Average Receivables	Annual Sales Divided by 365	Number of days of sales outstanding as receivables
Effectiveness of Assets	Inventory Turnover	Annual Cost of Goods Sold	Average Inventory	
	Asset Turnover	Annual Sales	Total Assets	
	Fixed Asset to Sales	Fixed Assets Net of Depreciation	Annual Sales	
Profitability	Return on Sales	Profit After Taxes	Annual Sales	
	Return on Assets	Profit After Taxes	Total Assets	
	Return on Net Worth	Profit After Taxes	Net Worth	
	Debt to Equity	Total Debt	Total Equity	Dollars of debt per dollar of equity funds
Borrowing Capacity	Cash Flow to Sales	Profit After Taxes plus Depreciation	Annual Sales	Rate of cash profit per sales dollar
	Time Interest Earned	Profit Before Interest & Taxes	Interest	
	Cash Flow to Debt Service	Profit After Taxes plus Depreciation	Annual Rate of Debit Repayment	Rate of cash profit to cash obligations

Figure 6-1

MANUFACTURING: FOOD AND KINDRED PRODUCTS:
Canned and frozen foods

Item Description (for accounting period 7/67 through 6/68)	A Total	B Under 50	C 50 to 100	D 100 to 250	E 250 to 500	F 500 to 1,000	G 1,000 to 5,000	H 5,000 to 10,000	I 10,000 to 25,000	J 25,000 to 50,000	K 50,000 to 100,000	L 100,000 to 250,000	M 250,000 and over
							SIZE OF ASSETS IN THOUSANDS OF DOLLARS (000 OMITTED)						
1. Number of establishments	1805	439	170	359	235	216	289	52	26	8	2	5	4
2. Number without net income	681	294	85	83	70	100	45	-	2	2	-	-	-
3. Total receipts (in millions of dollars)	6944.2	137.7	32.0	143.9	260.6	234.4	1256.6	617.8	591.8	484.7	383.0	922.3	1879.1
Selected Operating Factors in percent of net sales													
4. Cost of operations	73.8	70.8	71.2	76.5	86.6	77.1	78.7	74.9	76.5	80.1	87.0	68.5	65.4
5. Compensation of officers	.8	1.6	.7	4.1	2.7	1.4	1.3	1.1	.8	.5	-	-	-
6. Repairs	1.0	2.6	.9	.7	.8	.9	.9	.9	1.1	.7	-	1.1	1.3
7. Bad debts	-	-	-	-	-	-	-	-	-	-	-	-	-
8. Rent on business property	.6	.7	2.0	1.4	.7	.7	.6	.6	.8	.6	.6	1.0	-
9. Taxes (excl Federal tax)	1.9	2.8	1.7	1.6	1.9	2.5	1.7	1.6	2.0	1.4	1.1	2.4	2.0
10. Interest	1.3	1.7	.7	1.4	.9	1.5	1.2	1.5	1.2	1.0	1.4	1.9	1.1
11. Deprec/Deplet/Amortiz*	2.1	2.1	1.7	2.1	1.4	2.8	1.9	1.7	2.2	1.6	1.0	2.4	2.5
12. Advertising	2.6	3.2	1.1	.5	-	.6	.9	1.9	.8	3.1	.9	4.0	4.7
13. Pensions & other benef plans	.6	1.0	-	-	-	-	-	.5	.6	-	-	.8	1.1
14. Other expenses	11.6	14.5	19.8	11.5	5.5	10.2	9.4	10.8	10.5	7.5	7.5	13.1	15.5
15. Net profit before tax	3.6	*	-	*	*	2.2	3.0	4.5	3.4	3.2	*	4.4	6.0
Selected Financial Ratios (number of times ratio is to one)													
16. Current ratio	1.7	.5	1.5	.9	1.4	1.0	1.5	1.4	1.5	1.9	1.8	2.2	2.2
17. Quick ratio	.5	-	1.0	-	.5	-	-	-	-	.6	.6	.5	.8
18. Net sls to net wkg capital	6.1	-	9.0	-	18.0	42.9	8.3	7.4	6.8	6.9	7.9	4.0	4.1
19. Net sales to net worth	3.1	-	9.8	45.0	8.3	4.5	4.5	4.0	3.2	4.6	6.6	2.3	1.9
20. Inventory turnover	-	-	-	-	-	-	-	-	-	-	-	-	-
21. Total liab to net worth	1.0	-	2.9	17.2	1.7	1.9	1.4	1.4	1.1	1.4	1.7	.7	.6
Selected Financial Factors in percentages													
22. Current lia to net worth	64.6	-	211.6	1095.9	115.6	150.8	105.6	109.7	81.9	72.8	97.5	44.4	37.0
23. Inventory to curr assets	62.0	48.1	27.9	52.3	53.9	61.6	64.3	69.8	71.2	60.2	61.4	58.3	59.5
24. Net income to net worth	9.8	-	57.1	157.9	19.1	12.1	12.4	13.1	8.0	10.3	2.8	8.0	8.7
25. Retained earn to net inc	58.7	-268.2	100.0	99.6	94.7	92.8	89.7	94.6	84.8	77.6	100.0	49.2	31.4

*Depreciation largest factor

Figure 6-2
Illustrative Chart of Ratios for 199 Industries available in
"Almanac of Business and Industrial Financial Ratios," © 1970
Prentice-Hall, Inc., Englewood Cliffs, N.J.

on a cooperative basis and are generally available only to companies who submit their financial data. Collection Period—This ratio states the number of days required to collect the average accounts receivable dollar. The formula for computing it is:

$$\text{Collection Period} = \frac{\text{Average Accounts Receivable *}}{\text{Annual Sales}} \times 365$$

* Average Acounts Receivable is the average of the balance at the beginning and at the end of the year.

The collection period gives a good indication of the delinquency of customer payments. If, for example, sales are on a Net 30 basis and the collection period is 45 days, one can see that the average bill is paid 15 days late. Another important use to be made of this ratio is for predicting changes in the level of receivable with changes in sales volume. In the 454 day example, receivables can be estimated as 1½ months sales ($\frac{45}{30} = 1\frac{1}{2}$). When it is used this way, care should be taken to investigate seasonal shifts in collection period. Some companies have a 90 day collection period at Christmas time and a 45 day the remainder of the year. For companies with a seasonal trend, the chart shown in Figure 6-3 will instantly compare the receivable picture to previous years.

		Collection Period	
Month	2 Years Ago	Last Year	This Year
Jan.	42	39	46
Feb.	44	45	48
Mar.	40	46	52
Apr.	48	49	55
May	51	54	
June	50	50	
July	54	52	
Aug.	46	49	
Sept.	42	47	
Oct.	41	44	
Nov.	40	45	
Dec.	38	43	

Figure 6-3

TURN RECEIVABLE DOLLARS INTO CASH DOLLARS BY CHANGING TERMS OF SALE

To improve the collection period means more cash on hand. Several moves can be made to speed up collections. Tighter credit rules and tougher collection procedures are major steps and run the risk of lowering sales. Offering cash discounts will, if anything, attract new sales. The drawback is the cost of offering a cash discount. The cost to go from Net 30 to 1%, 10 days would be computed as follows:

1. With $100,000 outstanding and a 50 day collection period, the sales per day would be $100,000 ÷ 50 or $2,000 per day.
2. If, 1%, 10 days were offered, and the collection period became 20 days, the receivables then become 20 × $2,000 or $40,000. This means increased cash of $100,000 — $40,000 or $60,000.
3. The cost per year, if all sales were discounted, would be 365 × 2,000 × .01 or $7,300.
4. The percentage cost of the $60,000 would be $7,300 ÷ 60,000 or 12.2%.

At first glance a financial manager might discard the idea as too expensive. First he must consider—

a. He has increased his cash on hand which could immediately be used to pay off a 6% loan and, thereby, further improve his current ratio (explained below) and acid test ratio.
b. The improved current ratio and lower debt may allow him to get new long term debt to finance capital projects which would otherwise have been turned down.
c. The discount terms may attract more customers and offset the financial cost with greater sales.

IMPORTANT "BORROWING CAPACITY" RATIOS

The amount of debt which a company can employ without incurring excess risk or higher cost depends on the firm's financial condition. The most important ratios to measure ability to borrow are Current Ratio and Debt to Equity Ratio. The Current Ratio is the amount of assets which will be converted to cash within a year divided by the liabilities due within one year. It is, therefore, the ratio of potential cash within one year to known demands on cash within a year. A one to one ratio would mean no liquidity or safety margin. A two to one ratio would mean one dollar in reserve for every dollar obligated for payment.

So long as the ratio exceeds one to one, the current ratio can be improved by more efficient use of current assets as follows:

1. Lowering cash balances and using the extra cash to retire current liabilities.
2. Lowering the collection period and using the cash generated to reduce current liabilities.
3. Improving inventory turnover and applying the cash to current liabilities.

If the ratio is less than one to one, the above measures will actually worsen the ratio. However, in these circumstances, the financial manager is faced with the need to ration his cash resources in relation to the maturities of current liabilities, and any additional efficiency which he is able to achieve in the use of cash will assist in that effort.

The debt to equity ratio assesses a very fundamental fact—what part of the funds comes from outsiders and what part comes from stockholders. A lender is vitally interested in this ratio since a sure sign of financial trouble is excessive borrowing. To decide how much borrowing is excessive requires comparative data from similar companies, and an assessment of the relative risk involved in the cash flow of the companies.

Data necessary to make comparisons must be obtained from a variety of sources. The U. S. Department of Commerce publishes a pamphlet which lists many of these sources ("Guides for Business Analysis and Profit Evaluation", published by the U. S. Government Printing Office). If a precise comparison with a particular competitor is required, it will be necessary to calculate the relevant information from the competitor's published statement, or other available information.

HOW MUCH DOES MONEY COST—COST OF CAPITAL

When additional capital is to be invested in new products two questions must be answered. First—What return will there be on the invested money? Second—What will the additional capital cost the company? In Chapter 8 methods of measuring return on capital are shown. In this chapter the cost of capital is explained.

Money Costs More Than Banks Charge

If $100,000 were to be added to inventory for a new product line, what is the financial cost of carrying that inventory? If banks would lend the $100,000 need at 6%, the temptation is to say that the inventory costs 6% per year. However, the borrowing of the $100,000 has increased the debt to equity ratio and decreased the current ratio. This means additional borrowing will be harder to get. Eventually a company which borrowed for all its needs would reach its debt limit. At this point banks would say "No more loans until more equity funds are put in the company." New equity funds have a cost since new stockholders would want a 10% after tax return. Thus borrowing the $100,000 at 6% before taxes will lead to a need for other money at a 10% after tax cost.

How to Compute the Cost of Capital

The procedure for computing the cost of capital is as follows:
1. Recognize the difference between before tax and after tax cost. For example, a company paying a bank 6% interest has a .06 × .5 or 3% after tax cost assuming a 50% tax bracket.
2. List all major sources of capital shown on a balance sheet as shown in Figure 6-4.
3. Compute the before tax cost of tax-deductible types of funds (See Figure 6-4).
   a. For loans use the annual interest rates.
   b. For secured loans use the interest rate plus service charges.

Type of Funds	Computed Cost Before Taxes	Tax Multiplier	After Tax Cost
1. Trade Credit (lost discounts)	.09	.50	.045
2. Bank Loan	.06	.50	.030
3. Secured Loans	.120	.50	.060
4. Bonds	.064	.50	.032
5. Accruals	.000	.50	.000
6. Preferred Stock	.600	1.00	.600
7. Common Stock	.100	1.00	.100

Figure 6-4
Source of Capital-Cost Computation

EXAMPLE: If receivable financing costs 1% of invoices used as security plus 7% interest, the computation would be

$$\text{Total Cost} = (\text{Svc. Charge}) \times \frac{\text{Sales}}{\text{Receivables}} + \text{Loan Interest}$$

$$= 1\% \times \frac{1,000,000}{200,000} + 7\%$$

$$= 12\%$$

An alternative method of computing the cost is from past records. The total of the bank's service and interest charges for the past year is divided by the average loan balance. The average loan balance is obtained by totalling the twelve month balances and dividing by 12.

c. The cost of trade credit on which discounts were missed is a possible cost to be considered. If the discount period is shown as D.P. and the actual pay period as P.P., the cost in percent per annum is

$$\% \text{ cost} = \frac{\text{Discount } \% \times 365}{(\text{P.P.} - \text{D.P.})}$$

$$= \frac{.01 \times 365}{50 - 10} = .09$$

d. The cost of term loans, mortgages and bonds is computed by adding the interest rate to the amortized expenses of obtaining the debt. A 20 year 6% bond issue for a million dollars which had a $50,000 underwriting expense would be computed as:

$$\text{Cost } \% = .06 + \frac{(\quad 50,000 \times 1 \quad)}{(1,000,000 \qquad 20)}$$

$$= .064$$

    e. Other liabilities such as accrued payroll, accrued taxes and trade credit on which discounts are taken have no tangible cost.

4. Equity Funds have a cost which must be *imputed*. When a stockholder invests in a company, he expects a return on his money. How much he expects depends on the risk involved which in turn depends on the type of company. A utility stockholder will be happy if his money earns 7% while in an electronics company the figure might be 15%. The management's task is to earn this expected return. Thus the cost to the management is the 7%, 15% or whatever the stockholders expect of them. Preferred stockholders clearly state their expected return on the stock certificate. Common stockholders do not spell out their expectations. It is up to the financial manager to estimate them.

    a. *How to Compute the Cost of Preferred Stock*

        Since the dividend is paid out of after tax funds, the tax multiplier is 1.00 as shown in Figure 6-4. The cost is simply the coupon rate. The exception would be preferred stock with a redemption date (similar to a bond). In this case, the underwriting costs can be amortized as was explained for bonds above.

    b. *How to Estimate the Cost of Common Stock*

        The stock market offers the best means of measuring what percent return stockholders require. This is done by computing the price earnings ratio for all publicly held stocks in the same business and of the same relative size.[1] If ten times earnings were chosen, the cost of capital is 10%. For 12 times earnings, the cost would be 8.3%.

The weighted average is computed in Figure 6-5 by multiplying the fraction of total capital (A) by the after tax cost (B) of each kind of funds found on the balance sheet. The sum of the products is the cost of capital.

How to Use the Cost of Capital

The average after tax cost per dollar of capital can be put to several uses such as—

1. Use in determining satisfactory percentages of return on investment required for new capital investment.
2. Checking trends of the cost of money compared to the total economy.
3. Analyzing cost trends of the component types of capital.

To put the cost of capital in perspective one must think of the balance sheet in terms

---

[1] More sophisticated techniques involve determining separate rates of return for retained earnings and common stock. These methods are of academic interest only.

Type of Capital	Dollar Amt.	(A) Fraction of Total Capital	(B) After Tax Cost	(A) Times (B)
Trade Credit	75,000	.15	.045	.0067
Bank Loans	25,000	.05	.030	.0015
Secured Loans	50,000	.10	.060	.0060
Accruals	25,000	.05	.000	.0000
Bonds	50,000	.10	.032	.0032
Preferred Stock	50,000	.10	.060	.0060
Common Stock	225,000	.45	.100	.0450
	500,000			.0684

Figure 6-5

of capital. The asset side represents the uses of capital and the liability side represents the source of capital. Therefore, profit is the return on assets or uses of capital. Interest, dividends and retained earnings represent the distribution of the profit to the sources of capital. In this context cost of capital takes on a very definite meaning.

How to Compare the Cost of Capital to the Return on Capital

Figure 6-5 explains how to derive a Cost of Capital figure—specifically 6.84%. To what figure should this 6.84% be compared? The proper ratio is the Return on Capital. This is the after tax profits excluding interest from expenses.

The formula for computing it is—

$$\text{Return on Capital} = \frac{\text{Prof. After Tax} + (1\text{-Tax Rate} \times \text{Interest})}{\text{Total Assets}}$$

What does it mean when the Return on Capital is greater than, or less than, the Cost of Capital? The meaning is dependent on the circumstances in each case. First, it should be emphasized that the Cost of Capital is based on a calculation of historical relationships; it is a calculation of the cost of the amount of capital which has actually been utilized in the business. Thus, in Figure 6-5, the total capital of $500,000 is the amount actually employed in the business, without regard to the value of the assets which may have been acquired with that capital. It may be that this capital has been used in part to acquire a very valuable piece of property at a very favorable price; that value is not reflected in the Cost of Capital. Yet the cost of the common stock portion of the capital is a reflection, at least in part, of stockholders' expectations for the industry in which we operate. This expectation may well comprehend the earning power of valuable assets acquired in the past at low cost. In this case, the fact that the company was showing a Return on Capital substantially above its Cost of Capital may not be any basis for assuming that the stockholders are satisfied with the company's performance. It may merely reflect the stock market assessment of the true value of the capital being employed in the business. The converse can also be true, where a business has high cost assets on the books.

The above discussion points up a difficulty in using the historical Cost of Capital as a guideline in making future investment decisions. Particularly if a very significant move is made by a company (e.g., a major expansion, an acquisition, or a retrenchment), there may be a reaction in the price/earnings ratio of its stock, so that its cost of Capital for that decision is different than would have been calculated based on the formula given above. Thus, in the example given in Figure 6-5, if the company is only selling at eight times earnings, the common stock portion of its capital is costing 12.5% after tax, and the composite cost of capital would be nearly 8%. Conversely, if the company makes a move which is favorably interpreted on the stock market, and its stock moves permanently to 15 times earnings, the composite Cost of Capital would fall to 5.3%. Obviously, management is interested in knowing what will be the cost of adding new capital, rather than merely what is the cost of the capital already employed. As we have already indicated, this new capital cannot all be assumed to be borrowed capital—at some point there will be the need for new equity capital. It may be that the mix of new capital will approximate the existing mix between borrowed and equity capital. If that is the case, we must still decide whether our company can attract new equity money in competition with other companies with similar risks. Only if the company's future prospects compare favorably with others of similar size (particularly in the same industry) can we rely on the cost of capital which we have assigned to the common stock segment of the total capital.

The Effect of Cost of Capital on Cash Reserve Policy

A financial manager who knows what his cost of capital is can improve the company's return on investment by careful control over the use of cash resources.

Example. A company which holds large cash reserves in low interest treasury bills can improve its return on investment quite easily. If there is no use for the funds in the business, they can over a period of time be turned back to the stockholders as dividends. If the cash returns 2% after tax, and the overall cost of capital is 6%, the return on assets will improve if the cash is removed from the balance sheet. An example of this is shown in Figure 6-6.

Use of Cost of Capital to Make Capital Investment Decisions

In Chapter 8 the methods of organizing the capital spending program are shown. The calculation of the cost of capital can play a role in capital investment decisions. In reviewing alternative proposals showing various rates of return, the minimum acceptable rate must be spelled out. To set this "hurdle rate" the cost of capital must be known, although a somewhat higher rate may be set, in order to cover such expenditures as corporate overhead, which may not be included in rate of return calculations.

Moreover, the "hurdle rate" must be set at a level which will permit the company to

A. *Status with Excess Cash*

1.

Balance Sheet

Cash	50,000		
Marketable Securities	200,000	Debt	400,000
All Other Assets	750,000	Equity	600,000

2.

P & L Statement & Return on Capital

Return on Operations excluding Interest	$76,000
Return on Marketable Securities (2%)	4,000
Total Return on Capital	$80,000

$$\% \text{ Return on Capital} = \frac{80,000}{1,000,000} = 8\%$$

3. *Cost of Capital*

Type of Capital	(A) After Tax Cost	(B) % of Total Capital	A × B
Debt	.03	.40	.012
Equity	.10	.60	.060
		Cost of Capital	.072

B. *Status Without Excess Cash*

1.

Balance Sheet

Cash	50,000	Debt	400,000
All Other Assets	750,000	Equity	400,000

2.

P & L Statement & Return on Capital

Return on Operations excluding Interest	76,000
Return on Marketable Securities	—
Total Return on Capital	76,000

$$\% \text{ Return on Capital} = \frac{76,000}{800,000} = 9.5\%$$

3. *Cost of Capital*

Type of Capital	(A) After Tax Cost	(B) % of Total Capital	A × B
Debt	.03	.50	.015
Equity	.10	.50	.050
		Cost of Capital	.065

C. *Comparison*

	With Excess Cash	Without Excess Cash
Cost of Capital	7.2%	6.5%
Return on Capital	8.0%	9.5%

Figure 6-6
How Excess Cash Holds Down the Return on Capital and Increases the Cost of Capital

meet its goals for earnings growth, and profitability in relation to shareholder equity. These considerations may keep the "hurdle rate" considerably above the cost of capital.

SOURCES AND USES OF FUNDS

A periodic review of changes in capital structure is an important duty of the financial manager. This is done by making a Statement of Sources and Applications of Funds. It is generally done yearly as a part of a general financial review. The balance sheet is consolidated into not more than twenty asset and twenty liability accounts. The titles used are those commonly seen on simplified balance sheets such as the example in Figure 6-7. Last year's balance in each account is subtracted from this year's balance. If the account carried a debit balance, the difference is put in the debit column. The proper sign is also derived via this rule. If this year's balance is larger than last year's, the sign is plus, if less, the sign is minus. The converted difference is used to eliminate minus signs. Any negative debit is changed to a positive credit. Any negative credit is changed to a positive debit. Once this has been done, the dollar amounts in the credit column are moved to source column. The debit amounts go to the uses column.

A few examples of the meaning of the statement shown as Figure 6-8 are as follows:
1. To increase the accounts receivable is a use of funds since there will be that much less cash available.
2. To increase bank loans is a source of funds since there will be that much more cash available.
3. To increase the depreciation reserve on the buildings is to change profit and loss with a non-cash expense and thereby increase the cash. This is, therefore, a source.
4. To increase Retained Earnings is a source of funds since cash will increase.
5. To decrease Accounts Payable is a use of funds since cash will decrease.

The S & A Statement Tells the Financial Story

The financial manager seeks to make good use of the funds available to the company. The S & A Statement delineates all the sources of funds. These sources may be thought of as all the cash generated in the past year. The applications represent all the cash consumed in the past year. Figure 6-8 is an example of a 5 year spread of sources and applications of funds.

Inventory climbed each year and is shown as an application. Money was reinvested in fixed asset each year. This was another major application. Major sources were depreciation and retained earnings. The five year spread quickly points out important balance sheet changes and trends.

Important Checkpoints in S & A Statements

Listed below are several methods of using an S & A Statement as a financial barometer.
1. Add up all the sources which come from current assets and liabilities. Sub-

	Balance This Year	Balance Last Year	Difference Dr.	Difference Cr.	Converted Difference Dr.	Converted Difference Cr.	Uses	Sources
Cash	50,000 Dr	30,000 Dr	+20,000		20,000		20,000	
Acct. Rec.	200,000 Dr	245,000 Dr	−45,000			45,000		45,000
Invent.	300,000 Dr	270,000 Dr	+30,000		30,000		30,000	
Other Curr.	30,000 Dr	27,000 Dr	− 3,000		3,000		3,000	
Invest. in Subid.	80,000 Dr	80,000 Dr						
Land	40,000 Dr	40,000 Dr						
Bldg	180,000 Dr	160,000 Dr	+20,000		20,000		20,000	
Deprec. Res.	30,000 Cr	21,000 Cr		+ 9,000		9,000		9,000
Equipment	290,000 Dr	257,000 Dr	+33,000		33,000		33,000	
Deprec. Res.	80,000 Cr	57,000 Cr		+ 23,000		23,000		23,000
Automobiles	44,000 Dr	44,000 Dr						
Deprec. Res.	24,000 Cr	17,000 Cr		+ 7,000		7,000		7,000
Other Assets	12,000 Dr	12,000 Dr						
Accounts Payable	150,000 Cr	172,000 Cr		− 22,000	22,000		22,000	
Taxes Payable	48,000 Cr	49,000 Cr		− 1,000	1,000		1,000	
Notes Payable	80,000 Cr	112,000 Cr		− 32,000	32,000		32,000	
Accruals	74,000 Cr	62,000 Cr		+ 12,000		12,000		12,000
Other Liabilities	37,000 Cr	12,000 Cr		+ 25,000		25,000		25,000
Mortgages	121,000 Cr	132,000 Cr		− 11,000	11,000		11,000	
Term Loan		137,000 Cr		−137,000	137,000		137,000	
Preferred Stock	120,000 Cr			+120,000		120,000		120,000
Common Stock	194,000 Cr	188,000 Cr		+ 6,000		6,000		6,000
Retained Earnings	268,000 Cr	206,000 Cr		+ 62,000		62,000		62,000

Figure 6-7

All figures in thousands of dollars

	Sources					Applications					5 Year Recap	
	Year 1	Year 2	Year 3	Year 4	Year 5	Year 1	Year 2	Year 3	Year 4	Year 5	Sources	Applications
Cash	10.3				11.0		5.4	7.6	8.1		0.2	
Receivables	4.1	12.1	6.2	48.1						44.4	26.1	
Inventory						24.8	41.1	7.7	17.2	10.6		101.4
Fixed Assets						57.4	44.8	58.0	68.9	32.1		261.2
Depreciation	38.6	44.2	32.8	29.7	28.8						174.1	
Other Assets	2.0			2.0	7.1		16.0	4.0				8.9
Payables	18.7	19.1			27.4			1.2	39.1		24.9	
Accruals	6.5	3.5		4.8				2.0		4.1	8.7	
Bank Loans		6.8	12.8		6.8	23.8			41.1			385
Preferred Stock				50.0							50.0	
Common Stock												
Retained Earnings	25.8	21.6	28.7	19.8	30.1						126.0	
Totals	106.0	107.3	80.5	154.4	112.2	106.0	107.3	80.5	154.4	112.2	410.0	410.0

Figure 6-8

	1st Quarter	2nd Quarter	3rd Quarter	4th Quarter	1st Quarter	2nd Quarter	3rd Quarter	4th Quarter
Collection Period — Last Year Average 39 days Assume-Constant except 4th Quarter which is +20% or 47 days	39	39	39	47	39	39	39	47
Sales in Current Quarter — Quarterly Sales 91	$600M	$470M	$520M	$840M	$660M	$517M	$572M	$924M
Sales Per Day Current Quarter	6.59	5.16	5.71	9.23	7.25	5.68	6.28	10.15
Accounts Receivable — Collection Period × Sales/Day	257.0	201.2	222.7	433.8	282.8	221.5	244.9	434.3

Figure 6-9
Pro Forma Worksheet

tract all the uses which come from current assets and liabilities. If the balance is a positive number, it is the net addition to working capital. If it is negative, it is the net loss of working capital.

2. Compare all fixed asset accounts to all depreciation accounts. Did depreciation cover the cash required for new acquisitions?

3. Check the long-term trend of the inventory account. If it is a major use, what is the ratio of the change in inventory to the change of sales? This ratio should not exceed the cost of sales percentage.

PRO FORMA BALANCE SHEETS

The liquidity of the company shall be projected forward for several years advance to to assure sound planning. The short term cash budget works on the principle of old balance plus receipts less disbursements and is described in Chapter 2. Over longer periods of time receipts and disbursements become more difficult to estimate. The formulas become complicated and the assumptions more and more vague. A better method for long term projection is the Pro Forma Balance Sheet.

The Pro Forma Balance Sheet is completed in the following three steps:

1. Estimate Sales, production, purchase activity for future periods.

2. Based on these estimates predict the amounts of all major asset and liability accounts at the end of each future period except cash.

3. Subtract total assets other than cash from total liabilities to get the cash balance.

STEP 1—ESTIMATING SALES, PRODUCTION AND PURCHASES

Many firms require the marketing division to make sales forecasts which can be used for budget purposes. Such an estimate would be ideal for this purpose. If no such estimate is available, the financial manager can make one as follows:

1. For each major sales type or product line determine an annual growth rate.

2. Multiply each growth factor (1.06 for 6%) by current annual sales to determine next year's annual sales. Repeat again for each additional year.

3. Based on historical data break the annual figure into monthly or quarterly estimates. For example: 1st quarter 30%, 2nd quarter 20%, 3rd quarter 18%, and 4th quarter 32%. The choice of quarterly vs. monthly depends on whether a pro forma balance sheet will be generated for the end of each quarter or each month.

To obtain production and purchases per quarter or per month, the sales level, plant capacity, manpower needs and other factors must be taken into account. An estimate of production takes the form of 60% of the next quarter's sales but not to exceed $120,-000 which is plant capacity. The 60% is the inventory cost factor per sales dollar. Purchase requirements can be based on production estimates. An estimate of purchases takes the form of 48% of the next quarter's production.

STEP 2—ESTIMATING THE BALANCE SHEET ITEMS

Estimating procedures are applied to only certain balance sheet accounts. Those not estimated are assumed to be fixed. The criteria for deciding which accounts are to be treated as fixed are:

1. Relatively small dollar balances in the account.
2. No simple connection between the balance and sales or production levels.
3. No known pattern to variations in the account balance.
4. The account is known to carry a fixed balance.

Examples of accounts which should be treated as fixed are Investment in Subsidiaries, Deposits and Prepaid Items, Land, Preferred Stock, Common Stock, Exchanges Payable.

Estimating Receivables

The historical data on the collection period is used to determine receivables levels; three situations are possible:

1. The collection period may be steadily rising or falling.
2. The collection period may show a major seasonal pattern.
3. The collection period may be constant.

Use of these assumptions and the current collection period allows the estimation of the future collection periods. A sample worksheet is shown in Figure 6-9. Note that the Notes Column is used to write down the assumptions made. These notes are valuable for review of assumptions and techniques at a later date.

Computation of Receivables

From the sales forecast the quarterly sales figures are entered on the worksheet. These are then converted into sales per day by dividing by 91. Multiplying sales per day by the collection period gives the receivable balance.

Techniques to Improve the Accuracy

Depending on the accuracy desired and time available any of the following sophistications can be added:

1. Estimate the collection period by product lines or sales groups which match the sales forecast. A worksheet is filled out for each one and figures added to obtain total receivables.
2. Assume a compound variation in collection period. An example would be —Collection period steadily rising and also showing seasonal variation.
3. Allow for price level increases or decreases.

Estimating Inventory Levels

The most difficult item to estimate for manufacturing concerns is inventory. Several approaches are possible. Estimates can be based on man hours of labor, units produced, pounds throughout, or some other physical index. If physical indexes are used, they are generally first estimated in the production and purchase figures. Retail concerns can generally base inventory estimates on % of sales. Both methods are explained below. Physical index of man hours is used in Figure 6-10 and % of sales in Figure 6-11.

Estimating Inventory on Physical Index Basis

Based on non-financial factors such as level employment policy and equipment capacity, a production schedule is made out. The man hours in the example in Figure 6-10 show a plant which adds an extra shift during the fourth quarter. These man hours are converted into dollars by using a company-wide labor and overhead rate. This is computed on Line 3 and is added to raw material purchases to get total addition to inventory. The subtractions from inventory are calculated as a percentage of sales on Line 6. The additions netted against the subtractions give the net change in inventory on Line 7. This added or subtracted from the beginning inventory gives the new inventory balance on Line 9.

Estimating Inventory Based on % of Sales

The technique is similar to the previous example except that additions to inventory are based on sales. In Figure 6-11 the current sales are used to compute 30% of the addition to inventory on Line 2. The next quarter's sales are used to compute 70% of the addition to inventory. In both cases the inventory value to sales ratio of 62% is used. This means that each dollar of sales is valued at $.62 when it is put in inventory. The deletions from inventory are computed using the same 62% factor times the current quarter's sales. The net change is calculated and added or subtracted from the opening balance as in Figure 6-10.

How to Make Inventory Projections Even More Accurate

More involved computations will add to the accuracy. The choice of exact method will depend on the availability of detailed data, time available, and other factors which the financial manager may wish to take into account. Some alternatives are:
1. A breakdown of sales, production, and purchase schedules by product line with a worksheet for each.
2. Estimate minimum and maximum inventory levels for each product line. Minimums are based on protection against out-of-stock and maximums are based on physical limits of storage areas. Review all balances to make sure no minimums or maximums have been violated. If they have, schedules must be revised.
3. Allow for change cost levels of labor, overhead and materials in future periods.

Control of inventories requires continuous attention, if we are to avoid tying up unnecessary resources in this form. Naturally, the inventory forecasts developed in the

Figure 6-10
Inventory Estimate Based on Physical Index
(All figures in thousands)

Item	Line	Notes	1st Year				2nd Year			
			1st Quarter	2nd Quarter	3rd Quarter	4th Quarter	1st Quarter	2nd Quarter	3rd Quarter	4th Quarter
Sales Current Quarter			600	470	520	840	660	517	572	924
Raw Material Purchases		From Purchase Schedule	94	104	168	132	103	114	185	112
Factory Man Hours		Level Production except 4th Quarter which is +33%	30.0	30.0	30.0	40.0	33.0	33.0	33.0	44.0
Labor & Overhead Added to Inventory		Labor Rate 3.25 Overhead Rate 6.35 Addition to Inventory (3.25 6.35) × Manhours	286.5	286.5	286.5	382.0	315.2	315.2	315.2	420.2
Total Added to Inventory		Add Raw Matl. to Labor and Overhead	380.5	390.5	454.5	514.0	418.5	429.5	500.2	532.2
Total Depletions of Inventory		68.9% of Current Sales	413.5	323.8	358.3	578.8	454.7	356.2	394.1	636.6
Change of Inventory		Additions less Depletions	−32.9	76.7	96.2	−64.8	−36.2	73.3	106.1	−104.4
Old Inventory		Inventory Prior Quarter	184.4	151.5	228.2	324.4	259.6	223.4	296.7	402.8
New Inventory		Old ± Change	151.5	228.2	324.4	259.6	223.4	296.7	402.8	298.4

Figure 6-11
Estimating Inventory on Percent of Sales
(All figures in thousands)

Line		1st Year				2nd Year			
		1st	2nd	3rd	4th	1st	2nd	3rd	4th
1	Sales	600	470	520	840	660	517	572	924
2	Inventory Addition for Current Quarter	.30 × .62 × Current Sales	112	87	97	156	123	96	106	172
3	Inventory Addition for Next Quarter	.70 × .62 × Next Quarter Sales	204	226	364	286	224	248	401	315
4	Total Additions to Inventory	Line 2 plus Line 3	316	313	461	442	347	344	507	487
5	Total Deletions from Inventory	Current Sales times .62	372	291	322	521	409	320	355	573
6	Old Balance Inventory		488	432	454	593	514	452	476	628
7	New Inventory	Old balance plus additions minus deletions	432	454	593	514	452	476	628	542

fashion outlined above will only be a rough tool in judging the adequacy of the inventory control procedures. Where inventories represent a large investment, it will be necessary to make more detailed analyses.

One type of analysis is provided through the construction of an inventory control system which weighs the cost of a "run-out" (in terms of lost profit on a sale) against the cost of carrying enough inventory to lower the probability of run-out. In order to be reliable, this system will require data on experience with sales frequency, as well as cost data for the cost of carrying inventory, and the cost and profitability of sales. The data must be adjusted whenever major changes in them occur. Also, the results (the recommended inventory levels) must be modified when there is a major sales promotion. Such a system as this requires computer-assisted calculations in most instances, and can be utilized profitably only where the potential saving from lower inventory levels will justify the cost. This potential saving is measured by the cost of carrying the extra inventory.

A more general method of analyzing the adequacy of inventory levels is to compare levels (in relation to sales or cost of sales), with the relative levels of similar inventories maintained by competitors. While some competitors will have different sales mix or cost trends, the comparison will nonetheless serve as a goad to operating management to achieve reduction in relative inventory levels.

Estimating Other Current Assets and Miscellaneous Current Liabilities

Minor accounts which are not treated as fixed can be treated as varying with sales. Figure 6-12 shows a simple worksheet where each is treated as a percentage of sales of the current quarter.

Estimating Fixed Assets and Allowance for Depreciation

Future plans for capital spending must be forecast carefully. The evaluation of capital expenditures is discussed in the next chapter. The forecast of fixed asset balances involves more than a listing of those projects which management can now foresee. It also includes an estimate of those other expenditures which cannot now be foreseen precisely, as well as an estimate of retirements and sales that will take place during the forecast period.

For the next one or two years, it may be that the known new projects will provide a relatively complete list of likely additions to the fixed asset accounts. Longer term forecasts will require estimates of additions that cannot now be foreseen.

Retirements and sales of fixed assets are particularly difficult to forecast, unless they are occasioned by new capital investment which replaces an existing asset. Nevertheless, even in the absence of a capital replacement, there will be a certain level of retirements and sales associated with any large fixed asset balance.

Once the fixed asset balances have been forecast, it is well to assess the reasonableness of the totals. Will the forecast additions result in productive capacity throughout the period at a level consistent with the forecast growth in sales, after considering products which may be purchased for resale? What is happening to fixed asset balances in relation to earnings after taxes? Are large fixed asset costs being added with no apparent increase in profits? If the answers to these questions suggest unfavorable trends, the assumptions used in the forecast must be reexamined.

Depreciation Estimates

To obtain the accuracy required an estimate of depreciation must be made. The depreciation is subtracted from the sum of new purchases and the old balance in net fixed assets to get the new net fixed assets. The following eight steps should be used to schedule the depreciation:

1. A schedule of depreciation of fixed asset already being depreciated is made. This will show a declining dollar value as depreciable value of the oldest assets reaches zero. See Line 2, Figure 6-13.

2. A depreciation formula for new assets is chosen-straight line, declining balance, or sum-of-the-digits. The straight line has been used in Figure 6-13 since it simplifies the computation.

3. An average life of assets purchased is chosen. If purchases contain large amounts of automotive and building items, separate schedules should be made for these. Their life estimates (4 years and 30 years) would distort the average estimate.

4. Depreciation is assumed to start in mid-year of the year of purchase. Thus the depreciation in the year of purchase is one-half the following year.

5. A separate line is used for the depreciation on assets of each future year.

6. Total depreciation (Line 8) for the year is the sum of the depreciation on Old Balance and the five future years.

7. The Gross Assets are computed as the sum of Net Fixed Assets of previous year (Line 11) plus this year's purchases (Line 1).

8. The new Net Fixed Assets (Line 11) is the Gross Assets (Line 9) less Total Depreciation (Line 8).

Estimating Accounts Payable

The dollar amount in this account depends on the following factors:
1. The terms of sale of suppliers.
2. The payment policy of the company. Three alternatives are payment within the discount period, payment on net terms, payment after an extended period past the due date.
3. The daily dollar rate of purchases.

A two year projection of accounts payable is shown in Figure 6-14.

The procedure used to produce the estimate is as follows:
1. From Figure 6-10 show the purchases per quarter.
2. Divide quarterly purchases by 90 to obtain daily rate of purchases as shown on Line 2.

3. Determine the payment policy and convert it to days of payable outstanding. Allow a percentage for processing delay. Typically a company paying within 10 days shows an average of 13 days payables actually outstanding. The three days represent invoices in transit, check in process, and checks in transit.
4. Multiply the purchases per day (Line 2) by the days of payables unpaid (Line 3) to get the total variable payables outstanding.
5. Determine the amount of Basic Miscellaneous Payables by estimate or analysis. An accurate analytical method is shown in Figure 6-15. The total payables is plotted against purchases. A straight line is drawn through the area where the points cluster and projected back to the vertical axis. This vertical height represents the fixed basic amount of payables. This basic or fixed amount represents the continual purchase of operating supplies and overhead items. The amount of these purchases bears no relation to volume.
6. Total is determined by adding the basic amount to the variable amount (Line 5 to Line 4).

Estimating Bank Loans

Bank credit can take several forms and each would be handled in a separate way. The most important form is line of credit borrowing. These funds are used for "cash fill in" to offset period of heavy inventory or receivables. Since the pro-forma balance sheet serves to predict the cash balance, the amount of line of credit borrowing has a direct effect on the cash balance itself. The proper approach is to assume that half of the line of credit will be outstanding. This leaves one half as a contingency reserve. Once the pro-forma statement is complete, and cash balances predicted, the amount of bank loan can be revised upward or downward as required. If an annual clean up is required by the bank, in the quarter when activity is the lowest the bank loan should be assumed to be zero. Choice of the quarter when the line of credit is cleaned up is critical. The cash shortage may occur in the clean up period instead of in the period of peak sales and inventory.

A bank loan requiring installment or periodic payments can be estimated precisely. A bank loan which is secured by inventory or receivables can be estimated based on the inventory or receivable estimate. Banks or other lending institutions generally apply a reserve ratio to such loans. If 80% of the secured receivables can be borrowed, the loan balance would be set at .80 times receivables. Two important exceptions must be allowed for in such estimates as follows:
1. If certain accounts are disallowed as security in a receivable loan, the amount must be adjusted downward to allow for this.
2. There may be periods when all the borrowing capacity will not be used. This is determined after the pro forma statement is complete and the statement adjusted accordingly.

Item	Notes	1st Year				2nd Year			
		1st	2nd	3rd	4th	1st	2nd	3rd	4th
Sales per Quarter	From Sales Estimate	600	470	520	840	660	517	572	924
Other Current Assets	3.1% of Quarterly Sales	18.6	14.6	16.1	26.0	20.5	14.6	17.7	28.6
Accruals	2.7% of Quarterly Sales	16.2	12.7	14.0	22.7	17.8	14.0	15.4	25.0
Taxes Payable	1.8% of Quarterly Sales	10.8	8.6	9.4	15.1	11.9	9.3	10.3	16.6

Figure 6-12
Worksheet for Other Current Assets, Accruals & Taxes Payable

Item	Line	Old Balance	1	2	3	4	5
Annual Purchase	1		104	118	148	170	205
Depreciation on Old Balance	2		60	50	40	30	20
1st Years	3		12	24	24	24	24
2nd Years	4			15	30	30	30
3rd Years	5				16	32	32
4th Years	6					17	34
5th Years	7						14
Total Annual Deprec.	8		72	89	110	133	154
Gross Fixed Asset Balance	9	480	594	712	860	1030	1235
Depreciation Reserve Balance	10	180	252	341	451	584	738
Net Fixed Assets	11	300	342	371	409	446	497

Figure 6-13
Five Year Projection of Fixed Assets Balance

Item	Line	Notes	1st Year				2nd Year			
			1st	2nd	3rd	4th	1st	2nd	3rd	4th
Purchases	1		212	180	284	410	219	195	300	444
Purchases per Day	2	Purchases divided by 90	2.35	2.00	3.15	4.55	2.43	2.16	3.33	4.93
Days of Payables Unpaid	3		13	13	13	13	13	13	13	13
Variable Payables	4	Days times Purchases per day	30.0	26.0	41.0	59.1	31.6	28.1	43.3	64.1
Basic Miscellaneous Payables	5		14.0	14.0	14.0	14.0	14.0	14.0	14.0	14.0
Total Payables	6		44.0	40.0	55.0	73.1	45.6	42.1	57.3	78.1

Figure 6-14
Estimating Accounts Payable

Estimating Other Current Liabilities

Taxes Payable, Accrued Payroll, and other such accounts can be treated as either fixed or variable. If treated as variable, the formula would be—

$$\text{Taxes Payable (Estimated)} = \frac{\text{Taxes Payable (Base Period)}}{\text{Sales (Base Period)}} \times \text{Sales (Estimated)}$$

A representative base period is chosen to obtain the ratio Taxes Payable to Sales per Quarter.

Estimating Long Term Debt

Unless a specific new loan is planned or a specific type of debt set for retirement, the normal retirement rate should be used. If the purpose of the pro-forma statement is to plan for long term debt, different plans and methods can be explored once the basic estimated balance sheet is completed.

Thus the first pro-forma balance sheet should represent the status quo and variations introduced afterwards.

Estimating Preferred and Common Stock

As explained under Long Term Debt the status quo is the basic assumption. Thus no substantial changes would be projected. If employee stock purchase plans or stock options are in effect, an allowance can be made for an increase in Common Stock. Stock dividends have the effect of increasing common stock by the exact dollar amount that the Retained Earnings decrease. Since the total effect is simply to transfer dollars from one equity account to another, the stock dividend can be ignored.

The same reasoning would apply to a stock split.

Estimating Retained Earnings

The balance in Retained Earnings is effected by two variables—profits and dividends. The profits are estimated as part of the budgeting process. By applying the sales estimate to the operating budget, a profit figure can be generated for each future quarter. See Figure 6-16, Lines 1 to 5.

The operating budget is discussed in Chapter 8. To establish the amount of earnings to be paid out as dividends, a dividend plan must be chosen. The alternatives are as follows:

1. Pay out a fixed percentage of after tax earnings.
2. Pay out a fixed amount per year.
3. Pay no dividends.
4. Distribute more than is earned.

Figure 6-16 has been computed based on a 60% payout ratio. First the annual rate of earnings is computed on Line 7. This quantity is divided by 4 and multiplied by .60 to obtain the quarterly dividend. The previous balance in retained earnings is shown on Line 9. The old balance plus profits after taxes minus dividends gives the new balance shown on Line 10.

Preparing the Pro Forma Balance Sheet

With all the component figures available, the final sheet lays out the entire balance sheet except cash. Figure 6-17 shows how in Step 1 the total liabilities are computed by totalling the various estimated balances. In Step 2 the estimated balances in all asset accounts is subtracted from total liabilities to arrive at cash. Depreciation reserves are negative asset accounts and are added not subtracted. Step 3 involves all revisions of the first set of estimates required to bring the cash balance to optimum levels. As shown in Figure 6-17 the line of credit balance is lowered in the 1st quarter of the 1st year to reduce the cash balance to the optimum level. The loan balance is increased in the 3rd quarter of the 1st year to compensate for the low cash balance.

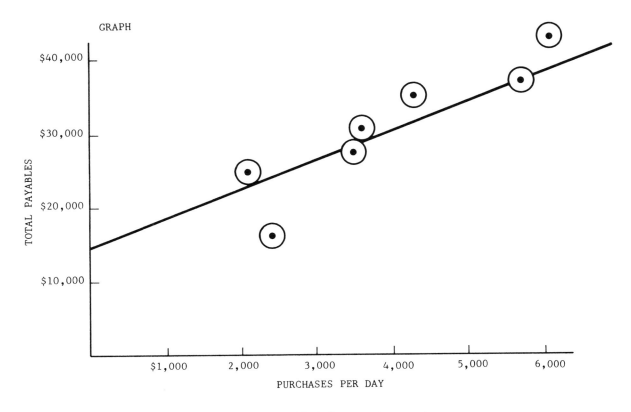

GRAPH

DATA - Compiled from past records

Monthly Purchases	Purchases Per Day	Payables (End of Month)
$ 69,000	$ 2,300	$15,000
105,000	3,500	27,000
126,000	4,200	35,000
174,000	5,800	36,000
60,000	2,000	24,000
102,000	3,400	31,000
180,000	6,000	43,000

**Figure 6-15
Estimating Basic Miscellaneous Payables**

Figure 6-16
Estimating Retained Earnings
(All figures in thousands)

Item	Line	Notes	1st Year				2nd Year			
			1st	2nd	3rd	4th	1st	2nd	3rd	4th
Sales	1		600	470	520	840	660	517	572	924
Variable Costs	2	From Operating Budget	402	310	347	514	447	330	358	567
Fixed Costs	3		183	183	183	183	192	192	192	192
Profit Before Taxes	4		+15	−23	−10	143	+21	−5	+12	+165
Profit After Taxes	5		+8	−12	−5	+72	+11	−3	+6	+83
Payout Ratio	6		.60	.60	.60	.60	.60	.60	.60	.60
Annual Rate of Earnings	7	Total Earnings for Year	63	63	63	63	97	97	97	97
Quarterly Dividend	8		9.5	9.5	9.5	9.5	14.5	14.5	14.5	14.5
Previous Retained Earnings	9		742.0	740.5	719.0	704.5	767.0	763.5	746.0	737.5
New Retained Earnings		Line 9 ± Line 5 − Line 8	740.5	719.0	704.5	767.0	763.5	746.0	737.5	806.0

Figure 6-17
Pro Forma Balance Sheet

Item	Line	Note	1st Year				2nd Year			
			1st	2nd	3rd	4th	1st	2nd	3rd	4th
Step 1										
Payables			44.0	40.0	55.0	73.1	45.6	42.1	57.3	78.1
Accruals			16.2	12.7	14.0	22.7	17.8	14.0	15.4	25.0
Misc. C.L.			82.0	82.0	82.0	82.0	82.0	82.0	82.0	82.0
Bank Loan (Line of Credit)			150.0	150.0	150.0	150.0	150.0	150.0	150.0	150.0
Common Stock			240.0	240.0	240.0	240.0	240.0	240.0	240.0	240.0
Retained Earnings			740.5	719.0	704.5	767.0	763.5	746.0	737.5	806.0
TOTAL LIABILITIES			1,272.7	1,243.7	1,245.5	1,334.8	1,298.9	1,274.1	1,282.2	1,381.1
Step 2										
Inventory			432.0	454.0	593.0	514.0	452.0	476.0	628.0	542.0
Accounts Rec.			257.0	201.2	222.7	433.8	282.8	221.5	244.9	434.3
Fixed Assets			380.0	385.0	390.0	395.0	400.0	405.0	410.0	415.0
Other Current			18.6	14.6	16.1	26.0	20.5	14.6	17.7	28.6
Other Assets			37.0	37.0	37.0	37.0	37.0	37.0	37.0	37.0
TOTAL ASSETS LESS CASH			1,124.6	1,191.8	1,258.8	1,405.8	1,192.3	1,154.1	1,337.6	1,456.9
Step 3										
Unadjusted Cash			148.1	51.9	−13.3	−71.0	106.6	120.0	−55.6	−75.8
Revised Bank Loan			100.0	same	220.0	280.0	same	same	260.0	270.0
Revised Cash			98.1	same	56.7	59.0	same	same	54.4	44.2

7

Procedures for a
Sound Capital Management Program

7

Procedures for a
Sound Capital Management Program

Decisions on capital expenditure proposals take on a measure of overriding importance because they touch every aspect of financial management. Capital expenditures usually mean higher charges for property taxes, insurance, interest, and depreciation. But, if judiciously made, they generally mean lower costs for maintenance and repairs, raw materials, labor, and supplies.

The treasurer or controller must help this firm select only those investment proposals that tend to reduce overall costs; he must strike a balance between the higher cost of making capital expenditures and the economies that result from them. Errors in purchasing fixed assets have a way of haunting a company for years; they are far more serious than, say, errors in purchasing inventory.

CONDITIONS SIGNALING NEED FOR ASSET REPLACEMENT

A discerning capital expenditure program requires a systematic approach to deciding when—and if—currently owned assets must be replaced. Don't assume that you should replace equipment only after it completely wears out. Careful studies of cost data may show a definite need to replace some equipment or a building immediately —despite several years of remaining useful life. "Equipment replacement" entails more than simply replacing worn-out assets with new facilities. Here are a few reasons why you may have to replace certain fixed assets, even though they are still serviceable.

High Repair Bills

Increased maintenance costs accompany the age and wear of equipment and buildings. With age, repairs become more frequent. These repairs may keep a facility in service, but only at the expense of higher operating costs.

127

As the wear on a turret lathe increases, maintenance and repair costs will also increase, and the number of defective parts may become greater. Likewise, wear on a plant floor requires increasingly frequent repairs. The repairs will provide a floor, but only at the expense of high maintenance costs. A completely new floor—or building—may be more economical in the long run.

Increased Downtime

An important sign of trouble is lost productive time due to equipment failure. Most companies keep track of the ratio of productive vs. non-productive time for each piece of equipment or class of equipment. A check of these records will yield a list of those machines with an unfavorable ratio. The next step is to break down these machines' downtime into cause grouping such as:

1. Machine repair
2. Set-up
3. Testing and pilot runs
4. Administrative delay
5. Other

If machine repair is an excessive amount, the cost of the excess time can be reported as a justification for equipment replacement. The cost per hour is the difference between the revenue nets and the variable cost per hour of operating the machine.

Inadequate Facilities

Inadequate facilities may result from an enlargement of company operations. Limited equipment capacity may retard production, cramped storage space may cause damage to products, and meager customer facilities may depress sales. The finance officer must ensure that the condition and capacity of his firm's fixed assets keep pace with expansion and growth.

Equipment Obsolescence

Regardless of whether operations are expanding, an improved model of an existing piece of equipment may offer operating economies sufficient to justify replacement. Automated office equipment and machine tools may shrink the time now spent in services and production. Replacement may also be desirable from the standpoint of meeting competition. If competition adopt the improved equipment, their savings may enable them to offer the same product at a lower price.

To make certain that it does not lose money by operating obsolete or inadequate fixed assets, a company should:

1. Conduct periodic reviews—preferably each year—to determine which fixed assets should be replaced.
2. Keep track of all new equipment placed on the market and explore ways to take advantage of improvements developed by equipment manufacturers.

3. Maintain comprehensive cost records that include all maintenance and repair costs. The accuracy of any investment decision depends on the accuracy of cost figures.

THE CAPITAL BUDGET

The capital budget is the basic control document for fixed asset expenditures. The long range plan will provide for capital expenditures in each of the years covered by the plan. However, these forecasts will be subject to constant change, both in timing and definition of the projects, until the year is reached in which the expenditure is expected to be committed. At that time, the capital budget will be prepared, covering all of the capital expenditures which are expected to be committed during the next year.

The control point for the capital budget is the point of commitment, not the point of expenditure. This is because capital expenditures can be committed in a variety of ways which will obligate the company to make the expenditure, and control is required over the basic decision, i.e., the commitment.

Linkage with the Long Range Plan

The capital budget is an integral part of the planning cycle of the company, and there must be a certain linkage between the programs covered in the long range plans and the specific implementing projects in the capital budget. But we must not establish such a rigid linkage that there will be no opportunity to make changes that clearly ought to be made; this would destroy the planning cycle. Instead, we must provide the mechanism to permit management to explain the changes which have occurred, and the reasons therefor. Only major changes should be the subject of explanation. In order to keep detail down to a manageable level, it may be desirable to have the explanation of changes from the long range plan given in general, qualitative terms only. The financial officer must judge whether this generality will retain effective control, without excessive workload.

Organization of the Capital Budget

The capital budget will be organized according to the organizational units and functions where responsibility for acquisition of the capital asset will rest. It will include all items which are expected to be committed during the year. Thus, there will be provision for certain minor items which it may not be possible to foresee at the beginning of the year. The great bulk of the capital budget will consist of identified items, for which at least preliminary justification exists; we shall have more to say later about justification for capital expenditures. If an item is too nebulous to be justified at the time of the preparation of the capital budget, we have two choices in dealing with it: if it is a small item, we may make a contingency provision, subject to later detailed justification; otherwise we may leave it out altogether, and require the budget to be revised when it becomes more certain. If inclusion of a contingency (only a small item should be considered for this treatment) will not materially affect the financing plan for the company, this treatment can be followed. Otherwise it is better to omit the item altogether. Then we shall be certain that all aspects of the revised budget will be considered when the item is presented, including the ability of the company to finance the changed total for capital expenditures.

Approval of the Capital Budget

The capital budget, as the basic control document for capital expenditures, should be approved by the Board of Directors. Approval of appropriations within the limits of the budget can be delegated to lower levels of management, so long as they are consistent with the capital budget and the long range plans of the company. Revisions of the capital budget should be approved by the Board in the same manner as the original budget was approved. Typically, individual appropriations will be permitted to overrun by expenditures of 10% without giving rise to the need for further approval. This overrun privilege should not be extended to the capital budget itself. We would normally expect that some appropriations would be completed for less than forecast, and some would overrun. Moreover, some projects which were contemplated in the budget will not ultimately develop, so that there should be some flexibility in the total budget. Nevertheless, if a large appropriation which is overrun by less than 10% results in an overrun on the total budget, this revision should be processed through the approval channels in the usual manner, since this variation will likely be material in the company's financial forecast.

THE APPROPRIATION

Once the budget has been approved, it is still necessary to have specific authorization to commit for the expenditure. This authorization is the appropriation. While the budget is the total of all projects expected to be committed during the next year, the appropriation covers the specific projects themselves. As we have already indicated, the budget may be based only on preliminary justification, or it may even include provision for a small amount to be committed for projects which cannot be foreseen at budget time. By the time the projects are ready for appropriation, there will be specific justification, and this justification will be presented in order to secure authorization for the commitment.

Approval Authority for the Appropriation

So long as the project being appropriated was contemplated in the capital budget, and is consistent with the budget, the authority to approve the appropriation can be delegated to lower levels of authority than those necessary to approve the capital budget or revisions thereof. Also, small appropriations will customarily be delegated to even lower levels of authority. Figure 7-1 shows three different procedures which can be followed depending on the size of the request. The smallest items can be authorized by the financial manager acting only. However, if he is in doubt he can hold the request for the next meeting of the capital appropriations committee. The committee should be made up of senior management personnel from manufacturing, finance, engineering and marketing. The next level (up to $5,000) can require an engineering survey if the committee or the financial manager requests it. It also would include comments by the controller's department about the cost figures shown. The larger requests require complete studies by engineering departments and the controller's office. The largest requests are the responsibility of the executive committee or the board of directors.

Size of Request	Originator of Request	Procedure
up to $500	Any dept. supervisor with superior's approval	Sent directly to purchasing. Not considered part of capital appropriations.
$500 to $5000	Department Manager	1. Submitted to financial manager 2. Industrial engineering approval optional 3. Financial manager may release to purchasing or submit request to committee
$5000 to $100000	Vice President	1. Submitted with complete industrial engineering report 2. Reviewed and approved by capital appropriations committee or passed to the executive committee.
over $100000	Vice President	1. Includes complete cost analysis and engineering report 2. Final approval by board of directors

Figure 7-1
Procedures for Capital Spending Approval

The Format of the Request

To establish uniformity in the review and approval of capital requests, standard forms are used. A sample of the front page is shown in Figure 7-2. Space is provided to recap important data. For major requests the form serves as a cover sheet for a detailed supporting data report which will be described below.

The Capital Appropriation Request Form

The form is divided into four sections. The first describes the capital asset; its function, its cost and its date of installation. Descriptive literature from the supplier should be attached. If several possible suppliers have been considered, only the one chosen should be described. If justification of the choice is required, it should be regulated to a

INVESTMENT REQUESTED   Date . . . .
    Description
    Supplier (include alternates)
    Installation Date
    Cost — Purchase
            Installation
            Other
                Less recoveries
    Total Cost

DOLLAR BENEFIT
                    Source of Savings   Description   Annual Amount
                1.
                2.
                3.
                    Added Revenue   Description   Annual Amount
                1.
                2.
                3.
                        Total annual dollar benefit   . . . .

JUSTIFICATION
    Net Cash Investment . . . .
    Net Cash Annual Benefit . . . .
    Profitability Index . . . .
    Payback Period . . . .
    Analytical conclusions

DISPOSITION
        Requested by   . . . . . .
                    Comments or Approval
    Manufacturing . . . .
    Engineering . . . .
    Marketing . . . .
    Finance . . . .
    Final Disposition

Figure 7-2
Capital Appropriations Request Form

supporting sheet. The justification section described below should justify only the
chosen piece of equipment. It should not be concerned with the choice of alternatives.
That choice is not the realm of the top executives.

   The Dollar Benefit Section shows the components of the savings which will result.
For major purchases, one or more Cost Worksheets (Figure 7-3) would be included

Capital Item Description . . . . .

Date . . . . .
Prepared By . . . . .

DIFFERENTIAL METHOD

Type of Cost	Explanation	Computation	Savings Column

COMPARATIVE METHOD

Type of Cost	Explanation of Change	Expense Before	Expense After

PAGE TOTAL

Figure 7-3
Cost Savings Worksheet

to explain each line. The Dollar Savings Section is used to explain increased profit (cash flow) resulting from the investment. Examples of this benefit would be less downtime, added sales volume, and higher productivity. A sample form is shown in Figure 7-4. It shows a computation for the income produced before and after the added capital investment.

The Justification Section shows the computation of decision information. As will be explained below several methods can be used.

The Disposition Section can be used if the Capital Appropriation Request is to be routed among the members of the Capital Projects Committee without calling meetings. Space is provided for all major functional areas of the company to approve the project. The reviewing officer should be encouraged to do more than merely initial and forward the appropriation request. He should check the estimates and assumptions about sales, production, and cost which are made in the report. The opportunities for consultation that naturally arise from this procedure provide additional valuable information for weighing all factors linked with an investment proposal. They provide a guarantee that advantages claimed in a proposal will be realistic and attainable. The adjunct to this arrangement is that it induces sponsors to be honest and precise in their estimates.

HOW TO COMPUTE SAVINGS

The objective in evaluating investment proposals is to determine how much money—if any—the firm will save by buying the proposed equipment. In drawing cost comparisons between present equipment and proposed equipment, include all pertinent costs, such as initial cost, operating cost, salvage value, interest, depreciation, maintenance, space, power, taxes, insurance, and labor. Below is explained one method for determining these costs.

Operating Costs

Determine the annual savings in operating costs by comparing those costs that differ for the present and the proposed equipment. If overhead, for example, is the same for both pieces of equipment, exclude it as a factor in determining annual cost savings. However, if the new machinery would produce the required number of items faster, this fact would have a bearing on labor, maintenance, and power.

The comparison of different operating costs might yield a list such as this:

	Present	Proposed
Direct labor	$ 6,000	$4,000
Indirect labor	3,000	2,000
Set-up time	500	250
Maintenance	1,600	400
Power	400	1,600
Taxes and Insurance	200	1,200
Total Annual Operating Expenses	$11,700	$9,450

Checklist	*Description*	*Amount*
Will the output increase?		
Will sales increase?		
Will prices be changed?		
How else will income increase?		
Total Effect on Income	. . . .	
Less Variable Costs	. . . .	
Net Added Income	. . . .	

Figure 7-4
Gains in Sales or Productivity Worksheet

(NOTE: This example does not compare costs for materials and materials handling, which should be included when applicable.)

The comparison shows an annual operating saving of $2,250 for the proposed investment over the existing facility. This appears to indicate that the proposed investment is sound. However, before giving the "go-ahead," the finance officer must consider certain other costs, such as interest and depreciation.

The Cash Flow Concept

Once operating savings are determined, the interest associated with different financing arrangements appears to be the other cost to consider. If, however, a few assumptions are made the value of the project can be kept separate from the method of financing. The merit of the project, particularly small and medium-sized ones, should not be confused with the financial arrangements which have been offered. For example, if a company requires a 10% return after taxes, an 8% before tax interest rate on a chattel mortgage would make a particular project look even more profitable than the operating savings indicate. The mathematics of the return on investment computations are such that the difference between 10% return and 8% times ½ for taxes (or 4%) are credited to the project as added income. When the time comes to purchase the equipment, the cash required may come from a 5¾% bond issue which is being issued. Thus the question 8% vs. 5¾% is an arbitrary one. It is better to assume cash payment and concentrate on the dollar savings from operations. There is an important side effect of this method. Leasing is a method of not paying cash for an asset but instead—paying for it over a period of time plus interest charges. Thus lease proposals cannot be considered in the same way as explained in a later section of this chapter.

Depreciation

Another cost element that the finance officer must compare for alternative investment proposals is depreciation. The Internal Revenue Service approves several methods of determining allowable depreciation. The most common are the straight-line method, the double-declining-balance method, and the sum-of-the-years-digits method.

If the useful life of the proposed equipment is 10 years, and the estimated salvage value is 10%, a sample calculation can be shown as follows. In using the straight-line method, financial accounting depreciates the cost of the asset, less its estimated salvage value, in equal annual installments over the asset's estimated useful life. The annual allowable depreciation of a $10,000 piece of equipment would be $900, determined this way:

$$\frac{\$10,000 - \$1,000}{10 \text{ years}} = \$900 \text{ per year}$$

The finance officer is also concerned with the depreciation charges on present equipment to determine how they compare with charges on proposed equipment. The depreciation charges on present equipment come from depreciation and fixed asset records. For illustration, suppose that the existing asset had an 8 year useful life, with a purchase price of $6,500 and a salvage value of $500. This means that the annual rate of depreciation is $750 ($6,000 divided by 8 years), yielding this comparison:

	Present	Proposed
Annual Operating Expenses	$11,700	$ 9,450
Depreciation	750	900
	$12,450	$10,350

The proposed investment offers a potential annual cost saving on the books of $2,000 over the present facility. The saving may not be enough to justify making the capital expenditure. The decision for or against the investment proposal may be decisively influenced by answers to these questions:

1. What are the chances of improved equipment coming into the market before the investment pays for itself?
2. What is the advantage of acquiring equipment with a greater capacity than the business now requires?
3. Will new products likely require new machines or processes?
4. What effect will each of the alternatives have on employment levels?
5. Which of the alternatives is more flexible, more adaptable to different types of work?
6. How do alternatives compare from the standpoint of reliability and safety?

Depreciation Under the Cash Flow Concept

The difference in depreciation between before buying and after buying is a non-cash expense. Every year after the purchase the added depreciation shows as additional expense on the tax return and will reduce taxes by one-half the difference. This assumes an income tax rate of 50%. This cash reduction of income taxes is a direct benefit of investing in the new asset. To arrive at the total after-tax cash return per year, the example shown above would appear as follows:

	Before Taxes	Cash Flow After Taxes
Operating Savings	$2,250	$1,125
Depreciation Increase	150	75
Total Annual Cash Benefit		$1,200

EVALUATING RETURN ON CAPITAL INVESTMENTS

The ability to achieve an adequate return on capital investments substantially determines management success. Financial management must never commit funds for plant or equipment before conducting tests for profitability. Here are several useful tests for assessing the investment merits of capital projects.

Production Savings Method

The production savings method reveals how many years it will take for a project to earn enough to return the original investment. In using this method, the financial analyst must know the amount of time the equipment is in use, the time savings per production operation, and the cost of operating the equipment. This information enables him to learn how long it will take a new asset to pay for itself through increased efficiency and lower operating costs, as this example illustrates:

Time per operation with present equipment	30 minutes
Time per operation with proposed equipment	12 minutes
Potential time savings per operation	18 minutes
Potential percentage of time savings	60 percent
Approximate usage rate of equipment	30 percent
Daily operating cost (255 days per year)	$55.00
Cost of proposed investment	$10,000

60 percent savings $\times$ 30 percent use $\times$ $55.00 $\times$ 255 days = $2,524.
$10,000 (cost of machine) divided by $2,524 = 3.96 years

The proposed investment—if made—will pay for itself in slightly less than four years.

Without considering the usage rate, the asset would pay for itself in about one year. But when an asset is idle, it is theoretically not returning any of the investment. The production savings method does not take taxes and depreciation into account. It is valid only in determining actual production savings as a return on the capital required to purchase the asset.

Payback Method

A more accurate method is to compute the length of time until the cash investment is recovered. First the net cash investment must be computed. The gross investment is $10,000, however the old asset will be sold for cash. Suppose it yields $500 and has a book value of $2,000. This results in reduced taxes due to the loss on sale of the asset. The cash tax benefit is ($2,000 — $500) $\times$ .50 or $750. The total cash benefit is $750 plus $500 proceeds of the sale. This amount is subtracted from the $10,000 giving a net cash investment of $8,750. The period of time (called the Payback Period) required to recover the $8,750 is computed by dividing $8,750 by $1,200. $1,200 is the *net cash* benefit computed above. The Payback Period is 7.29 years.

Profitability Index Method

The profitability index method—also known as the *discounted cash flow method* and the *present worth method*—shows the rate of return on the investment. This is the rate at which a firm would have to invest the capital required to purchase an asset to equal the rate of return on the proposed investment.

To use the profitability index (PI) you must know these facts:

1. Total investment expenditure and its time schedule
2. Annual cost savings
3. The asset's useful life
4. Annual depreciation allowance
5. Anticipated income tax rates on profits

Applying the PI. Assume that a firm plans to invest $1,000 in a new piece of equipment that is expected to provide savings of $400 per year. The asset's useful life is five years, after which it will be scrapped with no salvage value. To simplify the example, assume that taxes will take 50 percent of the annual profits, and that savings represent profits.

Using this data, you can figure the rate of return, or profitability index, with the help of the PI work sheet in Figure 7-5, by taking these steps:

1. Compute net profit (receipts less taxes but before depreciation).

Savings	Depreciation Deduction (20%) straight-line method	Net Taxable Income	50% Income Tax	Net Profit
$400	$200	$200	$100	$300

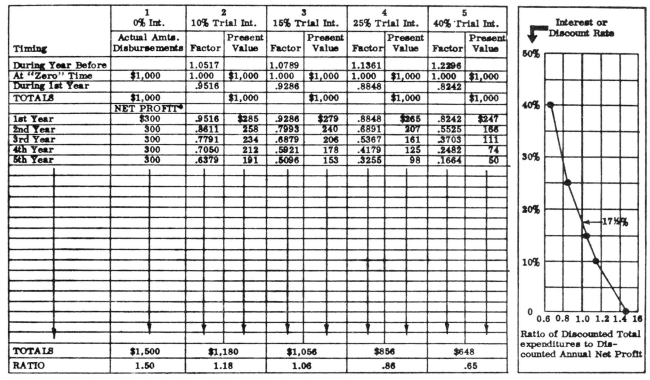

Timing	1 0% Int. Actual Amts. Disbursements	2 10% Trial Int. Factor	Present Value	3 15% Trial Int. Factor	Present Value	4 25% Trial Int. Factor	Present Value	5 40% Trial Int. Factor	Present Value
During Year Before		1.0517		1.0789		1.1361		1.2296	
At "Zero" Time	$1,000	1.000	$1,000	1.000	$1,000	1.000	$1,000	1.000	$1,000
During 1st Year		.9516		.9286		.8848		.8242	
TOTALS	$1,000		$1,000		$1,000		$1,000		$1,000
NET PROFIT*									
1st Year	$300	.9516	$285	.9286	$279	.8848	$265	.8242	$247
2nd Year	300	.8611	258	.7993	240	.6891	207	.5525	168
3rd Year	300	.7791	234	.6879	206	.5367	161	.3703	111
4th Year	300	.7050	212	.5921	178	.4179	125	.2482	74
5th Year	300	.6379	191	.5096	153	.3255	98	.1664	50
TOTALS	$1,500		$1,180		$1,056		$856		$648
RATIO	1.50		1.18		1.06		.86		.65

* Receipts Less Expenditures after Income Taxes but before depreciation.

Figure 7-5
Profitability Index Worksheet

Net profits for the $1,000 machine providing annual savings of $400 amount to $300. (Savings of $400 minus income tax of $100.) Enter this figure for each year of the machine's useful life on the PI worksheet.

2. At "zero time" in column 1 of the worksheet, enter the figure $1,000, the capital outlay required. (Zero time represents the time of the purchase.)

3. Using the worksheet, now find the total of disbursements in column 1 ($1,-000) and net profit ($1,500), and calculate the ratio of net profits to disbursements (1.5).

4. Repeat the steps for disbursements and net profit in columns 2, 3, 4, and 5, multiplying the figures in column 1 by the discount factor [1] for each year. This procedure gives "present value."

5. Using the graph in Figure 7-5, plot the ratios against the trial interest rates and connect the points with a smooth curve. The PI is the point where the curve intersects the heavy 1.0 ratio line. For this particular investment, the PI is 17.5 percent.

Significance of PI findings. The PI of 17.5 percent indicates that the proposed investment would be worth as much as investing $1,000 at 17.5 percent compound

[1] Discount factors are present value factors and are examples under "Significance of PI Finds".

interest for five years. Given the opportunity to invest $1,000 in such a way, *it is presently worth more than $1,000*. To find the present worth of the $1,000 to be invested in the new asset, use this formula:

$$S = P(1 + i)^n$$

Where: S = sum of money in the future
i = interest rate
n = number of years
P = present amount of money

Completing the formula we show that $1,000 invested at 17.5 percent compound interest is worth $2,336 five years later. Stated differently, $2,336 five years from now has a present worth of $1,000. All the finance officer does is to figure the future value of a certain amount of today's money invested in a certain way. In our example, $1 today will be worth $2.336 in five years. In other words, that dollar actually has a potential worth of $2.336. If not invested, of course, the dollar will still be worth $1.00 five years from now.

Figure 7-6 shows a tabulation of discount factors for $1 received once in some future year. The year is shown in the vertical column on the far left. For each discount rate the "value now of $1 then" is shown. For example $1.00 received in 10 years has a present value of $.82 if a 2% discount rate is used. That same dollar has a value of $.191 if an 18% rate is applied. Figure 7-7 has to do with a dollar received *every* year for a certain number of years. This is a stream of dollars in contrast to a single dollar in Figure 7-6. The factors shown are the "present value of one dollar received every year for a certain number of years." For example, one dollar received for two years at a 2% discount rate is now worth $1.97. At an 18% rate those same two dollars are now worth $1.566.

Assume that your company can install a new piece of equipment for a capital expenditure of $27,673 (net cost after investment credit). The machine has a serviceable life of 12 years (the time the machine can compete with new equipment), the asset will have an estimated salvage value of $2,767 (10 percent of its net cost). Most of this information is summarized in Figure 7-4.

Assume further that you will use the double-declining-balance tax depreciation. To determine the profitability of this investment, follow along with these steps:

1. Find 12 years on the bottom scale (reading from left to right).
2. Go up the chart to the point at which the 12-year line (service life) and the 10 percent salvage ratio intersect.
3. Read straight across from this point to the vertical scale on the left margin, to where the lines intersect at 3.8 percent. This is the "chart percentage."
4. Multiply the installed cost by 3.8 percent. You will get $1,052. This is the "chart allowance" (the formula allowance for next-year capital consumption, minus the tax value of the next-year interest and depreciation deductions carried by the project).
5. Subtract the $1,052 from the after-tax saving of $5,358 (Line 32 of Figure 4) to get the net available return on investment (in this case, $4,306). (See Line 34).

Figure 7-6

Present Value of $1

Years hence	1%	2%	4%	6%	8%	10%	12%	14%	15%	16%	18%	20%	22%	24%	25%	26%	28%	30%	35%	40%	45%	50%
1	.990	.980	.962	.943	.926	.909	.893	.877	.870	.862	.847	.833	.820	.806	.800	.794	.781	.769	.741	.714	.690	.667
2	.980	.961	.925	.890	.857	.826	.797	.769	.756	.743	.718	.694	.672	.650	.640	.630	.610	.592	.549	.510	.476	.444
3	.971	.942	.889	.840	.794	.751	.712	.675	.658	.641	.609	.579	.551	.524	.512	.500	.477	.455	.406	.364	.328	.296
4	.961	.924	.855	.792	.735	.683	.636	.592	.572	.552	.516	.482	.451	.423	.410	.397	.373	.350	.301	.260	.226	.198
5	.951	.906	.822	.747	.681	.621	.567	.519	.497	.476	.437	.402	.370	.341	.328	.315	.291	.269	.223	.186	.156	.132
6	.942	.888	.790	.705	.630	.564	.507	.456	.432	.410	.370	.335	.303	.275	.262	.250	.227	.207	.165	.133	.108	.088
7	.933	.871	.760	.665	.583	.513	.452	.400	.376	.354	.314	.279	.249	.222	.210	.198	.178	.159	.122	.095	.074	.059
8	.923	.853	.731	.627	.540	.467	.404	.351	.327	.305	.266	.233	.204	.179	.168	.157	.139	.123	.091	.068	.051	.039
9	.914	.837	.703	.592	.500	.424	.361	.308	.284	.263	.225	.194	.167	.144	.134	.125	.108	.094	.067	.048	.035	.026
10	.905	.820	.676	.558	.463	.386	.322	.270	.247	.227	.191	.162	.137	.116	.107	.099	.085	.073	.050	.035	.024	.017
11	.896	.804	.650	.527	.429	.350	.287	.237	.215	.195	.162	.135	.112	.094	.086	.079	.066	.056	.037	.025	.017	.012
12	.887	.788	.625	.497	.397	.319	.257	.208	.187	.168	.137	.112	.092	.076	.069	.062	.052	.043	.027	.018	.012	.008
13	.879	.773	.601	.469	.368	.290	.229	.182	.163	.145	.116	.093	.075	.061	.055	.050	.040	.033	.020	.013	.008	.005
14	.870	.758	.577	.442	.340	.263	.205	.160	.141	.125	.099	.078	.062	.049	.044	.039	.032	.025	.015	.009	.006	.003
15	.861	.743	.555	.417	.315	.239	.183	.140	.123	.108	.084	.065	.051	.040	.035	.031	.025	.020	.011	.006	.004	.002
16	.853	.728	.534	.394	.292	.218	.163	.123	.107	.093	.071	.054	.042	.032	.028	.025	.019	.015	.008	.005	.003	.002
17	.844	.714	.513	.371	.270	.198	.146	.108	.093	.080	.060	.045	.034	.026	.023	.020	.015	.012	.006	.003	.002	.001
18	.836	.700	.494	.350	.250	.180	.130	.095	.081	.069	.051	.038	.028	.021	.018	.016	.012	.009	.005	.002	.001	.001
19	.828	.686	.475	.331	.232	.164	.116	.083	.070	.060	.043	.031	.023	.017	.014	.012	.009	.007	.003	.002	.001	.001
20	.820	.673	.456	.312	.215	.149	.104	.073	.061	.051	.037	.026	.019	.014	.012	.010	.007	.005	.002	.001	.001	
21	.811	.660	.439	.294	.199	.135	.093	.064	.053	.044	.031	.022	.015	.011	.009	.008	.006	.004	.002	.001		
22	.803	.647	.422	.278	.184	.123	.083	.056	.046	.038	.026	.018	.013	.009	.007	.006	.004	.003	.001	.001		
23	.795	.634	.406	.262	.170	.112	.074	.049	.040	.033	.022	.015	.010	.007	.006	.005	.003	.002	.001			
24	.788	.622	.390	.247	.158	.102	.066	.043	.035	.028	.019	.013	.008	.006	.005	.004	.003	.002	.001			
25	.780	.610	.375	.233	.146	.092	.059	.038	.030	.024	.016	.010	.007	.005	.004	.003	.002	.001	.001			
26	.772	.598	.361	.220	.135	.084	.053	.033	.026	.021	.014	.009	.006	.004	.003	.002	.002	.001				
27	.764	.586	.347	.207	.125	.076	.047	.029	.023	.018	.011	.007	.005	.003	.002	.002	.001	.001				
28	.757	.574	.333	.196	.116	.069	.042	.026	.020	.016	.010	.006	.004	.002	.002	.002	.001	.001				
29	.749	.563	.321	.185	.107	.063	.037	.022	.017	.014	.008	.005	.003	.002	.002	.001	.001	.001				
30	.742	.552	.308	.174	.099	.057	.033	.020	.015	.012	.007	.004	.003	.002	.001	.001	.001					
40	.672	.453	.208	.097	.046	.022	.011	.005	.004	.003	.001	.001										
50	.608	.372	.141	.054	.021	.009	.003	.001	.001	.001												

Figure 7-7
Present Value of $1 Received Annually for N Years

Years (N)	1%	2%	4%	6%	8%	10%	12%	14%	15%	16%	18%	20%	22%	24%	25%	26%	28%	30%	35%	40%	45%	50%
1	.990	.980	.962	.943	.926	.909	.893	.877	.870	.862	.847	.833	.820	.806	.800	.794	.781	.769	.741	.714	.690	.667
2	1.970	1.942	1.886	1.833	1.783	1.736	1.690	1.647	1.626	1.605	1.566	1.528	1.492	1.457	1.440	1.424	1.392	1.361	1.289	1.224	1.165	1.111
3	2.941	2.884	2.775	2.673	2.577	2.487	2.402	2.322	2.283	2.246	2.174	2.106	2.042	1.981	1.952	1.923	1.868	1.816	1.696	1.589	1.493	1.407
4	3.902	3.808	3.630	3.465	3.312	3.170	3.037	2.914	2.855	2.798	2.690	2.589	2.494	2.404	2.362	2.320	2.241	2.166	1.997	1.849	1.720	1.605
5	4.853	4.713	4.452	4.212	3.993	3.791	3.605	3.433	3.353	3.274	3.127	2.991	2.864	2.745	2.689	2.635	2.532	2.436	2.220	2.035	1.876	1.737
6	5.795	5.601	5.242	4.917	4.623	4.355	4.111	3.889	3.784	3.685	3.498	3.326	3.167	3.020	2.951	2.885	2.759	2.643	2.385	2.168	1.983	1.824
7	6.728	6.472	6.002	5.582	5.206	4.868	4.564	4.288	4.160	4.039	3.812	3.605	3.416	3.242	3.161	3.083	2.937	2.802	2.508	2.263	2.057	1.883
8	7.652	7.325	6.733	6.210	5.747	5.335	4.968	4.639	4.487	4.344	4.078	3.837	3.619	3.421	3.329	3.241	3.076	2.925	2.598	2.331	2.108	1.922
9	8.566	8.162	7.435	6.802	6.247	5.759	5.328	4.946	4.772	4.607	4.303	4.031	3.786	3.566	3.463	3.366	3.184	3.019	2.665	2.379	2.144	1.948
10	9.471	8.983	8.111	7.360	6.710	6.145	5.650	5.216	5.019	4.833	4.494	4.192	3.923	3.682	3.571	3.465	3.269	3.092	2.715	2.414	2.168	1.965
11	10.368	9.787	8.760	7.887	7.139	6.495	5.938	5.453	5.234	5.029	4.656	4.327	4.035	3.776	3.656	3.544	3.335	3.147	2.752	2.438	2.185	1.977
12	11.255	10.575	9.385	8.384	7.536	6.814	6.194	5.660	5.421	5.197	4.793	4.439	4.127	3.851	3.725	3.606	3.387	3.190	2.779	2.456	2.196	1.985
13	12.134	11.348	9.986	8.853	7.904	7.103	6.424	5.842	5.583	5.342	4.910	4.533	4.203	3.912	3.780	3.656	3.427	3.223	2.799	2.468	2.204	1.990
14	13.004	12.106	10.563	9.295	8.244	7.367	6.628	6.002	5.724	5.468	5.008	4.611	4.265	3.962	3.824	3.695	3.459	3.249	2.814	2.477	2.210	1.993
15	13.865	12.849	11.118	9.712	8.559	7.606	6.811	6.142	5.847	5.575	5.092	4.675	4.315	4.001	3.859	3.726	3.483	3.268	2.825	2.484	2.214	1.995
16	14.718	13.578	11.652	10.106	8.851	7.824	6.974	6.265	5.954	5.669	5.162	4.730	4.357	4.033	3.887	3.751	3.503	3.283	2.834	2.489	2.216	1.997
17	15.562	14.292	12.166	10.477	9.122	8.022	7.120	6.373	6.047	5.749	5.222	4.775	4.391	4.059	3.910	3.771	3.518	3.295	2.840	2.492	2.218	1.998
18	16.398	14.992	12.659	10.828	9.372	8.201	7.250	6.467	6.128	5.818	5.273	4.812	4.419	4.080	3.928	3.786	3.529	3.304	2.844	2.494	2.219	1.998
19	17.226	15.678	13.134	11.158	9.604	8.365	7.366	6.550	6.198	5.877	5.316	4.844	4.442	4.097	3.942	3.799	3.539	3.311	2.848	2.496	2.220	1.999
20	18.046	16.351	13.590	11.470	9.818	8.514	7.469	6.623	6.259	5.929	5.353	4.870	4.460	4.110	3.954	3.808	3.546	3.316	2.850	2.497	2.220	1.999
21	18.857	17.011	14.029	11.764	10.017	8.649	7.562	6.687	6.312	5.973	5.384	4.891	4.476	4.121	3.963	3.816	3.551	3.320	2.852	2.498	2.221	1.999
22	19.660	17.658	14.451	12.042	10.201	8.772	7.645	6.743	6.359	6.011	5.410	4.909	4.488	4.130	3.970	3.822	3.556	3.323	2.853	2.498	2.221	2.000
23	20.456	18.292	14.857	12.303	10.371	8.883	7.718	6.792	6.399	6.044	5.432	4.925	4.499	4.137	3.976	3.827	3.559	3.325	2.854	2.499	2.222	2.000
24	21.243	18.914	15.247	12.550	10.529	8.985	7.784	6.835	6.434	6.073	5.451	4.937	4.507	4.143	3.981	3.831	3.562	3.327	2.855	2.499	2.222	2.000
25	22.023	19.523	15.622	12.783	10.675	9.077	7.843	6.873	6.464	6.097	5.467	4.948	4.514	4.147	3.985	3.834	3.564	3.329	2.856	2.499	2.222	2.000
26	22.795	20.121	15.983	13.003	10.810	9.161	7.896	6.906	6.491	6.118	5.480	4.956	4.520	4.151	3.988	3.837	3.566	3.330	2.856	2.500	2.222	2.000
27	23.560	20.707	16.330	13.211	10.935	9.237	7.943	6.935	6.514	6.136	5.492	4.964	4.524	4.154	3.990	3.839	3.567	3.331	2.856	2.500	2.222	2.000
28	24.316	21.281	16.663	13.406	11.051	9.307	7.984	6.961	6.534	6.152	5.502	4.970	4.528	4.157	3.992	3.840	3.568	3.331	2.857	2.500	2.222	2.000
29	25.066	21.844	16.984	13.591	11.158	9.370	8.022	6.983	6.551	6.166	5.510	4.975	4.531	4.159	3.994	3.841	3.569	3.332	2.857	2.500	2.222	2.000
30	25.808	22.396	17.292	13.765	11.258	9.427	8.055	7.003	6.566	6.177	5.517	4.979	4.534	4.160	3.995	3.842	3.569	3.332	2.857	2.500	2.222	2.000
40	32.835	27.355	19.793	15.046	11.925	9.779	8.244	7.105	6.642	6.234	5.548	4.997	4.544	4.166	3.999	3.846	3.571	3.333	2.857	2.500	2.222	2.000
50	39.196	31.424	21.482	15.762	12.234	9.915	8.304	7.133	6.661	6.246	5.554	4.999	4.545	4.167	4.000	3.846	3.571	3.333	2.857	2.500	2.222	2.000

6. To find the return on the proposed investment, divide $4,306 by $27,673. This gives you 15.5 percent.

THE LEASE OR BUY QUESTION

If the decision is yes on a capital project, should the asset be purchased or leased? Not only buildings but practically every kind of equipment is available for lease—office furniture, business machines, computers, production equipment, machine tools, earth-moving equipment, and cars and trucks. Leasing may be the more expensive way to acquire a fixed asset, but many companies turn to leasing rather than buying outright because they find other advantages that make up for the higher costs.

How an Equipment Lease Works

An equipment leasing transaction generally takes place this way: (1) the financial manager tells the leasing company what equipment is required, its cost and manufacturer; (2) the leasing company will submit a proposal of the terms and conditions of the lease; (3) after terms are agreed on, the leasing company will buy the equipment (if it doesn't already have it) and deliver it; (4) the equipment is used during the lease term and the agreed rental is paid on a monthly or other basis. When the lease expires, you either return the equipment or renew the lease. The lessee generally gets the benefit of all dealer guarantees, warranties, and services, just as if he had bought directly from the manufacturer. Many companies have set up direct leasing arrangements for their products. This arrangement generally may cause a lower rate, since some of the middleman's profit may be eliminated.

What the Lease Covers

Basically a lease will have (a) a description of the leased equipment, (b) the amount of the payments and when they are due, and (c) the duration of the lease. The lease may also provide for optional renewal. Other clauses generally cover identification of the equipment (such as putting company name on cars and trucks), maintenance and service, insurance, taxes, warranties, remedies, and recording.

Advantages of Leasing

A large equipment purchase can mean serious depletion of working capital, especially for a smaller company. Leasing gives the lessee the equipment he needs without tying up capital that might be invested better elsewhere. Leasing also—
1. Cuts losses due to changes and obsolescence.
2. Keeps initial cost down. The leasing companies' larger purchasing power generally lets them buy the equipment at a discount. In addition, they can probably get a better price for equipment turned back after the lease period is over. Both of these factors often help to reduce the rental charge.

3. Helps meet seasonal demand. If certain equipment is needed only in emergencies or at peak season, leasing can fill the temporary gap.
4. Avoids need to issue new stock. Leasing may make unnecessary the issuance of new securities to obtain funds for fixed assets, thereby avoiding an undesirable spread of company ownership.
5. Contributes to company growth. When management must postpone a purchase because cash is not available, growth is stymied. Leasing can provide what amounts to a new line of credit, and the increased income from the use of the new equipment may more than balance the cost of leasing.
6. Raises cash. It's possible to sell existing equipment to a leasing company and lease back the same equipment, or more modern equipment of the same type. This arrangement, called a sale and leaseback, can bring about tax savings. A profit on the sale is taxed at favored capital gains rates, and you can deduct the rent you pay as ordinary business expense.

Disadvantages of Leasing

Leasing is generally more costly. The total dollar outlay is higher than when buying for cash. Other disadvantages are that leasing—
1. Impairs credit. Banks generally treat a lease as a fixed charge, and consider it as a debt in evaluating a corporation's eligibility for a loan.
2. Fails to provide equity. When the average lease has run out, the lessee is left with nothing. He either returns the equipment or renews the lease.

Tax Aspects of Leasing

Ordinarily, payments under a properly-drawn lease should be fully deductible for tax purposes when incurred. The key to this situation is that the lease be properly drawn. Certain types of leases which have been carelessly drawn may be treated by the Internal Revenue Service as installment purchases of the property, thus losing the full tax deduction for the lease payment. The present strict rules arose from efforts of certain lessees to obtain essentially all of the benefits of ownership—including the right to re-purchase the property at the end of the lease term—while at the same time obtaining fully the tax deductions for all cash payments to the lessor. As a result of these cases, any of the following will cause a lease containing an option to purchase to be considered a purchase by the Revenue Service:
1. Portions of the payments are specifically applicable to an equity to be acquired by the lessee.
2. The lessee will acquire title upon payment of a stated amount of rental.
3. The amount to be paid for a relatively short period of use is an excessively large proportion of the total which must be paid to obtain transfer of title to the property.
4. The rental payments materially exceed the current fair rental value.

5. The purchase option is nominal in relation to the probable value of the property at the time the option is exercisable.
6. Some portion of the payments is designated as interest or readily recognizable as interest.

Whenever a lease involves essentially the entire useful life of the asset, or where there is a purchase option, it is advisable to obtain professional advice as to the proper lease terms.

TESTING CAPITAL INVESTMENT POLICIES

No amount of mathematical computations will give an advance guarantee of correct decisions, but certain calculations will help determine whether existing plant and equipment are serving their intended purposes. Two helpful ratios are the ratio of fixed assets to net sales and the ratio of fixed assets to net profits.

Ratio of Fixed Assets to Net Sales

If a firm has a sales volume of $2 million with fixed assets of $600,000, it is reasonable to believe it will enjoy greater profits than a competitor's firm with the same sales volume, but having a substantially greater sum tied up in fixed assets. The ratio of fixed assets to net sales indicates how many dollars are invested in fixed assets to produce one dollar in sales. This ratio varies widely among industries and within an industry. One firm may rent much equipment, another may own expensive labor-saving equipment, and accumulated depreciation charges may differ—all of which directly affect this computation. Use this ratio only in conjunction with other methods of investment analysis.

Ratio of Fixed Assets to Net Profits

Since fixed asset ratios are intended to show the profitability of capital investments, the ratio of fixed assets to net profits (before income taxes) offers a more meaningful description of return on capital investments than the ratio of fixed assets to net sales, which ignores operating costs.

A firm that installs automated machinery may have fixed assets of $1,000,000 and annual sales of $2,000,000. A competitor using less efficient machinery may have the same sales volume but only half as much tied up in fixed assets. The first firm has 50 cents in fixed assets for every sales dollar; the second firm only 25 cents.

At first glance, the second firm appears to have the more productive capital structure. But, if the first firm's lower operating costs yield a net profit of $200,000 and the second firm's net profit—largely because of higher labor charges—is only $100,000, the first firm has apparently invested wisely. If certain fixed assets are not used in the ordinary course of business, they and the profits they produce should be excluded from the computation. This procedure maintains the soundness of the ratio, and enables the financial analyst to judge the profitability of these assets separately.

8

Profit Planning Through
Budgeting and Cost Analysis

8

Profit Planning Through
Budgeting and Cost Analysis

||||||||||||||||||||||||||||||||||||||||||||||||||||||||||||||||||||||||||||||||||||||||||||||||||||||||||||||||||||||||||||||||||||||||||||||||||||||||||||||||||||||||||||

WHAT IS A BUDGET SYSTEM?

Systems for budgeting operations vary from company to company. Some companies prepare only a rough sales forecast (or sales budget) and an overall production budget. Most firms require more comprehensive budget programs embracing all company operations, as illustrated in Figure 8-1. By using a number of specialized budgets in an integrated budgetary control system, management can establish objectives, coordinate planning, and compare actual results with objectives.

The planning budget and the sales forecast are estimates of income. The remaining operating budgets are estimates of the expense required to attain budgeted income; they show the costs involved in manufacturing and distributing the number of finished products called for in the sales forecast.

This chapter highlights features of some of the more important operating budgets and shows how an effective system of budgeting and costing serves as a dynamic planning and control tool for financial management.

BASIC PRINCIPLES OF RELIABLE BUDGETING

No worthwhile operating budget can be prepared hurriedly. Most managements generally assign responsibility for preparing budgets well ahead of the dates new budgets go into effect. Some firms prepare manuals to aid operating personnel in formulating budgets. Whether through the medium of the budget manual or in other ways, the finance officer must acquaint all managers with the purposes and techniques of budgeting.

149

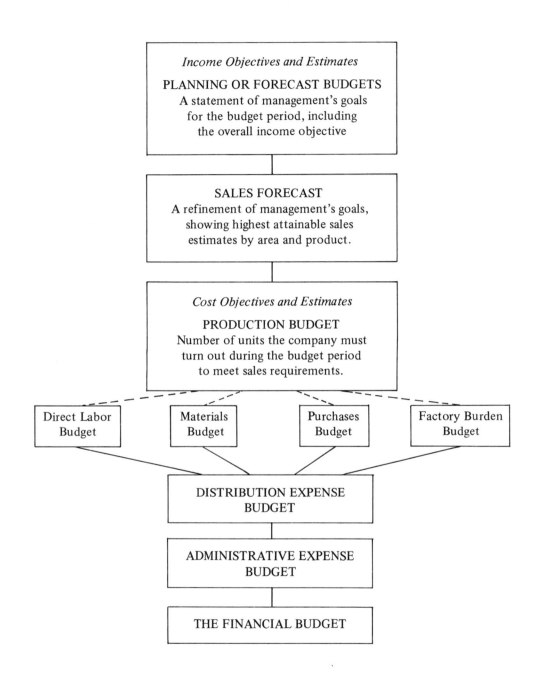

Figure 8-1
Components of a Comprehensive Operating Budget

Here are some fundamental principles that can make any system of budgetary control more effective:

Participation

The participation of key men at all levels is essential. Involving managers in budgetary preparation will (1) acquaint them with the goals of the company, (2) improve morale, and (3) knit the organization into a more unified group. Once a budget system has been operating for one or more years managerial participation is assured. Periodic review of spending performance compared to the budget makes managers aware of the structure and function of the budget. When asked to participate in setting the targets for the next budget, such managers have the valuable experience of prior budgets and reviews to draw on. Participation, then, is accomplished not on one day with one budget but over a period of time by *using* budgets.

Coordination

Budgets help define responsibilities and lines of authority. Budgeting works only if there is responsibility for results. It follows that budgets must be directed at the people who can do something about them.

Accurate Accounting

Maintain a well designed accounting system that records and presents complete facts—by department, by product, by sales area. A reliable accounting system permits a valid comparison of budget estimates with results. Accurate accounting for budgeting means responsibility accounting. Reports should be constructed for people (managers) who are in control of operations. The reports should deal with costs which the men in charge have control over.

Realism

Profit goals must be realistic—not just figures on a piece of paper. The budget must be an honest appraisal of the best that can be reasonably expected. It should be a demanding standard, yet an attainable one, and it should be adaptable to changing conditions.

THE SALES FORECAST IS THE FIRST STEP

The sales forecast gives an estimate of total income by describing how many of each of its products your company expects to sell. Since your entire budget structure will likely be based on this forecast, your central task is to arrive at sales estimates that are within a reasonable margin of error. This situation immediately raises key points to consider:

1. How much time should be spent in trying to develop accurate sales forecasts?
2. In how much detail should the forecast be prepared?
3. Should it be in dollars only or in dollars and units?

Aim for Flexibility

Accountants are tempted to spend a great deal of time and money increasing the accuracy of forecasts. Analysis of marketing conditions, business trends, and economic cycles may offer helpful insights for estimating sales, but the results of such extensive research are often disappointing. Developments within an industry arise unpredictably, and competitors act illogically (or so it may appear). When this happens, the bases of finely reasoned calculations may no longer apply to the new situation.

Obstacles to accurate sales forecasting, however, do not weaken the value of the forecast as a management tool. They simply highlight the need to make plans flexible enough to adapt to changing conditions. There exists a reasonable range of possibilities as to sales volume, based largely on last year's sales. The company must be ready to operate anywhere within that range. Thus the sales forecast, recognized as fallible, stands as a basis for sound decision making in response to new developments. To achieve flexibility, some companies prepare two or more alternative budgets for different levels of volume. At the department level, they may devise complete budgets for every probable level of volume. This procedure is called "variable budgeting."

Sales Forecasting Methods

Although complete accuracy is elusive, certain sales forecasting methods yield better results than others. The best results often come from tapping any one or a combination of the following sources:

1. *Management opinion.* The closest source of information is the most important one—the considered judgment of high level management. The value of that judgment depends largely on how closely management personnel are attuned to market conditions. In large companies, only a few executives—perhaps only the general sales manager—can give a knowledgeable projection of sales activities. Indeed, many companies, while relying heavily on the advice and suggestions of the financial officer, make the general sales manager directly responsible for compiling the sales forecast. The thinking is that the more directly the sales manager is responsible for the final sales estimates, the more earnestly he will try to achieve them.

2. *Sales force.* The man in the field is closer to the market than anyone. His opinion is often invaluable, particularly in specialty lines where sales are few in number but large in amount. And it is a sound idea to ask salesmen and their supervisors to contribute their comments.

This is often done with questionnaires. In addition to specific questions, the form should provide space for their personal appraisal of market trends and conditions. Since salesmen's opinions are sometimes overly optimistic or pessimistic, last year's actual and forecast figures should be provided for their use as a basis for making current estimates.

3. *Statistical analysis.* Though business forecasting is far from an exact science, a statistical analysis of historical data and current trends will make projected sales more reliable. A common application of statistical methods to historical trends is the preparation of market surveys. For example, a tricycle manufacturer wants to know the expected size of the population, in the three-to-five year age range, ten years from now. A projection based on today's population and the expected growth rates over the next 10 years would provide a realistic basis for planning the orderly expansion of production.

The financial officer must always remember, however, that statistical analyses are valid only if the basic trends or relationships on which they are formulated remain constant. Hence, a certain element of risk goes with any forecast based on statistical analysis, and must be taken into account in evaluating the results.

Present a clear picture. If a company sells hundreds or thousands of different items, it faces a special problem in presenting a clear picture of anticipated sales. The only practical solution is to base the forecast on broad product grouping, with additional subgrouping as required. This arrangement should parallel the classification of products in the accounts. In addition, specify an annual quote for each region or territory, with a monthly or quarterly breakdown. Figure 8-2 shows a portion of a completed sales forecast. Notice that the first quarter's sales are broken down by month whereas the balance of the year is done by quarters. This is enough detail for use in annual budgets. However, as the year progresses subsequent quarters can also be broken down by month. The added detail is used as input to performance reports used under the Management Information System concept as explained in Chapter 9. The forecast reveals estimated sales by product and by sales district. To be used in a Management Information Systems additional detail by product line, distributor, etc. can also be added.

The computer can help. Often the sales budget becomes a drudgery if done in too much detail. Management, however, can not settle for a forecast which is not clearly thought out. There are two important ways in which data processing can help solve both problems. A large amount of sales data from recent years is always available to feed to the computer for computing trends and—thereby—next year's sales. If there is a large number of products, the input can be segregated by product and the prediction made by product. This gives a maximum amount of detail and yet saves on clerical labor. A second method by which a computer can save clerical labor is in converting an annual budget by product to a monthly budget or annual budget by product to a sales by territory budget. By establishing a formula for distributing the annual among the months or among the territories, the computer can apply that formula to each individual product.

THE PRODUCTION BUDGET PREPARES THE WAY FOR MANUFACTURING

Once there is agreement on the sales forecast, you are able to devise a production budget by determining the amount of goods that must be manufactured (or purchased) to meet sales goals. The quantity of goods produced will equal the sales forecast less on-hand inventory for each product, as Figure 8-3 illustrates.

Product A—$5.00 per unit	Totals		Northern District		Southern District		Eastern District		Western District	
	Units	Amount	Units	Amount	Units	Amount	Units	Amount	Units	Amount
January	3,800	$19,000	1,000	$ 5,000	800	$ 4,000	1,400	$ 7,000	600	$ 3,000
February	4,200	21,000	1,200	6,000	900	4,500	1,500	7,500	600	3,000
March	4,850	24,250	1,500	7,500	950	4,750	1,750	8,750	650	3,250
Total First Quarter	12,850	$64,250	3,700	$18,500	2,650	$13,250	4,650	$23,250	1,850	$ 9,250
2nd Quarter	5,450	27,250	2,000	10,000	1,000	5,000	1,750	8,750	700	3,500
3rd Quarter	5,750	28,750	2,200	11,000	1,000	5,000	1,800	9,000	750	3,750
4th Quarter	6,250	$31,250	2,500	$12,500	1,000	5,000	2,000	$10,000	750	$ 3,750
	$30,300	$151,500	$10,400	$52,000	$ 5,650	$28,250	$10,200	$51,000	$ 4,050	$20,250
Product B—$2.00 per unit										
January	5,800	$11,600	2,000	$ 4,000	1,000	$ 2,000	2,000	$ 4,000	800	$ 1,600
February	6,900	11,800	2,500	5,000	1,200	2,400	2,200	4,400	1,000	2,000
March	7,900	15,800	3,000	6,000	1,300	2,600	2,500	5,000	1,100	2,200
Total First Quarter	20,600	$39,200	7,500	$15,000	3,500	7,000	6,700	$13,400	2,900	$ 5,800
2nd Quarter	8,300	$16,600	3,000	6,000	1,500	3,000	2,600	5,200	1,200	2,400
3rd Quarter	8,600	17,200	3,200	6,400	1,500	3,000	2,700	5,400	1,200	2,400
4th Quarter	9,200	$18,400	3,000	$ 6,000	1,700	$ 3,400	3,000	$ 6,000	1,500	$ 3,000
	$46,700	$91,400	$16,700	$33,400	$ 8,200	$16,400	$15,000	$30,000	$ 6,800	$13,600

Figure 8-2

PRODUCT A

	Sales Forecast R'qments	Less Finished Goods Inventory	Total Production Req.
January	300,000	240,000	60,000
February	225,000	10,000	215,000
March	200,000	50,000	150,000
Total 1st Quarter	725,000	300,000	425,000
2nd Quarter	600,000	200,000	400,000
3rd Quarter	550,000	100,000	450,000
4th Quarter	400,000	50,000	350,000
Total	2,275,000	650,000	1,625,000

PRODUCT B

	Sales Forecast R'qments	Less Finished Goods Inventory	Total Production Req.
January	150,000	75,000	75,000
February	100,000	25,000	75,000
March	90,000	20,000	70,000
Total 1st Quarter	340,000	120,000	220,000
2nd Quarter	300,000	100,000	200,000
3rd Quarter	280,000	140,000	140,000
4th Quarter	320,000	80,000	240,000
Total	1,240,000	440,000	800,000

Figure 8-3
Detailed Production Budget

To formulate a reliable production budget, management must (1) consider length of production period, (2) ensure coordination of activities, and (3) decide on inventory policies.

Consider the Length of the Production Period

The production period rarely matches the sales period, because the time lag between initial production activity and the completion of the first products may take weeks or months. This situation requires additional schedules describing the timing of the units to be started. If processing requires two months, then the starting of units must be moved two months ahead of the production budget date for units to be completed.

When production consists of many parts, it may be necessary to prepare a separate *parts production budget* showing the dates for parts to be started and parts to be completed. Copies of supplementary production budgets and schedules must go to the purchasing division well ahead of start-up dates if this division is to provide a timely supply of production materials.

Ensure Coordination of Activities

Translating sales demands into production effort can be exceedingly complex. The task requires, in addition to production plans, detailed planning for material and labor requirements, plant capacity, capital additions, and inventory policies. Though the production manager is primarily responsible for drafting and executing the production budget, the finance officer must help coordinate activities among production, finance, personnel, research and development, and sales.

Coordination between sales and production, for example, is indispensable for keeping these two divisions fully aware of each other's problems. It may be necessary to adjust the sales forecast to capitalize on those products that can be produced most efficiently. When revising the sales estimate for any product, selling and promotional expenses must also be revised.

Decide on Inventory Policies

A satisfactory production program rests on definite inventory policies. One of the main advantages of production budgeting is that it forces a consideration of inventory problems in advance. Inventory standards are often fixed in terms of (1) months' supply or (2) minimum and maximum inventory limits.

Months' supply: The months' supply method of determining standard inventory is usually budgeted sales requirements.

> EXAMPLE: Sales forecast for X Manufacturing Company calls for 10,000 units of Product A, a figure that anticipates a monthly sale of 833 units. If production requires a two months' supply of this item, then the standard materials inventory level for single components of Product A becomes 1,666.

Minimum and maximum limits. The minimum inventory limit is determined first, based on how fast the item moves and the time required to replenish it. This is the safety level below which the inventory should not be permitted to go for any item. The maximum limit is then set to prevent excessive accumulation of goods.

Standard inventory turnover. The restocking rate is regulated by setting a ratio for the size of the inventory to the number of units that will be withdrawn (sold).

> EXAMPLE: If 300,000 units will be sold during the year and sales require an in-stock inventory of 50,000, the materials inventory turnover ratio for single components of each product will be set at 6.
>
> $$\frac{300,000}{50,000} = 6 \text{ turnovers a year.}$$

NOTE: In establishing inventory standards be sure to consider (1) perishability of products, (2) storage facilities, (3) extra capital to finance inventory, (4) protection against material and labor shortages and price increases, and (5) a reporting system for keeping inventory information current.

GUARANTEE THE RIGHT QUANTITY OF MATERIALS

The quantities of materials (both components and raw materials) needed to meet production requirements are specified in the materials budget. Quantities of direct materials or parts are shown by month, quarter, or other convenient periods, taking such factors as normal delivery time, economic order quantities, and available storage space into consideration.

The materials budget may include material costs, but this information is usually reserved for the purchases budget. The sample budget in Figure 8-4 gives total quantities required, broken down by product, part, and period.

Estimating Material Quantities

Estimating material quantity requirements poses no problem when you know how many units of each kind of raw material you need for each manufactured unit. These unit rates are often developed during the initial engineering and development of the product. But quantity requirements can be a critical matter when unit consumption rates are unknown. In such a case, you can often devise reliable estimates based on historical ratios:

1. Ratio of raw material used to some measure of production, such as direct machine hours or direct labor hours.
2. Ratio of material cost to some measure of productive output, such as machine hours or direct labor hours.
3. Ratio of material cost to direct labor cost.

It is advisable to test estimates by comparing them with results of past years. If standard costs are not used as the basis for the estimate, they should, at least, be taken into account. If standard costs appear stringent, it may be necessary to budget a material usage rate that varies from the standard.

CALCULATE LABOR NEEDS

The direct labor budget describes estimates of direct labor requirements for carrying out budgeted production. The finance officer works closely with the production and personnel officers in planning the labor required to meet production goals. The direct labor budget gives him the information he needs for determining cash requirements for direct labor. And by revealing the total cost of direct labor, it affords him a means of controlling direct labor expenses.

The two chief ways for developing a direct labor budget are (1) to multiply standard hours for each unit by total number of units, and (2) to base labor costs on historical ratios.

Material Budget-Unit Requirements by Product and by Time Period

| | PRODUCT A | | PRODUCT B | | |
	Production Planned	Material R'qd.	Production Planned	Material R'qd.	Total Units Material R'qd.
Part #47					
January	60,000	60,000	75,000	NONE	60,000
February	215,000	215,000	75,000	NONE	215,000
March	150,000	150,000	70,000	NONE	150,000
Total 1st Qtr.	425,000	425,000	220,000	NONE	425,000
2nd Qtr.	400,000	400,000	200,000	NONE	400,000
3rd Qtr.	450,000	450,000	140,000	NONE	450,000
4th Qtr.	350,000	350,000	240,000	NONE	350,000
Grand Total for Year	1,625,000	1,625,000	800,000	–	1,625,000
Part #58					
January	60,000	60,000	75,000	75,000	135,000
February	215,000	215,000	75,000	75,000	290,000
March	150,000	150,000	70,000	70,000	220,000
Total 1st Qtr.	425,000	425,000	220,000	220,000	645,000
2nd Qtr.	400,000	400,000	200,000	200,000	600,000
3rd Qtr.	450,000	450,000	140,000	140,000	590,000
4th Qtr.	350,000	350,000	240,000	240,000	590,000
Grand Total For Year	1,625,000	1,625,000	800,000	800,000	2,425,000

(Note: Anticipate approximately 20,000 of this item of hand beginning January)

| | PRODUCT A | | PRODUCT B | | |
	Production Planned	Material R'qd.	Production Planned	Material R'qd.	Total Units Material R'qd.
Part #19					
January	60,000	40,000	75,000	75,000	115,000
February	215,000	215,000	75,000	75,000	290,000
March	150,000	150,000	70,000	70,000	220,000
Total 1st Qtr.	425,000	405,000	220,000	220,000	625,000
2nd Qtr.	400,000	400,000	200,000	200,000	600,000
3rd Qtr.	450,000	450,000	140,000	140,000	590,000
4th Qtr.	350,000	350,000	240,000	240,000	590,000
Grand Total For Year	1,625,000	1,605,000	800,000	800,000	2,405,000

Figure 8-4
Detailed Materials Budget

Standard Hour Method

By using a standard hour system, you can compute direct labor costs by multiplying the standard hours required for each unit of production by the total units called for in the production budget, then multiplying this figure by the average wage rate per standard hour. For example, if the production budget calls for 30,000 finished products, and each unit requires two standard hours to complete, you clearly have a direct labor demand of 60,000 standard hours. Multiplying this figure by the average wage rate of, say, $3.00 per standard hour, you get the direct labor cost to produce the desired number of finished product units—$180,000.

Standard hours for some companies are always loose, in others they are always tight. Such a situation requires budget planners to decide on the variations from standard hours that must be incorporated in the budget to meet annual goals.

Figure 8-5 shows a direct labor budget based on standard hours per unit, and broken down to reveal labor costs by product, time period, and workcenter. This arrangement helps to pinpoint responsibility for control purposes.

Labor Cost Ratio Method

Direct labor costs may also be determined by relating labor costs to some other measure of production activity, such as direct machine hours or direct material costs. Some companies simply have workcenter foremen estimate the direct labor hours required to meet the budgeted output for each workcenter, then combine the workcenter estimates to arrive at a total direct labor figure. In the case of new products, a rough estimate may be necessary.

ESTIMATING DISTRIBUTION COSTS

The distribution expense budget (also called selling expense budget) includes all costs involved in selling, distributing, and delivering products to customers. The primary objective of the distribution expense budget is to achieve a proper relationship between sales expense and sales volume or income. If sales estimates are revised because of production schedules, selling expenses may have to be changed. These costs should bear a close relation to sales volume rather than production volume.

Selling costs involve consideration of (1) the sales potential in each territory, (2) the number of salesmen's calls expected, and (3) the need for additional salesmen to sell additional units of a product. Salesmen's salaries might be budgeted on this basis:

Annual Sales Volume	Salesmen's Salaries Required
480,000 units	$192,000
510,000 units	204,000
540,000 units	216,000

In this schedule, it was determined that the present sales force could sell 480,000 units. Adding a new salesman would produce 30,000 units (the difference between 480,000 and 510,000) at an additional cost of $12,000 (the difference between $192,000 and $204,000). To add still another salesman would produce 30,000 units at a cost of $12,000, and so on.

PRODUCT A	Units to be Produced	Standard Hours per Unit	Total Standard Hours	Cost	Total Cost
January					
Workcenter 1	40,000	.5	20,000	$3.00	$ 60,000
Workcenter 2	10,000	.5	5,000	2.00	10,000
Workcenter 3	10,000	.5	5,000	2.00	10,000
February					
Workcenter 1	30,000	.3	9,000	3.00	27,000
Workcenter 2	42,000	.2	8,400	2.00	16,800
Workcenter 3	15,000	.8	12,000	2.00	24,000
March					
Workcenter 1	12,000	.1	1,200	3.00	3,600
Workcenter 2	34,000	1.0	34,000	2.00	68,000
Workcenter 3	18,000	2.0	36,000	2.00	72,000
Total	211,000		130,000		$291,400
PRODUCT B					
January					
Workcenter 1	8,000	.5	4,000	3.00	12,000
Workcenter 2	10,000	.2	2,000	2.00	4,000
Workcenter 3	1,500	.6	900	2.00	1,800
February					
Workcenter 1	10,000	.5	5,000	3.00	15,000
Workcenter 2	8,500	.1	850	2.00	1,700
Workcenter 3	9,000	.2	4,500	2.00	9,000
March					
Workcenter 1	50,000	.3	15,000	3.00	45,000
Workcenter 2	20,000	.8	16,000	2.00	32,000
Workcenter 3	15,000	.5	7,500	2.00	15,000
Total	132,000		55,750		$135,500

Figure 8-5
Direct Labor Budget — First Quarter Only

UNCOVER VARIANCES WITH A STANDARD COST SYSTEM

A standard cost is the expected cost of a product produced at a specified volume under a given set of circumstances. Variances above or below the standard are the profit or loss of internal operations. Standard costs help to strengthen the budget program by controlling current activities directly, whereas the budget serves as a yardstick against which to measure actual costs incurred. The standard costs themselves are based on the same data used in preparing the budget.

Using Standard Costs

There are many ways to use cost standards, but they all have these common objectives:

1. To obtain the cost of production in standard dollars.
2. To compare the standard cost data with actual costs.
3. To determine the variances between 1 and 2, and the reasons for such variances.

This can be accomplished in a variety of ways; the two chief methods use the Work in Process account. With both methods, standard costs are credited to this account when products are transferred to Finished Goods. One method, however, debits the account with *actual costs*, the other method debits the account with *standard costs*.

1. *Charging Work in Process with actual costs.* With this method, the accountant records all expenses (direct material, direct labor, and overhead) at their actual costs and transfers them to the Work in Process account at actual costs:

		DR.	CR.
STEP 1	OVERHEAD	18,200	
	Indirect labor		6,000
	Depreciation		5,000
	Electricity		5,200
	Rent		2,000
	To transfer factory expenses incurred		
STEP 2	WORK IN PROCESS	74,200	
	Materials		32,000
	Labor		24,000
	OVERHEAD		18,200
	To transfer actual costs to Work in Process		

Standard costs become part of the accounts under this system when completed units are transferred to Finished Goods at standard cost. To complete the operation and determine the variances, a physical count is made of the work in process inventory. Accounting then converts this count to equivalent completed units and multiplies this number by the standard cost per unit. The result is subtracted from the balance in the Work in Process account and any balance remaining in this account is the variance—the difference between actual and standard costs. Finally, the variance is closed to the Cost of Sales account. The variance can be subdivided into Labor, Material and Overhead by maintaining separate accounts for each category. A further subdivision is possible by maintaining separate Work in Process accounts for each department.

2. *Charging Work in Process with standard costs.* With this method, the accountant debits Work in Process with standard costs of the goods worked on during the period, and he credits this account with the standard costs of units transferred to finished goods. The accounts for direct labor, materials, and the summary account for factory overhead

are charged with actual costs, but transfers from them to Work in Process are made at standard costs.

Thus, the variances are developed in the materials, labor, and overhead accounts. Any debit balances remaining in these accounts at the close of a period are unfavorable, and credit balances indicate favorable variances. These balances are closed to variance accounts, which, in turn, are closed to Cost of Sales.

NOTE: If desired, charge these variances directly to variance accounts when incurred. Suppose the standard cost of an item is $2.00 and you purchase 1,000 at $2.20. The entry could be:

	DR.	CR.
Raw materials	$2,000	
Raw materials price variance	200	
Vouchers payable		$2,200

Computing Equivalent Production

If your company produces a large number of physical units, not physically identifiable one from the other, you undoubtedly use a process cost system of accounting which, in effect, averages costs over all units produced in a given time period—week, month, quarter. To gain the benefits of a standard cost system under these circumstances, your production departments must convert partially completed units to an equivalent number of completed units, a computation that gives you *equivalent production*.

Finding equivalent production is sometimes quite simple. This is the case when the materials, labor, and overhead involved in producing 100 units that are 50 percent complete is the same as for 50 units that are 100 percent complete:

Completed units transferred to next department	17,200
1,800 units in ending inventory (50 percent complete)	+900
	18,100
1,200 units in beginning inventory (40 percent complete)	−480
Equivalent production for period	17,620

Making separate computations. The computation above, however, applies only when materials, labor, and overhead go into the units uniformly throughout the production process. If, for example, materials are issued only at the beginning of the process, the following computation must be made for applying material costs to units:

Completed units transferred to next department	17,200
1,800 units in ending inventory (50 percent complete, 100 percent as to materials)	+1,800
	19,000

1,200 units in beginning inventory (40 percent complete, 100 percent as
    to materials)   −1,200

Equivalent production for period   17,800

If materials costs in this department are $32,000 for the period, and labor and over-head are $38,000, unit costs are determined as follows:

Direct Materials—
    $32,000 + 17,800 units = $1.798
Labor and Overhead—
    $38,000 + 17,620 units = 2.157

Cost per unit $3.955

The $3.955 unit cost is used to value the ending inventory and the units transferred to the next process where, starting from the $3.955 base, another computation of equivalent production determines unit costs in that process.

For a precise calculation of costs of equivalent production units, be sure to apply costs for any waste or shrinkage that takes place during a production process.

Pinpointing Variances with Budget Reports

Budget reports may be prepared for a section, a department, or an operating division. Although their complexity varies, all budget reports serve a common purpose: to indicate budgeted and actual costs and to explain any budget variances.

See that line management prepares budget reports as often as is necessary. You may need weekly reports for critical cost items, while monthly or quarterly reports may be adequate for evaluating overall performance. You'll also want to set standards for explaining variances. For example, it may be unnecessary to require explanation for variances from the budget of 5 percent or less. Benefits derived from the explanation might not justify the cost of the investigation. In the following example, however, variances are substantial enough to require explanation.

Departmental Budget Performance Report
Production Department "A", Quarter Ending 6/31

	Budget	Actual	Variance	Percent
Wages	$240,000	$288,000	$48,000	+20
Material	120,000	144,000	24,000	+20
Supplies	10,000	12,000	2,000	+20

EXPLANATION: Variances in all areas caused by increases in production schedule
                to meet shipping department requisitions.

If the basic budget estimates are sound, the use of reporting techniques forces personnel to be alert and efficient. Budget reports perform the inspection function of showing management the weak areas, and they are helpful in evaluating the administrative capabilities of personnel. Budget control and its accompanying standards are instrumental in implementing a standard cost system.

An effective budget control system depends on honest reporting. Don't let department heads feel that reporting an overrun cost is necessarily a reflection on their personal efficiency. In many cases, it may be out of their control entirely. The budget control serves to improve operating efficiency, not to find scapegoats.

Regardless how well managers understand the management information system, there will always be a certain amount of complaints if a manager consistently receives reports showing variances over which he has no control. This will be particularly so if the amount of these variances is significant. Much of this difficulty can be avoided by structuring the reports in such a fashion that certain of the costs which are controllable only at a higher level of management are reported in a separate section of the cost analysis. Thus, for example, certain interdepartmental charges may be accumulated in a separate section which is added to the manager's costs, but for which he is not specifically accountable. Continuing this system at the next higher level of management, a larger proportion of the total costs will become controllable, and therefore subject to that manager's accountability.

USE BREAK-EVEN ANALYSIS IN ADAPTING TO CHANGES

No matter how carefully you calculate the many elements that go into profit planning, changes beyond your control are likely to occur that drastically affect anticipated profits. During the budget year it may be necessary to expand the sales territory, to meet union demands for more wages, to buy new machinery, or to put unused plant capacity into production. In each instance, break-even analysis will indicate the effects of the new situation on profits. It does this in much the same way that it finds the profit-making level of any business operation.

Computing the Break-Even Point

The break-even point refers to that level of business activity where a firm neither makes a profit nor incurs a loss, where income is just enough to cover expenses. To make a profit, the firm must have sales volume higher than the break-even point; to avoid a loss, it must not sell below the break-even point.

To compute the break-even point, take the following steps:

Step 1. Separate all costs into fixed and variable categories.

Step 2. Express the variable expenses as a percentage of sales, and subtract that percentage from 100 percent. The difference represents the percentage of each sales dollar available for fixed expenses and profit.

Step 3. Take that last percentage and divide it into the total fixed cost. The resulting figure is the total sales required to absorb the fixed cost. This is the break-even point.

EXAMPLE: The Acme Corporation forecasts sales of $5,000,000, variable costs of $3,300,000, and fixed costs of $1,200,000. Sales at break-even point = variable expenses as a percentage of selling price + total fixed expenses.

$$\text{Variable expenses} = \frac{\$3,300,000}{5,000,000} = 66 \text{ percent of sales}$$

100 percent — 66 percent = 34 percent = sales required for absorbing fixed expenses.

$$\text{Fixed expenses} = \frac{\$1,200,000}{34 \text{ percent}} = \$3,530,000 = \text{break-even point}$$

Proof of computation:

Sales at break-even point	$3,530,000	
Less:		1,200,000
Variable cost at break-even point		
(66 percent of $3,530,000)		2,330,000
Total costs		*$3,530,000*
Profit or loss		None

Loss per sales dollar if sales fall below break-even point = $1.00 — 66 percent = 34 cents.

Applying the Break-Even Analysis

The Acme Corporation's sales forecast is $1,470,000 above its break-even point ($5,000,000 — $3,530,000). The fixed and variable expenses of $4,500,000 on sales of $5,000,000 will permit a net profit before taxes of $500,000 or 10 percent. But suppose that the cost of materials suddenly rises 10 percent and that management considers it necessary to maintain the current selling price. How much will sales have to be increased to maintain the present dollar profit? Break-even analysis supplies the answer:

CURRENT DATA:	
Fixed costs	$1,200,000
Variable costs as percent of sales	66%
Profit	500,000
Sales	5,000,000
ADDITIONAL COST BURDEN:	
Increase of 10% in variable costs (materials)	
ANALYSIS:	
New ratio of variable costs to sales (66% + 6.6%)	.726
Sales dollar available for fixed costs and profit	.274
Total	1.000

REQUIRED SALES:

($1,200,000 + $500,000) + 27.4% = required sales

$1,700,000 + 27.4% = $6,204,375

PROOF:

Sales		$6,204,375
Costs:		
Fixed	1,200,000	
Variable (72.6%)	4,504,375	5,704,375
Profit		500,000

To maintain the same profit of $500,000 while incurring a 10 percent increase in material costs, sales must advance from $5,000,000 to $6,204,375. If management considers this goal feasible, it can absorb the increase in variable costs; otherwise, it will have to adjust the selling price. Break-even analysis assumes these conditions: (1) a change in sales volume will not affect the per-unit selling price, (2) fixed costs remain fixed regardless of volume, and (3) variable costs vary directly with production. Since these conditions never exist in actuality, the analyst should frequently determine whether the degree of error is significant.

He should also recognize that some expenses, instead of falling neatly into a pattern of variable and fixed costs, contain elements of both. Though these "semivariable expenses" fluctuate with volume, they do not do so in direct proportion to changes in business activity. Examples include expenses for advertising and utilities.

TAKING STEPS TOWARDS PROPER BUDGETS

The budget is a piece of paper and represents the plan for making the profit required by stockholders. The budgeting process is far more dynamic than the simple act of writing a budget down on paper. Budgeting is a continual process of analysis, communication, interpretation, and correction. It involves the financial manager and the operating management. It is best conceived of as the following five step process:

1. Estimate sales and the level of production for the coming year.
2. Specify in detail the expenses which will be incurred in the coming year.
3. Compute the profits resulting from steps 1 and 2. If these are not acceptable, alterations in sales and expense targets are indicated.
4. Periodically during the budget period compare budget goals with achieved results. Analyze the causes of expenses which are out of line.
5. Take action to improve those conditions which cause variances from the budget.

Budgeting Is a Company-Wide Process

The five steps are not an accounting project. They are the responsibility of line management. The financial manager and his budget manager are responsible for gathering the estimates and presenting them in a finished budget. The important decisions, however, are the estimates which are made by the line management. The budgeting manager fills out the estimates and obtains the line managers' approvals.

Budgeting Payoffs

The involvement of line management leads to these important advantages:
1. Planning ahead is encouraged.
2. A coordinated plan of action is developed.
3. Performance targets are set.
4. Standards of performance are agreed upon.
5. Subordinates understand company goals.
6. The control of operations is simplified.

The Budgeting Timetable

The annual budget is prepared in advance of the start of the accounting year. While the new budget is prepared, results of the current budget are analyzed and corrective actions are taken. The life cycle of the new budget is interwoven with that of the existing budget. Figure 8-6 shows the timetable for budget preparation. Notice that time is allowed (Oct. 15 to Dec. 31) to adjust and rework a budget if it is not accepted. Also if a company's situation changes during the budget preparation period, there is time to change the budget. For example, acquisition of new products or new sales outlets could substantially change the upcoming budget. It is important that the budget reflect as much as possible the situation which will be encountered in the new year. The budget must not be allowed to become obsolete. Once the consensus of management is that the budget is obsolete, it will be ignored and its value lost.

Date	Party	Action
July 1	Financial Manager	Outline goals and timetable for next budget.
Aug. 1	Financial Manager & Marketing Manager	Complete an estimated sales volume by product or product line. Include price and unit information.
Aug. 15	Financial Manager & Production Manager	Complete production budget based on sales volume.
Sept. 15	Financial Manager & Staff	Complete dollar spending budget by month based on production budget.
Sept. 30	Financial Manager & Staff	Completed budgeted P&L. Put budget in documented form.
Oct. 15	President or Board of Directors	Adopt new budget.
Oct. 15 to Dec. 30	Financial Manager	Revise and resubmit for approval if required.
15th of each month during the following year.	Financial Manager & Operating Manager	Review budget performance against actual. Look for ways to improve performance. Explain differences between budget and actual.

Figure 8-6
A Sample Budgeting Timetable

9

Organizing a Management
Information System

9

Organizing a Management Information System

||||||||||||||||||||||||||||||||||||||||||||||||||||||||||||||||||||||||||||||||||||||||||||||||||||||||||||||||||||||||||||||||||||||||||||||||||||||||||||||||||||||||||||||||||||||

TAILOR THE SYSTEM TO THE MANAGEMENT TASK

The design of an M.I.S. is an expression of the way a company should be managed. According to management theory the firm accomplishes its goals in four distinct interlocking steps:

1. It plans future activity
2. It implements its plans
3. It executes its plans
4. It compares results against the plan and then plans, implements, executes and compares all over again

The fourth step is called the control phase when quantified results are compared to original plans. The plans themselves are generated as part of the annual budget. Included in the annual budget (or plan) are sales quotas, production quotas, expense rates, and purchase schedules. The amount of detail in the plan determines how much detail is available in the control phase. If a manager can only say "Something's wrong somewhere" but cannot pinpoint the troublespot, it is the result of hazy and incomplete planning. If the plans were made up in more detail, results would have more meaning and troublespots could be spotted quite easily. Thus a Management Information System is simply a detailed reporting of results against a detailed plan of organization.

What Is So New About M.I.S.?

The concept of M.I.S. is not really new. Responsibility accounting, budgeting, and variance analysis are all different aspects of the same idea. What makes M.I.S. important is the computer power which is available to management. For the first time detailed timely information about a multitude of topics can be produced for management at low cost and quickly. Daily, weekly and monthly reviews of planned versus actual can really take place. Thus managers need not suffer from a lack of information. As computer power grows managers are increasingly faced with too much reported information rather than too little. The purpose of a Management Information System is to consolidate report data into the smallest quantity of meaningful and inter-related facts and figures possible.

The structure of an M.I.S. becomes more involved when the systems analyst takes into account the different levels of management. Each level requires a different type of report. What is irrelevant detail to a general manager is important factual information to a department manager. Wherever possible summary reports should be backed up with expanded detail for a lower level of analysis.

DESIGN CRITERIA OF A MANAGEMENT INFORMATION SYSTEM

Listed below are the essential characteristics to aim for in an M.I.S.
1. Inter-related interlocking reports—All major factors effecting profit and efficiency should be covered in the reports. Cost consideration should be tied to volume; volume should be dovetailed with mix problems; and mix should be integrated with volume. The fundamental fact which underlies such a structure is that profit is the result of all three factors taken together.
2. Critical data in meaningful form—Managers must work with real facts which highlight important trends or events. Statisticians can produce mean values and standard deviations which as numbers are meaningful to other statisticians. Cost accountants can produce involved variance analyses which are true in what they state but difficult to comprehend. Managers must operate their sectors of the business with concrete real guidelines, not abstractions.
3. Detail data tied to summary figures—The information reported is used in different ways by different levels of managers. Reports must contain enough but not too much information for the user. The user should be thought of as a specific man with a specific level of responsibility.

HOW NOT TO BUILD A MANAGEMENT INFORMATION SYSTEM

Several important factors effect the way management can build and install an M.I.S. First, the system must be built on the job. By contrast, if a company wanted to install a new boiler, it would order one from a supplier. At the supplier's plant, designs are drawn up, steel is cut, parts are assembled, and a finished boiler is delivered ready for final installation. The old boiler operates until the replacement is installed and is easily removed once it is out of service. The M.I.S., by contrast, must be integrated into the existing flow of information. If an M.I.S. were designed and programmed at a supplier's plant (as with the boiler) it would not work when installed. It would fail because the data flow, time schedules, and exceptional conditions are only encountered where the system will be used.

Second, a total system must be conceived in total and installed in phases. The natural tendency of a manager is to ask, "What day will I get my M.I.S.?" If an M.I.S. is properly installed, the day never comes. As each phase is completed the data flow is more integrated than before, the master files are more complete, and reports are improved. But the next phase continues to unify the data and integrate the reports from a different aspect.

Third, the reports are specified first, the timetable second, the master files and data third, and the method of processing last. The most common cause of failure of an M.I.S. is concentration on the method of processing and the machinery used. Machinery must be kept in its proper place. By analogy, the book is more important than the printing press. Managers should emphasize reports when they talk about an M.I.S.

Fourth, an M.I.S. should not be a crash program. It should be a set of target dates spread over a period of months or years. Typically, a manager becomes enthused at the prospect of a comprehensive M.I.S. and pushes for a single early completion date. Too often, systems personnel are coerced into a single unrealistic delivery date instead of a set of phase completion dates.

THE INGREDIENTS OF AN M.I.S.

From a user's point of view there is only one ingredient to an M.I.S.—the reports which come out of it. However, from the systems analyst's point of view there are several important components to consider. These are shown in Figure 9-1 and are described in detail below.

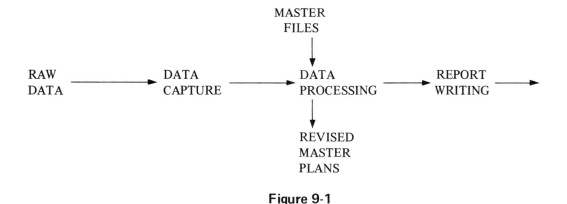

Figure 9-1

Input Data

All business concerns generate new data which is potential imput to an M.I.S. The titles and types of data vary with the type of business. Listed in Figure 9-2 are the most typical imputs found in a manufacturing concern. They are grouped according to the source of the information. Included in the list are budget and forecast data which make up the profit plan. Forecast and budget data require as much or more attention than the actual data. Forecasts and budgets must be generated in sufficient detail to meet the report requirements. For instance, if sales reports are broken down by product within product line within product group, the sales budget should be broken down in the same way.

	Actual		*Planned*
Sales Data			
	Units by Product Type	Sales Budget	
	Dollars from Billing Data		Units by Product Type
			Dollars by Product Type
Standard Cost Factors			Dollars by Territory and Region
	Labor per unit		Dollars by Product Group
	Material per unit		
Standard Rates		Expense Budgets	
	Labor Rates		
	Overhead Rates		
	Material Rates		
Actual Performance Data			
	Yield Data		
	Transfers of Inventory		
	Withdrawals from Stock		
	Man-Hours by Job or Cost Center		
	Vendors' Invoices		
	Scrap Reports		
	Quality Control Reports		
Order Data			
	Purchase Order Data	Inventory Standards	
	Received Quantities	Safety Stock Levels	
	Physical Inventory Counts	Min-max Points	

Figure 9-2
Typical Inputs for a Management Information System (Manufacturing)

Master Files

All data which is reused or updated periodically is held on master files. The data flow is then as shown in Figure 9-3. The master files are revised each time new data is put through the system. These updated masters are then used as the new master files for the next run. The data contained in the masters would include the following:

1. Constant information—such as code numbers, cost factors, titles.
2. Budget—The detailed budget figures are arranged according to their classifications, categories, etc.
3. Year-to-date figures—Figures are balance forward totals and are added to each time more data is input.
4. Forecast figures—These are laid out the same as budget data except that they are changed each time a new forecast is made.

Data Capture

The conversion of information (such as numbers, letters, symbols, quantities, units of measure, etc.) from raw data to imput data is data capture. It may take several forms. The most common is keypunching. Other possible methods include optical reading, direct entry on magnetic tape, byproduct punching into paper tape, keyboard entry to disk files. The important characteristics of data capture are:
1. *Control and Proof Figures*—Wherever possible data is entered in batches with pre-added batch totals supplied with the data. These totals assure that critical items are correct.
2. *Audit Trail*—The raw data source of data entered must be traceable at a later date. In case of error or question, the source of problems can be singled out.
3. *Low Cost*—The enormous amounts of data required for an M.I.S. make it important that the cost per character captured be minimized. Depending on the application data can be captured and controlled for from $3.00 to $10.00 per thousand characters.

Data Processing

The processing step consists of matching master records against imput data, performing computations, updating master files, and sending data to a printer mechanism. This kind of printer is a mechanical device which prints reports on instruction from the computer. Each type of processing must be individually designed for the problem at hand. This is the job of the programmer. The diagram shown in Figure 9-1 shows the report writing function separate from the data processing function. In actual practice the printing is often done at the same time as the data processing.

Report Writing

This step takes selected data from the master files and the imput data and directs it to the printer in a report format. The programmer has the choice of what is to appear on the pages of a report.

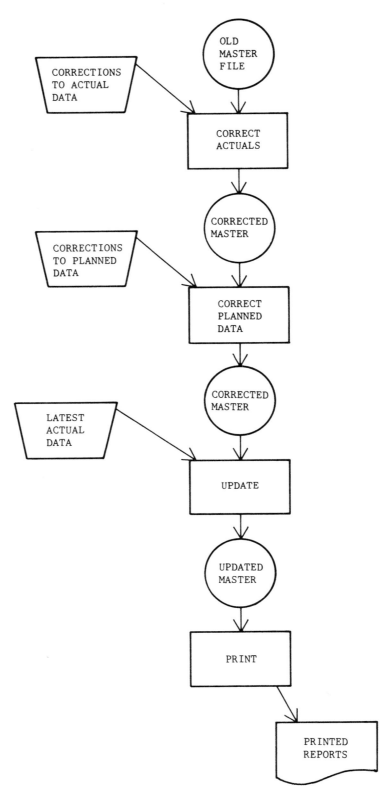

Figure 9-3
Flowchart of Master File Update

THE REPORTS TO MANAGEMENT

A Management Information System is judged by the reports it produces. These are the management tools used to control and direct the course of events within a business concern. Listed in Figure 9-4 are the most useful reports which flow from an M.I.S. The reports are grouped according to their frequency. Some are fairly common types and were produced before the idea of a Management Information System was conceived. The M.I.S. concept has added very important features to existing reports. The principal change is the addition of planned results for comparison to actual. A second important addition is the use of forecast annual figures for comparison to planned actual figures for comparison to planned annual targets. The method of forecasting is described separately in a later section.

Some Specific Reports

To illustrate the structure of management-oriented reports, samples of several reports listed in Figure 9-4 are shown in Figures 9-5 to 9-10. Each illustrated report is explained below.

Profit Contribution by Product Line

To aid in analyzing the contents of this report, definitions of the column heading are given below (See Figure 9-5).
1. *Product Group*—A grouping of several product lines.
2. *Product Line*—A group of several similar products. For example, a title of a product line would be "Instant Coffee." The titles of the products in that product line would be "½ oz. Foil Pack," "2 oz. Glass Jar," "6 oz. Glass Jar," etc.
3. *Month Sales*—Sales for one product line in the current month (April).
4. *YTD Sales*—Sales for one product line from January through the month of the report (April).
5. *Month Contribution*—Sales less variable cost for the current month for one product line. Variable cost should include all variable material, labor, overhead, commissions, advertising allowances, freight allowances, etc.
6. *Planned Contribution*—The month's annual planned contribution for one product line as detailed in the Annual Profit Plan.
7. *YTD Contribution*—The actual contribution from January to the current month (April) for one product line.
8. *Planned YTD Contribution*—The sum of the planned monthly contributions for one product line from January to the current month (April).
9. *Forecast Annual Contribution*—The figure shown is the sum of the two components. The first is YTD Contribution (#7 above) and the forecast amount for the balance of the year. The figure shown changes with each

Frequency	*Report*
Monthly	Receivable Aging
	Inventory Turnover Analysis
	Product Line Profit Contribution
	Fixed and Variable Budget vs. Actual
	Sales by Product Line vs. Plan
	Sales by Territory and Region vs. Plan
	Contribution by Product Line vs. Plan
	Contribution by Territory and Region vs. Plan
	Profit Center Performance vs. Plan
	Inventory Replacement Forecast
Weekly and Daily	Inventory Shortages Projected and Actual
	Equipment Utilization — Actual and Scheduled
	Open Order Status and Schedule
	Labor Cost and Manpower Hours

Figure 9-4
Reports Product by an M.I.S.

month's report. This is because the new actuals replace the amount previously forecast for the latest month. The forecast for the balance of the year can also change as the forecast is received each month.

10. *Planned Annual Contribution*—The sum of Twelve Planned Contributions (#6 above). This is a fixed number and remains the same for all twelve monthly reports.

Profit Contribution by Product Group

The sample report is shown in Figure 9-6. The column headings are the same as Figure 9-5. The figures shown are the totals for all product lines within each product group. Instead of a column for product line the report contains the name of the product manager responsible for the product group. If no one individual is responsible for each product group, the column could be used for descriptive information about the product group.

Sales by Territory

Figure 9-7 shows a sample of the report. Listed below are definitions of the column headings.

1. *Region*—The geographical area which includes several territories.
2. *Territory*—The grouping within a region of several salesmen. The grouping could be based on geography, type of customer, or type of product sold.

3. *Monthly Sales*—Actual current month sales.
4. *Planned Monthly Sales*—The month's planned contribution for one territory as detailed in the Annual Profit Plan.
5. *YTD Sales*—Actual year-to-date sales for one territory.
6. *Planned YTD Sales*—The sum of the planned sales for each territory for the months from January to the current month (April).
7. *Forecast Annual Sales*—The figure is the sum of actual year-to-date sales plus a forecast for the balance of the year.
8. *Planned Annual Sales*—The figure found in the Annual Profit Plan for the year's sales for a given territory.

Sales by Salesmen

Figure 9-8 shows a sample of this report. The column headings are the same as Sales by Territory. An important difference is the lack of forecast data for each salesman. A careful study would show that mathematical projections of the lowest level of sales would produce erratic results. The summaries by territory or region would show much better results.

Sales by Region

Figure 9-9 shows a sample of this report. The column headings are the same as those of Sales by Territory.

Profit Center Report

Figure 9-10 shows one format for such a report. The profit center is a different concept from a product group or a sales region. It is an activity whose income and expenses can be segregated accurately. As an example, a firm selling industrial items has six regional sales offices, a mail order department for special items, an export sales department, and a contract sales office. Taken together these nine sales outlets represent all the company's sales. The regional sales offices have their own warehouses as does the mail order department. Export and contract sales are shipped directly from the main plant. All sales data contains a code which tells which of the nine sales outlets should be credited with them. In such a situation, how should the profit centers be organized? The proper answer is to make all nine sales outlets profit centers. The sales can be segregated via the sales code mentioned above. The remaining problem is to segregate costs among the nine profit centers. Certain corporate expenses can not be charged among the profit centers. They are lumped together and charged off to the profit centers as G & A. The G & A is charged to profit centers as a percentage of sales.

Those costs which can be charged among the nine profit centers include the following:

1. Raw Material cost at standard
2. Labor Cost at standard

Month April

Product Group	Product Line	Monthly Sales	YTD Sales	Month Contribution	Planned Contribution	Actual YTD Contribution	Planned YTD Contribution	Planned Annual Contribution	Planned Annual Contribution
30	120	26,854	89,611	6,866	8,100	30,988	37,200	109,600	106,000
	130	7,550	10,091	3,946	4,444	11,614	13,100	41,700	47,000
	140	16,746	48,498	10,800	10,700	28,012	30,700	90,300	88,000
	150	37,400	143,004	20,054	23,000	72,100	70,400	244,000	234,000
40	210								
	220								

Figure 9-5
Profit Contribution by Product Line

Month April

Product Group	Product Manager	Monthly Sales	YTD Sales	Month Contribution	Planned Contribution	YTD Contribution	Planned YTD Contribution	Forecast Annual Contribution	Planned Annual Contribution
30	J.C. Haynes	87,550	301,014	41,666	47,500	142,714	151,400	485,600	475,000
40	P.M. Merk	211,515	584,177	127,462	111,800	349,645	317,000	984,000	1,012,000
50	S.T. Harms	107,712	384,843	64,872	64,700	212,717	241,000	712,100	644,000

Figure 9-6
Profit Contribution by Product Group

Month April

Region	Territory	Monthly Sales	Planned Monthly Sales	YTD Sales	Planned YTD Sales	Forecast Annual Sales	Planned Annual Sales
11	20	17,212	19,000	62,755	64,000	174,800	191,000
	21	12,119	8,000	57,451	49,000	147,500	135,000
	22	27,440	21,000	79,171	78,000	228,900	211,000
	23	23,667	24,500	92,342	86,000	236,500	238,000
	24						
	25						
12	30						
	31						

Figure 9-7
Sales by Territory

Month April

Region	Territory	Salesman	Month Sales	Planned Month	YTD Sales	Planned YTD Sales
11	20	1	9,520	10,500	34,035	33,100
		2	7,692	8,500	28,720	30,900
	21	1	2,100	4,900	27,231	27,100
		2	10,019	3,100	30,320	21,900
12	26	1				
		2				

Figure 9-8
Sales by Salesman

Month of April

Region	Monthly Sales	Planned Monthly Sales	YTD Sales	Planned YTD Sales	Forecast Annual Sales	Planned Annual Sales
11	183,241	189,000	725,187	640,000	2,880,000	2,711,000
12	171,482	191,000	611,111	712,000	2,790,000	2,950,000
13	12,742	21,000	84,992	87,000	794,000	861,000
14						
15						
16						

Figure 9-9
M.I.S. Report, Sales by Region

3. Manufacturing Overhead Cost at standard
4. Variable Distribution Cost at standard
5. Sales Salaries and Sales Promotion Expenses
6. Shipping and Warehousing Expenses
7. Office Expenses
8. Any other expense which can be traced to one of the profit centers
Figure 9-10 shows a sample of the monthly profit report for one cost center.

The report shows Contribution (sales less Cost of Sales) as the fourth line. Below that point are listed the expenses which are charged to the particular profit center. Deducting these leaves a Net Contribution. From this figure G & A is subtracted to give the profit by cost center. The report shows Planned, Monthly and YTD figures.

Month   April

Profit Center   Chicago Office

Profit Center No.   14

	Month Actual	Month Planned	YTD Actual	YTD Planned
Sales	97,424	91,400	387,441	391,000
less Returns	−1,281	−1,700	−9,155	−6,700
Net Sales	96,143	89,700	378,286	384,300
Cost of Sales	44,644	43,600	181,884	190,200
Contribution	51,499	46,100	196,402	194,100
Sales Promotion	2,788	2,690	10,816	11,000
Sales Salaries	9,445	8,200	37,913	31,900
Warehouse	12,817	11,700	46,448	49,100
Office Expense	8,475	7,950	35,745	33,000
Other Expense	8,871	7,100	28,692	29,200
Profit Center Cost	42,396	37,640	175,614	170,200
Net Contribution	9,103	8,460	36,788	39,900
Allocated G & A	3,897	3,660	15,498	15,600
Profit	5,206	4,800	21,290	24,300

Figure 9-10
Profit Center Report

Other Possible Reports

The report illustrated above has dealt with income and expense from a sales point of view. An M.I.S. is also very effective as a control tool for factory management. Reports such as Projected Stock-Outs, Critical Workcenter Loading Forecast, Material Re-order Projections can be valuable tools. They have been omitted since they apply only to industrial management. The sample principles of systems design and installation apply to them as to the reports illustrated.

10

Waging a Blitz on Costs

||||||||||||||||||||||||||||||||||||||||||||||||||||||||||||||||||||||||||||||||||||||||||||||||||||||||||||||||||||||||||||||||||||||

10

Waging a Blitz on Costs

The importance of cost-cutting becomes apparent when one considers that cost reduction has a greater potential impact (per dollar) on net income than would an equivalent dollar increase in sales. This is because the sales dollar carries with it some additional elements of cost, whereas a cost or expense reduction flows directly through to net income (before tax).

There must be a systematic approach to cost-cutting. It is not enough to initiate a cost-cutting program from time to time to bring costs down; there must be a continuous effort to keep them down and to find new ways to save money. Conditions change, so that an operation which was once as low cost as possible can become a candidate for still further substantial reductions.

How does one ferret out these cost-saving opportunities? First, it is necessary to identify some of the important areas where substantial costs are incurred, and therefore substantial savings may be possible. (This does not mean we ignore opportunities for saving lesser amounts; it does help to focus attention on large potential savings.) Some of these heavy cost areas are:

—Labor, both direct and indirect
—Taxes, particularly property taxes
—Maintenance materials and supplies
—Raw materials

DIRECT LABOR AND RAW MATERIAL COSTS

Savings of both direct labor and raw material costs are possible through good production control procedures. We shall have more to say about these procedures later in the chapter. Basically, we are concerned with the need to obtain a quality product at minimum cost. Of course, there is always the need to compromise in reaching that goal, since it is patently impracticable to manufacture a product which is 100% flawless (unless we are being compensated for this unusual quality control in a manner similar to that employed in the space programs.) Instead, there is an economic balance between product rejects and the quality control necessary to eliminate them. Some industries have even gone to the extreme position of having little or no quality control, since rejections by customers run at such a low level as to make further quality control uneconomic. In analyzing this problem it is necessary to have enough information about the economic and public relations consequences of lower quality in order to make a rational decision. Once this information is available, management can make the decision to override the economic facts and build a better-quality product. That is a proper management decision, but in making it the company will be deciding that there are intangible benefits to be derived from the higher quality which will ultimately be realized in a financial sense, even though they cannot now be quantified. The important point is to get management to make this decision in a positive manner, rather than having it made by default, or much worse, having it made by the sales organization. This latter organization will always want a higher quality product to sell, at the lowest possible cost. It will almost never be possible to satisfy both of the salesman's objectives.

CLERICAL COSTS

Indirect costs can also be a source of cost-savings. One example is clerical costs. These costs, which are largely within the financial manager's portfolio, can represent substantial monetary commitments. The design of accounting systems must comprehend the optimizing of accounting costs. But there is also the need to investigate the desirability of eliminating some management reporting which is unusually costly. Once we have determined that the information is being gathered in the most efficient manner, management must face the question as to whether it can afford the additional control which the information provides. Thus, it has even been possible in certain carefully controlled situations to eliminate standard inventory accounting control procedures for items which involve less than a minimum dollar value. Naturally, if such a course of action were adopted it would be necessary to ensure that the physical control procedures for these items were adequate, to prevent excessive pilferage. Again, in examining the question as to whether information systems are too costly, the decision must be taken by responsible management at a sufficiently high level to ensure objectivity. Managers are notoriously eager to obtain information which can be provided by a staff group which is not on the manager's payroll.

TAXES

Still another cost saving area is that having to do with taxes, particularly sales taxes and property taxes. The income tax laws are complicated, but the laws, regulations and customs which govern the sales and use and property tax fields are if anything even more so.

Sales and Use Taxes

Sales and use taxes are payable on a broad spectrum of transactions in most states. The sales tax is payable for transactions executed within the state, and the use tax is a compensating tax payable on purchases from outside the state. All states which levy these taxes have a bewildering variety of exemptions from these taxes. Often purchases for the purpose of resale are exempt, to give only one example. It is necessary to be particularly vigilant with respect to use taxes, since the tax may not be collected at the proper point, and the company can be subject to penalties for failure to pay the tax. Also, the firm collecting the use tax may not be totally familiar with the state law on the particular transaction, so that the tax may not be payable. In dealing with the sales and use tax area, there can be no substitute for a thorough knowledge of the law of the jurisdictions in which the company operates, together with the regulations which have been issued by the state taxing authorities.

Property Taxes

Property taxes present an even more difficult problem. Property tax assessments are based upon laws, regulations and customs which vary from jurisdiction to jurisdiction. In general, each taxpayer should be assessed on a comparable basis throughout the taxing jurisdiction. Since the local jurisdictions set their own assessed valuations, there is a system of equalization which is used by the states in order to establish comparable values throughout the state. Thus, if an equalization rate of 39 is assigned to a particular area, this means that the state judges that assessments in that area are made at 39% of value in relation to a scale of 100%. Value determinations are necessarily a highly subjective matter, since only a small percentage of the property in a given jurisdiction will have been sold on the open market during any particular tax year. Consequently, taxpayers must be alert to inequities in assessments and opportunities to make a request for reduction in assessed valuation. Such a request can be made on the basis of comparison with some other taxpayer's assessed valuation, or upon a general claim of inequity. In the latter case it will be important that the claim is supported by convincing evidence of a lower value.

Idle property is a special area where cost saving on property taxes can be achieved. Typically, the assessor will not reduce the assessed valuation on an asset simply because it is not presently being used for the purpose for which it was originally designed. It may be necessary to dismantle the asset in order to obtain the reduction. This decision is an economic one: is the tax sufficient incentive to incur the cost of dismantling an asset, given the probable future value of the asset?

When substantial items are being moved into a state at a time near assessment date, it is well to coordinate the move with the financial officer. If there are no overriding operating reasons for making the move at that particular time, it may be possible to save an entire year's tax merely by delaying the move for a period of a few days or weeks. Also, an eye to the tax calendar could be important when considering the completion date for a building or other large asset being constructed. The assessor may view the incomplete building in a much different light than the same building completed a few weeks later.

Capital Investments for Cost Savings

A final example of areas where cost saving may be obtainable is in the replacement of labor by machinery. This possibility exists in almost every function, from the controller's office to the assembly line. It is necessary to be continually alert to the availability of new automated devices, as the cost of labor continues to escalate. This course of action is fraught with a major problem, however. This is the problem of reliability. Too often a machine has been acquired to replace a man on the payroll, and the result has been to keep the man (or his equivalent) because the machine has not proven sufficiently reliable. It is unlikely that this situation will improve, in part because of the comments which we made above regarding quality control. The manufacturers of these machines have difficulty meeting the demand for their products, and they cannot afford to build in additional reliability, so long as they are enjoying the present high growth rates in demand.

Inspire intracompany competition for cost reduction. When all of the obvious areas for cost control have been investigated by the financial officer or suggested by him to line management, there is still another opportunity for achieving savings. This has to do with interdepartmental competition. It is often true that a manager may be able to demonstrate convincingly that he cannot achieve lower costs than he presently has. But if there is another division of the company which has a lower cost for this particular function, making the comparison with the manager will often obtain an unanticipated reduction. First, he may learn that there is a better way to perform the function than he was at first able to discern. Second, he may just try harder than he had before. While we mention comparisons with other divisions of the company, the same effect can be obtained if comparisons are possible with the operations of competitors. Here, obtaining data will be a difficulty, but the effort may not be entirely fruitless. It may be enough to be able to say that the management of Company Z says it performs this function for 10¢, as compared with our 13¢.

While the above are general areas in which cost-cutting can be implemented, the following are some more detailed specific suggestions.

EIGHT WAYS TO CUT OVERTIME COSTS

Business has always been concerned with cutting overtime costs. This concern becomes more vital as the Federal government indicates it may boost minimum rates for overtime pay. In reducing overtime, the objective, of course, is to get as much of the job done as possible during regular working hours. Here are ways to help do this; many of these ideas were gathered by the Manpower Research Council during a survey of 200 companies across the nation.

1. Speed up Worker Training

Skilled operators are hard to find—and the cost of training "new hires" to cut over-time is high. The only solution to this situation is to get the most out of your new employees by improving training procedures so that workers will quickly become fully productive in a variety of jobs.

2. Sharpen Supervision

Supervisors are essential to the success of on-the-job training. They must be able to instruct and bring out the best in their workers. The following checklist applies:
    A. Are the supervisors fully qualified technically?
    B. Do they understand the need to upgrade workers to do more skilled jobs?
    C. Are they good teachers?
    D. Can they inspire their workers to want to add more skills?
    E. And are they patient with a worker who is slow to catch on to a new operation?

3. Put Retired Workers on Call

If the work load is too much for the present workers to handle during regular working hours, consider using retired employees at regular hourly rates. The personnel department should go through the company files of retired employees to check age, health, qualification, etc. After selecting potential "returnees," they should be contacted and given notice of the company's intention. If they are interested, a physical examination should be conducted so that they are ready to go when called.

4. Get a Full Day's Work

Competitive companies must get a full day's work out of every man on the payroll. Campaigns against absenteeism and lateness can help. Hard and fast time limits for coffee breaks are important. These are things to take care of *before* peak periods arrive; otherwise, time-wasting habits will have become taken for granted and practically impossible to root out in a hurry.

5. Require Executive Approval of Overtime

Have all supervisors report to higher management any overtime they have approved in their departments. An even tighter restriction is to require approval in advance. This procedure may be time consuming, but worthwhile. This arrangement puts the spotlight on the supervisor. He is likely to think twice before asking for overtime pay for his department.

6. Use Faster Methods

To prove ways of getting more done in less time, ask the managers these questions:
  A. Do we perform some duties out of habit—duties that could be eliminated?
  B. Could anyone suggest any shortcuts in habitual procedures?
  C. Could inspections be simplified without lowering product quality?
  D. Could plant space be used more economically for more direct transferring of work from one machine to another and from one worker to another?

7. Use Proper Scheduling

To get things done when they should be done, managers must:
  A. List what must be done.
  B. Make someone responsible for each task.
  C. Set completion dates and require progress reports. Completion dates must be flexible, however. Periodically review the schedule.
  D. Make specific arrangements to get work done in regular hours during seasonal operating peaks, inventory-taking, vacation periods, etc.
  E. Have plans in readiness for subcontracting on short notice to meet peak loads or sudden big orders.
  F. Consider surcharges for passing on any overtime costs to customers when they require unusually quick delivery.

8. Choose the Right Workweek

Choice of the right workweek can trim overtime costs considerably for all workers covered by the wage and hour laws. What is a workweek? It is *any* continuous period of 168 hours. It can start at *any* hour of *any* day of the week. Below is an illustration of how one company, by changing its workweek, saved all of its overtime bills:

Company A's employees are required to work on Fridays and Sundays of alternate weeks. To accomplish this, the employees of Company A had been working a regular Monday-through-Sunday schedule of alternate overtime and non-overtime workweeks. A calendar of an employee's hours—with 48 hours scheduled for every other workweek and 32 scheduled in the alternate work-week—looked like this:

M	T	W	T	F	S	S		M	T	W	T	F	S	S
8	8	8	8	8	0	8		8	8	8	8	0	0	0

For the first workweek, at a rate of $1.25 an hour, the employee was paid $65; for the second week he received $40. His total wages for the two week period were $105.

The company changed its workweek to begin on Sunday and end on Saturday. Here's the new schedule:

S	M	T	W	T	F	S	S	M	T	W	T	F	S
0	8	8	8	8	8	0	8	8	8	8	8	0	0

The same employee now earns $50 each week—a total of $100 for the 2-week period.

The employee's actual schedule remains unchanged. He still works the same days, and has the same days off as under the previous schedule.

When setting up a new workweek, the financial manager should keep in mind that (1) it must be permanent—must remain fixed, and (2) it cannot be established just to evade the law—just to save overtime cost.

TRIMMING PAYROLL COSTS BY USING OUTSIDE CONTRACTORS

The use of outside contractors to reduce payroll costs (including those costs caused by overtime) has grown spectacularly in just the past few years. The most striking growth has been in the area of temporary help. Temporary workers—used strategically—can bridge manpower gaps that occur in nearly every type of business operation. Temporaries are "rented" workers—employees of a temporary employment contractor who leases out their services.

The Growing Variety of Services

Not all temporaries are clerical. Their assignments are varied: one may be a ticket taker, another an interim president, another a file clerk or engineer.

Below is a list of possible tasks temporaries can perform:

1. typing
2. shorthand
3. filing
4. plant maintenance
5. selling
6. casual labor
7. demonstrating
8. surveying
9. keypunch
10. inventory-taking
11. switchboard
12. moving
13. telephone solicitation
14. truck driving
15. calculating
16. bookkeeping
17. material handling
18. payroll
19. modeling
20. transcription
21. parking
22. sample distribution
23. lawn care
24. packing
25. addressing
26. machine operation
27. merchandise display
28. delivery
29. translating
30. reception
31. computer operation
32. chauffering
33. maid service
34. drafting
35. engineering
36. executive management
37. computer programming

The Cost-Saving Aspects of Temporary Help

Temporary help is now used by all types of companies, including virtually all of the nation's 100 largest firms. Growth of this service industry has been due to ten major reasons, all of which add up to economy or convenience for the user:

(1) Elimination of fringe benefits, since companies using a temporary help service are not responsible for these extra charges.

(2) Elimination of costs by paying employees for time not worked. For example, vacations, sick leave, maternity leave, jury duty, personal time off, etc.

(3) Convenience in obtaining needed personnel merely through a telephone call to another office, which fills the need.

(4) Gaining the use of "instant skills" without a long, involved training procedure.

(5) Elimination of costs of recruiting, advertising, record-keeping, testing, screening, and payrolling. A single check to the leasing contractor covers all the temporaries' salaries. Out of this check, the contractor pays social security, insurance, Federal and state taxes.

(6) Improved unemployment and workmen's compensation ratings and no claims. The president of a Chicago warehouse used a temporary-help company for two years and cut his firm's unemployment compensation rating by 80 percent. The actual cost reduction was equal to half of what he spent for temporary help.

(7) Problem-free termination of employment. When a firm no longer has a need for short-term personnel, there is no psychological problem created if the employees are those of a temporary help service.

(8) Overtime costs for permanent people are reduced or eliminated through the use of temporary help.

(9) More efficient use of one's own employees; high cost employees need not be used on low-paid jobs.

(10) Ability to use limited equipment on a double or triple-shift basis, thus getting maximum use from it. Temporary help can be brought in to use such equipment on a second- or third-shift basis.

Comparing Costs of Hiring and "Leasing" Temporary Help

In deciding whether to use a temporary help service, the financial manager has to know what it will cost to hire his own temporary help. Hiring his own temporary help often requires advertising, interviewing, testing, and related procedures and expenses. In some instances, this may be the only practical course to take. If a highly skilled worker is needed, he will often be better off hiring his own temporary—though the new range of skills available from outside agencies suggests a careful look here, too. However, for special mailings, peak loads, vacation schedules, etc., he can almost certainly end up ahead with a temporary help service.

How to Use a Temporary-Help Service

Every company's personnel needs are different. The decision on temporaries depends very much on the job requirements. If the job requires skills peculiar to the industry or business, company-hired temporary help or former employees may be the answer. If a temporary from an agency can do the job, the following procedures should be followed:

1. Compute the "actual cost" of carrying an employee on the payroll by adding fringe benefits, social security, and Federal and state insurance payments to his salary, sick leave, vacation, and any other pertinent costs.
2. Compare the above total with the amount a temporary help agency charges to supply you with workers of similar training and ability.
3. Check the union contract to learn if there are restrictions on hiring temporaries.
4. Contact one or more temporary help agencies and specify precisely what job skills are required. Do not be vague.
5. When temporaries report for work, have them checked very closely for job skills during their first day or week. If they are incompetent, return them to the agency. Many agencies offer a test period for which there is no charge if the worker is unacceptable.

WORKFLOW SYNCHRONIZATION PARES WASTED TIME

Every company loses some part of its profits through its employees' waste of time. The waste isn't always due to the employees themselves—much of it can be traced directly to lack of planning by management. Plugging these profit leaks requires a thorough analysis of the company's work patterns to determine the reasons for delays, whether they be in the plant or office.

These gaps of wasted time stem directly from a failure to anticipate and make provision for disruptions that cause breakdowns in the flow of the firm's operations. A synchronized flow can regain up to 50 percent of wasted time.

The Three Steps in Workflow Synchronization

Management *knows* when time is being wasted. The puzzling question is *where*— at what point or points in the chain of operations—does the lack of coordination occur which interrupts the workflow? Basically, there are three steps in workflow synchronization which enable a company to identify waste, find out where it is located, and set up procedures to keep it under control:

1. Determine the workload in man-hours and/or machine-hours.

2. See that supervisors know their workloads.
3. Set up a system of communications on the status of work.

Workflow Synchronization Tackles a Production Problem

Suppose 120 man-hours are allocated for a particular production job. The job must be completed in four days, so the foreman assigns four men to it (4 men working 8 hours for 4 days equals 128 man-hours). Completion of the job, however, runs beyond the schedule.

To find out whether the original job estimate is incorrect, or whether time is being wasted, management applies the principles of workflow synchronization by matching the estimate against performance in the machine shop. Management finds that:

A. One foreman supervises nine drill press operators.
B. As each operator finishes his job, he goes to the foreman for another assignment.
C. The foreman then goes to the layout area to select a job for the operator.
D. After determining the tooling requirements, the foreman walks to the tool room to requisition the necessary jig or tools.
E. The procedure takes anywhere from 8 to 23 minutes, and becomes even more time-wasting when two operators come to the foreman at the same time.
F. The idleness of the drill press operators accounts for 80 percent of the extra time required to complete the job.

The Solution to the Problem

A visual control is devised in the form of a work-assignment board.
1. Each man in the shop has a wooden pocket attached to the board.
2. Each pocket has a clock face attached to the front of it.
3. Each assignment sheet contains the time needed to perform the job.
4. As the foreman makes an assignment, he sets the clock hands to the time he estimates the job should be completed.
5. The foreman now has a comprehensive picture of the entire day's work for the machine shop. He can check the progress of each job, anticipate its completion, and have things in order for each worker's next job before he is through with his current assignment.

Synchronization in the Office

Workflow synchronization can be used in the office as effectively as in production areas. Disruption of operations can spring (among other reasons) from unpredictable breakdowns, poor coordination of interdependent departmental functions, improper physical layouts, or lack of proper training of employees for particular jobs.

Operations differ for each company. There are no standard or pat formulas; particularization is the essence of synchronizing workflow. What is common to all companies, however, is the need for a study of each firm's problems to devise remedial procedures.

AN EASY WAY TO HANDLE CASH COLLECTIONS

An interesting example of cost-cutting is found in the cash receipts area. It is the timesaving *remittance envelope system*. This system is easy to set up; simply use the envelope in which the customer mails his payment as the basic accounting document for recording cash, checks, discounts, and for posting accounts receivable.

Use of remittance envelopes varies from one firm to another. It is sufficiently flexible, however, to be applied to practically any company regardless of how sophisticated its bookkeeping operations may be.

How it Works

Accountants have always relied on the check as a source for making entries. The check cannot be retained, of course, since it must be deposited in the bank. For accounting purposes, then, an excellent substitute for the check is the customer's remittance envelope.

Here is a suggested step-by-step procedure:

1. Block-stamp the face of each envelope. The stamp should provide space for recording the amount of cash, discount, and a credit to accounts receivable.
2. Sort envelopes into alphabetical order and then number them consecutively using a numbering machine. The checks should bear a corresponding number.
3. Record the amount of the check on the envelope in the space shown in the block-stamp.
4. Record the entries in the accounts receivable ledger.
5. List the checks, using an adding machine, so that the total cash can be verified with the entries in the cash column of the ledger. The remittance envelope is used as the source document for both the cash receipts journal and the accounts receivable ledger.

Details of System Are Important

Making any system work depends a good deal on the people handling the routine operations. With this system, the details are very important. Accurate transcribing from check to envelope is essential to the success of this plan. Some factors to keep in mind when using the remittance envelope are these:

1. The customer's name should appear on the envelope with the return address. If it's missing, the cash clerk must enter it on the envelope.

2. Transcribe to the outside of the envelope any identifying invoice numbers and other data that will help the bookkeeper apply the check.
3. When a letter, note, or other correspondence accompanies the check, attach this data to the back of the envelope.

Benefits of the Plan

This plan has been used successfully by companies with over 2,000 active accounts. They find its chief benefits are that (1) checks can be deposited at once; (2) cash discounts can be verified with the postmark dates on the envelopes; (3) cash control rests with the person who opens the mail and numbers the envelopes and the checks. The person who opens the mail should not have access to any cash fund in the office. This is an important internal control requirement.

The remittance envelopes should be filed and held for at least one year so that they will be on hand if postmarks, correspondence, cash-item control numbers, etc., have to be checked.

PRACTICES THAT LEAVE PROFITS AT THE POST OFFICE

The increase in mail rates has boosted the cost of mailing packages. Rate increases on catalog mailing have also occurred. If shipments by mail constitute more than a small part of a company's shipping program, any one of the faulty mailing practices described below can become extremely costly during the course of a year.

Inaccurate Weighing

This may be caused by defective, inappropriate, or hard-to-read scales. It is best to have the scales checked and adjusted for accuracy by the manufacturer's service representative regularly. Avoidance of hard knocks, overloading, and storage in damp atmosphere will improve their accuracy and increase their life.

Overposting

Management should clamp down on the "better safe than sorry" mailroom philosophy. A package that is just under a rate-weight break, should be checked to see if the mailroom applies a correct, rather than a "safe" postage rate. Weight-to-postage conversion tables should be revised or changed when postal rates change. Mental or scratch-paper arithmetic to adjust to new rates often results in costly rounding-up.

Incomplete Knowledge of Rates

Postal and shipping rates are too numerous, complicated and changeable to be remembered by anyone. The use of a break-point chart posted in easy view which shows the cheapest shipping method for various weights and distances can also save money.

Heavy Packaging

The packaging expert should investigate the practicality of using lighter weight packaging materials. Slightly more expensive but lighter containers, or internal cushioning materials or both, might be feasible.

Wrong Insurance

Post Office insurance rates are established to meet the needs of one-time mailing situations. If a firm mails valuables in quantity over the course of a year, it can probably save money by using commercial insurance instead of Post Office insurance. Claims will be handled faster with commercial insurance. If annual losses are small, the financial manager may even want to assume the risk and use self-insurance.

VALUE ENGINEERING

Value engineering has become a systematic, widely effective technique for cutting product costs. Many companies claim startling results. For example, the Carrier Corporation of Syracuse, New York, applied value engineering in altering the design of a float valve and slashed its cost from $35 to $6.

What Is Value Engineering?

Value engineering—sometimes called value analysis or value control—finds new ways to produce a product of equal or superior performance at lower cost. The underlying principle of value engineering is that it is easier to boost profits by reducing costs than by increasing sales. These principles work as well for the small businessman as for the large corporation. Value engineering needs no elaborate organization, involves little expenditure, and requires minimum training. It does demand, however, the application of common sense, observation, investigation, and imagination.

Where to Begin?

Value engineering might begin with products that have been in full scale production for some time and may be improved with new technology. A list of these items, ranking them from high to low according to annual purchase or production costs is a good starting point. From this list items for which costs are out of line with prices of approximately similar items should be selected.

The Seven Basic Steps

The value engineering method involves seven basic steps. These steps, however, are not always distinct and separate; they often merge or overlap. Completing them answers these questions about a product: What is it? What does it do? What does it cost? What is it worth? What other product or products might do the job? Which is the least expensive? What is needed to implement?

The seven steps are:

1. *Product selection.* Select the product to which value engineering efforts are to be applied.
2. *Determine function.* Analyze and define the functions that the product must perform.
3. *Gather facts.* Learn the specifications, development, and inventory of the product. What are the costs of its operation?
4. *Make comparisons.* Find out whether other products can do the same job, and if so, how much each one costs to make or buy.
5. *Refine the idea.* What new concept emerges, after all functions, methods, and alternatives have been studied?
6. *Overcome obstacles.* Prove that the alternatives will not jeopardize the fulfillment of performance (functional) requirements and effect a changeover.
7. *Review results.* Compare actual with expected results to determine merits of changeover. Was the original information accurate and applicable? Were savings effected where expected? What was learned from the execution of the plan that can be used again?

Savings often result when a switch is made (1) from a heavy metal to a light one, or vice versa, when weight is not a factor, (2) from machining to casting of a metal item, (3) from casting to stamping, (4) from various metals to lighter-weight or more resistant plastics.

What Value Engineering Means to Defense Contractors

Value engineering is a must for defense contractors. It is needed both to increase their profits and to improve their chances for contracts. The Secretary of Defense places contractors' value engineering proposals under direct surveillance. To help contractors with value engineering efforts, the government formed a top-level Value Engineering Evaluation Group. This Group is expected to bring about annual savings of $500,000,-000 in defense procurement. The Defense Department estimates that $1 of value engineering should produce $10 of savings.

It is up to the financial manager to get a good value engineering program underway or to find ways to improve an existing program. To find out about value engineering, write for these two booklets: "Value Engineering—a Challenge to Management," single copies are obtainable free from the American Ordnance Association, Transportation Building, Washington, D.C., 20006; "Organizing and Operating Value Engineering Programs," Defense Department publication H-111, 40 cents a copy, from the GPO, Washington, D.C., 20402.

CHECKPOINTS FOR CUTTING COSTS IN OPERATING COMPANY CARS

Here are some checkpoints to help cut the cost of operating business cars. Most companies are able to trim expenses somewhere along the line by reviewing these points and comparing them with company practices. In all but a few instances, a negative answer calls for investigation.

Yes	No	
____	____	Do we have a preventive maintenance program, and are our drivers following it?
____	____	Do we follow manufacturers' maintenance suggestions?
____	____	Are we using premium where regular gas will do?
____	____	Have we considered gasoline credit cards as a cost control procedure?
____	____	Do we audit dealer repair orders?
____	____	Do our cars favorably reflect our corporate image?
____	____	Have we looked at floor mats and seat covers as a way to increase our resale value?
____	____	Have we determined whether there is a pattern of failure?
____	____	Are we using the lowest cost suitable oil?
____	____	Do we rotate tires regularly?
____	____	Have tire lease and rental programs been investigated?
____	____	Do we have a safety program and is it up to date?
____	____	Have we compared our car cost with other companies like ours?
____	____	Do we ask manufacturers' representatives to help us specify the right equipment and options?
____	____	Is our mileage-rate payment to employees fair?
____	____	Have we investigated automobile leasing programs completely and without bias?
____	____	Do we know the best time of year to trade cars for best resale value?
____	____	Have we investigated the cost savings of compacts?
____	____	Do we buy cars of a color and trim that help resale?
____	____	Do we encourage automobile dealers' cooperation through prompt payment of invoices?
____	____	Can small automobile dealers understand our forms, such as invoices, purchase orders, and so forth?
____	____	Have we looked at our trade-in program recently?
____	____	Do we consider the driver, the terrain, and the driving conditions when we specify make, model, and optional equipment?
____	____	Are we buying optional equipment that gives the best resale value?
____	____	Do we consider total cost—what we'll have to pay for operation, service and repairs—when deciding the make and model to be purchased . . . or do we buy the make on which we get the lowest bid?
____	____	Is an engine governor practical for our cars?
____	____	Have we considered ways of reducing our insurance cost, license fees, and taxes through the purchase of different models or makes?

Yes   No

―――――   ―――――   Have we analyzed cost of outside dealer maintenance vs. our own
                              shop maintenance?
―――――   ―――――   Would we be money ahead to keep our cars longer, or replace
                              them sooner?
―――――   ―――――   Should we operate various segments of our fleet under different
                              plans, or is one plan best for the whole fleet?

PREVENTING EMPLOYEE DISHONESTY

Though many companies drive hard for production, sales and direct cost reductions, they do surprisingly little about setting up systems to prevent losses sustained through dishonesty of their employees. Their accounting systems are small help since most losses stay hidden in the books and never come to light—or at least not until it's too late.

The controller must be sure that he is taking proper precautions to prevent or reduce stealing by employees. A review of internal procedures and controls might very well help spot and correct weaknesses in your current system.

The following approaches are important when checking and reviewing a preventive program:

1. Subdivide or allocate work so that no one person has sole control over any transactions, assets, or the records accounting for them.
2. Establish the flow of the work so that one employee, acting independently, automatically verifies the work of another.
3. Provide the physical and mechanical facilities such as check-protectors to safeguard the work performed as far as practicable.
4. Remember that certain danger points require special vigilance. These are places where employees have access to cash, securities, notes, inventory readily convertible to cash, and memoranda or records representing cash.

A Blueprint for Action

In designing a system of internal check, observe these principles:

1. Maintain separate responsibility for physical handling of assets and record-keeping of assets.
2. Assign responsibility for physical handling of individual assets to a single individual. For example, only one employee should have access to a given drawer in a receiving cage.
3. Protect physical assets from unauthorized or improper use. For instance, keep as much inventory as possible in an enclosed space and issue it only on duly authorized requisitions.
4. Make all disbursements by check, preferably written by a check protector.
5. Segregate approval of disbursements from authority for making payments;

payrolls should be approved by one person, but payroll checks prepared and issued by others.

6. Prenumber all original memoranda supporting receipt or disbursement of cash, inventories, or other assets.

7. Limit access to areas where assets are kept.

8. Require double signature on checks, notes, and acceptances, and dual approvals of important transactions.

9. Bond all officers and employees in positions of trust.

10. Require every employee in a position of trust to take a vacation at least once a year, during which time another employee fills his job, and rotate employees from job to job.

11. Perforate or indelibly stamp "Paid" with the date, all documents in which payment has been made.

12. Avoid the use of dual positions, such as cashier-bookkeeper, shipping clerk-store clerk, etc.

13. Take a complete physical inventory at least once a year, and maintain perpetual inventory control.

Generally, the cost of preventive measures is small compared with the savings effected. But controls become more and more costly as they near 100 percent efficiency. Therefore, at some point it may be more economical to rely on internal and external audits, rather than controls geared to prevent all loss.

11

Managing the Legal Aspects of Finance

11

Managing the Legal Aspects of Finance

THE FINANCIAL OFFICER & LEGAL COUNSEL

Business is conducted under a legal framework which is important to the financial officer. If the business is incorporated all the powers granted the financial officer are derived from local, state, and federal corporate law. State law is the most important source of corporate law. The laws vary considerably from state to state. This fact points up the importance of competent legal counsel for corporate officers. The legal expert is an important advisor. The background information provided here or in any course of instruction on business law should never be used as a substitute for legal advice. It should only make the businessman aware of legal aspects of his problems.

TYPES OF BUSINESS LAW

All business is subject to at least three sets of laws. They are listed and explained below:

    A. *Statutes*—Governing bodies of the state and nation pass laws which affect business. An important body of law of this type is corporate law which is enacted and enforced at the state level. Such laws enable the creation and operation of corporations as legal entities. Federal statutes involve other areas, such as bankruptcy law.

    B. *Administrative Law*—The regulatory boards and commissions are set up by legislatures and are empowered to issue regulations. These regulations can be enforced as law in the courts and schedules of fines and prison sentences are spelled out as penalties. Some major examples of bodies issuing these types of laws are Internal Revenue Service, Federal Communications Commissions, and the various state utility boards.

205

C. *Uncodified Law*—This type of law is popularly known as common law. Common law is the legal precedent set by prior court decisions. Since these decisions are based on even earlier decisions, the real root of common law is the historical sequence in which mankind decided what was right and what was wrong. The great failing of common law is that it cannot anticipate sudden change and technical progress. For example, common law had no answers for the first legal problems involving airplanes. Wherever possible states have tried to replace common law with new codes (statutory law) which clearly define areas where common law has been found ambiguous or inapplicable.

Faced with these three types of laws the financial officer must depend on experts to interpret them. Several major areas of administrative law are so important to businessmen that the financial officer often develops his own expertise. One example is federal and state tax law. Other rulings of the ICC for freight companies, or the Federal Communications Commission for broadcasting companies are common knowledge to the managers. With these exceptions legal problems are generally not to be handled by line management.

THE CORPORATE FORM OF BUSINESS

Of the three forms of business (proprietorship, partnership and corporation) the type least used is the corporation. Surprising as it may seem proprietorships and partnerships outnumber corporations. However, since corporations tend to be large while proprietorships and partnerships tend to be small, the corporations employ the most people and account for a major share of the business transacted in this country. In order to understand the corporate form, a clear idea of what a corporation is is required.

The Corporation as a Legal Entity

A difficult aspect of corporations is its lack of physical being. The corporation exists only on the documents of incorporation and in the legal statutes which recognize this incorporation as meaning something. The building and machines *belong* to the corporation, the officers *work for* the corporation, the stockholders *own* the shares of the corporation; but no physical thing *is* the corporation. The corporate officer must, therefore, perform his duties with several facts in back of his mind:

1. The legal entity, the corporation, must suffer the effects of officers' actions.
2. Officers are responsible for their actions to the board of directors. The board of directors is responsible to the stockholders.
3. When an officer acts, he acts for the corporation, not as an individual. His corporation is responsible for his deeds unless his acts are determined to be against public policy or illegal.

The Financial Officer's Obligations as a Corporate Officer

Stemming from his position as a corporate officer, there are certain specific obligations which the financial officer has. These arise from the laws and the regulations of the Securities and Exchange Commission and the several states regarding the obligations of officers and directors of companies whose stock is held by the general public. These obligations have become much more specific—and to some extent more onerous—in recent years as a result of actions taken by the Securities and Exchange Commission to protect the interests of the public.

These obligations have to do with disclosure of important information to the public. The financial officer's function is particularly involved in this matter, since much of the information in question is financial information.

Information contained in a prospectus. Except for small issues, whenever a public offering of securities is made, these securities must be registered with the Securities and Exchange Commission, and a prospectus must be furnished to prospective purchasers of the securities. The securities cannot be sold until the SEC has permitted the prospectus to become effective. The SEC rules require a very detailed description of the securities and business of the company, as well as detailed financial statements supported by the public auditor's certificate. The officers and directors signing the prospectus are entitled to rely on the auditor's certificate as the work of an expert, but each of them must exercise due diligence in acquainting themselves with the information supporting the statements made in the prospectus. The degree of diligence required of the officers and directors varies with the nature of their individual responsibilities; thus, the financial officer would be expected to know a great deal about the financial information, and to have discovered a major misstatement of fact in the prospectus in connection with that information. There can be very severe penalties for failure to exercise due diligence in connection with the issuance of a prospectus.

The use of inside information. As an important member of the management of the corporation, the financial officer has access to a good deal of important, often confidential, information. Naturally, much of this information cannot be disclosed to the public because disclosure may give a competitor an undue advantage, or result in the loss of a commercial opportunity. Therefore, during the time when the information is not disclosed to the public, those persons possessing information which is significant enough to influence the average investor's judgment on the price of the stock, cannot buy or sell the stock. This prohibition applies to any employee possessing such information. In addition, directors and officers (and certain large shareholders) cannot both buy and sell the company's stock during any six month period. If they do, any shareholder can sue to have the corporation recover the excess of the sale price over the purchase price for any such sales and purchases which took place during any six month period. This latter penalty is applicable on a mere showing that the sale and purchase took place; there need be no evidence of wrongful intent. The sum total of these two restrictions is that the financial officer must be extremely cautious about making any purchase or sale of the corporation's stock at a time when there is significant undisclosed information, and he should refrain entirely from having both a purchase and a sale fall within a six month period.

Dealing with securities analysts. An important part of the financial officer's duties has to do with answering questions from analysts, or making presentations to them. Formerly, it was considered permissible, and in fact desirable, to give the securities analysts "private showings" of corporate information which was considerably more detailed than was released to the general public. Now, many companies are adopting the practice of inviting the press to these briefings. Also, when securities analysts call the corporate officers and ask for specific information, the officers are faced with a delicate question, as a result of the cases mentioned above. It is dangerous to give a single analyst, or a group of analysts significant information which is not at the same time available to the general public. Therefore, some companies will accompany any significant disclosure to analysts with a press release to the public. This is not intended to imply that every question which a securities analyst may ask falls in the category of significant information. It may be that certain detailed information is not released, because it is not particularly significant, and it is necessary to hold down the bulk of the annual report. If a shareholder or analyst requests such information, it probably can be given without the need for further public disclosure, provided it is in fact not significant.

NEGOTIABLE INSTRUMENTS LAW

An important subject for financial managers is the legal aspects of notes, drafts and checks. Each day, millions upon millions of dollars are transferred as a normal part of business. The transfers occur mostly in the form of negotiable instruments. Explained below are the important features of the Uniform Commercial Code's section on negotiable instruments. The Uniform Commercial Code has been adopted by the great majority of the states. Those states which do not have the Uniform Commercial Code have statutes which generally follow the same fundamental ideas. However, specific differences in specific states are best explained by a lawyer.

What Is a Negotiable Instrument?

In order for a "promise to pay" or an "order to pay" to be considered negotiable it must have the four characteristics explained below:
1. The promise or order must be *written* and must be *signed* by the *maker*.
2. The written message on the instrument must be an *unconditional* promise or order to pay a *specific sum of money*. Furthermore, no other conditions can appear in the message.
3. The instrument must be payable either on *demand* or at a *definite* time.
4. The *payee* must be clearly specified. That means that the instrument must be payable to the "bearer" or to the order of a named person.

Why Is Negotiability Important?

Payment of debts once was always made in cash. The substitution of checks for cash has permitted the phenomenal growth of business in the past two centuries. However, the check must be "very nearly cash" for the creditor to accept it in payment. The essence of negotiability is that the paper is "very nearly cash." It can be passed to a third, fourth, fifth, party with each holder convinced that what he holds is "very nearly cash." The banking system passes checks through third, fourth, and fifth parties at high speed and with little effort because the checks are negotiable.

The negotiability of notes is equally important. Creditors are able to accept the written promise to pay since they are able to pass the note on to third parties for cash. A common method of handling short term notes is discounting with a bank acting as collecting agent. In this case the payee endorses the note over to his bank with his bank's permission. The bank credits the payee's account with the face amount plus face interest to maturity less the bank's interest (or discount charge). The bank holds the note until maturity when it delivers it to the maker's bank for payment. In this case, the maker's bank would be termed the *drawee*. The drawee is a third party directed by the maker to pay the amount specified on the due date.

The Obligations of the Drawee

The drawee is in most cases a bank or financial institution. The payee maintains an account with the bank. Typically this is a checking account and the drawer's instructions to pay are in the form of a check. Three common types of checks are:

1. *Regular Checks*—The maker directs the drawee (bank) to pay a certain amount to the payee (named recipient).
2. *Certified Checks*—The drawee sets aside the face amount and guarantees that the funds will be available to pay the check.
3. *Cashier's Checks*—The bank is both the maker and drawee and is itself liable for payment of the amount specified.

It is important to realize that with a regular check the drawee is under no obligation to pay the payee simply because the check exists. For example, a forger in St. Louis, Missouri could sign and deliver a check naming a Pittsburgh bank (with whom he has no account) as drawee. The act of signing the check in St. Louis does not obligate the bank in Pittsburgh in any way. The bank does become obligated when it accepts the check. As a practical matter, accepting a check means having it delivered by the bank's clearing house and not rejecting it within a prescribed period of time.

What Is a Holder in Due Course?

In order for fourth, fifth and sixth parties (people not named as payee on the face of the instrument) to accept a negotiable instrument, they must be protected. They considered the instrument to be "very near cash." Within certain limits the Uniform Commercial Code offers such protection to holders in due course. In order for a holder to be a holder in due course he must pass the four following tests:

1. He must be the holder which means, have possession of the instrument. If it is lost he must be able to prove that he was the holder when the instrument was lost.

2. He must have received the instrument "for value." That is he must have a legitimate reason for receiving it.

3. He must have received it "in good faith." This means that he must have received it with the belief that it represented a legitimate payment.

4. He must at time of acceptance have no knowledge of defenses against or defects in the instrument.

If a holder qualifies as a holder in due course, he is in effect guaranteed that the instrument was cash-like to him. For example, suppose A writes a check payable to B, B endorses the check over to C, and C endorses the check over to D. When D presents the check at the bank, there are insufficient funds to cover it in A's account. If C and D are holders in due course, D returns the check to C and receives repayment, C returns the check to B and receives payment. Because they qualified as holders in due course, they cannot be held liable for the check's uncollectibility.

When a Holder in Due Course Is Not Protected

There are conditions under which an instrument was void or null since inception. These conditions constitute "real defenses" of the maker against claims made against him by holders in due course. Listed below are the conditions under which "real" defenses exist:

1. Forgery
2. Signature of an authorized agent
3. An incomplete instrument on its face
4. Alteration of the face
5. Blanks later filled in on the face
6. Checks written to complete illegal contracts such as gambling, extortion, etc.

In such cases the holder in due course still has a claim against whomever he received it from. The real defense prevents him from making his claim directly against the maker.

Conditional Contracts on the Face Make an Instrument Non-negotiable

If a maker writes a note which adds conditions to a contract, the instrument becomes non-negotiable. It is a popular opinion that writing special terms on the face of a check reinforces the legal position of the maker. This may help the maker but it forces the payee to accept a non-negotiable instrument. This denies to the payee the rights which he would have as a holder in due course. For example, a farmer may purchase a tractor and pay for it with a note which states "The seller agrees to repair the tractor free of charge until this note is paid one year from date of purchase." This makes the note conditional and non-negotiable. The seller would be wise to refuse the note and request another form of payment.

How an Officer Should Sign a Check

When a corporate officer signs a note (or check) he does so as an authorized agent. If the corporation fails to pay the notes, the officer is not held personally liable. He could possibly be held liable if his signature and the instrument were construed to be a personal one and not that of the corporation's. By contrast the same faulty signature could work to the detriment of the payee. If a payee accepted a corporation's note which was signed by an agent, the board of directors or president of the corporation might deny liability on the premise that the signature was a personal signature, not an agent's signature.

There are several proper methods of signing as an agent. The three most acceptable forms of signature are shown below:

1. AJAX CORP.
   by A. Smith, Agent
2. AJAX CORP.
   A. Smith, President
3. A. Smith, President
   AJAX CORP.

The important characteristics of all three are that they clearly identify the principal, the agent and the relationship between the two.

How to Salvage a Check Refused for Insufficient Funds

If a check is returned to the payee because the bank does not have sufficient funds in the account, the payee may be able to obtain a partial payment. The bank named as drawee is not obligated to make a partial payment to the extent there are funds left in the account, but it may make a partial payment. The bank could make the payment directly or the payee could deposit enough funds in the account to make the check good. If the unauthorized deposit method is used, the payee surrenders his rights to the unpaid balance. However, if the drawee is considered insolvent or has absconded, the best course may be to settle for a partial payment. In bankruptcy cases, the federal or state government may attempt to seize the bank accounts for unpaid taxes. In these situations, speed is of the essence.

The Proper Way to Stop Payment on a Check

If a check is stolen, lost, or in dispute the corporate financial officer should see that payment is stopped. (If the payment is in dispute the financial officer should not stop payment without the advice of counsel.) The instructions should be given to the bank immediately via phone call. A follow-up written confirmation should be sent to the bank. The written confirmation will obligate the bank for six months. Some banks have shortened the term of the stop payment order by notice to depositors.

Financial managers should check with their bank for this possibility. If the bank pays the check by mistake, ignoring the stop payment order, the bank is liable for the amount of the check. It can be made to redeposit the funds in the maker's account. It then can test the legality of the stop payment order. If it is determined that the check was negotiable and the payee was a holder in due course, it can overcome this stop payment. If not, the bank suffers the loss.

Financial managers (if the stakes are large enough) may not want to depend on the bank to stop payment. The suggestion might be made that all the funds be withdrawn from the account rather than stop payment. However, several states have construed such a move to be an act of fraud. Such a case could be prosecuted in criminal court to the detriment of the financial manager and his corporation. Unless specifically recommended by a lawyer, the withdrawal of funds is not advisable.

The Bank Statement May Contain Hidden Liabilities

As previously explained, forged checks are not the responsibility of the maker. However, carelessness in handling a bank account can result in a maker being charged with checks forged against his account. The bank as drawee expects the drawer to challenge promptly any forged, altered, or mishandled checks charged to his account. The courts have not set any fixed period of time but the Uniform Commercial Code states an outside limit of one year. Banks often specify on their forms and statements a much shorter period of time before their liability ceases. If the drawer can be shown to have agreed to this shorter period, the court would probably rule for the bank. The financial officer can prevent any difficulty by (1) having all bank statements checked immediately upon receipt and (2) by checking the bank's stated time limit for notification and challenging it in writing if it is deemed too short.

Is a Certified Check as Good as Cash?

It is a commonly held belief that when a bank certifies a check there is no way to prevent the payee from turning it into cash. In fact, what a bank does when it certifies a check is to guarantee that the stated amount is in the account and will be set aside until the certified check is cashed. However, between the time when a check is certified and the time it arrives at the bank for payment, other things can happen. Specifically, the drawer can direct the bank to dishonor the certification. To do this the drawer must sign an agreement to indemnify the bank against loss, and pay all legal fees resulting from the defense of the act of stop payment. Often the bank will ask the drawer to post a bond equal to twice the amount of the check. Thus the payment can be stopped. This applies only to checks certified by the drawer prior to presentation to the payee. If the payee takes the check to the bank and has it certified, there is no way payment can be stopped. The financial officer should, if possible, have all certified checks certified after receipt if he doubts the drawer's intention or financial strength.

A Reference Chart for Negotiable Instruments

As with all other legal matters, the only real answers can be provided by a competent lawyer supplied with specific facts about a definite problem. However, as a learning tool the reference chart of terms and mechanics of negotiable instruments under the Uniform Commercial Code is shown in Figure 11-1. The upper portion shows the important characteristics as the instrument passes from the drawer to a holder in due

1 *Drawer*	

To be negotiable
  1. Written and signed
  2. Unconditional promise to pay
  3. Payable on demand or on a definite date
  4. Named payee
	Maker—Instructs drawee to pay to the payee a definite sum on a definite date
	Drawer—same as maker
	Guarantor—Back up the promise of the maker

2 *Payee*	

Holder in Due Course
  1. Holder
  2. For Value
  3. In good faith
  4. No knowledge of defect
	Indorser—Promises to new holder to pay. Can be qualified
	Guarantor—Backs up the promise of the indorser.

3 *Holder in Due Course* Same Condition	Rights to Holder in Due Course—Has the promise to pay of all prior holders (indorsers) plus the maker
4 *Drawee* 1. Must accept promptly or reject promptly 2. Will dishoner if overdue 3. Has no liability until acceptance 4. Can 'stop pay' on order	Acceptor—The drawee after he has accepted the instrument

Figure 11-1
Negotiable Instruments Reference Table

course to the drawee. The bottom section shows a summary of definitions of important terms.

12

The Proper Handling of Debt

215

12

The Proper Handling of Debt

THE BANK AS A SOURCE OF FUNDS

The bank loan is the most common form of outside financial aid, and it is also the cheapest. A company that cannot get a loan from a bank must turn to other and more expensive sources of short-term capital. Often, however, a company might receive financial support if it has observed the basic rules and practices that help to ensure an adequate line of bank credit.

Select a Bank That Knows the Industry

A lot of banks may look alike; their names may sound alike—but they are actually not alike. Certain banks are much better for a company's borrowing purposes than others because they specialize in various types of loans. To find the bank that can help, the selection should be based on these four attributes:

1. *Special know-how.* The financial manager should seek a bank that knows the peculiarities of his operation. Whatever business he is in, there is probably at least one bank with a reputation for serving it especially well. Very likely this bank will do more than lend money—it will give very sound operating advice as well.

2. *Its size is a factor.* In choosing a bank, the financial officer should consider the size of the bank. If he needs big money, he obviously should not go to a small bank. On the other hand, if his credit needs are modest, a small bank where a financial manager has access to the key officers might be just the place.

3. *Reputation for aggressiveness.* What's the bank's reputation for aggressiveness in lending? What is its ratio of loans to deposits? What types of loans won't the bank make?

4. *The people in charge.* It always pays to be forthright with a banker and to tell him exactly how much money is needed and for how long a time. It is not advisable

to reduce the figure in the false hope that this will improve the chance of getting the loan.

When a borrower fails to ask for the amount really needed, or agrees to repay the loan in one year (when he could have just as easily obtained an 18-month term), he jeopardizes his relations with the bank. He may have to ask for more money or more time for repayment and create the following problems:

1. The bank will wonder why, at the time he sought the loan, he wasn't astute enough to ask for the amount needed or to allow enough time for repayment.
2. The bank will tend to lose confidence since, in effect, he has failed to live up to his commitments.

Provide a complete financial report. The loan applicant should give the banker a long-form, not a short-form report. The long form should consist of four sections.

The first section describes the business and its branches, lists the officers, and tells what the business does.

The second section compares the balance sheet of the current year with the previous year and gives a statement of changes in working capital. It also gives the various balance sheet ratios and the reasons for any substantial increase or decrease in working capital.

The third section compares the statement of income of the current year with the previous year, and gives the reasons for any significant increase or decrease.

The fourth section gives the scope and details of the accountant's audit, explaining what he did to substantiate each figure in the balance sheet.

Explanations avoid doubts. If the reasons behind the figures are clearly stated, no room is left for speculation or misinterpretation. The banker will have an understanding of the company that will be helpful in advancing proper credit. Figures that are unexplained can be misleading and subject to different interpretations. And bankers usually view *apparently* unfavorable figures in the worst light. A cardinal rule is always to state the reasons behind unfavorable figures whenever they may be misinterpreted.

Supply supplementary information. It is advisable that the banker be supplied with the following information at the start (he'll undoubtedly ask for it, anyway):

1. The company's estimates of earnings for the following year on an actual basis and on a cash flow basis.
2. The method and rate of depreciation.
3. Research and development expenses and how much of this money is required to advertise and market new products.
4. Life insurance policies that designate the company as beneficiary.
5. Thumbnail sketches of key personnel.
6. If substantial credit is involved a visit to the borrower's establishment by the bank officer is indicated. This gives the banker a chance to meet the management and see the business in action.

HOW TO MAINTAIN A LINE OF CREDIT

A good credit line is not only hard to get—it's just as hard to keep. A bank doesn't renew a loan automatically; it first reviews the borrower's financial condition. Questions are asked, and the wrong answers will either reduce a credit line or cause it to be withdrawn altogether. To protect a credit line, investigate these sensitive areas before the bank probes them.

Has the Company Maintained Its Profit?

When a company's net worth is reduced, banks often feel that the credit line should also be reduced. They view dips in earnings as portents of a severe loss in some future year. If a firm *has* sustained a loss, the bank will want to know why. And if the loss stemmed from excessive expenses or some other instance of faulty management, the bank will want the condition corrected before continuing the loan arrangement.

Has There Been a Decrease in Liquidity?

If so, was it due to a general slowdown in collection of accounts receivable? If collections have slowed because of a change in credit terms—for example, the extension of payments from 30 days to 60 days or 90 days—the bank will look for greater profit to offset this strain.

Perhaps more funds are now tied up in inventory. This could be the harbinger of greater profits if the buildup consists of a new line or favorable material purchases. On the other hand, if battered or obsolete goods burden the inventory account, convert them to cash.

Have New Loans Been Added?

This is a red flag to a bank—unless the borrower first got its approval to take on additional loan obligations. The bank based the credit line on its evaluation of the financial statement. The appearance of additional loans may prompt the bank to lower sharply its original evaluation of the firm's ability to retire debt.

AUGMENT AVAILABLE CREDIT WITH JOINT LOANS

Every company tries to operate within the credit line extended by its bank, but this isn't always possible. Growth companies, especially, may need more capital than they can get from their bank alone, but they may readily qualify for a participating loan—one provided by both a bank and a finance company.

How the Bank-Finance Company Loan Works

There are many variations of these participating loans; a typical one works this way—
1. The joint loan is made on a revolving basis, with the borrower assigning his accounts receivable as collateral.
2. The customer remits payment to the finance company. (Sometimes the customer makes payment directly to the borrower.)
3. Both the bank and the finance company have recourse to the borrower.

4. The finance company administers the loan and the bank contributes up to 50 percent of the borrowed funds.

Advantages to the Borrower

He obtains the amount of working capital needed—or at least much nearer that amount than from the bank alone—and at an interest rate that is generally lower than if the entire amount were borrowed from a finance company. And, under most arrangements, the borrower gets the following services and information from the finance company.

1. All of the assigned accounts are verified on a monthly basis.
2. All receipts accompanying invoices are carefully checked with the delivery company or railroad.
3. Overdue items, discrepancies, and the like, are noted and investigated.
4. The customers' credit is studied thoroughly. A concentration of shipments to any one customer is watched and analyzed.
5. Accounts receivable are aged at least once a month. Those that are past due more than a certain number of days are charged back to the borrower. Delinquent accounts are investigated to find the reasons for nonpayment.
6. Trends of sales, gross profits, expenses, turnover of receivables, and ratios of sales to inventory are plotted and observed.

The supervision outlined above is conducted primarily for the protection of the lender. But in a very real sense, the benefits from these procedures also accrue to the borrower.

Borrow More With a Joint Factor-Bank Loan

An innovation in participating loan plans consists of the factor-bank participating loan. This recently devised arrangement is distinctly different from the usual bank-finance company participating loan. This is a typical arrangement:

1. The borrower sells all of his accounts receivable to the factor on a non-recourse maturity basis.
2. At the same time, the borrower assigns to the bank a continuing right to the proceeds of his accounts receivable held by the factor.
3. The borrower then borrows the amount agreed on directly from the bank at banking rates.
4. At the beginning of each month, the factor sends to the bank a statement of the borrower's account, showing the total sales factored during the previous month and the average due date of the invoices.
5. On the specified average due date, the factor sends its check for the matured balance directly to the bank. The bank then applies the proceeds as a reduction of the loan.
6. The factor provides the following services for the borrower: (a) buys the accounts receivable, thereby relieving the borrower of the risk involved

in credit sales, (b) does all the accounts receivable bookkeeping, (c) collects money due from the borrower's customers.

The Merits of the Plan

The borrower can obtain a higher amount of credit from the bank than otherwise, since the factor guarantees to the bank the solvency of all the customers represented by the accounts receivable purchased by the factor. As for cost, the borrower pays the factor a commission of from 1.0 to 1.5 percent on sales for his services, and, as with the bank-finance company loan, he pays regular interest rates on amounts advanced by the bank. This is cheaper than the straight factoring arrangement.

Comparing Assignment of Receivables Under Individual and Joint Loans

A company can often boost its bank line of credit by pledging receivables as collateral, without bringing a finance or factoring company into the picture. But this procedure often fails to gain either the maximum line of credit or the cheapest rates.

Banks limit the amount they will lend on accounts receivable to a predetermined ratio of the borrower's investment in the business. Finance companies generally exceed this ratio by a substantial margin. For example, a company with a capitalization of $50,000 and receivables of $200,000 could typically borrow only $100,000 against the receivables from a bank. But it could probably borrow as much as $180,000 from a finance company, and even more from a factoring company.

As for costs, some banks raise interest charges on loans made against accounts receivable. In some instances, bank loans against receivables reach almost to the 12 percent maximum of the 7 percent to 12 percent range. When a borrower's interest approximates 12 percent, he should consider arranging for a participating loan.

GET QUICK CASH THROUGH INTERIM FINANCING

A company that wants to grow big in a hurry often needs money in a hurry. Sometimes, just when it needs the money most, it finds that its bank credit is already extended to the limit. How can it get cash quickly in such a situation? One possible answer is interim financing.

What is Interim Financing?

This is simply a high-interest short-term loan. It is especially useful for the company that (1) enjoys a strong competitive position, (2) is already using a full credit line at its bank, and (3) has a good chance to make substantially greater profits if it can get a sizable amount of money on short notice.

If a firm is in this situation, it may be able to use one of two interim financing arrangements.

1. The "standby" commitment. Using this procedure, the borrower approaches a

bank for the capital. The bank may not want to lend the money directly since it considers the project too risky. To meet this objection, the borrower finds an interim financier to "stand by," that is, to agree that in default, he will take over the loan. The bank is then fully protected, and will agree to make the loan. To get this arrangement, the borrower must furnish collateral to the firm that guarantees the loan.

2. *The direct loan.* Using this method, the borrower deals with only one party, usually a commercial finance company, that provides the necessary money after a stipulated amount of collateral is pledged. Interim financiers prefer the usual type of collateral, but they may accept such things as second mortgages or improved land.

What Does It Cost?

The cost will depend on the risk involved in the use of the money and on the loan arrangement. When a firm borrows from a bank on a "standby commitment," it pays interest on the bank loan plus a fee of two to five percent to the financier who guarantees the loan. When borrowing directly from a finance company under the direct loan arrangement, the usual interest rate runs from 10 to 12 percent. If the firm can get part of the money from a bank, some interim financiers will provide the rest at a lower-than-usual rate. On the other hand, the annual interest rate will be more—as much as 15 percent—if repayment is not personally guaranteed by the president, vice president, or some other responsible officer. No matter how one looks at it, interim financing is expensive.

An Interim Financing Checklist

The following factors will weigh heavily in the decision of the lender whether or not to grant the loan.

1. *What industry is the firm in?* Manufacturing industries get top rating. Service industries are less likely to get interim financing.

2. *How does its management rate?* An impressive record with no signs of management negligence is a big point in your favor. Also, proven ability to carry out profitable ideas counts heavily.

3. *What financing has it already obtained?* Most companies that borrow from an interim financier have already received other loans. Whether the firm will be considered as overfinanced depends on its past performance, the scope of the project, and expected profits.

4. *Is an officer of the firm risking his own money?* Chances of getting the loan are improved if the interim financier knows that one or more officers of the firm intend to put their own money on the line as well as his.

When Not to Use Interim Financing

Knowing when not to use interim financing is as important as knowing when to use it. Generally, interim financing is not applicable unless the borrower:

1. Has exhausted every possibility of getting a bank loan.

2. Has tried accounts receivable financing.
3. Needs a lot of money. Interim financiers do not like to make loans for less than $250,000. A loan as low as $50,000 is possible, but rare. Commercial finance companies can provide more information to companies interested in interim financing.

MORE WAYS TO GET SHORT-TERM FINANCING

Pledging and Selling Notes and Contracts

A company can pledge or sell notes and contracts receivable to banks or sales finance companies. The lender often keeps possession of the paper; the borrower can usually do so only under a trust agreement. Two types of instruments are involved—conditional sales contracts and notes receivable. The latter is usually secured by a chattel mortgage.

When a company markets goods under a conditional sales contract, it may sell the contract, (if the customer has good credit) to a bank or finance company. The bank will immediately pay the amount of the contract and later collect from the customer.

When a firm uses notes receivables secured by chattel mortgages to sell goods, it may likewise turn these over to a bank or finance company for cash. The notes may sometimes be held by a third party under a deed or trust. This arrangement enables the borrower to keep the paper and collect directly from the customer.

Under both the conditional sales contract and notes receivable financing, recourse by the lender in case of nonpayment by the borrower's customer is handled in one of three ways:

1. Full recourse. The lender has full recourse if the buyer fails to pay.
2. No recourse. The lender absorbs the bad debt.
3. Limited recourse. The lender may: (a) have full recourse until a certain number of payments are made, and not after that; (b) require the borrower to handle the sale of any repossessed goods; (c) require the borrower to repurchase the materials for the amount of the unpaid balance; (d) hold the borrower liable only up to the amount of reserve held by the lender.

Bills of Lading

A buyer can borrow to pay for a shipment by pledging bills of lading with a lender while the goods are in transit. When the goods arrive, the borrower (buyer) can get the bill of lading on a trust receipt, pick up and sell the goods and pay off the loan at a later date. Or, he can put the goods in a public warehouse and turn over the warehouse receipt to the lender.

Sight Draft with Bill of Lading Attached

A seller can borrow on bills of lading by drawing a sight draft on the buyer and discounting this note with the bank. The bank has recourse against the borrower if the goods are refused. The seller is protected because the bill of lading is not released to the buyer until the goods are paid for.

Bank Acceptance

Rather than wait from one to three months for payment, a seller can draw a draft on the buyer's bank and get payment almost immediately. For example, if a manufacturer in New York wishes to use a bank acceptance in selling to a merchant in Texas on 90 days' time, the manufacturer will send the bill of lading and a draft to the merchant's bank. The bank will accept the draft because it has assurance that the draft will be paid at maturity. This assurance rests either on the high credit standing of the Texas merchant or on the fact that the bank holds the bill of lading or some other document as collateral. After acceptance, the bank is liable to the drawer of the draft, but it looks to the merchant for payment. When the New York manufacturer receives the banker's acceptance, he can discount it at his own bank or sell it on the open market.

FOR LONG TERM FINANCING CONSIDER A LIFE INSURANCE COMPANY LOAN

A growing company may find that its financial needs outstrip its supply of short-term funds. It can turn to a commercial bank for intermediate financing—two to five years —but if it needs credit for 10, 15, or 20 years, it must look elsewhere. A good place to start is with a life insurance company.

Types of Life Insurance Company Loans

Life insurance companies provide three types of business loans: (1) unsecured term loans, (2) commercial and industrial mortgage loans, and (3) restrictive covenant loans. Most loans run from 10 to 15 years and are written for large amounts—up to $5,000,000.

Unsecured Loans

The long-term unsecured loan is backed solely by the borrowing company's credit. Obviously, the company must have a long history of capable management and robust earnings, and it generally must be large, because many life insurance firms will not consider making a loan for less than $1,000,000. A few will grant loans for as little as $150,000, but this is rare.

Mortgage Loans

A company planning to construct or buy a plant might consider an insurance company mortgage loan. In reviewing the application, the insurance company will be vitally interested in the type of building it is asked to finance. If it can serve multiple uses, the chances are much better than if the applicant is seeking a loan on specialized property. Another matter to consider is that state laws generally prohibit insurance companies from lending more than 75 percent of the appraised value of the property, so the borrower must be ready to put up 25 percent of the required cash.

In the case of an unsecured loan, the life insurance company may want to be the sole lender. If so, the borrower must retire all existing debt. This is not necessarily a disadvantage. It may enable him to tie his financing arrangements together in one neat package, with the loan from the insurance company representing the only continuing financial obligation.

Restrictive Covenant Loans

These loans are a special type of unsecured loan. The insurance company seeks protection by contractually guaranteeing liquidity and financial strength of the borrower. The borrower signs an agreement containing any of several restrictive covenants such as:
1. Cash dividends will not exceed 60 percent of net earnings.
2. Net working capital must exceed a fixed dollar minimum.
3. The current ratio must not fall below a specified minimum.
4. No assets may be pledged as collateral.
5. Short term debt may not be used for more than nine consecutive months.
6. Annual capital investment may not exceed annual depreciation. The terms of the agreement can be tailored to the individual needs of a borrower. The insurance company will also alter some of the restrictions, so that the fixed minimums can be exceeded with written permission of the lender. In such cases the burden would be on the borrower to explain how and why such permission would be to the long range benefit of both the lender and the borrower.

How to Qualify for an Insurance Company Loan

Insurance companies look for a sound balance sheet and impressive earnings record. A borrower should be ready to supply financial records for a ten-year period, and include (1) an analysis of sales by each product line or company division, (2) a detailed history of all members of top management, and (3) a full description of the plan to use the money.

Loan rejections are frequent, sometimes running as high as 90 percent of applications received. The following are the three chief causes for rejections:

1. *Low earning power.* Lenders often look for a demonstrated earning power of two times the debt obligation after depreciation. One and one-half times is the legal requirement, but many insurance companies consider this not enough.

2. *Poor credit analysis.* The borrowing firm's credit position is not competitive. Financial officers often fail to assess their own company's financial strengths and weaknesses against companies of similar size in the same industry. As a result, some borrowers do not meet the highly selective standards of the lenders.

3. *Thin management.* No lender wants to advance money to a "one-man operation."

The departure of the key executive or two may drastically affect management capability and company performance. Borrowers must be able to show depth in management.

How to Approach an Insurance Company

Assume that the financial manager has assessed his company's attributes and believes that it stands a good chance of getting an insurance company loan. How does he make contact with the loan department of an insurance company? Does he simply make a telephone call and explain his needs? He can, but he is more likely to have success if he works through an intermediary, such as a broker, banker, or investment banker.

He should try to select an intermediary who has a close working relationship with the insurance company. He'll know what the lender looks for in borrowers, and can tell the borrower exactly how to present the application. He may steer him to a different lender, or he may advise that the plan be altered or to forget about the plan completely. This prevents a formal rejection and leaves the firm free to try elsewhere without word spreading that it has been turned down.

If the investment banker or other intermediary takes the loan request to the insurance company, the applicant has a good chance of success. The investment banker, in effect, places his personal endorsement on the credit worthiness. Since he has his own reputation to protect in the financial community, he handles only those deals that he feels have a fairly good chance of going through. As an experienced negotiator and expert in this aspect of finance, the investment banker is likely to get better terms than an unrecommended applicant. His services will cost one-half of one percent of the loan amount, but generally this is money well spent.

SBA OFFERS 10-YEAR LOANS

The Small Business Administration (SBA) provides 10-year loans of as much as $350,000 to qualified firms: (a) those who do not exceed a certain size, and (b) those who cannot get money from private sources at reasonable rates. This source of credit is worth investigating, since 95 percent of all firms qualify under SBA's definition of "small" business.

SMALL BUSINESS CLASSIFICATIONS

Manufacturing	From 250 to 1,000 employees, depending on the industry.
Retail	Annual sales of $1 million or less; exceptions include automobile dealers, where limit is $3 million.
Wholesale	Annual sales of $5 million or less.
Service	Annual sales of $1 million or less; exceptions include hotels, up to $2 million.
Construction	Average annual receipts of $5 million or less for preceding 3 fiscal years.
Trucking	Annual receipts of $3 million or less.

The nearest SBA office can supply specific standards applying to a given business. Classifications may change, and certain industries or lines of business are ineligible. These include lending or investment agents, newspapers and magazines, radio-TV broadcasters, and firms which derive a good deal of their earnings from the sale of alcoholic beverages.

Getting an SBA Loan

To get an SBA loan, the borrower must demonstrate prospects of long-range growth. Loans are not made on a temporary basis to solve pressing financial problems. In making its decision, the SBA will take into account such factors as amount of capital invested in the business and the collateral offered.

SBA loans are available only to businesses that cannot get bank credit. Before trying SBA, therefore, a borrower should go to at least two banks to see if they will make the desired loan, either on their own, or in participation with the SBA. If the banks are unwilling to provide the loan under any conditions, it is advisable to ask them to state this fact in writing, and apply for a direct loan from the SBA.

When the bank is willing to participate in a loan, the SBA may provide for cash needs under one of the following plans:

1. *The 90 percent participation plan*. The SBA participates or guarantees up to 90 percent of the loan, with the bank supplying the remainder. The loan applicant files three copies of SBA Form 4 and all supporting papers with the bank. The SBA and the bank jointly decide, usually within three weeks, whether to grant the loan. Maximum loan amount is $350,000, and must be repaid in 10 years.

2. *The 75 percent participation plan*. With this plan, SBA limits its participation to 75 percent instead of 90 percent. The company deals directly with the bank, on whose judgment SBA relies. If the bank is willing to lend $25,000, the SBA will automatically lend as much as $75,000. The maximum loan amount and duration are the same as for the 90 percent plan.

3. *The early maturities participation plan*. This plan meets a banker's preference for making loans that mature in two years or less, but the borrower still gets a 10-year loan because the SBA continues its share for eight years. There are many modifications of this plan. Sometimes the duration of the bank's participation depends on how much of the total loan it provides. The bank is repaid in 7 years if it puts up 70 percent of a 10-year loan, in four years if it puts up 40 percent, and so on.

SBA forms are more detailed than most bank forms. The bank has the advantage of prior knowledge of the company's activities. Moreover, the bank rarely makes loans with maturities as long as those offered by the SBA. Before filling out a loan application, a talk with an SBA representative will result in his advice on procedures to follow to improve the chances of qualifying for the loan.

IS AN SBIC THE ANSWER?

Small Business Investment Companies (SBIC's) are a relatively new kind of financial institution. Set up by Congress in 1958 and licensed by the Small Business Administration, they lend money to growth companies with a new worth of up to $5,000,000 in return for debentures running as long as 20 years. These debentures are often convertible into common stock at a predetermined price. Loans cannot exceed 20 percent of the SBIC's capital stock and surplus.

How to Select an SBIC

Not all of the more than 600 SBIC's can serve a given firm's needs equally well. Some specialize in particular industries, such as chemical, drugs, foods, or electronics; some operate nationally; others regionally or locally. Some SBIC's will make only large investments of as much as $1,000,000; others will invest as little as $20,000 or $30,000. And some offer professional management consulting services as well as capital, while others do not.

The loan arrangement is such that the borrower is taking on a business partner. The partner should be someone who knows the line of business and can help with problems. Careful selection of the SBIC whose policies and services match the needs is of primary importance.

How an SBIC Selects Borrowers

Getting an SBIC loan is a two-way matter, of course. An SBIC screens a loan application very carefully. After choosing the SBIC that best fits his needs, the financial manager must do everything possible to improve his chances of getting the loan. SBIC administrators offer the following guidelines, based on several years' experience in financing company expansion.

1. *Prepare a written prospectus.* Set forth briefly but accurately the history of the company. Include: (a) its present and proposed products and services, (b) the nature of present and proposed markets, (c) organization structure, (d) qualifications of principal executives, (e) nature of labor supply, (f) names of principal raw material suppliers and principal customers, (g) prospective sales and earnings, and (h) long-term financial requirements.

The managers of any SBIC will be favorably impressed if the prospectus is well organized and informative. The statement saves everybody time by permitting all persons to get the available facts quickly.

2. *Give a frank appraisal.* Give the SBIC a frank appraisal of the company's present condition. In this analysis be sure to include (a) the company's strengths and weaknesses, (b) past and present operating problems, (c) major decisions recently made or contemplated, (d) results of past decisions, and (e) anticipated results of present decisions.

3. *Make a long-range forecast.* Many companies applying for long-term financing fail to give the SBIC specific, long-term sales prospects. Vague forecasts based on wishful thinking damage the chances of getting a loan.

4. *Ask for enough.* Give the SBIC a realistic estimate of the funds needed. As in borrowing from a bank or any other lender, the borrower does not improve his chances by asking for a minimum amount. It is wise to ask for enough capital to carry out his long-range forecast. If he asks for less capital than needed, the SBIC may doubt his business judgment, or he may run into financial troubles at the very time his plan is about to succeed.

5. *Show management continuity.* The success of any business depends on the hard work, imagination and competence of its people, especially its executives. It is important to show the SBIC that the ranking officers are committed to the future of the company. The best way to do this is to demonstrate economic interests. Key men in a growth company should be paid primarily by incentive plans rather than by drawing high salaries. SBIC representatives will be favorably impressed if the officers draw modest salaries, yet stand to make substantial gains in stock options or bonuses *provided* the company makes intended profits.

What Is the Cost?

Since loans are generally given in return for convertible debentures, the applicant will want to know how much of an interest he must give up in return for the capital. This is naturally a matter of legitimate concern, but more important is the potential value of the retained share in the company. It's obviously better to have 60 percent of a growing company with profits of $200,000 than 90 percent or even 100 percent of a company having $50,000 or $100,000 in profits.

The important variable in financing with an SBIC is not the percentage of equity given up for additional capital, but the amount of potential growth in the value of the equity retained. Because an SBIC is active in high-risk financing, it seeks strong inducements in the form of an equity in the borrower. This arrangement helps the SBIC to weather the losses it suffers from the companies that fail to overcome the risks involved in growth.

Though a greater risk requires a greater inducement, an SBIC never seeks to control or operate the borrower's business—except in an emergency to protect its investment. Its aim is to invest in the growth of a company and to keep present management hard at work.

OTHER SOURCES OF LONG-TERM FINANCING

Ford Foundation Loans

Though little known in corporate circles, the investment department of the Ford Foundation makes loans for as long as 15 years and in amounts from $1,000,000 to $5,000,000. The Foundation reviews a borrower's application in much the same way as any other lender. It closely examines earnings projections, cash flows, audited records, and management. It likes to see a full description of operations and products and credible projections of earnings and profits. About 85 percent of loan applications are turned down for various reasons, but they all add up to the usual central weakness: the borrower did not demonstrate repayment potential.

Equipment Financing

Though equipment financing resembles extended trade credit, it serves a purpose similar to a long-term loan when a company needs to finance the purchase of equipment or machinery. Manufacturers offer this type of financing to promote sales. The buyer makes a down payment of from 20 to 33 percent of the cost of the equipment, and pays interest and principal in monthly installments. The seller either retains the title or obtains a lien on the equipment until final payment.

Sale and Leaseback

Though not in itself a loan, a company can raise cash by selling a fixed asset and leasing it back. The transaction has business and tax advantages that merit consideration, especially if the value of the asset is higher than its remaining depreciation. In this situation, a corporation (1) raises working capital without increasing debt or issuing stock, and (2) gets a rent deduction substantially higher than the depreciation deduction. The rent deduction, of course, depends on cash outlay, whereas depreciation does not. But it may be to a company's advantage to pay this price for freeing capital that would otherwise be tied up in equipment, land, or buildings.

13

Financing with Stocks and Bonds

231

13

Financing with Stocks and Bonds

‖‖

For a business to be successful it must grow. It may experience temporary dips in income or retrenchments in operations. Unless it soon resumes an expansion pattern it will start losing ground to competitors.

A business grows by getting more capital to invest in plant facilities, research and development programs, marketing programs and new products. It gets most of this capital through greater depreciation allowances and improved earnings. It also gets capital by borrowing from banks and insurance companies. But many businesses reach a point where these capital sources are not enough to meet ever-increasing demands. When this happens they must obtain funds through the distribution of stocks or bonds, a procedure called "going public."

QUALIFYING FOR UNDERWRITING

Before a company can go public, it must meet certain requirements. Though there is no fixed set of rules, there is general agreement among investment bankers on several points. (Investment banking firms specialize in selling stocks and bonds; they are often called *underwriters*.) The first thing they consider is whether the company has a superior product (or service) and a capable management. Both features point toward long-range growth and help to generate investor confidence.

What the Investment Banker Wants to Know

Since an investment banking firm's reputation is closely linked to the performance of its underwritings, it may engage an independent research organization to survey the company's products and business prospects. These studies will be made at the client's expense. Not until all this information is in does the underwriter decide whether to proceed further.

233

Specifically, the underwriter looks for answers to questions such as these when appraising the investment merits of the client company.

1. How does the trend in sales and earnings for the past several years compare with other firms in the industry?
2. What is the current financial position as reflected in the balance sheet and by the financial ratios?
3. How do the firm's products and services compare with similar products and services?
4. Is the company keeping pace with competition? How much is spent on product research and development? What new products are in the offing? Can the need for additional funds be justified in light of past performance and products?
5. What is the caliber of top management? How long have key personnel been employed? Are those at the middle management level getting the experience they need to take over top jobs?

An astute underwriter will assess not only the client company but its industry as well. Stock of a company in one industry is sometimes easier to sell than stock of a company in another industry, regardless of the basic merits of each company. There is often a current "glamor" industry that generates investor confidence. Stocks of companies in a popular industry sell readily; sometimes they are fully subscribed before the new offering becomes effective. Conversely, stocks of companies in industries not currently favored by investors may be quite difficult to sell, even though the companies may show considerable promise. The underwriters will note closely investor acceptance of stock issues by other companies in the same industry before deciding whether to market your offering.

THE UNDERWRITER'S JOB

Occasionally, a company makes a public offering without an underwriter's guidance. The results are frequently unsatisfactory if not disastrous. The many eager friends and associates who presumably had $5,000 to invest turn out to want only $500 when the time comes to actually put out the cash. In addition to not finding enough buyers, an equally serious hazard is that of running afoul of SEC regulations. No financial manager issues stock often enough to become familiar with the many complexities of the procedure. Setting up a special department for registering and marketing a new issue is generally more expensive than employing the services of a professional.

Underwriter Services

Registering and marketing a new issue are only two responsibilities of an underwriter. A competent underwriting firm offers its clients these basic services:

1. *Marketing advice.* Underwriters give companies contemplating new issues advice in the practical field of securities distribution. The task is not merely to sell securities, but to sell the right type and number of securities at the right time, on the basis of the needs of the company and the demands of the market.

Especially in a first issue, the financial manager needs expert advice on the best type of stock to offer and at what price. An able underwriter knows whether to sell common stock or preferred stock. If the business is just speculative enough to weaken the protection normally associated with preferred stock, thereby making preferred stock buyers wary, the underwriter may suggest an offering of common stock to attract the more aggressive buyer—those more interested in capital gains than in dividends.

An underwriting firm has the "feel" of the market; it knows buyers' attitudes toward prices and the types of securities that currently appeal to stock buyers. This knowledge is essential for a successful distribution because the capitalization structures and earnings ratios of new issues must compare favorably with all other securities competing for investment funds.

2. *Stock sponsorship.* A responsible underwriter not only quickly distributes a new issue, he also makes a secondary market after completing the initial sale. He does this by buying back shares now owned by investors and reselling them to other buyers. The price of a new issue tends to drop sharply if the underwriting firm is reluctant to repurchase shares it has just sold. Should the underwriter take the extreme measure of putting a "no bid" on the stock, that is, refuse to buy back shares, stock brokers in general will shun the stock, leaving it worthless.

A new issue coming on the market must compete against more than 40,000 other stocks clamoring for buyers, and most of the stocks already outstanding are better known. This means that almost all new issues must be sponsored to a certain extent, as a means of supporting their offering prices. An underwriting firm sponsors a new issue by bringing it to the attention of its customers and recommending it for investment.

Should the financial manager be concerned about the price of individual shares in the secondary market? His company has already received the full proceeds of the stock sale, as provided in the contract with the underwriter. One answer is that a falling price may suggest little confidence in the company's management and business future. The manager must look forward to the time when he may need more equity financing. The price of the next offering can be no higher than the current market price of the stock. The investing public will remember the price performance after the last stock issue. Thus it is in the company's long term interest to assure stable price performance.

3. *The underwriter bears the risk.* The most important function of the underwriter is the risk which he takes in contractually agreeing to pay for the entire stock issue whether he sells it or not. Without this inducement few companies would be able to offer their stock to the public. The underwriter's efforts to guide the client towards the proper price, timing and type of issue are in his own self-interest. The financial manager must be a counterforce to insure that the terms of the underwriting are the best available. In the case of small issues of unknown stock or if the financial manager holds out for terms unacceptable to the underwriter, the underwriter may suggest a "best efforts" sale. This means that any unsold stock is returned to the company with no further obligation of the underwriter. This means that the company, not the underwriter, bears the risk. "Best effort" sales are often the only deals available to companies when they first go public. If the financial manager accepts such a plan, he should be sure that the sale will occur in a strong market when new issues have the best chance of acceptance.

Underwriting Syndicates

Often a new unseasoned stock needs a "breadth of market" which is a term indicating a wide range of stockholders with a wide range of investment goals. Thus some stock will not be available for sale immediately after the new issue. If most of the stock were presented for sale, the price would probably plummet. To avoid this many buyers are sought. This is best accomplished by dispersing the stock among several sales outlets. These several sales outlets contractually join together in a selling syndicate. The syndicate lasts until all of the new stock is sold. Syndicating brokers agree to purchase a part of the new issue through the "managing broker" and resell it to their customers. The managing broker earns a management fee and selling brokers earn their commission. The commission is the spread between the underwriter's price and the sales price of the issue. The syndicate is called a purchase group. Among themselves they sign a "Purchase Group Contract" which sets forth the rights and obligations of each member. The underwriting agreement is a contract between the originating broker and the company selling stock. The two are legally separate but as a practical matter are closely related. A financial manager would be wise to investigate the credentials of both the originating brokers *and* his syndicating brokers before signing the underwriting agreement.

Another reason that stock sponsorship may be of overriding importance is the liquidity that an active market provides for the original owners of substantial shares of stock. (Liquidity refers to the ease of converting a security to cash.) To provide a market for these large shareholders is sometimes a chief factor leading to the public offering in the first place. And many investors will not purchase a stock for which there is a limited market.

WHAT TO CONSIDER IN SELECTING THE UNDERWRITER

Selecting the right underwriter is perhaps the most important step in bringing out a first issue. Underwriters specialize in different types of issues. Many underwriters do not handle initial issues at all, whereas others specialize in "originating." These firms have skilled staffs of experts who work closely with the management of a company that plans to offer a new stock issue.

To find this type of underwriter requires some investigation. A good place to begin is with a commercial banker. He can supply helpful information about various underwriting firms. He can also contact accounting firms and lawyers who specialize in securities work, and who therefore have an intimate knowledge of the underwriting business.

One of the first things to consider in making the selection is the size of the underwriting firm. If a firm is local in nature, a small underwriter with a local network of securities offices will be the most likely prospect. A large underwriting firm with offices from coast to coast is generally interested only in introducing issues of larger companies who are known nationally.

Another and equally important matter to consider is the underwriter's reputation. If he is esteemed by the financial community, a new issue takes on a certain luster and becomes easier to sell. Conversely, a firm with a record of unsuccessful underwritings is likely to dampen investor interest in a stock.

Cost of a Public Offering

It costs more to sell common stock than preferred stock or bonds. According to figures compiled by the Securities and Exchange Commission, the median cost of floating an issue of common stock amounts to 10.28 percent of the gross proceeds, whereas the cost of selling preferred stock amounts to 4.34 percent, and of bonds, 1.49 percent.

Costs of an underwriting for common stock can be divided into two major divisions: the underwriting firm's compensation (determined by its risk and selling expenses), and all other expenses connected with the underwriting, such as filing fees, attorney's fees, printing costs, and so on.

Underwriter's Compensation

The underwriter's risk and selling costs chiefly determine the discount, or spread, which the underwriter negotiates with the issuing firm. The discount is greater for common stocks than preferred stocks or bonds, for untested companies, for first offerings, and for small offerings. Generally, the underwriter's discount ranges from a little over 4 percent for common stock offerings between $10,000,000 and $20,000,000 to 21 percent for offerings under $500,000.

In addition to his discount the underwriter may ask for options that give him the right to purchase stock at preferred prices. For example, the option may permit him to purchase from one to three percent of the total shares at the initial offering price during the first year following the underwriting, with the price increasing by three percent above the initial offering price for each of the next three years. This arrangement is preferable to a higher spread because it creates less of a cash drain. It also serves as a good selling point by reflecting the underwriter's confidence in the company.

Other Expenses

In a recent initial stock offering involving total proceeds of $3,000,000, company expenses (excluding underwriter's discount) were as follows:

SEC registration fee	$ 300.00
Registrar and transfer agent's fee	2,032.00
Blue-sky filing fees and expenses	2,750.00
Cost of printing registration statement and prospectus	8,500.00
Attorneys' fees and expenses	22,178.00
Accountants' fees and expenses	9,231.00
Miscellaneous expenses	552.00
	$47,043.00

These expenses total a little more than 1.5 percent of the gross proceeds of the underwriting. Each cost item varies for different offerings, depending on the amount involved and the particular problems that arise. Here is a general explanation of how the cost of each item is determined:

1. The SEC registration fee is 1/100th of one percent of the total offering; the minimum fee is $25.00.

2. Registrar and transfer agent's fees are based on a fixed fee for each certificate registered and transferred. The securities law generally requires that a company appoint an independent transfer agent and registrar before it offers stock to the public. The minimum charge for this is usually around $1,000.00.

3. Blue-sky filing fees and expenses largely depend on the number of states in which the underwriter qualifies the issue. ("Blue-sky laws" is a name given to state securities laws. Stock offerings must be registered in all states in which the securities will be sold.)

4. Cost of printing registration statement and prospectus normally runs from $5,000 to $11,000. The prospectus may be mimeographed at a cheaper rate, but underwriters invariably insist it be printed for greater sales appeal. The urgency to get the prospectus to the public as soon as the offering becomes effective puts printers under burdensome time schedules, raising the costs of financial printing.

5. Cost of printing stock certificates depends largely on the elegance of the certificate. Simple lithographed certificates will do, but management usually selects a more impressive certificate. An initial underwriting generally requires at least 4,000 certificates.

6. Attorneys' fees and expenses for offerings above $1,500,000 range from $13,000 to $29,000. Most of the fees go to the counsel responsible for the registration statement. This is usually the counsel for the underwriter, but the company's own attorney may do the work. The contract with the underwriter usually limits how much of the underwriter's legal costs the company will absorb.

7. Accountant's fees and expenses vary according to the size and complexity of the company and whether a new audit is necessary. A company can save the expense of an extra audit by preparing the registration statement at the time of its annual audit. Of course, this is not always possible.

8. Miscellaneous expenses include telephone, telegraph and various other expenses.

WRITING THE REGISTRATION STATEMENT AND PROSPECTUS

After selecting the underwriter who agrees to market your offering, the financial manager will supply him with additional information for his examination. This will include audited financial reports for the current year and the three preceding years.

It's a good idea to have these prepared by an accountant who knows the requirements of underwriters and the SEC. The underwriter will also need a history of the business, its products, volume, profits, research developments, and so on. If the underwriter's investigation of the company's management and operations turns up nothing unfavorable, he will go ahead with the preparation of a registration statement for the SEC.

Facts That Go into a Registration Statement

The registration statement must give "full and fair disclosure" of the securities being offered for sale. In addition to the information mentioned, it should contain the names and addresses of directors, officers, experts who helped prepare the statement, and numerous exhibits, including copies of resolutions, bylaws, charters, and all research contracts and purchase and sale contracts accounting for more than 15 percent of the business. It also contains—

1. A full description of corporate properties (plant and equipment).
2. An explanation of the capital structure and intended uses of the proceeds of the offering.
3. A list of patents and copyrights and dates they expire.
4. A description of raw material sources, principal markets, customers, competitors, pending legal proceedings, and proposed mergers or acquisitions.
5. An analysis of available labor, showing present employees and describing salient features of union contracts.
6. A description of all financial transactions between the directors, the officers, and those stockholders who own 10 percent or more of the stock.
7. A description of the financial arrangements between the company and the underwriter.

The Prospectus

The prospectus is a condensed registration statement. It contains basically the same information but is not quite so detailed. For example, it contains no exhibits. A copy of the prospectus goes to all prospective stock buyers; they ordinarily do not get a copy of the registration statement.

General Tone of the Registration Statement and Prospectus

These two documents present the company to the investor. The general tone of the registration statement and prospectus is almost negative. If a company is unseasoned, the prospectus clearly labels the offering a "speculation." The "competition" section describes major competitors. It must make clear—if such is the case—that some competitors enjoy a stronger market position and a greater financial strength. Comparative facts and figures must clearly support any assertion that the company is a "leader" in this field.

Certifying the Registration Statement

As we have noted, the financial statements must conform with SEC regulations governing content and format. They must also be certified by a CPA who is completely independent of the company, and who meets specific qualifications. The SEC's ruling on this point states:

> "The Commission will not recognize any person as a certified public accountant who is not duly registered and in good standing as such under the laws of the place of his residence or principal office."

To enforce this rule the SEC keeps a current file of accountants authorized to practice in each state. State societies of CPA's cooperate by furnishing copies of directories as they are published. When the SEC cannot identify the certifying accountant in this way, it asks for evidence of his qualifications. If not satisfied of his authority to certify, the SEC requires the registrant to submit a financial statement certified by some other accountant whom it can recognize as qualified.

In addition to the accountant's certification, the registration statement requires the signatures of the underwriters, the president, the principal finance officer, a majority of the directors, and any other experts whose testimony appears in the statement.

When all documents are in order, the issue can be filed with the SEC. First, however, the company and the underwriter must determine the number and price of the shares. Though price information is a basic part of the registration statement, the underwriter may wait almost until the final day before making the tentative per-share price a final one.

PRICING THE STOCK

Stocks of closely held companies are often priced too high for sale to the public; most investors prefer medium- to low-priced stocks, particularly for new issues. To give the underwriter a salable commodity, the financial manager may find it necessary to rearrange the company's capital structure.

Recapitalizing for More Shares and Lower Price

A recapitalization frequently precedes a public offering. When applied to common stocks, this procedure results either in a decrease or increase in the number of shares. A simple stock split combined with an increase in authorized capital stock serves two purposes: (1) it brings the price of the stock down to an attractive level, and (2) it provides the required number of additional shares for public distribution. The following example shows how it works—A closely-held company (Company A) has decided to go public. Company A and the underwriters place a valuation on the proposed offering of $6,000,000. If present stockholders own 3,000 shares, each of these shares takes on a value of $2,000 based on the agreed valuation of $6,000,000. Company A and the underwriter face a problem because it is impossible to sell the issue at $2,000 a share (except perhaps by placing it privately with an institutional investor, such as an insurance company).

The underwriter proposes to split the 3,000 shares 50 for 1, changing the total stock outstanding to 150,000 shares. Company A then increases the authorized capital stock (with the consent of the stockholders) to 200,000 shares. This procedure provides 50,000 shares to sell the public at $30 a share (6,000,000 divided by 200,000 shares). The additional shares leave the current stockholders with less than complete ownership, but they will maintain their controlling interest in a company whose net worth is fattened by $1,500,000 (50,000 times $30).

Determining Suitable Price-Earnings Ratio

Investors will use this ratio to compare the investment merits of a new issue with those already on the market. If the average price-earnings ratio is 17 to 1 for stock in a company's industry (i.e., market price per share is 17 times greater than earnings per share), the new offering must compare favorably against this yardstick. The underwriter will probably suggest a lower price-earnings ratio than the industry average if a company is a relatively small one whose products are not as well known as those of its competitors.

If a somewhat modest offering price is put on the stock, news of its value is likely to radiate among other brokerage firms and investors. A fast-moving stock naturally gets much more attention than one that is sluggish. This does not mean selling the stock at bargain-basement prices. The issuing company has an obligation to get the best price possible that does not impair market performance.

Allowing for Market Conditions

Stock market behavior is also important in setting the price. An underwriter will study market conditions and the general reaction of investors to new securities. He may make a last minute canvass to assess trends. What he learns will influence the final price he recommends for the issue.

FILING AN ISSUE WITH THE SEC

After the registration statement and prospectus are written and certified and a price has been determined for the stock, the next step is to file with the SEC. We should mention here that the SEC never approves or disapproves the investment merits of new offerings, nor does it attest the accuracy and completeness of information in the registration statement and prospectus. The Commission merely signifies that the information it requires has been submitted in the proper form and *appears* correct and complete on its face.

The Securities Act of 1933 requires a 20 day waiting period between the time of filing a statement with the Commission and the time it becomes effective. This gives the Commission time to examine the statement. If it appears that a statement contains a falsehood or omits a material fact, the Commission requires correction through a device called a *deficiency letter*, or *letter of comments*. If the issuing company and the underwriter differ with the SEC concerning the alleged deficiencies, the next step is to arrange a conference to resolve these differences.

The rush of statements flooding the SEC often makes the time lag between registration and clearance run much longer than 20 days. To speed the processing of proposed stock offerings, the Commission sometimes gives summary treatment to registrations of companies with histories of reliable performance in registering shares, and limits detailed reviews to those statements that arouse suspicion and to companies that have never before registered securities. Though proposed securities cannot be marketed until the registration statement becomes effective, a company can make *offers* to sell through a preliminary prospectus, or "red herring," prior to Commission release of the statement. Any corrections the SEC requires before releasing the final prospectus must be furnished to all those who received the preliminary prospectus.

Requirements of the 1964 Securities Law

If a company has total assets of more than $1,000,000 and if any class of its equity securities is held by more than 500 persons, it comes under the jurisdiction of the Securities Acts Amendments of 1964. One of the purposes of this law is to broaden the coverage of companies whose securities are not traded on one of the registered stock exchanges.

Along with filing their registration statements with the Securities and Exchange Commission, companies covered by this law must:

1. Keep their registration statements up-to-date by filing periodic reports with the SEC.
2. Comply with SEC's proxy regulations which prescribe the form and content of the proxy statement, the form of the proxy, and the manner of solicitation.
3. Comply with provisions imposing duties and liabilities on corporate insiders—directors and officers of the corporation and any person who owns more than 10 percent of any class of its equity securities.

An "equity security" not only means stock, but also includes such securities as (1) bonds convertible into stock, (2) bonds carrying warrants or rights to subscribe to or purchase stock, (3) any warrant or right to subscribe to stock. The SEC controls the activities of insiders by having them file periodic statements with the Commission showing the amounts of securities owned and any changes of ownership. The law prohibits insiders from selling their company's stock "short." If insiders buy and sell stock within six months, the company can sue for any profits realized on the sale.

Exceptions

Even though an unlisted company meets the assets and stockholder tests, it will not have to comply with the additional provisions of the law if it is—

1. An investment company registered with the SEC under the Investment Company Act. (Such a company is already subject to similar registration and disclosure requirements.)
2. A saving and loan association, cooperative bank, or similar institution having share accounts. (But such a company is not exempt if it has outstanding any permanent stock, guarantee stock, or similar certificate evidencing nonwithdrawal capital.)
3. A non-profit organization operated exclusively for benevolent, charitable, fraternal or like purpose.
4. A cooperative association as defined in the Agricultural Marketing Act.
5. A mutual or cooperative organization that supplies a commodity or service primarily for the benefit of its members and is not operated for profit.

Liabilities for False Information

Civil and criminal liabilities for willful violations effectively enforce Federal securities regulations. The Commission has the authority to investigate suspected violations, to institute court action to enjoin further violations, and to secure court orders compelling compliance with Federal regulations. The law gives securities buyers the right to bring legal action against the issuing company, the underwriter, and all others responsible for the offering if there is reasonable evidence that the registration statement or prospectus contains an untrue statement or omits a material fact. Conviction for a willful violation of Federal securities regulations carries a maximum penalty of five years imprisonment and a fine of $5,000.

CHECKLIST FOR A FIRST PUBLIC STOCK OFFERING

If a company decides to offer ownership to the public, it will take a step that will completely alter its character and direction. And the change is irrevocable; going public is not an action subject to recall. But, if properly planned and executed, the first public offering can be the gateway to continuing growth. For a successful underwriting your company must take such steps as these:

1. Appoint a committee to outline details of the issue.
2. Select an attorney experienced in SEC registrations to advise the company and to work with the underwriter.
3. Make arrangements with an accounting firm to conduct an audit and to certify financial statements.
4. Enlist the services of a reputable underwriter.
5. Furnish company counsel the following:
   Charter and amendments (or partnership agreement, if unincorporated).
   Bylaws and amendments.
   All research contracts and purchases and sales contracts accounting for more than 15 percent of the business.

Union contracts.

Details of previous stock issuances.

Description of stock option plans for officers and employees.

Salaries of officers and directors.

Five-year business history of executive officers.

6. Furnish public accountants all accounting records and financial statements for the past three years.

7. Amend the corporate charter, if necessary.

8. Hold a meeting of the company counsel, the underwriter, and public accountants to discuss the effects of each and to establish a time schedule for completion of assignments.

9. Get an estimate of the underwriter's discount and other expenses.

10. Write registration statement and prospectus with company counsel, underwriter, and accountants; decide whether recapitalization is necessary and determine the price of the new issue.

11. Try to get a "gentlemen's agreement" from the underwriter to purchase the issue outright when the registration statement becomes effective (rarely does an underwriter sign the actual underwriting contract with the issuing company until after the SEC approves the registration statement).

12. Make preparations to meet "blue-sky" law requirements in those states in which the stock will be offered.

13. Sign and file the registration statement and prospectus with the SEC.

14. Prevent publicity and news "leaks" during the waiting period. SEC may delay the effective date if it thinks the company is promoting its stock.

15. File amendments to make the registration statement conform to comments in any "deficiency letter" received.

16. Concurrent with filing amendments, submit a "request for acceleration" to avoid statutory 20-day waiting period following the filing of an amendment.

17. Sign contract with underwriter when SEC lets registration statement become effective, and collect company proceeds of public offering from underwriter (in other than "best efforts" agreements).

FINANCING WITH BONDS

Along with the sale of stock to the public, another principal method of financing corporate growth is through the sale of bonds. To issue bonds safely and successfully, a company should have a steady record of earnings and its profit margin should be at least double the fixed charges of the contemplated issue.

Though both bonds and stocks raise large sums for a corporation, these two financial instruments are quite different in character:

1. Whereas stock represents equity interest or ownership in a business, a bond is a formal debt obligation.

2. Because of their status as creditors, bondholders have no voting power and no voice in corporate management, as stockholders do.

3. Unlike stocks, bonds have a maturity date on which the principal comes due. By a specified date, the corporation must return the principal lent to it by the bondholder.

4. Interest on bonds is a fixed charge. This debt must be paid regularly. Dividends on stock are not a fixed charge; moreover, they are paid only when earnings permit, at the discretion of board of directors.

TYPES OF BONDS

The bonds most commonly used are mortgage bonds, debenture bonds, and collateral trust bonds. The mortgage bond is backed up by a specific pledge of assets, while debentures are unsecured in the sense that there is no specific pledge of property.

The mortgage bond requires three documents: the indenture, the bond itself, and a mortgage covering the pledged property. Since the debenture is unsecured, it requires only two documents: the bond and the indenture. Collateral trust bonds involve the pledge of securities; they are characterized by an actual transfer of pledged property to a trustee. Here are further details on three types of bonds.

Mortgage Bonds

In the mortgage that is included with these bonds, the corporation pledges specific assets or offers a general lien on all corporate assets. The bond is the actual promise to repay; the mortgage is security for the promise.

The pledge of specific property creates a lien against that property in favor of bondholders. In the case of a first mortgage, bondholders have first claim on the property designated by the mortgage in case of default by the issuing corporation, and proceeds from the sale of the property go to repay the company's indebtedness to bondholders. Most large bond issues are issued under general or blanket mortgages covering all corporate assets. A blanket mortgage may give bondholders more protection than a specific mortgage since it provides a claim against all real property owned by the corporation.

Even greater protection is afforded bondholders by including an after-acquired-property clause in the blanket mortgage. This clause gives a lien not only against all real property currently owned by the corporation, but also against all property subsequently acquired.

If a company attempts to sell a second issue of bonds, an after-acquired clause may hinder its efforts. Existing bonds will already have a first lien on all property owned or to be acquired by the company. This situation will tend to reduce the attractiveness of the later issue because its purchasers must content themselves with a second lien as security. One solution is to issue open-end mortgage bonds. Under open-end mortgages, a company may later issue additional bonds under the same indenture and as part of the same issue. If the original bonds give a first mortgage, all subsequent bonds of the same issue will offer the same security. The situation is quite different in a closed mortgage. Under this arrangement, additional debt financing can generally provide only a junior lien. Perhaps the most typical bonds are those secured by limited open-end mortgages. This arrangement enables the corporation to issue only a part of the total allowed under the indenture. The company can later issue the remaining bonds under the same indenture.

Debenture Bonds

A debenture is any bond not secured by a specific lien. It is issued only against the general credit of the borrowing corporation. Though debentures are unsecured in the sense that there is no specific pledge of property, they are secured by any property not otherwise pledged. This means that if the debentures are the insurer's only outstanding debt obligations, their holders will have first claim to earnings and assets in event of bankruptcy or reorganization. An indenture may specify, however, that the debentures be subordinated to other debt, such as a bank loan. In the event of liquidation or reorganization, subordinated debentures cannot be paid until the senior debt designated in the indenture is paid.

The quality of a bond depends more on the issuing concern's earnings record than on the security pledged to protect the bond. As long as a company continues to earn steadily, holders of its debentures are in as good a position as holders of any mortgage bonds the firm may have outstanding. And if debentures are the only debt, they are "secured" by all the corporation's assets. Holders of mortgage bonds are in a stronger position than holders of debentures only in event of the issuing concern's failure.

Debentures, then, are simply promises to pay lenders a certain sum at a specified date, with interest at a fixed rate. They are very much like notes, with the exception that they are issued under an indenture or deed of trust. Companies with a great deal of debt already secured by mortgage often issue debentures because they have no additional property to pledge as security. This is often the case when a company has bonds outstanding under a blanket mortgage containing an after-acquired-property clause. Many established companies in basic or essential industries can sell debentures simply because they are regarded so highly that investors require no pledge of specific assets to protect their investments. In fact, debentures in such companies as these are frequently rated equal or superior to the mortgage bonds of other firms.

Collateral Trust Bonds

To issue these bonds, a company must have securities to pledge as collateral. The securities may be bonds or stocks of other companies the firm owns, the securities of firm's subsidiaries, or a combination of the two. The firm must transfer title of the pledged securities to the trustee under the collateral trust indenture, and actually deliver the stocks of bonds to the trustee. The firm does, however, retain all rights in the securities, and it receives all interest and dividends paid while the securities are in trust.

By pledging securities, a firm provides investors with tangible collateral; bondholders acquire specific assets in event of default. At the same time, it runs no risk of losing any fixed assets in case of a breach of the indenture.

SPECIAL FEATURES OF BONDS

All of these bonds we have been describing—mortgage bonds, debentures, and collateral trust bonds—may be designed to fit the needs of the issuing company and the bondholders by including special features in the indenture. Modern indentures frequently contain redemption, conversion, and sinking fund provisions.

Redemption

Most indentures give the issuing firm the right to redeem or "call" bonds before maturity. The redemption feature enables the corporation to pay off bonds before maturity (saving interest charges), or to refund the bonds by issuing less costly securities in their place.

A bond issued at 100 would typically have a redemption price stipulated in the trust agreement of 106. If such a bond had a coupon rate of 5% (which was the prevailing rate at the time of issue), it is possible to compute what the price would be if prevailing interest rates went to 4%. The formula is shown in Figure 13-1 and shows a price of 125. At such prices, the issuing company would want to redeem the bonds at 106 and get rid of the 5% interest rate. It would at the same time offer a new issue of bonds at a price of 100 and a 4% coupon. As the bond started to rise in price towards 125, knowledgeable bond buyers would realize the danger of redemption at 106 and would refuse to pay a price too far above 106. Thus the bond's price would never get to 125. Thus the redemption feature is very favorable to the issuer and unfavorable to the investor. An issue with a straight redemption clause would, therefore, be unpopular with the investors and if one were issued the investors would expect some other compensation for accepting the redemption clause such as higher interest rate, shorter maturity, warrant for stock, etc.

Since the issuing company wants some control over redemption, the typical redemption clause is a compromise. A common stipulation is that redemption can not take place for at least five years. A more involved one would specify a redemption price of 110 after five years and 106 after ten years. These redemption clauses offer the bond buyer protection against redemption and make the new bond more salable. Such bonds are referred to as "Non-callable for 5 Years."

Conversion

Convertible bonds give their holders the right to exchange the bonds for the preferred or common stock of the issuing corporation. Conversion is at a fixed basis as described in the indenture. The conversion provision adds a speculative interest to bonds. Bondholders have the preferred position of creditors, plus the opportunity to share in profits by exchanging their bonds for stock. This makes the bonds more attractive to potential investors, and therefore more salable. The convertibility feature is found more often in debentures than in mortgage bonds and other secured issues.

The mechanics of convertibles are best explained by the following example. Company A has a common stock which has risen in price for each of the past 5 years and is currently priced at $18 per share. Company A issues a 5% convertible debenture which is callable at any time. The nominal unit of sale of bonds is $1,000. The conversion rate is stated as $25. This means that a bondholder may present his bonds (having a par value of $1,000 per bond) to Company A and receive one share of common stock for

Formulas and Definitions in Bonds

Par — The nominal number 100. All bond prices are measured relative to this number.

Par Value — The standard par value in dollars is $1,000 which is the same as a par of 100.

Yield — The true total return per yield from owning a security.

YIELD FORMULA

M.P. = Price at Maturity
T   = Years to Maturity
C.P.   = Current Price
I   = Coupon Interest per year in dollars

$$\text{Yield} = \frac{I}{CP} + \frac{(MP - CP)}{T X\ CP}$$

NEW PRICE GIVEN CHARGED MARKET YIELDS
(assuming bonds with no retirement date)

CY = Coupon Yield (% return at par)
P = Price (The indicated market price)
MY = Market Yields (prevailing interest rates for securities same grade)

$$P = 100 \times \frac{CY}{MY}$$

applied to example in text: $P = 100 \times \frac{5}{4} = 125$

Figure 13-1

every $25 of par value of bonds. This means one $1,000 bond would be convertible into 40 shares of common stock. With the stock at $18, no investor would be interested in converting a $1,000 bond into (40 times $18) or $720 worth of stock. Thus the investor would initially pay $1,000 for the bond to get the 5% interest rates. If six months after issuance the stock was at $16 and interest rates were down to 4%, the bond price would rise towards 125 (or $1,250 per bond). If after another six months interest rates went to 5½ % and the stock price was still $16, the bond price would fall to the point where its yield was 5¼ % (a price of 91). If after another year the stock price went to $30, the bond price would at last, start to follow the stock price. The bond would sell at (40 times $30) or $1,200 per bond which is called 120. At this point, Company A would call the bond according to the redemption clause. The bondholder then has two choices and he can present the bond for redemption and receive the redemption price of $1,000 per bond or he can present the bond for conversion and receive about $1,200 worth of common stock. Naturally, most investors take the new common stock which the company issues since it is worth more. The net result after two years is that Company

A had the use of the funds for two years at the relatively low cost of interest and then turned bondholders into stockholders and kept the cash.

Sinking Fund

A sinking fund provision in the indenture imposes on a corporation the obligation to set aside a certain sum from earnings periodically for the purpose of reducing the bonded indebtedness. Trustees frequently use these funds to retire a portion of the outstanding bonds if they are callable. Otherwise, the funds may be invested in other securities, or in the bond issue itself, until needed for the eventual payment of the bonds at maturity.

Under modern indentures, sinking fund payments are fixed in a variety of ways: (1) a fixed annual amount, sometimes not beginning until a certain number of years from the date of the indenture, (2) a fixed percentage of the bonds outstanding, (3) an amount that varies with earnings but with a fixed minimum, (4) an amount that varies entirely with profits, (5) gradually increasing amounts, (6) an amount contingent on payments of dividends of the common stock.

A sinking fund provision in the indenture gives bondholders added assurance that the issuing corporation will meet its obligation to them. But if a company's earnings record is good and the prospect for future earnings relatively certain, and if the total bonded indebtedness is a normal part of the capital structure, a financial manager ordinarily need not include a sinking fund provision to be assured of a market.

MECHANICS OF ISSUING BONDS

The issuing company can go from brokerage house to brokerage house in search of the best deal. This arrangement is called direct negotiation, and differs from an alternate arrangement, called competitive bidding.

Direct Negotiation

If the investment banker's preliminary and detailed investigation looks promising and his proposals are satisfactory, a preliminary underwriting commitment can be drawn up. The underwriter and the financial officers prepare the registration statement and prospectus for the SEC, as well as in qualifying the bonds for sale in the various states according to blue-sky laws. The bond indenture, or sales contract, makes this preparatory work even more complex than for a stock issue.

The company and the underwriter must agree on all provisions of the bond issue—maturity, type, price, interest, and so on. It is quite unlikely that, in the initial discussions, both parties will agree on terms. Since the underwriter's and issuer's objectives are the same—to offer a salable issue in line with going market conditions—these negotiations of differences usually don't pose serious problems.

Sometimes an investment banker refuses to underwrite an issue but agrees to handle it on a "best efforts" basis. This arrangement is even more unsatisfactory than with stock. Stocks are by their nature speculative, and therefore attract speculative buyers. Bonds, on the other hand, represent a conservative investment and attract buyers chiefly interested in protecting their principal. Bonds distributed under a best-efforts arrangement, therefore, appeal to neither buyer. Without a firm commitment from the underwriter to buy your issue outright, it is advisable to withdraw the offering.

Competitive Bidding

In selling bonds under a competitive bidding arrangement, a corporation invites bids from all investment bankers interested in underwriting its issue. The corporation specifies the amount of the issue and the maturity, but usually lets the bidders name both price and interest rate. The bidder offering the most attractive interest rate gets the bid.

The development of competitive bidding has been largely the result of government regulations intended to safeguard the general welfare in the public utility field. Nearly 90 percent of utility issues and rail issues are sold through sealed bidding, or competitively. The merits of selling bonds by competitive bidding versus direct negotiation has long been a subject of lively debate.

The government argues that competitive bidding increases competition among investment banking houses and thereby enables a company to get long-term funds cheaper than through direct negotiation. Companies that are subject to these rules seem reasonably satisfied, but few industrial companies use this procedure, though they are free to do so.

A disadvantage in competitive bidding is that the company must largely go it alone in preparing its issue for the market. The investment banker has no incentive for going to the expense and trouble of helping when he has no assurance he will be underwriting the issue. He might be willing to help for a fee, but the acceptance of a fee precludes submitting a bid, under the rules of the regulatory commissions. This means that only those houses having no interest in submitting a bid would be willing to offer their services.

The Role of the Trustee

If you are selling your bond issue to the general public, instead of placing it directly with one or a few large buyers in an arrangement called a private placement, your corporation must appoint a trustee to represent the bondholders. The trustee holds the copy of the indenture and sees that the rights and interests of the bondholders are enforced, as provided in the indenture. Prior to 1939, trustees were often merely agents of the issuing corporation; they frequently put investors' interests last, so that investors were not always assured of full protection. To correct this situation, Congress passed the Trust Indenture Act of 1939. This Act requires that a trustee be a corporation with capital and surplus of at least $150,000. Banks often serve as trustees.

A trustee may not own more than 5 percent, nor control more than 25 percent, of your corporation's securities. He must make periodic reports to bondholders on the company's condition. He is expected to take all necessary precautions to protect investors. In event of default, the trustee must notify bondholders and take appropriate steps to protect their interests.

The Indenture

We mentioned that the indenture is a contract of sale. It sets forth the rights of bondholders and the powers and duties of the trustee as their representative. The indenture's provisions apply to all bonds in the issue and serve as a three-way contract between the corporation, the trustee, and the individual bondholders. The bondholders automatically become parties to the agreement on buying the bonds.

The Trust Indenture Act of 1939 requires full and fair disclosure of all relevant facts to prospective buyers in a public sale; it prohibits misleading or deceptive provisions. The Act also provides that all indentures be approved by the SEC. To be acceptable to the SEC, an indenture must confer on trustees the rights and powers to fully protect investors.

Points the Indenture Covers

Since the indenture generally remains in force over a period of many years, it must provide for all foreseeable contingencies and carefully outline the duties and responsibilities of all parties. Most indentures run several hundred pages, the size of a hefty book. The contents of indentures naturally vary with the type of bond being issued, but indentures always—

1. Set forth particular covenants of the borrowing corporation, such as agreements to preserve the corporate existence and properties, to pay taxes and other assessments, to keep the property insured, and comply with state laws.
2. Describe the property pledged as security for the bonds, if the bonds are mortgage bonds.
3. Describe redemption rights, procedures for redeeming bonds, and the operations of the sinking fund, if one is required.
4. Describe the conversion privilege and procedure.
5. Explain the remedies of the trustee and of bondholders in event of default by the corporation in meeting interest or principal payments of sinking installments, and for the breach of any covenant.
6. Describe what takes place in event of bankruptcy, assignment for the benefit of creditors, receivership, reorganization, or dissolution of the corporation.

Special Provisions for Debentures

Indentures covering issues of debenture bonds are very much like those under which mortgage bonds are issued, although there are some major differences. Every trust indenture under which debenture bonds are issued contains some provisions or restrictions designed to protect the bondholders' investments without jeopardizing the corporation's freedom to expand and manage its affairs for the benefit of its stockholders. Some of the most common of these protective provisions are:

* The holders of debentures shall receive the same privileges, guaranties, and security given the holders of any secured bonds issued subsequent to the debentures.
* The indenture may prohibit the company from further borrowing until earnings bear a certain relationship to the amount of interest payable annually for all outstanding debt. There is sometimes a provision that net tangible assets must be a certain number of times more than funded debt before the company can assume additional debt obligations. The indenture may also prohibit the company from paying cash dividends of common stock unless (1) earned surplus or net current assets surpass a certain minimum figure, (2) current assets are a certain number of times the current liabilities.

PROS AND CONS OF SELLING BONDS

Selling bonds is only one of several methods a company can select to obtain long-term capital. Each method has its merits and faults. Some of the pros and cons of a public bond sale are listed below.

Advantages of a Bond Sale

1. Provides the use of large sums of capital for many years.
2. Distribution costs are generally much lower than for sale of stock.
3. Stockholders' equity remains undiluted.
4. A redemption feature permits the repurchase of bonds at attractive prices.
5. Interest charges are tax deductible.

Disadvantages of a Bond Sale

1. Principal and interest must be paid regardless of business conditions.
2. Company management is placed under restrictive agreements.
3. The debt/equity ratio and the company's financial rating may be weakened.
4. The company's stock may be affected adversely.
5. Complete financial information must be made public.

14

Managing Dividends and Surplus

‖‖‖

14

Managing Dividends and Surplus

WHAT DIVIDEND POLICY SHALL YOU ADOPT?

Power to declare a dividend rests solely with the board of directors, but almost in-variably the board acts on the recommendation of the finance officer. In most companies, only the controller or treasurer is able to examine the many complex factors that affect dividend payments and come up with sound recommendations. These recommendations present facts and figures on net income, financial requirements, the amount and type of dividend payment, and other information the board must weigh in declaring dividends.

Most companies pay quarterly dividends; a few pay dividends monthly, semi-annually, or annually. Stockholders seem to prefer spreading dividend income by receiving quarterly payments rather than semi-annual or annual dividend checks. But dividend policies involve more than scheduling dividend payments, in fact, some corporations pay no dividends at all. Generally speaking, a firm may adopt any of the following dividend policies:

No Dividends

The financial manager may recommend that the company declare a policy of paying no dividends, even though earnings are sufficient to give stockholders a return. Such a recommendation can be justified under these conditions.

1. The company is young and growing, or it is well-established but trying to branch into new fields or acquire subsidiaries.
2. The company has consumed its line of credit, or it prefers not to pay high interest rates on borrowed capital, so it plows earnings back into the business.

255

3. Stockholders are content to leave their investment in the firm to realize capital gains.

A "no-dividend" policy may be good for a time, but after a period of paying no dividends, a firm may have to declare some type of dividend—if only a stock dividend—to maintain the price of its securities.

If earnings are good and continue to mount, a firm has no choice but to declare a dividend eventually. The tax laws provide penalties against corporations that accumulate surplus beyond reasonable needs. Stockholders can sue to compel directors to pay dividends if directors are acting unreasonably in not paying dividends.

Regular Dividends

Many corporations pay regular quarterly, semi-annual, or annual dividends. Businesses following such a policy are typically those in industries that enjoy stable earnings. American Telephone and Telegraph was once known as "The $9 Company" because of its consistent $9 dividend, which it paid even during the depression years. The dividend amount remained unchanged until the firm split its stock. A company with highly variable earnings would obviously be hard-pressed to maintain steady dividend payments.

If a company establishes a policy of regular dividends, the dividend payments must be conservative so that the firm can maintain the payments even if business falters. The dividend amount, however, must also be adequate. Companies paying regular, but low, dividends often pay extra dividends from time to time. This policy enables them to maintain their policy of regular dividends while permitting their stockholders to share in higher earnings.

Companies that pay regular dividends put forth such arguments as these to support their policy:

1. A record of regular dividend payments is a favorable influence on prospective investors.
2. Knowing how much the company will pay out in dividends facilitates long range planning.
3. Regular dividends tend to raise gradually the market price of the firm's securities.
4. Regular dividends enhance the firm's credit standing.
5. Regular dividend payments increase stockholder confidence in the firm and in its management. Stockholders usually prefer some dividend—even if comparatively small—to no dividend at all.
6. Small but regular dividends result in lower tax payments for stockholders than occasional large dividends.

Studies show that overall corporate profits fluctuate far more than overall dividend payments, indicating that most corporations pay dividends consistently regardless of earnings. Corporations following regular dividend policies make concerted efforts to maintain the same dividend until it becomes clear that there will be no recovery in earnings. And only after sustained increases in earnings do these firms increase the size of dividend payments. Most concerns with a policy of paying regular dividends experience relatively little decline in stock prices, even when market activity fluctuates markedly.

Irregular Dividends

Not all companies can afford a regular dividend policy. Many new and growing companies, as well as firms with highly unstable earnings, fall into this category. Such concerns often pay dividends, but management makes no definite commitment to investors. The firm that follows a policy of irregular dividends typically needs capital to finance expansion and growth; it may need capital as a reserve against future periods of lower earnings. If it has ample funds after providing for growth, the firm pays a dividend; otherwise, it does not pay a dividend.

FACTORS EFFECTING DIVIDEND POLICIES

Profits, expansion plans, state laws, stockholders' preferences—these are but a few of the factors affecting dividend payment policies.

Importance of a Firm's Profit Level

Since dividends depend ultimately on profits and since a firm must generally expand to remain competitive, the finance officer must accurately determine earnings and know the amount of funds his company needs to finance expansion. He must also know what the firm's financial position will be at various points along the route to its objectives. If a company is financially weak and has a maturing debt that it cannot refinance, it obviously must conserve all available cash to meet the payment. And a concern with handsome earnings but with an expansion opportunity that it can finance only through retained earnings should certainly pay lower dividends, or curtail its dividend payments entirely, to finance the expansion project.

This means that when making dividend payment recommendations to top management, the financial manager must give weight to these factors:

1. The company's current working capital and cash position.
2. The current level of earnings and the profit margin.
3. Total outstanding debt obligations.
4. The firm's expansion rate and its plans and prospects for the future.
5. Earnings stability.
6. Access to debt capital.

State Rules

Dividends sometimes depend on state laws governing dividend payments. The various states have many conflicting laws on the subject. Here are a few rules that generally apply to dividend payments:

1. A company may pay dividends only from retained earnings. Paying them out of capital surplus merely distributes the investment in the company rather than its earnings.
2. If a company lacks sufficient current earnings to pay dividends, it may use past accumulated earnings in its retained earnings account. Unless a corporation has a long record of serious financial difficulties, it generally has ample funds in retained earnings to pay dividends—even if current earnings are off.
3. A company may not pay dividends while insolvent (as long as its liabilities exceed its assets).

Potential Increases in Stock Values

In setting dividend policy, the finance officer takes potential increases in stock values into consideration. For example, if it appears that retained earnings will increase earning power, resulting in more long-range benefit to stockholders through higher stock prices than paying high dividends now, the finance officer may recommend that the firm retain a greater proportion of earnings, keeping its dividend payments relatively low.

Tax Position of Stockholders of Closely-Held Corporation

The tax position of a corporation's stockholders may have a great influence on dividend policy. A closely-held corporation whose owners are in high income-tax brackets may pay relatively low dividends to protect its owners from high tax liabilities. The owners of such companies usually want to take capital gains rather than receive dividend payments subject to higher tax rates.

Ratios

Certain ratios can help determine an appropriate dividend policy. The payout ratio is probably the most important, but ratios of net worth to total debt, and fixed assets to net worth, are two other ratios that also affect dividend payout.

Payout Ratio

For purposes of financial analysis, most companies express the amount of dividend payments by means of a "payout ratio," which is actually a percentage and not a ratio. To obtain the payout ratio, divide dividends paid per share by earnings per share for the year in question, and express the result as a percentage. The payout ratio for preceding dividend periods is important in arriving at an appropriate dividend for the current period.

It is advisable to evaluate a company's dividend payments by comparing its payout ratio with those of other firms in the same industry. The percentage of profits paid as cash dividends amounts to about 65 percent for manufacturing corporations, 75 percent for electric power companies, and 85 percent for railroads.

Ratio of Net Worth to Total Debt

This ratio reveals the extent to which a firm is financed by creditors as opposed to stockholders. The ratio of net worth to total debt expresses the number of dollars of stockholder investment supporting each dollar of debt capital, indicating the degree to which the company is financed by equity capital and by debt capital. Ratios vary from company to company and industry to industry, but financial analysts generally believe that the owners should have at least a 50 percent equity in their business; that is, one stockholder dollar for every creditor dollar. If business dips, a company having less than half equity in its assets may not be able to meet regular fixed charges. This ratio tends to vary directly with risk. A company with a volatile earnings record would contain a higher proportion of equity.

Ratio of Fixed Assets to Net Worth

This ratio shows the degree to which a firm's equity investment finances the cost of its fixed assets. The ratio operates on the theory that the equity investment should provide at least the fixed assets necessary to carry on the business and should contribute something to current assets as well. If the ratio is higher than 100 percent (more than one fixed asset dollar to one net worth dollar) the equity investment does not fully cover the cost of fixed assets, and dividends may have to be curtailed or eliminated until conditions improve.

MEDIUMS IN WHICH DIVIDENDS ARE PAYABLE

The finance officer recommends to the board of directors not only the amount and frequency of the dividend payment, but also whether it should take the form of cash, stock, property, scrip, or bonds.

Cash Dividend

Cash dividends are first in popularity in terms of the frequency of their use and the satisfaction they give the stockholders. Though cash dividends are paid from retained earnings, a corporation needs more than an adequate retained earnings account to pay the dividend—it needs cash in the bank. Retained earnings results from profits, but these profits may be tied up in receivables, new inventory, fixed assets, or the like. Consequently, before choosing the type of dividend, the treasurer must examine the cash and working capital position as well as the retained earnings account.

He must also consider the need to meet other obligations over the longer term. As mentioned earlier, earnings retention must receive priority attention if the firm is expanding so rapidly that it must continually plow back sizable funds in additional current and fixed assets, if it must maintain an aggressive program of debt reduction, or if it is subject to marked variations in earnings. In any one of these cases, he may find it necessary to postpone or limit cash dividends, or he may elect to pay a stock dividend.

Stock Dividend

In paying a stock dividend, the corporation distributes additional shares of stock to existing stockholders on a pro rata basis; that is, so many shares of new stock for each share of stock held. The accountant must also "capitalize" an equal amount of earnings. He does this by transferring the amount of the stock dividend from the corporation's retained earnings account to its capital stock account.

> *An example is:* a corporation has $1 million in capital stock and an earned surplus account of $150,000. It pays a dividend of $50,000 in stock. It then has $1,050,000 in capital stock and $100,000 in retained earnings. The effect of this entry is to reduce by $50,000 the amount available for similar stock issuances or cash distributions.
>
> A corporation must have enough unissued stock to cover the stock dividend. If there is not enough stock, it is necessary to amend the certificate of incorporation to increase the amount of authorized capital stock. This involves going to the stockholders to get their approval.

A stock dividend leaves the stockholder's position essentially unchanged. It takes nothing from the corporation and adds nothing to the interest of the stockholder. A stock dividend does, however, enable a corporation to offer tangible evidence that the stockholder's investment is earning a profit, which in turn is being reinvested for presumably still greater profits. Here are some other reasons, along with conserving cash, why a firm may prefer a stock dividend.

1. *To increase the marketability of its stock.* When a share of stock rises in price beyond a certain point, investors are reluctant to buy it. It has been shown, for example, that an investor will more readily buy 100 shares of a $20 stock than 20 shares of a $100 stock. When a corporation feels the price of its stock is too high, it can reduce the price by paying a substantial stock dividend. This improves the stock's marketability and often brings about an upward trend in its price.

> There is a difference between a stock dividend and a stock split. Though a 100 percent stock dividend and a two-for-one stock split both reduce the stock price by half and give the stockholder twice as many shares as he had before, there is a basic difference between the two. In a stock split, earnings are not capitalized; the capital stock account and the retained earnings account remained unchanged. Also, stock splits almost always require stockholder approval to amend the corporate charter.

Generally a publicly-held firm should be wary of a large stock dividend unless it can raise the actual cash dividend payment. If it has been paying $4 on each share and then pays a 100 percent stock dividend, it should be prepared to pay, beginning soon thereafter, more than $2 per share on the shares that will then be outstanding. Stockholders will expect this after a large stock dividend and if not forthcoming, investor enthusiasm for the company's stock may languish.

Similarly, in the case of periodic small stock dividends, the company should be in a position to continue the same dividend rate on the larger number of shares outstanding after the payment of the stock dividend. Marketability may be adversely affected if no cash dividend at all accompanies the small stock dividend. This should be done only when the need to conserve cash is compelling and, even then, only when the stockholders are generally less interested in current cash income than in capital appreciation.

2. *To maintain a long-established dividend rate.* Some corporations prefer to pay periodic small stock dividends instead of raising a long-established dividend rate. If the funds available for dividends increase by, say, ten percent, they will elect to pay a 10 percent stock dividend and maintain their traditional dividend, instead of raising the dividend or paying an extra dividend.

Tax Advantage of the Stock Dividend

Though the merits of certain aspects of stock dividends are debatable, stock dividends do offer one real advantage for the stockholder: he does not pay a tax on his stock dividend unless he sells the stock. However, his cost basis of the stock changes. He computes the cost basis of his stock by dividing the amount he originally paid for his stock by the number of shares he has after receiving the stock dividend.

For example, if a stockholder bought 100 shares of stock for $12,000 ($120 a share) and the corporation subsequently paid a 50 percent stock dividend, the cost basis of each share became $80, or $12,000 divided by 150. Under the tax law, he would then realize a gain if he sells any stock at more than $80 a share—not $120 a share. He will likewise not incur a loss unless he gets less than $80 a share.

To determine whether any gain or loss on the sale of stock is a long-term or short-term gain or loss, the stockholder has to know the date-basis of the stock. If the sale is more than six months after the stockholders date basis (date of purchase), a long-term gain or loss results and the transaction is subject to capital gains tax instead of ordinary income tax. The date basis of the stock dividend is the same as the date basis of the original stock.

Dividends Payable in Stock or Cash

In recent years the practice has developed of giving the stockholders the option of selecting stock or cash. In some cases provision is made that all dividends are to be paid in cash, unless the stockholder notifies the company that he wants stock; in other cases, provision is made that all dividends are to be paid in stock unless the stockholder notifies the corporation that he wants cash. The option to receive either cash or stock subjects the stockholder who selects stock to immediate taxation, unlike a straight stock dividend which is nontaxable.

Property Dividends

If a corporation owns disposable assets that are physically divisible, it may distribute those assets to stockholders as dividends, provided there is retained earnings. Stock dividends usually consist either of securities in subsidiaries or of stocks or bonds of other companies held as investments. A concern holding a large block of another firm's stock may prefer to distribute the stock as a dividend rather than to sell it on the open market, which would likely drive down the price of the stock.

Stockholders are not obliged to accept property dividends, but they cannot elect to receive an equal amount of cash instead. If a stockholder refuses a property dividend, the corporation may offer to hold the property in trust for him or to sell it for his benefit.

Scrip Dividends

Scrip dividends are notes or other written promises to pay a certain amount at a specified date. The notes are called *dividend certificates,* commonly known as *scrip.* They usually bear interest at a fixed rate until redeemed for cash by the issuing firm. Companies rarely issue scrip dividends; when they do so, it is usually under these conditions:

1. The cash supply is temporarily weak.
2. Management wants to maintain an established dividend record without paying out cash immediately.

WAYS OF SHELTERING RETAINED EARNINGS

Dividend policies reflect management's decisions on the most profitable ways to use earnings—for financing expansion, paying dividends, retiring outstanding debt, or for other purposes. If the management sees profitable use for more cash, it should restrict dividends in order to accumulate substantial sums to meet these future needs. This may be difficult to do if the stockholders notice the retained earnings account getting bigger every year. To head off stockholder criticism, the financial manager can appropriate a portion of earnings for specific purposes.

Earnings can be appropriated for a variety of purposes: to record decreasing values in assets, to provide for estimated increased liabilities, and to set aside a portion of retained earnings for a specific future use. Current usage favors the use of the term *reserve* to refer only to the appropriation of retained earnings. The use of the term reserve to describe reductions in asset values or to provide for increased liabilities is declining in favor of words which are more descriptive of the purpose for which the provision is made.

Asset Valuation

These accounts provide for losses in the value of such assets as receivables, investments, marketable securities, plant and equipment, patents, and certain intangibles. For example, accounts receivables often diminish substantially in value as a result of bad debt losses. By setting aside an allowance for bad debts, a firm indicates the true value of its receivables—their book value less anticipated bad debt losses. Other valuation accounts include provision for depreciation.

Liabilities

Provisions for liabilities include those future liabilities that can be estimated with reasonable accuracy. The most common liabilities for which such provision is made are those for taxes, insurance, and interest.

Retained Earnings Reserves

These reserves provide for expansion and investment projects and for contingencies. They allocate certain amounts from retained earnings to specific projects, thereby indicating that that amount of retained earnings is not available for any other purpose—as for paying dividends.

Improper Use of These Amounts

Valuation accounts and provisions for future liabilities are created by charges to income, thus, these accounts could be used improperly to equalize profits by debiting income during a year of high profits and crediting income during a year of low profits. Worse, they could be used to conceal income entirely by crediting income directly to them or charging losses against them without disclosure. The chief financial officer must be alert to such a misstatement of income.

Effect of the Tax Laws

Under the Federal Tax law, an estimated deduction may be taken only if there is a liability to support the deduction. This generally means that charges to these accounts are disallowed except when:
1. The statute gives specific permission.
2. All transactions anticipated in the account have been concluded during the year.
3. The setting up of the provision is a typical procedure in accounting for the item in question, such as in the evaluation of depreciable assets.

The general rule is to allow a taxpayer to deduct losses only in the accounting period when they actually occur. Although it may be good business practice to set up a provision for a future liability which may arise, the provision itself is not deductible; only the expense incurred is deductible.

MECHANICS OF DIVIDEND PAYMENT

The board of directors should adopt a formal resolution when they declare a dividend. Such a resolution usually indicates (1) the rate or amount of the dividend, (2) the time of its payment, (3) the class of stock on which the dividend is declared, (4) the record date for determining who is entitled to the dividend, and (5) the medium in which the dividend is to be paid. Figure 14-1 illustrates a formal resolution declaring a regular dividend.

RESOLVED, That a regular ("annual," "quarterly," or "semi-annual") dividend is hereby declared out of the undivided profits of this corporation, payable on _____, 19_____, as follows: A dividend of _____ percent (_____%) on the outstanding Preferred Stock, and a dividend of _____ dollars ($_____) per share on the outstanding Common Stock without par value.

Figure 14-1
Declaration of Regular Dividend

Using a Disbursement Agent

A corporation may distribute its own dividend payment or it may use the services of a disbursing agent. A disbursing agent offers these services:

1. Prepares a stockholder list. (If the disbursing agent is the transfer agent—which is usually the case—he will prepare this list from the stock books.)
2. Prints and mails the dividend checks, using the corporation's checks signed by the proper corporate officer.
3. Keeps a record of checks that have not cleared the bank after a certain date and periodically sends an "Outstanding Checks" report.
4. Returns uncashed checks after a specified period, usually two to six years.

Before the disbursing agent does anything, however, he must first get a certified copy of the directors' resolution declaring a dividend. He usually needs this resolution well before the record date so that he can print the dividend checks on time.

Disbursing Agent vs. Internal Disbursements

The choice depends on the size of the company and the extent to which it makes use of electronic data processing equipment. Small companies can prepare dividend payments annually if they have few stockholders, or use simple business machines if they have a few hundred stockholders. For the medium-sized corporation, however, the manual system is far too costly, while the completely automated computer systems of the large corporations may be too elaborate. Many corporations this size use transfer agents who can do the job quicker and cheaper than the corporation itself. The transfer agent, because he does similar work for many companies, can profitably apply expensive data processing equipment to this task.

Other medium-sized firms distribute their own dividends by using a partially automated system, consisting of such machines as the addressograph and punched card tabulating equipment. A semi-automated system such as this cuts the heavy labor costs of the manual system and requires only a modest inventory in machinery. This machinery can also be used in many other business applications. Many large corporations with 1,000 or more stockholders handle their dividend payments economically by using EDP to do the job.

Payment Procedure for a Partially Automated System

Regardless of the system used—manual, partially automated, or fully automated— the procedure must always begin with a list of stockholders. The transfer agent can furnish such a list. If a firm keeps its own stock transfer records, its transfer department must prepare the stockholder list.

This requires an addressograph stencil for each stockholder whose name appears in the stock ledger. The stencil should show the stockholder's name and address, account number, and the number of shares he owns. The stencil must be kept current and must agree completely with the information in the stock ledger.

A dividend payment system known as the *register sheet method* has worked well for many years. The basic steps of this procedure are as follows:

1. *Preparing register sheets.* A typical register sheet has room for about twenty entries. Each entry gives the stockholder's name, number of shares owned, amount of the check, check number, and when cancelled. These sheets are run through the addressograph which prints the stockholder's name and address and the number of shares owned.

2. *Stenciling checks.* The dividend checks are connected in strips and divided into sections equal to the number of names on each register sheet. The checks are run through the addressograph and printed with the names and addresses of stockholders (and number of shares owned) in the same order as they appear on the register sheets.

3. *Check-writing machine.* The register sheet and its corresponding strip of checks are inserted in a check-writing machine simultaneously. The operator prints the check number and the amount of the dividend on both the check and the register sheet. The official signature of the proper corporate officer is printed on the check by means of a signature plate which is locked in the machine.

4. *Correcting checks.* As the checks are withdrawn from the machine, they are examined to make sure that they have been drawn for the correct amount and that they have not been spoiled by the machine. Spoiled or incorrect checks are marked "void" and held aside. New checks are then drawn for those voided.

5. *Checking totals.* The number of shares shown on the register sheets is reconciled with the total number of shares outstanding. The amount represented by the checks is reconciled with the total dividend payment. Three copies of these reconciliation statements are made—one to be pasted on the last register sheet, one for the disbursing department, and the third for the treasurer.

6. *Cutting and mailing checks.* The checks are pulled apart and inserted, with any other enclosures, into envelopes. The name and address printed on the check permit the use of window envelopes and eliminate the addressing chore.

7. *Payment dividend record.* The register sheets are bound as a permanent record of the dividend payment.

8. *Changes of address.* Change of address notices received after the dividend checks have been run off are honored by typing envelopes for these stockholders.

9. *Return of cancelled checks.* As dividend checks are cashed and returned to the corporation, the return date is entered on the register sheet. Follow-up letters are written to stockholders who have not cashed their checks, urging them to do so. The cancelled checks are kept until the statute of limitations has run on the debt. Some corporations keep them permanently.

To automate the register sheet method, the checks can be written on punched cards. The checks are prepared and prepunched with check numbers. The signature of the

---

To the Stockholder of

_____ Corporation:

The two percent (2%) stock dividend declared on _____ , 19_____ , is payable today to stockholders on record at the close of business on _____ , 19_____ . This stock dividend has been declared to capitalize a portion of the earnings which the Board of Directors deems desirable to retain in the business.

If your holdings of $10 per value Common Stock on the record date amounted to an even multiple of fifty shares, only a stock certificate is enclosed. If you held forty-nine shares or less, only a fractional interest order form is enclosed. Otherwise, both a stock certificate and an order form in enclosed.

If you have received an Order Form, the information set forth below should be read carefully. The Order Form represents an interest in your stock and has a definite value.

Very truly yours,

Figure 14-2(A)
Letter Accompanying Order Form for Purchase or Sale of Fractional Shares

corporate officers may also be preprinted. Using punched card checks simplifies the reconciling procedure (step 5 above) and can speed up other steps of the process.

Giving Notice of Declaration

The enclosed Order Form is not transferable, but entitles you, on or before _____ , 19_____ , to instruct _____ Trust Company of New York, Agent, either:

    (a)   to purchase for your account the additional fractional interest required to make up one full share, bill you for the cost, consolidate the fractions and deliver to you a certificate for a full share, or

    (b)   to sell your fractional interest and send a check for the proceeds to you.

For example, if you held fifteen shares of $10 par value Common Stock on the record date, you are entitled to 15/50ths of a share as a stock dividend. You have the option of instructing the Agent to purchase an additional 35/50ths of a share for you, which would then entitle you to one additional full share; or you can instruct the Agent to sell your 15/50ths of a share and send you a check for the proceeds.

To exercise either such right, you should mark an "X" in the appropriate box on the Order Form, sign it, and return it in the enclosed envelope to _____ Trust Company of New York. _____ Trust Company of New York, as Agent, will execute such Orders as soon as practicable, for the account of the individual stockholders, at a price determined by the Agent in its discretion which will be based on the currently prevailing market price for _____ Company shares on the New York Stock Exchange. The value of the fractional interest will, of course, vary depending upon the market price of the stock at the time your Order is executed. _____ Trust Company of New York, as Agent, may match and offset purchase and sale Orders. No charge will be made to stockholders for performing these services. The Corporation has agreed to reimburse the Agent for these costs.

All shares held to cover fractional interests with respect to which _____ Trust Company of New York, Agent, does not receive completed Order Forms from the holders thereof before the close of business on _____ , 19____ , will be sold in due course for the account of such holders, and the proceeds distributed to them. The order form will therefore become valueless after _____ , 19____ .

Figure 14-2(B)
Instructions for Completing the Order Form

Though it is generally not necessary to inform stockholders of a dividend declaration when the dividend will be paid in cash, many corporations consider a written or published notice desirable as a service to stockholders. Notification enables stockholders thinking of selling their shares to do so with full knowledge of the dividend situation. Dividend notices usually contain such information as the declaration date, the rate or amount of the dividend declared, the record date to determine who is entitled to the dividend, and the payment date. When a corporation declares an extra dividend or a higher regular dividend, a written notice ensures that every stockholder will know of this favorable company action.

When dividends are declared and payable in other than cash, a notice is generally necessary. If, under the arrangements of a stock dividend, for example, stockholders are entitled to receive less than a full share of stock, the corporation must send stockholders a letter (Figure 14-2) explaining its policy on stockholders' fractional interests and giving instructions on filling out a buy-or-sell order form that usually accompanies the letter. The stockholder uses the order form to instruct the corporation or its agent either to buy the additional fractions necessary to make up one full share, or to sell his fractional share and send him a check for the proceeds.

15

Proper Records Management

15

Proper Records Management

RECORDS RETENTION MADE EASY

The financial officer of the company is responsible for maintaining historical financial records. In small and medium sized companies this role is broadened to include responsibility for *all* corporate records. One major area of record retention excluded from this analysis is manufacturing records including product designs, blueprints, drawing, and production reports. It is assumed that few financial managers involve themselves in this area.

Separate Records into Permanent and Transient Types

The first major step to be taken is to classify certain records as Permanent and all others as Transient. Permanent records are all documents which should be kept either permanently or more than 8 years. By contrast, transient records are all those which should be discarded in less than 8 years. The Permanent class includes records which could be destroyed after 8 years but instead are retained. This system recommends that they be retained indefinitely. The example in Figure 15-1 illustrates the economics involved. The annual call refers to the annual review of the entire permanent file to find the 3,000 records on which retention period has expired. The unit cost of retaining those 3,000 records one more year is one forty-fourth the cost of removing those 3,000 records. This indicates that it is uneconomic to remove these records. The reasonable action to take is to leave the permanent file intact once it is established.

The arbitrary cut-off point of 8 years is chosen with good reason. As will be shown in a later section, 95% of the records can be discarded in less than 5 years. Recommended retention periods of more than 8 years for specific records are not based on law or regulation. Such documents are termed semi-permanent.

A.	Records Generated per year	100,000
B.	Per Cent Transient Records	90%
C.	Permanent Records 10% of 100,000	10,000
D.	Portion of permanent records which need not be retained indefinitely	3,000
E.	Unit cost of retaining a permanent record an additional year	$.0015
F.	Total File Size of Permanent Records	200,000
G.	Unit Cost of Culling Total File To Discard Type D Records (above)	.001
H.	Total Cost of Annual Cull .001 × 200,000	$200
I.	Records Discarding per Annual Cull 200 ÷ 3,000	.067
J.	Records Discarding per Annual Cull 200 ÷ 3,000	.067
K.	Payback Period for Annual Cull .067 ÷ .0015	44 years

FIGURE 15-1
Economic Computation of Permanent Records Retention

Individual firms must put their value on semi-permanent documents. The cost of reviewing the documents and the decisions to keep them is higher than the cost of indefinite storage. Thus they are included with permanent documents.

How to Start a Records Retention Program

Four steps are required to get the program started. First, an inventory should be made of records on hand. Second, a permanent file of records on hand must be set up. Third, an efficient storage plan must be laid out and the records to be retained must be restored. Fourth, the procedures and timetable for system maintenance must be laid down.

The Records Inventory

An inventory is the most difficult step. Financial managers tend to put off starting programs for just this reason. Storerooms are dusty, overcrowded, and confused places. Personnel resist such assignments. Below are listed some hints on how to make the inventory easier.

1. Hire temporary help to handle the heavy dirty work.
2. Set aside for one week an area ten times the size of the storeroom for disassembling, segregating, and repacking records. The greatest cause of inefficiency is often lack of space.
3. If records are obviously not to be retained (example, twenty-year-old cancelled check) discard them without bringing them to the work area.
4. Do not allow large accumulations of miscellaneous or "unknown" categories of records. The financial manager must ask himself this question. "If I don't know what I have saved, how can I ever use what information is contained in the records?"
5. Put consecutive numbers on all files saved as a cross-reference to the inventory sheet.

A sample of the inventory sheet is shown in Figure 15-2. The left hand side contains descriptive data. The right hand side focuses on reason for retention (if any) and disposition.

Cont. Ord.	Quantity	Dates	Description	Gov't Contract	ICC	State Board of Taxation	Normal Retention	Action
241	1 Box	1964 1966	Memo Change Invoices					Discard
244-47	4 Boxes	1965	Purchase Orders Issued					Discard
242-3	2 Boxes	1966	Sales Correspondence and Sample Follow-ups					Discard
240	1 Box	1966	Job Cost Sheets and labor sheets	✓				Retain 3 years
270-2	3 Boxes	1965	Invoice copies				✓	Retain 3 years

Figure 15-2
Records Inventory Sheet

Creating a Permanent File

Any of several types of records can be used for record retention records. Examples are cardex, 3 × 5 cards, or IBM cards. The use of tab cards add flexibility in the reports which can be generated. Figure 15-3 is card format specification for a unit record system. The report should be run semi-annually or annually in two different sequences—by expiration date and record type. Figure 15-4 shows a sample report. The expiration date sequence shows those files which can be discarded. The tabulation by record type should be retained as a means of locating specific boxes of records. The container numbers are assigned sequentially and boxes are stored sequentially. Thus, a given type of record would be found in several different containers distributed throughout the entire set of containers. Empty containers should be set aside for the reuse and their cards removed from the active file.

Storage Plans and Methods

The most efficient and low cost storage medium is corrugated cardboard, metal frame, single drawer file boxes. A later section of this chapter discusses the application of

Card Columns	Title	Description & Instructions
1 to 3	Container No.	One card per container
4 to 5	Oldest Year	Date of oldest records
6 to 7	Latest Year	Date of newest records
8	Partial/Complete	P if same record title and date
9 to 12	Month/Year of Discard	Date after which discard may take place
13 to 14	Record Type	Predetermined code to categorize type of record
15 to 70	Description	Descriptive data about the specific records

Figure 15-3
Unit Record Format for Record Retention System

RECORD TYPE Code	Description	Container No.	Oldest Date	Newest Date	Discard Date	Description
01	Payroll Chk	128	67	67	12/69	Salaried & Hourly Payroll
01		187	66	67	12/69	Hourly Payroll
02	Checks	191	64	65	12/68	1st National Account
02		722	65	65	12/68	1st National Account
02		819	65	66	12/69	State Federal Bank

Figure 15-4
Records Retention Report

micro-film as a storage medium. For the purposes of routine retention systems, cardboard and metal file boxes can be used. Such boxes are available in a range of sizes. Most firms are able to standardize on two or three sizes shown below:

STANDARD SIZE DESCRIPTION

Name	Inside Dimension in Inches		
	HEIGHT	WIDTH	DEPTH
Check & Envelope Size	5	8½	26
Letter Size	8½	11	26
Legal Size	11	14	26

Special sizes are sometimes necessary where large quantities of unusual sized documents are encountered. A common problem of this type is sales invoice copies, and receiving documents of unusual size. Corrugated blocks and dividers can be used with standard sizes, thereby eliminating the need for special sizes.

Consecutive numbers should be used. They should be assigned in blocks. For example—all check-size boxes should run from 100 to 300. The boxes should be stored in container number sequence to aid in locating a given box. Stocking height is optional. Some firms prefer space efficiency to convenience and stack eight to ten feet high. In such cases, clerical help can not be expected to retrieve particular boxes and help must be provided for climbing and lifting. Clear work space must also be provided in the records room for examining records once they are brought down from the high stack. Low stacking provides walk-up filing which clerical help can use themselves. As a general rule low stacking is advisable for small installations where no one can be assigned to handling the high stacks.

Maintaining security of confidential records is an easily-solved problem. Many financial managers never organize their old records because they fear that confidential information will be exposed to view in a records retention room. A little mechanical ingenuity can solve this problem. A carpenter can build a wire cage or the confidential boxes can be stored in steel shelving with locked barriers built across the front. This keeps the boxes under control of the master system but out of reach of unauthorized personnel.

Keeping the System Operating

A small amount of training plus an annual update are all that are needed to maintain the system once it is started. Explaining and enforcing the following rules will insure a good records retention system:

1. Remove and photostat original documents and return to their place immediately.
2. Maintain the filing sequence in the boxes the same as is used in active files.
3. Set a fixed date for annual update of the system. Discard obsolete transient records, and add the most recent year's records.
4. Any additions or deletions to the record room must be reflected by changes in the permanent file.

The proper length of time to retain a record depends on several factors. The most important are:

1. The management policy of the individual firm
2. The type of business—some industries are under control of regulatory bodies
3. The type of record.

One important fact should be understood. *No company has to throw away anything.* For many years companies were very conservative about old records and retained ten or more years of records. Efficiency experts finally pointed out the waste involved in too many old records. Up-to-date standards have been published which call for retention periods mostly in the two to four year range. They will be detailed later in this chapter. However, any company can choose to keep its records twice as long as recommended. A financial manager planning on keeping extra records should be aware of the cost of such a decision.

Cost of Retrieving Old Records

The cost of record retention is shown below in an example. It is first computed on a cost per year per thousand records:

COST PER THOUSAND RECORDS

Capacity of each file box	2,500 records
Stacking factor	5 boxes high
Records per stack—5 × 2500	12,500
Cost per square foot of floor space	$3.00
Square footage per stack	4.5 sq. ft.
Aisle and unused space factor	1.4
Total square footage 1.4 × 45	6.3 sq. ft.
Total cost per stack $3.00 × 6.3	$19.90
Annual storage cost of space $18.90 ÷ 12.500	.0015
or	$1.50/M

The calculation of *cost per record retrieved* is the second step and requires data about the size of files and frequency of use. The number of records on hand can be estimated at 2,500 per transfile. The frequency of use requires an estimate by the financial manager or the department managers under him. The question to be asked is simply: "How many records per month does your department use from the record room?" The cost computation is shown as follows:

COST PER RECORD RETRIEVED

Records on hand	125,000
Storage cost per year 1.5 × 125	$187.50
Annual Cost of Systems Maintenance 100 hrs. @ 3.00/hr.	$300.00
Total Annual Cost $187.50 + $300.00	$487.50
Total Requests for Records per year	75
Cost per Record Retrieved 487.50 ÷ 75	$6.50
Fixed Cost per Record Retrieved 300 ÷ 75	$4.00
Variable Cost per Record Retrieved 187.50 ÷ 75	$2.50
Variable Cost of Clerical Time to Retrieve one record 1 hr. @ $3.00/hr.	$3.00
Total Cost 4.00 + 2.00 + 3.00	$9.50

Cost of a Change in Retention Policy

Once cost benchmarks have been set, a decision on the length of retention period can be made. The table in Figure 15-5 tabulates the per unit and total annual costs for three different retention policies. This shows the cost effect of various decisions. The alternatives "Double Minimum Period" and "Triple Minimum Period" mean saving records twice or three times as long as the minimum recommended time.

Alternative	Per Record Stored	Per Record Retrieved	Annual Cost
Minimum Period	.0063	9.50	$787.50
Double Minimum Period	.0052	13.00	975.00
Triple Minimum Period	.0042	15.50	1,162.50

Figure 15-5
Tabulation of Costs Under Various Alternatives

Accounting Records
    1. General Ledger
    2. Subsidiary Ledgers posted to General Ledger

Stockholders Records & Corporate Records
    1. Board Meeting Minutes
    2. Charter, Bylaws, etc.
    3. Stock transfer records

Contracts and Miscellaneous
    1. Pension Agreements & Records
    2. Patent Agreements, licenses, etc.
    3. Any contract having perpetuity
    4. Property Records — Deeds, Leases, etc.
    5. Copyright and agreements

Tax Records
    1. All Federal Returns plus cancelled checks paying taxes
    2. All State Returns involving money.

Figure 15-6
Permanent Records to Retain Indefinitely

Recommended Retention Period

The list of record types shown in Figure 15-6 are the permanent types and should be saved indefinitely. In particular firms special records may qualify for permanent retention. By arranging a coding in the upper left-hand corner of the document, file clerks can be trained to set aside such records for permanent retention. Transient records should be grouped according to the types shown in Figure 15-7. They can then be filed and discarded in accordance with the minimum periods shown. These periods apply only to firms not under special regulations. Listed below are companies which would be subject to such special regulations:

1. Firms doing business with the Federal Government under control of Armed Service Procurement Regulations.
2. Firms in the transportation industry and subject to control by the Interstate Commerce Commission.
3. Firms subject to particular regulations promulgated by special regulatory bodies either state or local.

Record Types	*Term in Years*
1. Bank Statements	2
2. Cancelled Checks	3
3. Cash Receipt Records	3
4. Insurance Policies — Liability	5
5. Paid Bills	3
6. Payroll earning records	6
7. Payroll Registers	3
8. Payroll tax reports	4
9. Petty Cash and travel expense reports	3
10. Purchase Orders Issued	3
11. Receivable Ledgers by Customer	2
12. Sales invoices, credit memos, etc.	3
13. Shipping & Receiving Records	3
14. Time sheets or cards	2

Figure 15-7
Transient Record Retention Schedule

Other special situations requiring unusual retention are as follows:

1. All records supporting federal income tax returns until either—
   a. Three years elapse from the date of the tax return without the taxpayer signing a voluntary time extension for the convenience of Internal Revenue.
   b. The tax audit is completed and all tax payments are made.
2. Payroll records in cases involving unsettled workmen's compensation claims.
3. Any records involving legal action taken or threatened where the firm may have liability for damage.

CAN MICROFILM HELP?

Major advances have been made in applying microfilm techniques to business's record retention problems. Cost studies have shown that all records retained eight or more years are less expensive in microfilm form than in original form. Such a cost comparison is shown below.

From Figure 15-1, Unit cost of retaining an
    original record one additional year $.0015
Labor to take one picture (production rate-400/hr)   .0025 hrs
Labor cost per hour including camera $4.00
Labor cost per frame $4.00 × .0025 $.0100
Film cost per frame   .0020
Total microfilm cost per frame $.0120

Payback period of Microfilm $.012 — .0015   8 years

The microfilm was first applied to the banking industry for use in recording paid checks. Since that time, new formats of microfilm images have been developed which offer unusual possibilities.

Microfilm Techniques

Described below are some of the major methods using the photographic image for business records.

Rollfilm—The basic method of microfilming employs a roll of film mounted in a mechanized camera which automatically takes a picture of all documents fed into the machine. Each roll contains thousands of images. The systemization of film requires that documents have a sequential logic to them (such as date, invoice number, etc.) since a roll is a very sequential storage medium.

Microfiche—Acetate cards have been developed which can contain one hundred related images on one card 5 inches by 8 inches. These cards are kept in a file drawer in subject sequence. A user finds the proper subject card and inserts it in a viewer which enlarges the image to page size. Dial controls on the machine allow the user to project the desired image from the one hundred available on the viewing screen. Applications involving repeated use of the same are best suited to microfilm. Printed copies of selected images can be made on special microfiche printers. Important applications have been made in manufacturing operations calling for blueprint copies. See Figure 15-8.

Aperture cards—A single film image implanted in a tabulating card is called an aperature card. The advantage of this system is that the cards will run through ordinary sorters and collators. Thus it is possible to pick images from large card files based on the code contained in the card. Engineering drawings have also provided a major use for this technique. An important advantage of this over microfiche is that changing a record involves only one new photograph since there is only one on a card. See Figure 15-9.

Magnetic tape to microfilm—A new field microfilm involves direct conversion of what was previously computer printer output directly to microfilm *without printing*. The printer has always been the slowest part of large computer systems. To avoid it report data is written in magnetic code on a normal magnetic

Figure 15-8
Microfiche in Use
(Courtesy IBM Corporation)

tape. The tape is fed to a special computer which converts what would have been a page of print to images on a cathode ray tube. Microfilm images are made of the page images appearing on the tube at very high speed. This technique will be very important to the business world in the near future.

Microfilm Applied to Record Retention

As explained above, records held more than eight years can cost less if microfilmed. Before proceeding with a microfilm system the financial manager should consider the following advantages and disadvantages of microfilm over original records.

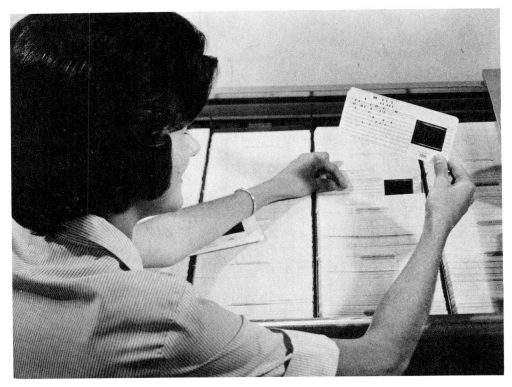

Figure 15-9
Aperture Card in Use
(Courtesy IBM Corporation)

Advantages of Microfilm:
1. The deterioration and damage of records in microfilm form is much less than in the original paper form.
2. The cost of generating a second copy which could be stored safely away as protection against fire is much lower with microfilm.
3. Microfilm is inherently neater and more appealing to employees.
4. Contractors can be hired to do all the microfilming using their facilities.

Disadvantages of Microfilm:
1. Indexing of documents is more complicated since searching long rolls of film is laborious.
2. Special equipment to make microfilm and other special equipment to view microfilm is required.
3. Photographic reproduction of colors is an unknown variable.
4. A bad image or two in the middle of a roll means either:
   a. Re-indexing and re-photographing the original documents on another roll or
   b. Re-photographing the entire roll.

16

How to Handle Tax Problems

‖‖‖

16

How to Handle Tax Problems

Taxes figure prominently in day-to-day operating decisions. The finance officer is responsible for seeing that the company pays only its share of taxes, and no more. He must therefore have a great sensitivity to the tax implications of contemplated decisions.

TAX IMPACT OF ACCOUNTING TRANSACTIONS

One of the important areas which has a direct impact on taxation is within the finance officer's direct control. The Federal income tax regulations require that, in general, net income for tax purposes must be determined on the basis which the taxpayer regularly uses in his books. Naturally, there are a number of exceptions to this general rule, but the general rule is of considerable importance, and particularly so where there is a question of asserting an additional tax against the taxpayer. Despite the fact that the Federal government has evolved its own peculiar rules of tax accounting, the manner in which many transactions are reflected in the company's books will often be determinative of the treatment which they will be accorded in the company's tax return.

Foremost among such transactions are those items which may arguably represent either capital or expense, as for example, a repair item. If the company capitalizes such an item on its books, there is little opportunity for it to argue that the item should be expensed on the tax return. Consequently, it is important that the accounting staff use care in recording expense items properly in the expense accounts. Where divisional management has a profit-and-loss responsibility, there may be a tendency to capitalize items which could properly be expensed, so as to avoid a direct charge to divisional profits. This tendency can be avoided by having accounting policy clearly determined by the financial officer, and not by the subsidiary line organization.

Clearly, it is to the company's advantage to expense an item on its income tax return rather to capitalize it; but accounting policies must be supportable by reasonable conformance with the requirements of the tax laws, or audit problems will arise with the Internal Revenue Service. Nevertheless, reasonable rules consistently followed will be accepted. Commonly, companies will expense small items, even though they are of a capital nature, so as to reduce the clerical workload in accounting for them.

Avoiding the Accumulated Earnings Tax

While the avoidance of the accumulated earnings tax is not solely the financial officer's responsibility, since it has to do with corporate policy, it will be the financial officer who will have to advise corporate management of the dangers which this penalty tax presents.

In essence, the accumulated earnings tax is a tax on earnings which have been accumulated beyond the reasonable needs of the business. The tax is imposed as a deterrent to corporations who avoid distribution of earnings so as to permit their shareholders to avoid taxation on such distributions.

The question as to whether earnings have been accumulated beyond the reasonable needs of the business is one of fact, and there are no clear rules to determine when such a situation exists. It is clear that the corporation may anticipate its reasonable cash needs and accumulate resources to meet those future needs (such as debt repayment, new capital improvements, etc.). However, if the corporation has large liquid resources, and has not made taxable distributions of earnings, there is a potential problem. It should be emphasized that nontaxable stock dividends will not help in alleviating the problem. The best protection against the tax is a good plan for the future development of the corporation, supported by actual progress in implementation. This will clearly establish that the corporation has a need for substantial capital in the future.

Examine Inventory for Subnormal Items

It is often worthwhile to examine carefully what has been carried in inventory. A close look will probably reveal several categories of items which, because of deterioration and obsolescence, have seriously depreciated in value. These items should be written down to their true value when computing the closing inventory for the year. The taxpayer may also subtract the direct cost of disposing of this inventory from his closing inventory valuation.

How to Write Down Inventory

Assume the opening inventory was $50,000 and the closing inventory also comes to $50,000. Purchases for the year are $200,000 and net sales $600,000. In the closing inventory a number of broken items which ordinarily would be valued at $10,000 will have a selling price of only $4,000.

If the cost of disposing of these items is $1,000, the closing inventory becomes $43,-000 ($50,000 minus a $6,000 loss in value and $1,000 for disposing of the items).

Shown below is a profit comparison using (1) normal value, or (2) subnormal value in figuring closing inventory:

(1) Normal Value			(2) Subnormal Value
$600,000		Net Sales	$600,000
	$ 50,000	Opening Inventory	$ 50,000
	200,000	Purchases	200,000
	$250,000	Total	$250,000
		Less: Closing	
	50,000	Inventory	43,000
200,000			207,000
$400,000			$393,000

By revaluing the inventory to reflect the sales price of the substandard items rather than their normal value, the gross profit is $7,000 lower and the tax bill has been cut by $3,500, based on a 50 percent total tax rate.

Be Ready for IRS Queries

The more a company reduces its closing inventory, the more it cuts its tax bill. But the closing inventory is just where the Internal Revenue agent takes a close look.

Inventory Count

Unless the financial manager can prove that the inventory count is legitimate, he may face a lot of paper work and duplicate effort to reconstruct the job. He must be prepared for these questions:

1. Did the company really take a physical count of its inventory?
2. Did the employees do all the counting of the inventory, or did management assign an independent auditor to work on it?
3. Did he follow accepted procedures in taking the company's inventory?

Valuation Methods

If the company used the lower-of-cost-or-market method of valuation, the financial manager may have to show the cost of each item before reducing it to the market price. He may also be asked to: (1) explain how he arrived at the stated market price, (2) show a comparison of the market valuations with prices of sales or purchases at recent dates, (3) produce the records that prove the figures used two or three years ago.

THE EFFECT OF VARIOUS SELLING PROCEDURES ON TAXES

Tax planning in connection with sales is concerned primarily with keeping income in the lowest brackets. There are tax rules as to when the proceeds from various types of sales are taken into income for sales (1) on open account, (2) on consignment, and (3) on approval.

Sales on Open Account

The majority of sales are made on open account. There is no absolute rule on when a sale has been completed, but the general practice is to consider that the sale is complete when title has passed. For income tax purposes, most sales are taken into income when the product has been delivered. The date of delivery is determined by the invoice or bill of lading.

When a seller knows that his tax rate for the following year will be higher, he should —when possible—speed up late-in-the-year deliveries to take sales into income before the end of the year. If next year's income is likely to be taxed at a lower rate, he should slow down the making of each delivery.

Sales on Consignment

The principal business reason for selling on consignment is to be able to repossess the goods in the event of the bankruptcy of the distributor. Sales are not taken into income until the consignee sells them. Goods on consignment are carried in the inventory at cost rather than selling price.

From an income-tax standpoint, the use of consignment sales postpones the realization of income until the sale to the ultimate user has taken place. If $10,000 worth of canned goods are sold on consignment to a broker in December, a large portion, if not all, of the income will be deferred to the next year when the broker actually sells them to the trade. On the other hand, if they are sold on open account in December, the income must be reported in that month.

In the absence of other overriding business considerations, a manufacturer who usually sells on consignment may find it to his advantage to sell on open account in a particular year. If the tax rate in the following year will be higher, he thereby accelerates income into the current year when it will be taxed at a lower figure. If the current year is the last one in which an unused net operating loss carry-over is available, maximized sales income in the current year will prevent it from being taxed at all.

Sale on Approval; Sale, or Return

The parties to a sale may "agree that the buyer shall temporarily take the goods into his possession to see whether they are satisfactory to him, and if they are not, he may refuse to become owner." They also may agree "that the property shall pass to buyer on delivery but that he may return the goods if they are unsatisfactory."

The first type of agreement is called a sale "on approval," or "on trial," or "on satisfaction." The second type is called a "for sale, or return." These types of transactions are generally used when a fairly new product is involved or where the product is perishable. The buyer does not want to bind himself to keep the product if he finds it does not sell or is not suitable.

In a sale on approval, title does not pass until the buyer decides to take the goods. He is usually accorded a reasonable time, such as 30 days, to make his decision. From an income-tax standpoint, this is akin to a consignment sale. Since title to the goods remains with the seller, the goods are included in the year-end inventory, and the sale is treated as income when the buyer accepts the goods.

In the case of a sale or return, transaction title passes immediately and the seller must take the sale into income upon delivery. If the goods are returned, they may be deducted the same as any other return.

From the practical standpoint, there is little difference between a consignment sale, a sale on approval, and a sale or return. In all cases, the goods have been delivered and it is not known for some time whether there has been a final sale. So far as the purchaser is concerned, it generally makes little difference to him which arrangement is used.

From an income-tax standpoint, however, the difference is substantial. When the sale is on consignment or on approval, the income from the sale is deferred until the goods have been accepted or sold to the ultimate user. When the transaction is a sale or a return basis, the income must be taken up immediately even though a large portion of the goods may be returned in a later tax year. A seller who has been using the sale or return method may defer a large portion of his year-end sales to the next year by the simple expedient of shifting to the sale on approval or consignment methods. The converse is true of a seller who has been selling on approval; he may accelerate sales income into the current year by shifting to the sale or return method.

Tax planning in connection with sales is essentially a short range proposition. The results of at least ten or eleven months' operations should be known before any steps are taken to accelerate sales into the current year or defer them to the following year. The tax bracket the taxpayer is in, proposed or effective legislation increasing or decreasing tax rates, and the presence or absence of net operating loss carry-overs, together with sound business requirements, must all be taken into consideration.

Using the tools described here, an alert management can often realize substantial tax savings through the proper handling of sales for income tax purposes. In some cases the savings will simply shift taxes from one year to the next; in others, permanent savings can be affected.

USING ACCELERATED DEPRECIATION

In addition to straight-line depreciation, which permits the deduction of the cost of an item ratably over its useful life, the two methods of accelerated depreciation are: (1) the double declining-balance method, and (2) sum-of-the-digits method.*

The Double Declining Balance Method

Under this method, the depreciation rate is double the straight-line rate of depreciation, applied to the unrecovered cost each year. The depreciation deduction starts off

---

* For a complete description of depreciation methods and other money-saving tax strategies, useful to both the corporation and the individual, see Prentice-Hall's *Encyclopedia of Tax Shelter Practices.*

high and goes down each year; at the end of useful life there will still be part of the cost unrecovered. For example: A machine has a depreciation basis of $12,000 and a useful life of 10 years. The straight-line rate is 10 percent; declining balance rate is double that, or 20 percent. First year's deduction is 20 percent of cost or $2,400. Unrecovered balance of cost is then $9,600. Second year's deduction is 20 percent (rate stays constant) of $9,600, or $1,920, and so on.

At the end of 10 years, depreciation deductions total only 89 percent of cost. There are two ways to recover the final 11 percent. They are:

(a) Abandon the asset as worthless or dispose of it for what it will bring, taking a deduction, normally against ordinary income, for the loss. Remember, however, that although the tax basis may be virtually nil because of depreciation deductions, the economic value of the asset may substantially exceed that basis. A sale of such asset normally results in an income gain under the tax law.

(b) Switch to straight-line depreciation at any time during useful life and thus recover all the cost. After seven years of declining-balance depreciation, you have recovered $9,483.48, leaving $2,516.52 still to recover. It is possible to switch to the straight-line method and depreciate the unrecovered cost, less salvage value, over the actual remaining life of the asset as determined at the time of the switch.

What about Salvage Value?

Under the double declining-balance method, don't adjust for salvage value as is done with other depreciation methods. However, property may not be depreciated below its salvage value. An explanation will clear up the apparent inconsistency of these two statements.

In the declining-balance method, an asset cannot be depreciated below a minimum value, while under other methods, salvage value is subtracted before applying depreciation. Though the yearly deduction will vary in amount, depending on the method chosen, the total depreciation taken under all three methods will be approximately the same.

Ten Percent Allowance

In calculating depreciation on property (except buildings) having a useful life of at least three years, it is permissible to subtract an amount from the salvage value equivalent to ten percent of the cost of the property. An example is a machine with a useful life of ten years costing $10,000, and the salvage value at the end of that period is $1,000 (10 percent of cost). The total depreciation deduction over the life of the asset will be $10,000—not $9,000—since the salvage value up to 10 percent of the cost can be disregarded.

The Sum-of-the-Digits Method

This method gives almost as high deductions in early years as the double declining-balance method and, although deductions diminish each year, it allows a 100 percent write-off over useful life. This method is applied by using a decreasing fraction of original cost each year for the depreciation deduction. The denominator of the fraction is constant; the numerators go down by one each year. The denominator is found by adding the numbers of all the years of useful life of the asset. For example: A machine has a depreciation basis of $12,000 and a useful life of 10 years. The first year's deduction is 10/55 of $12,000 or $2,181.82. Second year's deduction is 9/55 of $12,000 and so on. The denominator is 55 because the machine has a 10 year life, and $1 + 2 + 3 + 4 + 5 + 6 + 7 + 8 + 9 + 10 = 55$. (For simplicity salvage value has been disregarded).

To get the sum of years-digits for the denominators of the fraction use this simple formula:

$$S = N \; \frac{N+1}{2} \quad \text{When: } S = \text{sum of the digits}$$
$$N = \text{number of years of estimated useful life}$$

Substituting in the formula for the example:

$$S = 10 \left(\frac{10+1}{2}\right) = 10 \times 5.5 = 55$$

Not all assets qualify for accelerated depreciation. The double declining balance and sum-of-the-digits methods apply only to:
1. New *tangible* property or
2. Property constructed or reconstructed by the taxpayer, and
3. Property having a useful life of at least three years.

Accelerated vs. Straight-Line

The following table shows the cost recovery rate through depreciation allowances of a $10,000 asset with a 10 year useful life and no salvage value, under each of the three methods discussed:

	STRAIGHT-LINE		DECLINING-BALANCE		SUM-OF-THE-DIGITS	
	Annual	Cumulative Cost	Annual	Cumulative Cost	Annual	Cumulative Cost
Year	Deduction	Recovered	Deduction	Recovered	Deduction	Recovered
1	$1,000	$1,000	$2,000	$2,000	$1,800	$1,800
2	1,000	2,000	1,600	3,600	1,600	3,400
3	1,000	3,000	1,300	4,900	1,500	4,900
4	1,000	4,000	1,000	5,900	1,300	6,200
5	1,000	5,000	800	6,700	1,100	7,300
6	1,000	6,000	600	7,400	900	8,200
7	1,000	7,000	500	7,900	700	8,900
8	1,000	8,000	400	8,300	500	9,400
9	1,000	9,000	300	8,600	400	9,800
10	1,000	10,000	300	8,900	200	10,000

Note this from the table: At the half-way mark of useful life the tax recovery of cost is about—

½ under the straight-line method,
⅔ under the declining-balance method, and
¾ under the sum-of-the-digits method.

Advantages of the Accelerated Methods

In the first five years, the sum-of-the-digits method gives deductions that are greater than straight-line by $800, $600, $500, $300, and $100, respectively. In the last five years, the straight-line method yields exactly the reverse situation. However, if the company takes the in-pocket saving afforded by the sum-of-the-digits method and invests it at compound interest, it will have a net gain over the straight-line method because of the greater period of compounding.

For instance, the $800 advantage of sum-of-the-digits in the first year compounds for 9 years, whereas the $800 advantage of straight-line in the tenth year doesn't compound at all. Assuming a 50 percent total tax rate and compounded earnings of 2 percent after taxes, the extra after tax net profit from using sum-of-the-digits depreciation on the above asset, instead of straight-line depreciation, would be $160.00.

The Limited-Declining Balance for Used Property

Used property can be depreciated under the 150 percent-declining-balance method—a special method that the Revenue Service recognizes. Though it is not as good as double-declining-balance, it is still better than straight-line, particularly in the early years. Here's how it works.

Assume that the cost of used machinery is $50,000, it will be used for five years, and has an estimated salvage value at the end of that time of $15,000. The base for straight-line depreciation is $40,000 since $5,000 of the salvage value can be ignored ($50,000 × 10%). For 150-percent-declining-balance, however, the depreciation base is $50,-000, because salvage value is not taken into account. But an item can never be depreciated below the salvage figure. Compare the results:

	Straight-Line		150%-Declining-Balance	
Year	Annual Depreciation	Amount Recovered	Annual Depreciation	Amount Recovered
1	$8,000	$ 8,000	$15,000	$15,000
2	8,000	16,000	10,500	25,500
3	8,000	24,000	7,350	32,850
4	8,000	32,000	5,145	37,995
5	8,000	40,000	2,005*	40,000

But since the item may not be depreciated below the salvage figure ($10,000), the deduction is limited to $2,005.

* The rate applied to the $12,005 unrecovered cost would give a deduction of $3,602.

The table shows that, in the first two years, there is a much larger deduction with the 150 percent method than with the straight line. After that, it falls off fairly rapidly. But even at the end of the fourth year, the total depreciation recovery is greater with the 150 percent method than with straight-line.

Coordinated Loan Payments with Depreciation Rate

Institutions will finance the acquisition of machinery and equipment, geared to accelerated depreciation rates. Under these arrangements, buyers of equipment can stretch out their financing for periods more nearly co-extensive with the life of the equipment than with the customary type of loan. Payments, instead of being in equal installments, are in unequal installments, heavy at first and gradually declining, thus bearing a direct relationship to the allowable depreciation deduction. Although the interest rate on this type of loan is higher than on the customary short-period loan, the ability of the taxpayer to fund the purchase of his equipment and pay off the cost of earnings before taxes, may make the additional interest worthwhile. Straight-line depreciation also has its advantages. It may be advantageous to finance the higher maintenance costs of later years by the larger straight-line deductions in those years. The financial officer must assess the relative merits of various depreciation schedules in light of each situation, and select the one that will benefit his company the most.

Special First-Year Depreciation

There is one other depreciation deduction which is available to taxpayers in the first year in which tangible personal property is acquired. This is the 20% special first year allowance. It is limited to $10,000 of cost, so that it is not of great benefit to large corporations. The property must have a useful life of at least six years. The allowance is available in full, even though the property was not in service for the entire year.

MAKE FULL USE OF REPAIR EXPENSES

Though the law says that repairs to business property are deductible, there are many things to consider in qualifying for the *best* tax benefit. To take full advantage of the repair deduction, the finance man must know: (1) the difference between deductible repairs and nondeductible capital expenditures, (2) what he needs to back up the deduction, (3) how to time the repairs deduction.

Difference Between Repairs and Capital Expenditures

This distinction is not always clear, but here is a useful guide:
A *repair* is an expenditure for keeping the property in an ordinarily efficient operating condition. It does not add to the value of the property, nor does it appreciably prolong its life. It merely keeps the property in an operating condition over its probable useful life for the uses for which it was acquired.

A *capital expenditure,* on the other hand, is a replacement, alteration, improvement, or addition which prolongs the life of the property, increases its value, or makes it adaptable to a different use.

The essential difference is that a repair merely maintains the status quo and is therefore a maintenance charge; a capital expenditure adds something to the property or extends its useful life, and is therefore considered an addition to capital investment which should not be applied against current earnings.

The distinction, however, will always be elusive. There are instances where the following items were allowed as repairs in one case, but not in another:

Alterations	Electric wiring
Placing new floor over old	Waterproofing basement
Plastering	Reconditioning elevators

The conflicting decisions may actually be helpful in that they give the tax man more leeway in shaping and reporting transactions. Most firms prefer the bird-in-hand approach of claiming deductions as early as possible. If, however, a deduction for repairs would be wasted in the current year, it would be better to capitalize a borderline item.

How to Support a Deduction

Because the line between repairs and capital expenditures is often hazy, it is essential that records clearly indicate the nature of the work done. Not only may repairs be disallowed as a deduction, but there is at least one case where the court refused to allow depreciation on claimed capital expenditures because there was no proof that the expenditures were not deductible as repairs when they were made. Failure to keep adequate records could thus make it impossible to classify an expenditure as either a repair or an addition. This will mean a complete loss of any income tax benefit from the expenditure.

Sometimes extensive repairs and improvements are made at the same time. If the repair items are merely part of the general plan of improvement, the entire amount spent for both repairs and improvements must be capitalized. But even if the repairs and improvements are not part of a general plan, some of the deductions may be disallowed unless the exact cost of the repairs can be shown as a separate expense. The company must make the segregation; the courts won't. To get the full deduction for repairs, be sure to (1) keep all vouchers, receipts, invoices, cancelled checks, etc., to prove the amount of the expense; (2) instruct the maintenance officer to have repairmen clearly indicate on their invoices the nature of the work done; (3) have separate contracts and ask for separate bills for each type of work, when repairs and improvements must be made at the same time; (4) see that the transactions are clearly recorded on the books.

Timing the Repairs

As with many other types of tax strategy, timing repairs for the best tax benefit calls for having deductions fall in high income-tax years. If a corporation expects to pay more taxes next year, it should consider deferring repairs until that time. On the accrual basis, repairs are always deducted in the year the work is done—not when it is paid for. However, the cost of materials can be deducted this year, even though they are not used until next year.

ELECTION OF MULTIPLE SURTAX EXEMPTIONS

The first $25,000 of corporate profits is taxed at a lower rate than the balance. The first $25,000 is subject to the normal tax, while the balance is subject to both the normal tax and a surcharge. Until 1964, a time-tested way of reducing corporate taxes had been to set up separate corporations for each separate business activity. Each separate entity was entitled to its own separate tax exemption, which sheltered that much more income from the surtax.

Six percent penalty. Under the 1964 tax law, companies can still elect to file separate returns and take separate surtax exemptions. However, they must now pay a price for this tax break—a penalty of 6 percent on the first $25,000 of income. This, in effect, increases the normal tax from 22 percent to 28 percent.

Three Alternatives

Controlled corporate groups may now be faced with three alternatives:
1. A parent-subsidiary group (a parent corporation and its 80 percent-owned subsidiaries) can file a consolidated return, claim one surtax exemption and tax-free treatment for inter-corporate dividends.
2. The controlled group can forego the use of multiple surtax exemptions and divide one exemption among the group. If it's a parent-subsidiary group instead of a brother-sister setup (two or more corporations 80 percent-owned by an individual, estate, or trust), it can also elect tax-free treatment of inter-corporate dividends.
3. The controlled group can elect to pay the 6 percent penalty tax and claim multiple surtax exemptions.

Which Is the Best Way?

Since brother-sister groups cannot file consolidated returns and cannot elect tax-free treatment of inter-corporate dividends, they have no choice but to claim multiple surtax exemptions and pay the six percent penalty. Failure to elect multiple surtax exemptions can cost up to $5,000 for each separate exemption the group could have claimed (48 percent minus 28 percent times $25,000).

Parent-subsidiary groups have a little more leeway, although they too will normally be better off electing multiple surtax exemptions. This is true even though they can elect tax-free treatment of intercorporate dividends, because intercorporate dividends are entitled to an 85 percent deduction on dividends received, regardless. Depending on the situation, it could take a very substantial amount of tax-free dividends to make up for the loss of the extra exemptions—even with the penalty. An example follows: Assume Parent Corporation wholly owns Subsidiaries A, B and C. Each corporation (including

Parent) earns $75,000 a year, and each subsidiary pays its entire net after taxes to the Parent Corporation as a dividend. What will the total tax be (a) when claiming one exemption—allocated entirely to Parent—tax-free dividend treatment, and (b) when claiming multiple surtax exemptions?

One exemption: The group will pay a total of $137,500.

Multiple exemptions: Each subsidiary will pay $31,000. Parent will pay a tax of $40,504, a total of $133,504.

The group is $3,996 better off electing multiple exemptions. Remember, however, that each situation must be figured separately. A slight change in the facts can change the results.

How and When to Elect

While electing multiple surtax exemptions will probably be best in most situations, it may not be best for all. In fact, in borderline situations, it may be difficult to determine the best course to take. Fortunately, Congress came to the rescue by providing a unique tax-planning opportunity when it set up the mechanics for making the elections and terminating it.

The election to claim multiple exemptions can be made as of any December 31. It becomes effective for that taxable year and continues effective until terminated. Likewise, an election to terminate may be made as of any December 31 and becomes effective for that taxable year. If a controlled group elects and then terminates, it must wait five years before it can again change its election. However, this penalty is not as severe as it looks because the law contains a special timing privilege. The election doesn't have to be made in a hurry. A controlled group can make the election any time within three years of the due date of the income tax return for the year of the election. Furthermore, a termination can be filed within three years of the December 31 deadline to which it is to apply. This arrangement means that a financial manager can take advantage of hindsight to make sure that he is doing the right thing. If yours is a borderline situation, wait and see what happens. You have three years to make up your mind. Section 1551 of the Internal Revenue Code disallows the exemption if the extra corporation was formed merely to get the exemption.

HOW TO HANDLE BAD DEBTS

A debt incurred in trade or business is deductible in the year it becomes worthless. A corporation may claim the full amount of the loss as an ordinary deduction, except for worthless securities, where a special rule applies. Whether a debt is uncollectible is a matter of evidence. The burden is on the taxpayer to show, not only that it is worthless, but that it became worthless during the tax year.

Proving Worthlessness

Though no general rule can be laid down to indicate when a debt becomes worthless, these factors are generally accepted as ample evidence:

1. Bankruptcy of debtor
2. Debtor out of business
3. Collateral worthless
4. Debtor without assets
5. Disappearance of debtor
6. Insolvency of debtor
7. Ill health of debtor
8. Receivership of debtor

Some factors indicating a debt is not worthless are:

1. No serious effort to collect
2. Sales still being made to debtor
3. Debtor still in business
4. Debtor earning substantial income

To support a claim that a debt is uncollectible, it is important to keep a collection record of the debt, including copies of correspondence with the debtor, notations of phone calls or interviews, financial statements of the debtor, and other data showing efforts to collect.

If efforts to collect are fruitless, and if it appears worthwhile, the account can be turned over to an attorney for collection. Many attorneys handle collections on a purely contingent fee basis. In most cities, collection agencies operate quite successfully. At the end of the tax year, the financial officer should get a written opinion from the attorney as to whether the particular accounts in his possession have become worthless. He need not take legal action against a debtor to obtain a tax deduction if it appears that the costs of collection would exceed the debt, or that a judgment would not be satisfied. The law does not require the taxpayer "to do a vain thing, to institute some expensive proceeding to legally ascertain what he already knows."

Deducting Business Bad Debts with the Reserve Account

Corporations using a reserve account may deduct a "reasonable addition" to the reserve. What is "reasonable" depends on the facts in each case. It is proper to base a determination on (1) past experience or (2) current valuation. When using current valuation, the accountant merely analyzes the receivables at the end of the tax year and makes a reasonable estimate of their overall collectibility.

Under normal conditions, the best way to figure the addition to the reserve is to base it on past experience over a reasonable period. This is how a finance officer might compute a reasonable reserve based on a moving three-year average:

Year	Charge-offs	Recoveries	Net Charge-offs	Receivables December 31
1963				$ 400,000
1964	$20,000	$2,000	$18,000	500,000
1965	25,000	1,450	23,550	600,000
1966	30,000	1,800	28,200	. . . . . .
Aggregate totals			$69,750	$1,500,000

Percentage of net charge-offs to accounts receivable	4.65%
Accounts Receivable December 31, 1966	$ 650,000
Reasonable reserve for bad debts based on experience (4.65% × $650,000)	$ 30,225
Reserve at beginning of year	24,000

Less charge-offs	$30,000	
Add recoveries	1,800	
		28,200
		($4,200)
Reasonable addition to reserve based on experience (deduction for tax purposes)		34,425
Reserve for bad debts at December 31, 1966		$ 30,225

A company is not entitled to an addition to the reserve and also to a separate deduction for bad debts. Unusually large additions to the reserve should be explained in a rider to the return.

Some companies have established a policy of charging normal trade accounts on which no payment has been received for more than six months (or for more than a year) to the reserve. If this practice is followed consistently, and recoveries are credited to the reserve, it will probably be approved by the Revenue Service.

A SICK PAY PLAN CAN OFFER TAX SAVINGS

A company can save valuable tax dollars on the money it pays an employee when he is out sick, *provided* it meets certain conditions. Generally, payment to an employee absent from work because of sickness or injury is taxable for social security tax purposes. But the payment is tax free if made under a "plan or system."

What Is a Sick Pay Plan?

The law is vague on this point. Nowhere is a sick pay plan defined; the plan need not even be in writing. There are certain procedures, however, that the law recognizes as characterizing a plan:

Coverage

The employer must either include all employees generally, or all employees of a class, such as "salaried" or "clerical" employees, or employees of a particular "plant" group.

Terms

The employer must establish definite payment amounts, duration of payment, and waiting periods, if any.

Notification

The terms and conditions of the plan must be communicated to the employees. A bulletin board notice would be adequate.

TAX CONSEQUENCES OF EMPLOYEE INCENTIVES

The steeply graduated personal income tax has made it increasingly difficult for high-paid executives to retain significant take-home pay from straight salary payments. Competition for executive talent has given rise to a variety of employee incentives which offer tax advantages to the executive. Often these incentives do not give rise to a deductible expense to the corporation; the decision to offer them is largely one of having to compete for employees in a very tight market for executive talent.

For the employee to realize the benefits of the particular incentive plan, the plan must conform to the requirements of the Internal Revenue Service. As companies have become more innovative in designing employee benefit plans, the Service and Congress have hedged the available tax benefits with more and more restrictions.

Group Life Insurance

An employer can pay the premiums for life insurance on employees' lives. The first $50,000 of such coverage can be provided without any contribution on the employee's part, and the employee will not have to include the cost of acquiring the insurance in his personal income. For coverage in excess of $50,000, the employee is taxable on the amount by which the cost of such insurance (as provided in the Regulations) exceeds the employee's contribution.

> EXAMPLE. An employee who is 51 years old has $100,000 insurance provided by his employer. He makes a contribution of 50¢ per $1,000 per month for this coverage. The taxable income attributable to this coverage is calculated as follows:

Total insurance	$100,000
Tax-free portion	50,000
Coverage subject to tax calculation	$ 50,000

Cost of coverage per Regulations (Age 51) .68 per $1,000 per month

Taxable income ($0.18 $\times$ 50 $\times$ 12) $108

It can be seen from the above example that an employee can incur taxable income from group life insurance even though he pays the entire cost of the insurance (i.e., there is no employer contribution), if the cost to him is less than the cost set by the Commissioner in the Regulations for the employee's particular age. This situation can arise if the older employees' contributions are subsidized to a degree by the younger employees in the group.

Stock Options

Employee stock options have become a popular form of employee incentive. If the option plan is properly qualified with the Internal Revenue Service, the employee realizes no taxable income when the option is granted or when he exercises it. Options which are not qualified with the Service may give rise to taxable income, represented by the value of the option at the time it was granted. Qualified plans must follow certain narrow rules:

—The option must be exercisable within five years after it is granted.

—The option price must be at least 100% of the fair value of the stock on the date when the option was granted.

—The plan must be approved by the stockholders.

—The option cannot be exercised so long as the employee has a prior qualified option which is exercisable at a higher price.

When an employee exercises a qualified option, he can realize capital gain treatment on any gain if he holds the stock for a further three years. If he sells the stock within the three-year period, the gain realized up to the date of exercise of the option will be ordinary income; the balance of the gain will be capital gain. The employer will not obtain a tax deduction for the option unless the employee makes a disposition within the three-year period after exercise. In this case, the employer would have a deduction for the amount of gain which the employee is required to report as ordinary income.

There are also stock purchase plans which permit employees to buy stock at a discount of as much as 15%. The rules are similar to the stock option rules, except that the employee will always realize some ordinary income on disposition of the stock if the sale price is at least as great as the acquisition price.

Profit Sharing Plans

Employees are fully taxable on distributions from profit sharing plans if the distribution is made in cash. However, these plans are popular with employees and employers. To the employee, the "bonus" in a lump sum (or several annual installments) represents a windfall of disposable income which he can use for discretionary purchases. To the employer, these payments afford full tax deductions, and they do not incur the additional fringe benefit payment costs in the way an equivalent salary increase would. Also, by making the employee's continued employment a condition to the payment of deferred installments, the employer makes it more difficult for employees to move to another company. (The employee, of course, is not taxed on these deferred installments until they are received.)

Thrift Plans

The popular thrift plan is only one of a range of possible qualified employee trusts which can be set up. In the thrift plan scheme, the employee and employer typically will make contributions which can be used to make investments in securities (including the employer corporation's securities). If properly qualified with the Internal Revenue Service, the employee can accumulate interest and dividends in the trust without any current tax exposure. Thus, his personal estate can grow remarkably, and be distributed to him at a time when he may well be in a lower tax bracket. At the same time, the employer receives current tax deductions for contributions, subject to certain maxima set forth in the regulations.

TAKE FULL ADVANTAGE OF CHARITABLE DEDUCTIONS

Since every corporation is deluged with requests for donations from charitable organizations, the finance officer must know how to combine charitable giving with maximum tax savings. Here are some suggestions:

Consider Giving Inventory Instead of Cash

A donation of inventory, means a deduction of the selling price of the goods instead of their cost. This works to the donor's advantage because the spread between cost and value, which would be taxable profit if sold, becomes a tax deduction.

An example is a corporation in the 48 percent bracket. If it gives $1,000 to charity, it gets a deduction worth $480, making the net cost of the gift $520. Now let's say it gives inventory which would sell for $1,000. The inventory costs the corporation $500. Result: The corporation deducts as a contribution the $1,000 market value of the property, though it paid only $500 for it. Instead of incurring a net cost of $480 for the contribution, the corporation incurs a cost of only $20 ($500 inventory cost minus $480 taxes saved).

To prevent a double deduction (i.e., both the gift plus the cost of producing or acquiring it), remember to make one of these two adjustments: (1) If the company produced or acquired the item in the year it donated it, its cost should be removed from the cost of merchandise bought or produced for manufacture or sale; (2) if it was produced or acquired in a prior year, this year's opening inventory should be reduced by the appropriate amount.

Converting a Contribution to a Business Deduction

Sometimes a payment made to a qualified charity may actually qualify as a business expense. This applies when the donation is made with reasonable expectation of business benefit commensurate with the expense. Suppose a company makes payments to a local hospital (a qualified charity) in return for the hospital's binding agreement to provide hospital facilities and services to the company's employees. The payments are deductible as a businses expense.

Deducting a donation that is made for consideration as a business expense is not only correct under the law, but also desirable. Charitable contributions are subject to the five percent limit; business expenses, of course, are deductible without limitation. If the donation qualifies as both a charitable contribution and a business expense, it is deductible only as a charitable contribution. In the example above, what makes the payment a business expense is that the charity gives considerations for the payment.

Apply Excess to Following Years

A corporation's deduction for contributions cannot exceed five percent of its taxable income. This maximum deduction for a corporation having a taxable income of $100,000 is $5,000. But a contribution in excess of $5,000 need not be lost in such a case because the excess can be carried over to the next two years. The tax man must remember, however, that the deduction for each of these years (contributions plus the carry-over) cannot exceed the five percent limit.

Examples of Qualified Organizations

To qualify as a charitable deduction, the contribution must go to a qualified organization, such as one of the following: American Cancer Society; American Legion; American Red Cross; Boy Scouts of America; Carnegie Institute; churches and synogogues; community chests; Four-H Clubs; hospitals; Navy Relief Society; Salvation Army; United Service Organizations (USO); YMCA; city or county civil defense organizations.

Organizations That Do Not Qualify

Contributions to the following are among those that have been held not deductible: American Institute of Certified Public Accountants; Anti-Cigarette League; Bar Association (but tax-exempt State Bar exercising governmental functions qualifies); fund to attract industry to a city; Scientific Temperance Foundation; organizations substantially active in propaganda influencing legislation. For a complete listing, the Treasury Department issues a booklet entitled "Cumulative List of Organizations—Contributions to which are Deductible," available from the Superintendent of Documents, Government Printing Office, Washington, D.C. 20402.

17

Managing the Insurance Program

17

Managing the Insurance Program

The proper planning and administration of an insurance program are essentials for any business operation. Insurance not only offers protection against loss, but a well conceived insurance program also helps to produce profits by maintaining control over a sizable business expense. Recognition of the all-important function of insurance is reflected in the fact that the task of acquiring insurance coverage is generally the responsibility of a major financial executive.

This chapter is not intended to produce insurance experts, but it will help a financial manager judge whether he is getting the most insurance for the least dollars.

INSURANCE MINIMIZES RISK

If there were no such thing as risk, there would certainly be no need for insurance. Unfortunately, since every acquisition entails a possibility of loss, risk is inescapable; it may be minimized, but never eliminated. Minimizing risk is the function of insurance.

How Insurance Spreads Risk

Suppose statistics show that every year one plant of every 1,000 is so gutted by fire as to be unusable. Suppose further that a company's plant and equipment are valued at $500,000. How much cash could be set aside each year to replace a loss by fire? $15,000? $30,000? $50,000? Even at $50,000/year, it would take 10 years to accumulate the full replacement value. Even then, fire might strike again the first week after starting up the new plant. The "law of averages" protects no single enterprise; a loss can occur any time, regardless of the absence or frequency of past losses.

Contrast this situation with the economy—not to mention the security, peace of mind, and enhanced credit standing—of insurance. Insurance can offer full protection at a fraction of the cost of the possible loss by combining a large number of assets

305

exposed to risk, thereby taking advantage of what statisticians call the "law of large numbers." The basis of this law is that under certain conditions, events will occur with a definite probability, so long as the number of events considered is large enough.

When Not to Use Insurance

The more severe the loss, the more important the insurance. It follows then that minor losses pose little if any need for insurance protection. What constitutes a minor loss depends, of course, on the financial strength of the particular enterprise. A firm with a billion dollars in assets might be justified in self-insuring a loss amounting to one percent, or $10,000,000, of its exposed value. A small company, on the other hand, may not be able to risk a loss of $1,000.

Insurance may also be unnecessary when the cost of premiums is exorbitant in relation to the protection gained. This sometimes occurs in insuring old equipment. For example, the cost of insuring an old truck may amount to 15 percent of the cost of replacing it. Or the saving between a $50-deductible insurance policy and a $100-deductible insurance policy may amount to $30 or more—60 percent of the possible recovery.

TYPES OF INSURANCE COMPANIES

As with many other situations, buying skill is important in purchasing insurance. The amount of protection and satisfaction depends on a knowledge of the financial and legal characteristics of insurers. There are four major types of insurance organizations: stock companies, mutual companies, reciprocals, and Lloyds groups.

Stock Company

A stock insurance company is organized like any other incorporated business. The capital by which the company functions is supplied by the sale of shares of stock, and the stockholders share in the profits or losses of the business.

Mutual Company

Mutual companies are organized without the use of capital stock; in place of stockholders there are policyholders. Like a stockholder, each policyholder is part owner of the business. Net earnings are sometimes distributed among the policyholders in the form of dividends, resulting in lower net-premium costs. In the event of an overall loss, however, a mutual company may levy an assessment upon the policyholders to offset the loss. Large, financially sound mutual insurance companies protect their policyholders from assessments by issuing only nonassessable policies. The policyholder may not enjoy such protection, however, when insured by a small mutual company with limited assets.

Reciprocal

The reciprocal is an association of insureds, usually of preferred risk, which is operated by a manager. The manager usually receives a percentage of the gross premiums, ranging from 25 to 40 percent, with which he pays the management expenses. The remaining portion of the premiums is used to meet loss expenses. Any amount left over is returned to the policyholders as dividends. Members are subject to additional assessments in the event of a net loss.

Lloyds Association

A Lloyds association is a group of individual underwriters, each liable for the amount of insurance for which he subscribes. The insurance is written by individuals, as contrasted with insurance by a mutual or stock insurance company. There are many Lloyds associations, all of which are patterned after Lloyds of London, the most prominent association.

The membership of a Lloyds association is quite selective and deposits are required for the security of policyholders. A central committee makes an annual audit of members' accounts. The necessity of upholding its reputation compels this association to see to the prompt payment of its members' obligations. Lloyds type of insurance is very flexible in that it is a negotiated price insurance and very unusual policies are written.

Relative Position of Each Type

Of total property and liability insurance outstanding, stock companies account for about 70 percent, mutual companies for about 26 percent, reciprocals for about 3.5 percent, and Lloyds associations for the remainder, or about 0.5 percent. In the life insurance field, mutuals are dominant, accounting for about 70 percent of all life insurance, while stock insurers have the remaining 30 percent.

WHAT TO CONSIDER IN SELECTING AN INSURANCE COMPANY

The deciding factor in the choice of an insurance carrier should be the insurer's specialization, his adaptability, his financial resources, and the quality of his management.

Specialization

Many insurers specialize in certain types of coverage and offer the advantages of greater experience in those lines. Some specialize in machine-building industries, others in textiles, still others in oil and gas, and so on. Factory mutuals have high underwriting standards and stress loss prevention. For those firms that qualify, the cost of protection is usually very low. Lloyds associations specialize in those companies that other insurers consider too risky. Firms engaged in unusual operations or firms with loss records can often get insurance coverage from Lloyds groups, though the premiums may be quite expensive.

Adaptability

Insurance policies are not always fixed; a buyer often arranges with an insurer to include provisions that meet special needs. It is also possible to bargain over rates, especially if the policy is a large one. The buyer may be able to include in the contract the stipulation that part of the premium will be refunded if losses do not go over a certain amount. He may also get a reduction in cost by agreeing to handle certain administrative details in processing claims. Other factors being equal, the willingness of an insurer to make special arrangements may be the deciding reason for the selection.

Reliability

Since the purpose of taking out insurance is to get a guarantee from an outside source that loss claims will be indemnified, the ability of the insuring company to pay becomes crucially important. Insurance brokers are not fair judges of the reliability of the many insurance organizations they represent. What the buyer needs is a source of reference for checking on the financial strength of a proposed insurance company and on the efficiency of its management and claims service.

Financial Strength

The most frequently used reference book is *Best's Insurance Guide with Key Ratings.* This guide uses the amount of policyholders' reserves and unattached surpluses and arrives at the following ratings of financial strength:

AAAAA = $25,000,000 or more surplus
AAAA+ = $20,000,000 to $25,000,000 surplus
AAAA = $15,000,000 to $20,000,000 surplus
AAA+ = $12,500,000 to $15,000,000 surplus
AAA   = $10,000,000 to $12,500,000 surplus
AA+   = $ 7,500,000 to $10,000,000 surplus
AA   = $ 5,000,000 to $ 7,500,000 surplus
BBBB+ = $ 3,750,000 to $ 5,000,000 surplus
BBBB = $ 2,500,000 to $ 3,750,000 surplus
BBB+ = $ 1,500,000 to $ 2,500,000 surplus
BBB   = $ 1,000,000 to $ 1,500,000 surplus
BB+   = $ 750,000 to $ 1,000,000 surplus
BB   = $ 500,000 to $ 750,000 surplus
CCC   = $ 250,000 to $ 500,000 surplus
CC   = $ 250,000 or less surplus

Sound Management

In assessing the quality of an insurance company's management, *Best's Insurance Guide* studies the company's underwriting practices, economy of management (ratio of expense to premiums), adequacy of reserve, net resources adequate to absorb unusual shocks, investments, diversification and liquidity to arrive at the following ratings:

A+ = Excellent
A = Excellent
B+ = Very Good
B = Good
C+ = Fairly Good
C = Fair

The ratings are then combined and read as follows: A:BBBB+ which means that the company has excellent management and a surplus of $3,750,000 to $5,000,000. Naturally, the size of the insurance company selected also depends very much on the size of the policy desired.

FROM WHOM SHOULD INSURANCE BE BOUGHT

A buyer can get insurance either from an independent broker or directly from the insuring company. There are certain advantages claimed for each type.

Buying from a Broker

Most property and liability insurance is purchased from independent brokers who generally represent several insuring companies. The insuring companies maintain no direct control over the business of the broker except to decide what policies they will accept or reject. The broker's clients are his and the insurer cannot appoint another broker to take over his accounts. Correspondence from the insurer to the insured customarily goes directly to the broker, who then contacts the insured.

Dual Capacity

Although the insurance broker is generally looked upon as the agent for the insured, in certain respects he is also the agent of the company. In the field of fire insurance, when a broker places insurance for a customer, he is the agent for the company which is thereby bound on its contract to the insured.

The broker is often deemed the agent of the insured by receiving insurance premiums, but when a company delivers a policy to a broker for the insured, it is deemed to have authorized the broker to receive payment on behalf of the company. Thereafter, if the broker absconds with the premium, the company cannot look to the insured for payment a second time, even though the policy provides that the broker is deemed the insured's agent.

Buying from the Company

Buying directly from the company, often called direct writing, is the traditional procedure for life insurance and is being used more frequently for property and liability insurance. The buyer may purchase his insurance directly from the company through the mail, or he can buy it from a commissioned salesman who is employed by the company to promote, solicit and enter into insurance agreements on behalf of the company. The salesman, therefore, is not an independent business man like the insurance broker; the policies he writes belong to the insurer, not to him.

Conflicting Viewpoints

There are conflicting viewpoints about the relative merits of buying insurance from brokers or from direct writers. The differences between the two procedures have narrowed in recent years. Direct writers now offer a wide variety of insurance through the use of subsidiaries, and insurers using independent brokers have adopted the central billing techniques and continuous policies inaugurated by the direct writers.

Arguments in Favor of the Independent Broker

Proponents of the independent broker system claim that their system offers the insurance buyer certain advantages. Among them are the following:

1. *Convenience.* Since an independent agency generally represents several insurers, sometimes as many as 20, he can offer a greater variety of coverage than the direct writer. This simplifies the insurance buying task for the customer.

2. *Better service.* An independent broker has incentive to serve a customer who is "his" exclusively.

3. *Better claims representation.* Usually, the broker's influence with the company will be greater than the individual policyholder's because of the total business that the broker places with the company. Some companies even allow some of their independent brokers to settle routine claims and thereby provide more prompt claim service.

4. *Greater knowledge.* Because he deals with a variety of policies, the independent broker often has a greater knowledge of insurance than the direct writing agent, who more often writes only a limited line. Most local brokers can be relied on for continuous, authoritative answers to questions relating to all types of insurance.

Factors in Favor of the Direct Writer

Proponents of the direct writing system cite the following advantages for their method of distribution:

1. *Lower cost.* The premiums offered by the direct writing employee are usually considerably lower because of the economies made possible by direct contact with the insured. These economies result from the use of continuous policies that need not be rewritten each year, direct billing through the use of electronic data processing equipment, and reduced commissions on the purchase of policies.

2. *Good service.* The direct writer has a chance to become a specialist instead of dividing his attention among several insurers. Also, centralized services for routine office tasks free his time, and make advertising increase his sales effectiveness, leaving him more time for customer service.

PROPERTY AND LIABILITY INSURANCE

Regardless of the type of insurance coverage a buyer can find several insurers eager to sell a policy. The problem is not one of insurance availability but of gaining an understanding of the many varieties of insurance coverage. Even the "package" policies are complex and many-sided. Here are a few of the basic types of insurance that every firm needs for protection against property damage, loss of earning power, and liability claims.

Fire Insurance

Many states prescribe a standard fire policy by statute. The purpose of such statutes is (a) to protect the insured against obscure or tricky language, (b) to secure uniformity in insurance contracts, and (c) to protect insurance companies from fraud by their local agents.

The standard fire insurance policy on a building indemnifies not only against direct loss from actual burning caused by fire and lightning or explosion, but also against damage due to smoke, water, chemical fire extinguishers, destruction by firemen, or collapse of parts of a building. A policy insuring the building's content covers the same risks.

For an additional premium, "extended coverage" can be purchased. It protects against damage by hail, windstorm, explosion without fire, fallen aircraft, riot and civil commotion, malicious mischief and vandalism, breakage of glass, collapse of floors, walls or roofs, etc. The standard fire policy does not compensate for the cost of demolition or the cost of replacement. For this additional coverage, the insured must pay additional premiums and have demolition and increased cost of construction endorsements added to the policy. The standard fire policy also includes losses of accounts, bills, evidence of debt, and so on.

"Hostile" and "Friendly" Fires

A "hostile" fire is a fire that escapes from its intended place and becomes a destructive force. A "friendly" fire is a fire that burns where it is supposed to burn and yet causes some destruction of property. Standard fire policies generally pay only for losses caused by a hostile fire.

Example 1. Insured & Co.'s baking oven is damaged by overheating. The damage is not recoverable under the standard fire policy.

Example 2. An acetylene torch is used for welding in the insured's plant. Sparks from the torch fall on merchandise causing damage by fire. The loss is recoverable. It is possible to have an extended coverage endorsement attached to a fire policy to cover property destroyed by friendly fires. The additional cost is nominal.

The Coinsurance Clause

In most areas, coinsurance clauses appear in fire and other insurance policies that provide protection against property loss. It requires the owner to carry insurance equal to a stated percentage of the actual value of his property—generally, replacement cost at the time of loss less depreciation. If he doesn't carry this percentage, his recovery is cut proportionately. The following illustrates this point:

> EXAMPLE: The owner of a building worth $200,000 had a fire policy that contained an 80 percent coinsurance clause. This means that he had to carry at least $160,000 in insurance (80 percent times $200,000). Instead, the owner carried $80,000 or 50 percent of what he was required to carry. The result was that when a fire caused a $20,000 damage to the building, he collected only $10,000.

The purpose of the coinsurance clause is to prevent insurance buyers from insuring only a small part of the value of their property. Since partial losses occur much more frequently than total losses, premiums would have to be raised substantially if the general practice was to insure only a small portion of the property value. Rather than raise rates or provide a differential rate, insurers generally use the coinsurance clause to discourage under-insurance by sharply reducing recovery in event of loss.

Grounds for Suspending Insurance

Occupancy of the insured building is one of the requirements of the standard fire policy. If the insured leaves the building unoccupied and unattended for more than 60 days, the standard fire policy stipulates that insurance will be suspended for any time exceeding this period. To maintain uninterrupted coverage, he must get the insuring company's written endorsement containing coverage during the vacancy period. The oral assurances of an insurance agent is not enough.

Standard policies also include a fraud and concealment clause that generally stipulates that the policy is void if the insured has willfully concealed or misrepresented any material fact or circumstance concerning the insurance, or is guilty of any fraud or false swearing, whether before or after the loss. However, the insurer must show that the misrepresentation is both false and material, that he was in fact mislead thereby. If he would have granted the policy regardless, the court will usually not permit him to void the policy.

Boiler and Machinery Insurance

If a firm uses boilers, machinery, or pressure vessels, it must protect against the possibility of eruption, rupture, or explosion. It must also acquire protection against such an occurrence.

A boiler and machinery policy serves both purposes by automatically including regular inspections, written reports on the inspections, and follow-up by the insurance company when their inspections reveal faulty conditions and mechanical defects. Boiler and machinery insurance also protects against the following losses: (a) damage to the insured's property, (b) liability for damage to the property of others, (c) liability for bodily injury of others, (d) expediting expenses and (e) legal expenses.

One of the prime considerations in purchasing boiler and machinery insurance should be the quality, competency, expertness, and breadth of the scope of the inspection and engineering department of the insurance company under consideration. Qualified inspectors will frequently offer recommendations that lengthen the useful life of the boiler, and sometimes they will suggest ways to reduce fuel costs. The periodic inspections and the savings resulting from the inspector's recommendations are often worth many times the annual premium payments.

Inland Marine Insurance

Inland marine insurance provides protection against loss of goods that are stored away from the company's premises or that are in transit. It includes (1) insurance on goods in transit by rail, express, mail, motor truck, aircraft, and partly by water; (2) insurance on certain types of goods, wherever they may be, against any risk, even though not actually in the course of transportation; (3) liability insurance to protect transportation carriers, warehousemen, processors, and others from the consequences of legal liability.

Inland marine policies are known as "floaters" because they protect property frequently moved around, regardless of location, except where certain places may be specifically excluded in the policy. Some floaters are named-peril contract and others are all-risk policies.

Business Interruption Insurance

This form of insurance pays for loss of income due to physical damage to business property. A fire policy and other policies will pay only for the property damage incurred. But the indirect or consequential loss that results from business interruption following the fire is often much greater than the amount of the direct property loss.

Business interruption insurance, in the event of a fire or some specified event that causes a plant shutdown or discontinuance of business activities, reimburses the insured for certain continuing expenses and estimated profits. The amount of insurance coverage is established on the basis of business records for the previous year and an estimate of profits and certain expenses for the current year.

Public Liability

The firm is expected to maintain a safe place for customers and employees. If someone gets hurt because of a safety hazard on the premises or because of an action by an employee, the company may face a liability judgement of several hundred thousand dollars. Such a judgement could wipe out the entire assets of many firms.

In buying general liability insurance, there is a choice of (1) named peril liability policies, (2) comprehensive general liability insurance policy, and (3) package insurance.

Named Peril Liability Policies

This type of insurance requires one policy for each peril or each location and is therefore the most expensive (many policies instead of consolidated coverage) and the least efficient (serious gaps in coverage may occur). This type of insurance has little applicability for most businesses.

Comprehensive General Liability Insurance

This policy offers comprehensive liability coverage. Here's what it does:

1. It embraces all of the separate lines of named peril liability and all blanket hazards in all locations in all operations. (A "blanket" policy is one that "blankets" all locations for a given peril.)
2. It affords excellent contingent (unknown hazard) protection, thereby protecting from contingent liability that at present is unknown and undistinguishable.
3. It includes, if desired, liability coverage against the hazards of ownership, use, and maintenance of owned, hired, and non-owned vehicles and automobiles operated by employees.
4. It offers the following services and protection for covered claims:
   A. Investigation of the claim.
   B. Out of court settlement of the claim within policy limits (if there is liability as determined by the investigation).
   C. Defense of suit based on claim.
   D. Payment of judgment within policy limits.
   E. Prosecution of appeal in connection with an adverse judgement (subject to election by the insured) and representation of insured upon an appeal by claimant.
   F. Payment of premium for bond on appeal.

     G. Payment of all court costs.

     H. Payment of interest on the judgement.

Exclusions in a comprehensive general liability policy typically include workmen's compensation (this peril is covered by workmen's compensation insurance); liability for ownership, maintenance, and use of aircraft and watercraft; damage to property of others that is in the insured firm's custody; liability resulting from blasting or nuclear operations or from war.

Package Insurance

While the comprehensive general liability insurance policy may be called a package policy, the latest trend in packaged policies is to combine general liability, boiler machinery, property loss (fire, extended coverage, and so forth), crime, automobile, and inland marine coverages.

The annual premium for a comprehensive general liability policy is usually less costly than the combined premium of the separate named peril liability policies, and the packaged liability coverage is usually still less costly.

Workmen's Compensation Insurance

State laws require a firm to indemnify an employee injured in the course of his employment. The company must provide him not only with medical, surgical, and hospital care, but also with a weekly payment based on a percentage of his income. To protect itself against this type of loss, a firm must obtain a workmen's compensation policy. There is a Universal Standard Workmen's Compensation and Employer's Liability policy used in 47 of the 50 states. The policy's protection is in two parts, A and B:

    1. Coverage A includes the bodily injury liability and benefits that accrue to a qualified injured employee under workmen's compensation laws. The policy is so written that the workmen's compensation laws of a given state automatically become a part of the insurance contract.

    2. Coverage B is known as employer's liability. It includes all employer liability arising out of and in the course of employment not covered in Coverage A. This coverage protects a firm from liability suits and judgements brought by employees for accidents not covered by workmen's compensation or occupational disease laws.

How Premiums Are Computed

Premiums are based on payroll, broken down to show payroll amounts by employment classification. Rates vary from less than 0.1 percent of payroll for safe occupations (clerical and professional) to 25 percent for the most hazardous occupations (certain types of construction).

GETTING FULL MILEAGE FROM THE PROPERTY AND LIABILITY INSURANCE DOLLAR

Buying Deductible Insurance

Using an "inspection" fire insurance underwriter appraising a building and its contents separately are ways to cut costs. Some policies contain duplicate coverage. The right approach can save 15 percent or more on the annual cost of insurance.

Consider Deductible Insurance

Most experienced insurance buyers insure only against major losses that they cannot bear financially. Since most claims are small, the frequency of claims decreases as the amount of the claims increases; deductible insurance eliminates small, high-overhead, nuisance claims. If a buyer can absorb, say, a $20,000 loss, it will generally be to his advantage to take out a $20,000 deductible policy.

Modified Arrangement

A modification of the deductible arrangement is the franchise. A franchise clause is a policy stipulating a deductible amount. If a loss equal to or exceeding this amount occurs, the insurer pays the entire amount of the loss. Franchises are used more often in physical damage insurance than in liability insurance.

The insured must consider more than lower premium costs in calculating whether a deductible or a franchise offers savings over the long run. The basic question is whether the *net costs* will be less. The answer requires detailed information on losses over several years. Though deductibles generally provide net savings (this is almost invariably the case with automobile insurance), complete data and expert knowledge are required to know when to use them.

Buy Fire Insurance from Inspection Underwriters

There are two kinds of fire insurance underwriters: non-inspection and inspection. The non-inspection underwriters base rates on rating scales issued by standard rating organizations. The inspection underwriters, however, operate as a syndicate and conduct a more frequent and detailed inspection of the insured's property. They generally insure only fire-resistive buildings equipped with sprinkler systems. Since they are more selective than regular fire insurance underwriters and since their periodic inspections serve as an effective loss-prevention program, their rates offer worthwhile savings.

Use Appraisals to Avoid Over-Insuring or Under-Insuring

Very few insured properties have the exact amount of insurance they need. The best way to find out the right amount of insurance is to get the property appraised. Appraisals are normally made by insurance companies, architects, or professional engineers.

1. Insurance companies have competent appraisers, but their interests may not always be identical with the insured. When using insurance companies for appraisals, it is best to call in a professional appraisal engineer occasionally to provide for a system of checks and balances and to correct any errors that might have been made.

2. Architects are familiar with current square-foot and cubic-foot constructions costs of similar buildings and facilities, and can therefore serve as able appraisers.

3. Professional appraisal engineers are generally the most reliable. They are experts in appraising buildings and equipment. In case of a dispute or arbitration over insurable values at the time of loss, they will represent the owner, whereas insurance company appraisers will represent the insuring company. Their services are rather expensive, but this should not be a deterrent to their use.

Items to Include and Exclude

In appraising a building for insurance purposes, the cost of footings, foundations, and on-ground floor slabs should be included, because in the event of a total loss, it is unlikely that they could be reused. Also include architect's fees, since such services are necessary to replace or restore a building.

Exclude from the value of the building such non-insurable or excluded items as cost of underground sewers, pipes, drains, and tanks; excavations and backfilling; objects outside the buildings such as flag poles, fences, sidewalks, drives, and retaining walls, plus site development.

But include in the value of the building all fixed or attached items, for the insurance rate on buildings is approximately half that on contents. Insurance companies are flexible in classifying what is building and what is contents, and it behooves the insured to look into this matter. Any item that is securely fixed to a part of the building can usually be classified in the building category.

Insuring for Cash Value or Replacement Cost

The firm can insure a building either for actual cash value, which means replacement value less depreciation (also called actual value, sound value, actual sound value, or depreciated value), or for replacement cost or undepreciated or current value.

To determine the insurable cash value of a particular building, follow these steps: (1) determine current replacement cost, (2) determine the depreciation and non-insurable or excluded items, and (3) subtract the latter from the yearly adjusted replacement cost.

The current replacement cost of a building can be a part of an appraisal, by applying cost indexes to the original construction cost, or by applying a square-foot or cubic-foot cost of comparable buildings. Insuring for replacement cost is vastly superior to insuring for cash value; it makes it possible to repair or rebuild the same structure with new materials.

Check to Avoid Duplicate Coverage

Duplicate coverage means duplicate premiums. It also hinders settlement when loss occurs; sometimes each insurer tries to make its policy excess over the other, or to deny liability altogether. A periodic review should be made to uncover laps in coverage. The following are possible overlaps:

Boiler and Machinery Policy

The extended coverage section of a fire insurance policy gives insurance protection against furnace explosion and explosion of accumulated gases in the combustion chamber or chimney passages of any furnace or boiler. The insured can eliminate this coverage from the boiler insurance policy. If he has a comprehensive general liability insurance policy for an amount equal to or exceeding the boiler and machinery policy, he can eliminate from the boiler and machinery policy the bodily injury coverage.

Fire Insurance Policy

If contents securely fastened to the building have been classified in the insurable value category of the building, they should not be listed or carried in the insurable value schedule of contents.

Transfer Risk

It is possible to transfer the risk of loss to somebody else. Automobile insurance for leased vehicles should be handled by the lessor. He can probably get cheaper rates because he is a bigger buyer. When using leased buildings or machinery or outside contractors, transfer the insurance risk to the owner or to the supplier of the service.

Self-Insure

A large firm that is willing to administer a program of risk management, can be its own insurer for a part of potential losses. This arrangement is quite different from non-insurance; it involves setting aside a separate fund—partly from saved insurance premiums—to meet losses. For this procedure to be practical, a business must have many separate units to spread the risk and to enable a reasonably accurate estimate of losses. Though large companies can make greater use of self-insurance, small companies can also save money by self-insuring those risks that are scattered. Even the smallest company will generally find it worthwhile to self-insure its plate glass.

Tighten Control Over Workmen's Compensation

Every employer who must pay the cost of covering his workers must be vitally concerned with the cost—a cost that continually edges up as rates for workmen's compensation are increased.

Here are some questions and answers to help control losses and cut costs while maintaining proper coverage:

1. What can be done to control rising losses from workmen's compensation resulting from poor "experience" rating?

   A. Use the free services of the insurance company's safety engineers. Make use of their experience and knowledge on safety to find out the causes for the increase in accidents.

   B. Establish an active safety committee to make sure that supervisors and rank-and-file employees are aware of unnecessary losses resulting from accidents.

   C. Consider hiring an industrial nurse. In some states, insurance costs are lower if one is on the staff.

   D. Have employees take physical examinations before they are hired. This assures a healthy staff and less chance of getting an employee who has disabilities.

   E. If the insurance company is not providing good loss prevention service and follow-up on court cases, get another company. Ask them to show what they can do to control losses caused by accidents.

2. What can be done to cut compensation costs besides cutting accidents?

Here are some suggestions from which to choose the ones that best suit particular needs and situations.

   A. Look into the differences in costs between insurance sources: self-insurance, mutual, stock.

   B. Check into a *retrospective rating plan,* which is really *cost-plus insurance.* The insurance company provides the usual services, but the final cost depends on the actual maximum and minimum losses.

   C. Have insurance rates reviewed. It is possible to pay more than required because of improper insurance classification. A better rate may be available because of changes in economic conditions, or because the firm has taken on new products or operations.

   D. Make sure that policies are combined for the greatest possible discounts and see that there is only one compensation carrier.

   E. When reporting employee salaries to the insurance company, don't give any more information than is necessary. Don't include gross payroll or overtime payments in the report, because by this error the insured could end up paying more than required.

3. If an affiliated or subsidiary corporation is established, will it be protected under the present compensation policy?

A. No. A policy covers only the employer listed under the insured name. The insured should report at once any newly created or acquired companies, subsidiaries, or affiliated corporations.

4. If an independent contractor is hired, should the financial manager insist that he show certificates proving that he has purchased workmen's compensation insurance?

A. Absolutely! In most states the firm is held liable if the contractor doesn't have any insurance. The company would be paying a lot more for insurance coverage because the insurance company will include the payroll of the uninsured independent contractor with internal earnings when it computes the total premium.

5. Is there anything that can be done?

A. Yes, follow up the insurance carrier's effort to settle cases. If the policy is a retrospective rating, the carrier won't worry about the size of settlements.

B. Yes, make it clear to the carrier that witnesses will be available to testify in the company's behalf if cases go to court. This strengthens the adjuster's hand in settling cases. Few cases go beyond the hearing stage, but the company's willingness to fight large settlements can make a big difference.

C. Yes, keep a list of the attorneys for plaintiffs in unsettled cases. Very often, a lawyer who specializes in getting fat settlements will receive word-of-mouth recommendation among employees and end up with a large clientele. These are the cases to concentrate on or the attorney will think the company is a "soft touch."

GROUP HEALTH INSURANCE

In addition to protecting the firm against loss from property damage and from general liability suits, carriers now provide various types of insurance protection for individual employees. Group health insurance covers more employees than any other type of insurance. Though it was introduced more than 50 years ago, modified policies and new policies are continually becoming available.

Four Major Policies

There are available four major types of health insurance policies: (1) basic service plan, (2) comprehensive major medical—first dollar coverage, (3) supplementary major medical, and (4) superimposed supplementary major medical.

Basic service plan. This is the Blue Cross-Blue Shield type policy. The work *basic* indicates that this plan takes care of basic needs and is not comprehensive. Some of its distinguishing characteristics are: (1) limited number of days of hospital coverage—usually 180 days, (2) a 30-day waiting period before re-entry in hospital after 18 days have been used, (3) semiprivate ward accommodations, (4) no deductibles, (5) treatment of allergy, common cold, and so forth, excluded. Though this plan provides excellent basic coverage, it is not adequate for serious illnesses.

Comprehensive Major Medical (First Dollar Coverage)

As its name indicates, this plan offers very broad coverage starting with the first dollar of expense. It provides both basic and comprehensive coverage. Some of its distinguishing characteristics are: (1) 100 percent of the first $1,000 expenses paid in full, (2) coinsurance that pays 80 percent of all expenses over the first $1,000 with top limits of $5,000, $10,000, $20,000 or higher, (3) no waiting period for re-entry into hospital, (4) treatment for allergies, common colds included, (5) mental illness and psychiatric treatment included whether in hospital or not.

Supplementary Major Medical

The supplementary major medical plan insures only the catastrophic part of medical expenses. The coverages include hospital, surgical, medical, laboratory, and diagnostic services. Some of its distinguishing features include (1) large beginning dollar deductible—up to $1,000 or higher, (2) coinsurance that pays 80 percent of all expenses over the deductible, (3) top coverage of $20,000 or higher, (4) no waiting period for re-entry into hospital, (5) treatment for allergies, common cold, and mental illness included. For people who can afford the initial medical bills, this is the most economical type of health insurance.

Superimposed Supplementary Major Medical

This policy is identical to the supplementary major medical policy except that the deductible is "all of the expenses that will be paid by the Basic Service Plan" over which it is superimposed. Sometimes, to lower the premiums and to prevent small nuisance claims, the deductible is written as "all of the expenses that will be paid by the basic service plan plus $100 out of pocket money." When a superimposed supplementary major medical policy is purchased in conjunction with a basic service plan, the employee actually has a hybrid comprehensive major medical coverage.

The field of health insurance is so fluid that buyers need not purchase a canned type of policy. They can formulate unique plans, coverages, and specifications. Most commercial insurance companies, and even Blue Cross-Blue Shield to some extent, will sell any type of policy or coverage.

Advantage of Two-Year Premium Rate

It is wise to avoid being misled into buying insurance with a low initial first-year cost, only to find the rates raised materially after the first year. The actual experience of insurance companies is that the first year is a high acquisition cost year, and costs each year thereafter tend to increase up to the tenth year. If the age and sex grouping of employees remains constant, premiums should also decrease. To get the contract, however, some insurance companies charge less than their exact first-year acquisition costs, then increase rates after the first year. To avoid facing this situation, it is best to ask for a level premium rate for two years.

Ask for an Accounting of Losses or Claims

In the specifications for purchasing group insurance, the financial manager should ask for an accounting of dollars paid out in losses or claims. The firm should pay only for its own losses or claims and not for some other groups' losses. Keeping track of loss experience, and premiums will verify the fairness of the rate charged.

Good management also dictates that the carrier supply the insurer with complete information on net cost, including gross premiums and dividends, losses or claims, reserves, and administrative costs (i.e., retention costs). The proportion spent for administrative costs ranges from 40 percent to 5 percent, the average being 17 percent to 10 percent. The 17 percent is usually the first-year acquisition cost, with the percentage declining until the tenth year when it usually stabilizes at 10 percent. However, because of the volume of insurance purchased, large industries have been able to reduce the retention factor to as low as 7 percent the first year and 5 percent after the tenth year of insuring with the same company.

Decide whether to administer the plan. The insurance company will usually give the insured a premium discount of from one to two percent if it is self-administered. Whether to do this or not will depend partly on the scope and complexity of the plan. Some companies have found their administration costs running to five percent and more for certain complicated plans.

WHAT DISABILITY INSURANCE CAN DO FOR YOU

How long should a company continue to pay an executive his salary when he becomes disabled for an extended period? One month? Six months? One year? And regardless of length of time, should it give him his whole salary or only part? If only part, how much should his salary be reduced?

To avoid facing these perplexing and costly decisions, more firms are now carrying long-term disability insurance. This insurance serves two purposes: (1) It takes care of needed employees; (2) lets an employee know exactly what he'll receive should he become disabled.

Basis of Coverage

The insured can buy long-term disability insurance on one of the following bases:

Salaried Group

This covers all employees who are paid for working during a set period—weekly, biweekly, etc. (Hourly workers are usually considered under collective bargaining agreements).

Organizational Level

This covers employees only above a certain level—division managers or foremen and above, for example.

Salary Level

This covers employees above a specified salary level; many plans include only employees making $7,500 or more.

What Does It Cost?

Cost of disability insurance is determined by the following:

Age

Quite naturally, the older the age of the group, the higher the premium rate, though this factor is of minor importance under age 50.

Amounts of Indemnity at Risk

Employees receive a percentage of their salaries. The higher the percentage, the higher the premium.

Length of Waiting Period

The employee receives no benefits until a certain time has elapsed following the date of disability. The shorter the waiting period, the higher the rate. It is possible to tie in the waiting period with management's policy of paying a disabled employee's salary for a period before the disability insurance takes over.

Length of Benefit Period

The longer the benefits are paid for a given disability, the higher the rate.

These and other factors preclude the citation of specific costs. Generally, however, the cost will run one-half percent or more of the covered payroll for a policy with these specifications: a six-months' waiting period; payment of 50 percent of salary to a maximum of $150 a week; a lifetime benefit period for accident; a two-year benefit period for sickness.

GROWING NEED FOR DIRECTORS' AND OFFICERS' LIABILITY INSURANCE

There has been—and will probably continue to be—an increase in suits by dissident stockholders alleging negligence of some sort or other. The charges range from inefficient or lax administration causing unnecessary losses, to unauthorized or imprudent loans and unwarranted dividend payments.

These suits are not based on directors' or officers' dishonesty, fraud, or criminal acts, but on their personal liability for general negligence, error, or omission in managing corporate affairs—their own wrongful acts or failure to discover the wrongful acts of others. When stockholders' charges are substantiated, the awards by the courts often are sizable. And even if the charges are not proved, the legal fees for defending the suit often run high.

If a director is held liable for his official act (or failure to act), the corporation isn't necessarily relieved of responsibility. Since directors who act in their official capacity are agents of the corporation, (assuming no laws to the contrary), the corporation might very well be held liable for its directors' wrongful acts.

Bases of Stockholders' Suits

Here are some of the reasons why dissident stockholders sue corporations. The risks described are covered under a standard directors' and officers' liability insurance policy.
1. Misstatement of the company's financial condition.
2. Overstepping of authority under the corporate charter or by-laws.
3. Failure to press claims against persons or companies which result in loss to the corporation.
4. Compensation for executives alleged to be excessive.
5. Unnecessary losses to the corporation caused by inefficient or lax administration.
6. Failure of directors to exercise diligence or show good faith in their official capacity.
7. Failure to reveal vital and material facts to stockholders.
8. Unwarranted payment of dividend.
9. Advancing loans that were imprudent or unauthorized.
10. Conflict of interest with the corporation.
11. Incurring penalties for income tax.

Features of the Policy

The policy has two parts: The first part provides for reimbursing the company for any amount expended by it to indemnify officers and directors; the second part provides for direct indemnity to officers and directors for a loss sustained.

The Deductible and Coinsurance Clauses

Most policies contain a minimum deductible amount—usually $25,000—and a coinsurance clause whereby the company receives 95 percent of any loss above the deductible, and carries 5 percent of the loss itself.

An example would be: A company has coverage of $1,000,000 and $25,000 deductible. It is sued and must pay $225,000. It would collect $190,000 on its insurance policy ($225,000 minus $35,000 i.e. $25,000 + 5 percent times $200,000). Its net cost on the judgement would be $35,000.

Excluded Claims

These are some of the claims that the policy will not cover: (1) libel or slander; (2) damages sustained on account of a public offering; (3) anything more than money damages; (4) affirmative dishonesty or actual intent to deceive or defraud. The exclusion of libel or slander can be covered in a general liability policy for both the corporation and the director/officer. Dishonest or fraudulent acts by an officer or director may be insured under a fidelity bond.

Excluded businesses

Generally, the following types of business either cannot obtain, or have difficulty obtaining, director/officer insurance: aircraft manufacturers; airlines, steel companies, real estate syndicates, finance companies, drug manufacturers, and construction firms.

Premium Rates

Rates vary according to the size of the corporation, number of senior executives, and amount of coverage. A three-year premium for a $1,000,000 policy ranges from $10,-000 to $30,000.

18

The Data Processing Payoff

327

18

The Data Processing Payoff

‖‖

ORGANIZING THE DATA PROCESSING FUNCTION

The data processing function grows in size and importance every year. As it grows it becomes more difficult to fit into the organization chart. In its infancy the "tab" department was a minor function found in one of two places on the organization chart. It reported either to the head of the accounting function or to the head of administrative services. The highest data processing man was generally three or more levels removed from the president or general manager. This relationship has changed as shown by Before and After in Figure 18-1.

The change in status is due to two factors—growth of size and growth of breadth of applications. The change in size is easy to understand. The data processing budget has grown to the point where it must be under the control of a senior officer. The increase in applications outside the accounting area has made data processing a company-wide function. Production control and sales statistics were major applications after payroll, payables and receivables. As the major functions of the firm became more dependent on data processing it could no longer remain hidden in the lower levels of the financial organization.

Guidelines for Data Processing Organization

The nature of programming and systems development dictates the guidelines for structuring a data processing organization. Discussed below are the major ones common to all industries and organizations.

   1. Allow for the idea of dual leadership. Systems development is a project-oriented effort. Project groups are formed, expanded, contracted, and disbanded as the situation demands. Often members of a project report to different supervisors. While they are members of the project, they have a

329

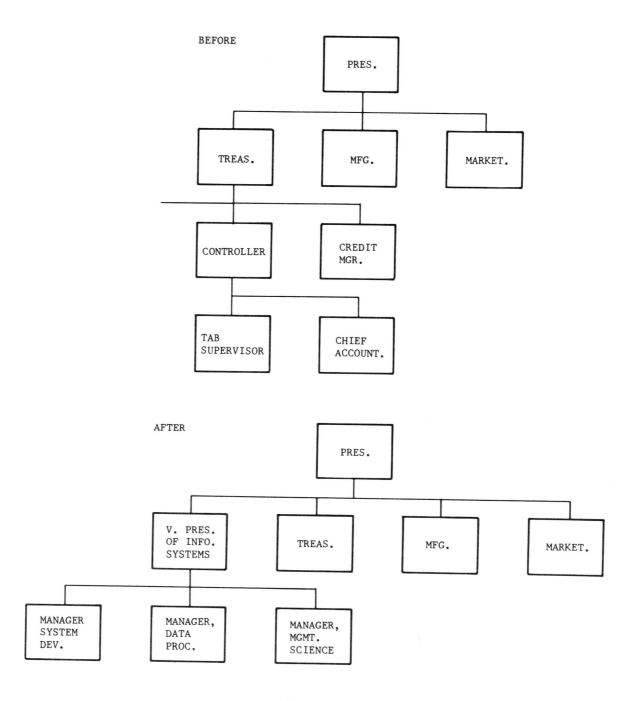

Figure 18-1
Organization Charts Showing the Growth of Data Processing

project leader. Thus any one programmer or analyst may have two supervisors at the same time—an administrative supervisor and a project supervisor.

2. Maintain separation between development and operations. Computer installations can be "tested-to-death." This results when the man charged with developing new systems is given control over systems which are currently operating. The internal priorities are then set and inevitably new crash programs take precedence over routine operations. Test time on the computer rises and output falls. To prevent this clear organizational lines must be drawn which separate development from operations.

3. Tie project teams to the organization chart. Where project teams cross departmental lines, the project leader may be in a position where he does not have a supervisor. Project teams floating free within the organization must be prevented. Figure 18-2 shows an example of what should be done. Project leader must report to one of the department managers. In Figure 18-2 the Department A manager was chosen since most of the project team was from his department.

4. Use committees to initiate programs and projects but not to supervise them. The committee is often able to cross organizational boundaries and reach consensus on what should be done. The committee, however, is the worst possible way to get things done. Committees tend to seek compromise solutions which make double and triple work for those who carry out the assigned work.

Fitting Data Processing into Large Organizations

Simple rules or guidelines are difficult to follow in complex organizations. The financial manager may be faced with some or all of the following questions:

1. Should branch offices or plants have separate data processing groups?
2. Should branch or plant data processing groups report to the data processing manager or to the branch or plant manager?
3. As data processing systems are integrated into manufacturing operations should control and responsibility for them be taken away from the data processing manager and given to manufacturing management?
4. Are all new systems best developed by the data processing department, or do some user departments have to develop their own systems?

To fit the guidelines to real situations, questions like these must be answered. The proper answers are listed below.

#1 & 2. The home office data processing group should have control and responsibility for the systems employed in branches. The operation of data processing equipment in branches should be under the control of the branch manager. If a branch becomes large enough for its own systems and programming effort, it might be limited to systems maintenance. If, however, a corporation decentralizes and each division has profit respon-

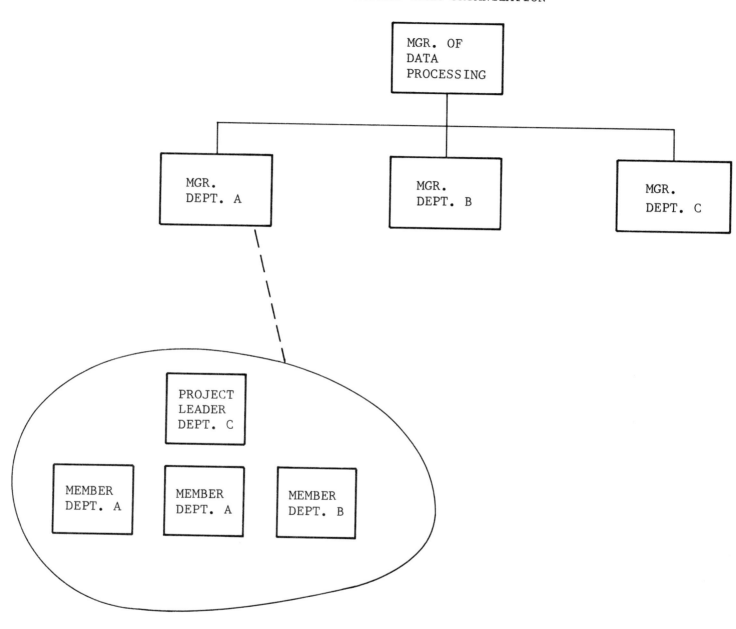

Figure 18-2
Project Team Organization

sibility, the central data processing group must become a coordinating group. Each division manager should be free to develop his own data processing team. The corporate group's effort then becomes advisory and liaison.

#3. Data processing is becoming a primary means of communication and control in many companies. Systems have been installed which provide on-line production control, process control, and even cost control. The operations of such systems cannot be left to "outside specialists." The data processing people cannot operate such systems since they are "outside specialists." They must train manufacturing personnel to handle input data, interpret output, and take corrective action. During the installation phase the responsibilities would be broken down as follows:

Manufacturing	*Data Processing*
1. Provide personnel for training in operation	1. Conduct systems analysis and prepare systems design
2. Provide systems specifications to data processing	2. Choose hardware to be installed
	3. Design and test programs required for system
	4. Train manufacturing personnel

Once the system is operational the responsibilities would be as follows:

Manufacturing	*Data Processing*
1. Handle all routine operations	1. Oversee technical aspects of operation
2. Investigate errors and exceptions	2. Provide liaison with data processing hardware manufacturer and their technical support
3. Initiate all requests for improvements or alterations to the system	3. Supervise alterations and improvements of the system

#4. Situations exist where user departments are in the best position to supervise their own systems development. Listed below are conditions which indicate consideration of decentralized systems development.
  A. If the system functions on hardware which is separate from and not similar to the firm's general purpose computers.
  B. If the installation is physically isolated from the main data processing installation.
  C. If the user's technology and specific problems are unique in comparison to those found in the rest of the firm.

Organizing Inside the Data Processing Group

Two fundamental approaches to organization are possible in the data processing department. Since the department is a service group, it can be organized in accordance

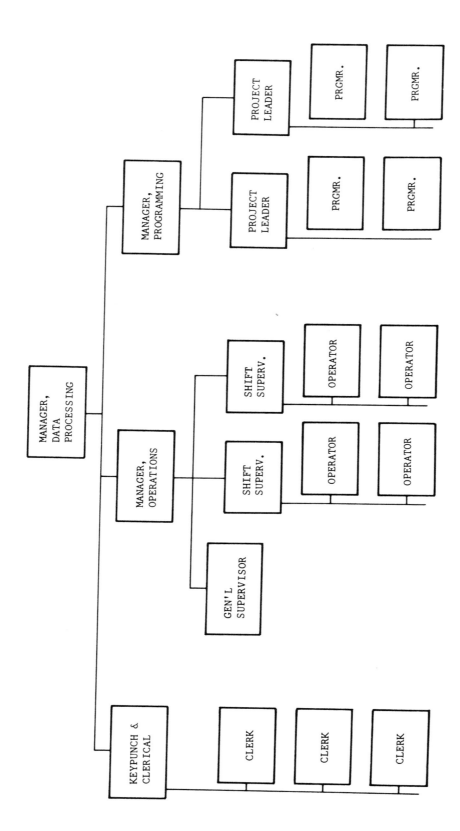

Figure 18-3
Typical Small Organization

with who is served. This is termed application-oriented organization. Since several types of work are done in data processing, the department can be organized based on internal function. This is called function-oriented organization. In practice most firms use a combination of the two approaches. For example, the operation of the computers (production) is often centralized while the systems group is broken down by user or type of application. As a general rule the type of organization varies with the size of the department. Three different organizations are described below, based on the size of the data processing effort. Though the organizations described are typical, their real purpose is to illustrate the factors bearing on the decision of how to organize.

Small Size

The chart in Figure 18-3 typifies the small computer installation. The total staff size is about twenty people. The computer equipment is centrally located at the company headquarters and processes a wide range of applications. Because of the simple situation—one computer with one general mission—the organization is functional. The clerical effort is consolidated with keypunch. The second supervisor is in charge of the operation of the hardware. The third supervisor is responsible for all software including applications and systems.

To provide focus on particular applications the programming effort is sub-divided into project teams. These are flexible groups which can respond to changes in the organization's needs. When individual projects are initiated, a project leader performs the feasibility study and systems analysis himself. Once a new project is cleared for programming, programmers are assigned to work under the project leader. As the project nears completion most of the programming effort is shifted to newer projects. It is left to the project leader and the remaining staff to complete the testing and install the system.

Medium Size

This organization chart (Figure 18-4) shows a second layer of supervisors two levels below the data processing manager. This organization includes about fifty people. The computer hardware includes one or two computers at the central data processing installation. The Western Branch represents a separate computer at a geographically isolated location. It provides special information and applications for the Western Branch. It could also represent a special purpose installation such as inventory control, credit management, or production scheduling.

The Western Branch manager represents a departure from functional organization. The importance of the Western Branch application is highlighted and organizationally guaranteed by placing it under its own manager. Within the Western Branch is found the major functional groupings found in the small installation of Figure 18-3. Thus the organization is a combination of application orientation and functional orientation.

The other major change from the small to medium size is the separation of systems from programming. Since project development requires passing new projects from systems

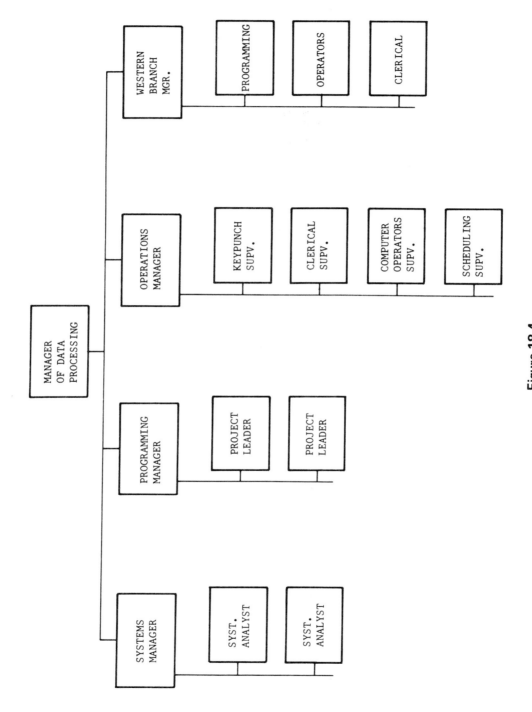

Figure 18-4
Typical Medium-Saized Organization

to programming, care must be taken to delineate responsibilities of each group. The systems department is responsible for all feasibility studies, systems design, user training and conversion, and systems specifications. Normally the systems department turns over to programming a detailed set of specifications which describe the programs to be written. The systems analyst also designs tests which will verify that the new programs meet the specifications. Pre-planned tests are the major means of quality control available to the systems department. The programming group first takes the specifications and generates a working program. Then by running the pre-planned test data through the programs, the programmers can test the accuracy of the results.

Project teams combining systems and programming personnel are still possible in this organization. They should be encouraged since they focus attention on the problems at hand. As pointed out in the Guidelines for Data Processing Organization, project leaders must be assigned to report to one of the line managers. This keeps lines of responsibility clear even though the interpersonal relationships become complex.

Large Size

When a data processing group reaches 100 people, its corporate mission is even more complicated than when it was Medium Sized. As shown in Figure 18-5, the simple functions of keypunch, machine, and systems found in Small Size no longer appear on the chart. Such job titles would appear under the block "Manager, Division A" since the organization has been decentralized. Each division has its own self-sufficient group.

The other major job titles reporting to the Data Processing Manager are varied to match the particular company's situation. In the example in Figure 18-3, a Manager of Data Processing Standards and Training performs a specialized job. In spite of decentralization, this company has decided to standardize each computer installation at the division. Thus corporate procedures, standards, and equipment specifications are needed. There is also a need for the training of systems, programming, and operations personnel to insure uniformity of approach. If the company had allowed the branches autonomy in running the branch operations, this group would have been deleted.

Since part of the data processing involves corporate-wide reports, a corporate systems and programming group is required to develop and maintain such systems. The chart also shows a new concept (timing sharing) being developed in a large project group. Because of the potential magnitude of the project, it is allowed to report directly to the Data Processing Manager. If the project were of lesser importance, it could be put under the control of the Corporate Systems Manager.

CONTROLLING DATA PROCESSING OPERATIONS

The production phase of data processing is often neglected. Many times the best programmer or systems analyst is put in charge of the entire effort. The profitable techniques of production control are never applied to data processing. These methods can be borrowed from any well-managed factory, modified, and applied to computer operation. Several prerequisites to a smooth operation must be satisfied first. They are:

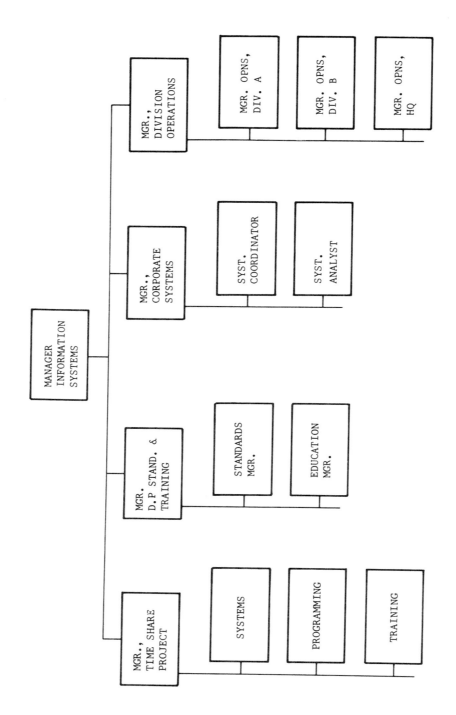

Figure 18-5
Typical Large-Sized Organization

1. *Predictable Performance*—All jobs accepted as operational must run in a predictable manner. They should not require operators' decisions or intervention. If jobs fail to run properly, they should be returned to the systems department.
2. *Quality Control Built In*—Control totals should be available to check the accuracy of the output.
3. *Complete Up-to-Date Documentation*—Each job should have step-by-step instructions. All unusual conditions should be accounted for and instructions included as to the proper action to take.
4. *Input Data Quality Controlled*—All input data must be uniform. No critical fields should be left blank. Alphabetic characters should not be found where numbers are expected and vice versa.

The importance of uniformity and predictability can not be over-emphasized. A machine shop can not turn out precision metal parts if:

A. Its machines can not be set to do the same thing exactly and repeatedly;
B. Its raw material reacts to the machining process in different ways at different times for unknown reasons; or
C. The management is not able to differentiate acceptable results from unacceptable results.

The same rules apply to data processing. Without uniform processing and clear standards of performance, there is no sense in proceeding. Control procedures can only make a functioning operation more efficient; they can not help if the basic operations are faulty.

Control Procedures That Work

Controls seek to measure input of labor against useful output. Fair standards of performance are required. Each job which runs on a computer must have its individual standards. These standards are developed in two ways. Past history of running time for each job provides one basis for standards. If running times vary with the quantity of input data, standards must be variable. Historical data which relate running time to volume is often not available. In this case the best basis for variable standards is a timing analysis by the programming or systems department. Based on the known elements involved in particular programs, a fairly precise estimate of running time can be made. The result would be X minutes of running time per thousand records read.

Gathering Time Data

The next step towards control requires gathering accurate and timely actual results. The labor effort must be measured for the following functions:

1. Computer running time
2. Keypunch labor time
3. Systems and programming time
4. Auxiliary machine time (sorters, collators, etc.)

　　　5. Bursting and decollating time
　　　6. Computer machine operator time (required only
　　　　　　if it differs substantially from #1)

This data should be gathered via time sheets as shown in Figures 18-6 and 18-7. The Equipment Usage Report (Figure 18-8) should be handed in daily on active equipment and weekly on machines which are used only occasionally. Examples of occasionally used equipment are:

　　　1. data transmission devices
　　　2. automatic burster-decollators
　　　3. off-line sorters, interpreters, etc.

The sheets should be attached to a clipboard or some other convenient device attached to the computer itself. All daily-type sheets should be reviewed at the end of each day by the operations manager or his assistant. Any omissions or errors must be brought to the attention of the person responsible for the error. This type of system fails for only one reason—management's failure to insist on proper input for all machine usage by all employees.

Keypunch time can be handled on either the Equipment Usage Report or the Time Charge Report (Figure 18-9). If one operator is assigned to one machine and no one else normally uses it, the Time Charge Report is preferred. If keypunch operators perform other duties, such as sorting or clerical, another method is needed. In this case an Equipment Usage Report is turned in for each keypunch machine and verifier. While the operator is operating these machines, she charges her time on the Time Charge Report to the line "Running Chargeable Machine". She fills out one line on the Equipment Usage Report for each job she works on. The total hours posted to this sheet for the day should equal the time she charges to "Running Chargeable Machines" for the day on her own time sheet. This technique allows flexibility in charging people's time if they are not tied to one machine.

Time Control Reports

With standards defined and actual data captured, reports can be generated which are the real tools of control. Figure 18-10 shows a Monthly Machine Hours Report in summary form. The Job Number column is empty since each line represents a total for a particular machine running a particular type of work. Figure 18-11 is the matching detail report which backs up the summary report in Figure 18-10. The actual hours are split into two components—On Standard and No Standard. The objective is to put all production on standard. The installation of controls, however, should not be delayed until all jobs have standards. By highlighting No Standard jobs the report provides a natural control on production running without standards. There are jobs and operations for which standards are impractical. The detail report can segregate these jobs as shown in Figure 18-11 under the heading "Special."

Date _____/_____/_____
    month day yr.

Machine No. _____

Initials	Job No.	Type or Phase	Meter Start	Meter Stop	Clock Time in hr min	Clock Time out hr min	Comments
1.							
2.							
3.							
4.			190.24	191.08	5 10	6 27	
5.			191.08	191.42	6 27	6 58	
6.	9999	50	191.42	191.42	6 58	8 00	Idle–found machine with switch off
			191.42		8 00		

Submitted by_____

Checked by_____

Figure 18-6
Daily Timesheet

Name_____

Emp. No._____

Week Ending _____|_____|_____
　　　　　　mon.　　day　　yr.

	Project	Phase	Weekly Totals	Daily Hours						
				M	T	W	T	F	S	S
_____		│	●							
_____		│	●							
_____		│	●							
_____		│	●							
_____										
_____										
_____										
_____										
_____										
_____										
_____										
_____										
_____				●						
Sk Lv, Vac, Holiday	0001	00	●							
Travel	0002	00	●							
Administrative	0003	00	●							
Training	0004	00	●							
Other	0005	00	●							

Total Weekly Hours_____ ●

Figure 18-7
Weekly Timesheet

Figure 18-8
Equipment Usage Report

MACHINE _____ 0 0 2 _____

DATE _____ 07/12/×4 _____

JOB NO.	TYPE OF RUN	ELAPSED TIME		Meter Readings		COMMENTS	INITIALS
		Hours	Min.	Start	Stop		
1182	01	1	05	18.07	19.11		
0717	06		42	19.11	19.82		
—	10	3	15	19.82	23.07		

TYPE OF RUN CODES
01 Native – Test
02 Native – Production
05 Emulation – Test
06 Emulation – Production
10 Maintenance
12 Downtime

Figure 18-9
Time Charge Report

EMPLOYEE NO. __081__   NAME __J. Jones__   WEEK NO. __27__

JOB CODE	COMMENTS	WORK CODE	TOTAL HRS.	MON.	TUE.	WED.	THU.	FRI.	SAT.	SUN.
0184		02	8.0	4	2	2				
		03	20.0	4			8	8		
		02	8.0		6	2				
			.							
			.							
			.							
			.							
			.							
			.							
			.							
7400	SICK LEAVE & PERSONAL TIME		4.0			4				
7410	ADMINISTRATIVE DUTIES		.							
7415	OPERATING CHARGEABLE MACHINE									
7425	ALL OTHER		.							
	TOTALS		40.0							

TYPES OF WORK CODES
01 Keypunch
02 Systems Design
03 Program Development

04 Program Test
05 Production
06 Verify

07 Tab Sort
08 Clerical
09 Tab Collate

10 Tab Reproduce
11 Tab Interpret
12 Tape Library

Month — July, 19___

	Job Machine	Type of Run	CURRENT Actual	Planned	%	YTD Actual	Planned	%
On Standards	1	Native Production	182	174	104	358	339	106
No Standard	1	Native Production	54	—	—	88	—	
On Standards	1	Emulation Prod.	112	118	95	174	200	87
No Standard	1	Emulation Prod.	49	—	—	112	—	
On Standards	1	Native Testing	62	80	77	117	118	100
On Standards	1	Emulation Testing	71	40	177	140	131	107
On Standards	1	Downtime	28	30	93	60	50	120
On Standrads	1	Maintenance	35	30	117	72	82	88
No Standard	1	All Other	8	—		9	—	

TOTALS FOR MACHINE

			CURRENT			YTD		
On Standards			490	472	104	921	920	100
No Standard			111	—	—	209	—	—

Figure 18-10
Machine Hours Summary

Month — July, 19___

Status	Job	Machine	Type of Run	CURRENT Actual	Planned	%	YTD Actual	Planned	%
On Standards	181	1	Native Production	5	4	125	12	9	133
	185	1		3	4	75	7	7	100
	192	1		8	7	87	19	19	100
	197	1		6	4	150	8	7	114
	234	1		14	10	140	24	22	109
	261	1		4	5	80	7	6	114
	291	1		12	13	92	21	20	105
	311	1		7	9	78	15	16	94
	444	1		28	28	100	70	65	108
	445	1		42	40	105	68	68	100
	446	1		53	50	115	107	100	107
	TOTALS ***			182	174		358	339	105
No Standard	190	1	Native Production	11	—		28	—	
	411	1		6	—		11	—	

Figure 18-11
Machine Hours Detail Report

19

Writing Better Reports to
Management and Stockholders

||||||||||||||||||||||||||||||||||||||||||||||||||||||||||||||||||||||||||||||||||||||||||||||||||||||||||||||||||||||||||||||||||||||||||||||||||||||||||||||||||

347

19

Writing Better Reports to Management and Stockholders

‖‖‖

REGULAR AND SPECIAL REPORTS FOR MANAGEMENT

The finance officer reports on a wide range of subjects—on expenses, sales and profit, return on investment, performance against goals, inventory turnover, receivables turn-over, break-even point, and many others. Merely reporting figures, of course, is not enough. Readers must not be forced to plod laboriously through statistics, analyzing and interpreting as they go. Rather, the significance of the facts must be immediately clear.

The ultimate criterion of a good report is that it be useful. The qualities that charac-terize a useful report depend in part on the type of report—on whether it is a regular report or a special report.

Regular Reports

Regular reports are repetitive; they follow a standard format in most cases and cover a definite time—usually a quarter. They relate facts about continuing operations and recurring problems. They show the immediate effects of business activities in terms of sales, expenses, profit, and similar indexes. They usually give figures for the company as a whole and for each major division or operating center as well, and they present data uniformly.

Regular reports often contain ratios and "better or worse" comparisons with previous reporting periods and budget estimates. They are simple, yet thorough. A lucid com-ment section, or a supporting memo, goes a long way toward helping readers under-stand the wholly statistical data of the usual stream of regular reports.

Special Reports

Special reports are analytical and may be addressed to the board of directors, to the company president, to the finance committee, or to other management representatives. They include after-the-fact analysis as well as appraisals of current performance and predictions of probable future performance. Special reports show cause-and-effect relationships. Those who prepare the reports must find and expose problems, explaining them in terms of their causes and probable future effects.

In many cases, special reports pertain to certain organizational segments that are either experiencing difficulties or making an exceptionally good showing. They all discuss factors that are crucial to overall performance, and normally give at least the following information:

1. Background data, including historical cost figures and other facts to familiarize management with the subject of the report.
2. Current information to bring management up to date on the subject.
3. An analysis of the factors leading up to the current status of the problem, pinpointing organizational responsibility and showing which division, branch, or even which individual has succeeded or failed in meeting assigned performance standards.
4. Recommended course of action for eliminating existing problems or generally improving performance.
5. Estimates of probable improvements under alternative courses of action.

Though much of the information for analytical reports is taken from the regular reports, the analytical report must provide management with new information and with new insight into business performance.

Avoid Rehashing

Too often, management receives reports based on no more than superficial data. The writer does little but rephrase stale information the reader has seen before. There may be nothing wrong with the way he writes the report, but the writer fails seriously in not thoroughly investigating and assessing the facts surrounding the subject.

Suppose a company experiences declining earnings over a substantial period. Management begins preparing the budget for the coming year, and asks the finance executive to provide a critical review of past operations as a guide. Management doesn't want a rehash of previous reports. Management wants new facts. It wants conclusions supported by logical reasoning. It wants to know *why* income has slipped and what can be done to correct the situation. To come up with a plausible solution, the report writer must break down earnings and expenses by product and division, pinpoint weaknesses, and recommend action calculated to return the firm to a favorable earnings position.

WRITING THE REPORT

As with any written communication, the first thing the financial report writer must do is to keep the reader in mind—who he is; what his needs are. Other important elements in report writing are style, consistency, conservatism, and timeliness.

Audience

A report's content and length will depend partly on who will be reading it. Each management level requires different information presented in a slightly different way.

Most top executives, for example, prefer their reports in summary form. This preference is particularly true for those reports dealing with overall company problems or performance. But these "summaries" must still point out high and low efficiency; they must still highlight performance in critical operations and in vital organizational units. Top management generally prefers that narratives accompany statistical reports. Figures may tell the story to an experienced accountant, but they don't always tell all they should to sales and production managers.

Financial reports to middle management are also most effective if presented in summary form, in much the same way as reports to top management. The report writer must keep in mind that middle management deals more with day-to-day operations and with more isolated problems than top management. Reports to the middle management level should help solve the problems at that level.

Lower-level managers (supervisors and foremen) coordinate and control direct line operation. Reports to this level must assist them in performing line duties. Reports to foremen and supervisors should be simple, phrased in non-technical accounting terms, and limited in scope to factors having a direct bearing on line operations.

Style

The principles that apply to any type of effective writing apply equally to financial writing and reporting. Above all, the writing should be simple, without pedantic expressions and words intended more to impress the readers with the writer's vocabulary than to convey information. Little words and simple phrases carry weight, whereas big words and tangled phrases have a stultifying effect.

The skillful report writer writes directly to the reader. He combines the personal pronouns *I, we, me, you, yours,* and *our* with active verbs to form clear, snappy sentences. Instead of writing, "An inspection of the books was made by the undersigned . . . .", He writes, "I inspected the books in Division A. . . ." He writes with confidence; he comes to the point. Readers appreciate his style.

The writer organizes his thoughts before beginning to write. He presents facts in logical order, in the order of their importance to the reader, if possible. He eliminates details that are of no use to the reader and avoids long, drawn-out conclusions. When he has said what he wants to say, he stops.

The writer pays careful attention to form, but doesn't hem himself in with it. Titles and headings are descriptive—or left out altogether. Column headings and captions identify material. Highly technical language or expressions colloquial to the finance organization have no place in reports going outside finance.

Consistency

Financial and accounting data should be treated consistently. If a report begins by comparing costs with revenue in a particular way, that comparison should continue throughout the report—and in succeeding reports on the same problem. Most executives become accustomed to certain formats and styles. A change in format or style from one report to the next can be quite confusing. Standard report forms make it easier for the reader to compare succeeding reports.

Conservatism

Be conservative in reporting financial affairs—particularly when giving an estimate. An overstatement of favorable trends and events may lead to an understatement of the importance of unfavorable circumstances. The convention of conservatism assures management that it is receiving representative cost data, and makes reports useful in evaluating trends.

Timeliness

Financial reports are valuable when the events leading up to them are fresh in the minds of the readers. Some financial reports are outdated before they are completed. Several weeks may pass before the finance organization can gather information to substantiate a report. If the problem is a complicated one, it may take more time to analyze the information and write a report. By this time, the problem may be too far along to do anything about it.

The analyst must gather information speedily and analyze it quickly. Timeliness is more important than absolute accuracy. Holding up reports until "all the facts are in" can detract greatly from their value. Financial data are never exact anyway; some estimating is nearly always involved. A responsible estimate is part of the analyst's job. When estimates are necessary, the reader should not be burdened with lengthy justifications.

HOW TO GIVE REPORTS EYE APPEAL

Regardless of accuracy in factual details, a report fails to serve its intended purpose if it is unnecessarily complicated and uninviting. The only way to bring to the surface all the significant facts hidden in accounting reports is to make them easy to read. Good reports should have "eye appeal" by employing some of the techniques described below.

20 Ways to Make Reports Easier to Read

Many of these suggestions are incorporated in the model expense statement in Figure 19-1. An asterisk indicates the illustration of a given rule.

1. *Use color.* Quick identification is facilitated by using differently colored pages, sections, dividers, tabs, and even binders.

2. *Use short titles.* Too many titles, subtitles, and lines of explanatory data don't always enlighten the reader and often frighten him away.

3. *Use uniform columnar headings.* By using the same headings in many different reports month after month, the reader is helped to find his way to the right column almost unconsciously. This "column-for-column" technique also expedites the preparation of reports.

4. *Use leadoff captions sparingly* *. Captions that qualify or explain the particulars of the report should be eliminated whenever the reader thereby loses no significant information.

5. *Use a uniform format.* This helps both the reader and the preparer of the reports. The reader soon becomes so accustomed to the standard sequence and arrangement that he requires the minimum of reorientation as he turns from page to page or moves from one month to the next.

6. *Put particulars in the middle.* The distance the eye must travel in relating the printed word to the printed figure should be as short as possible. If the report uses several columns requiring a very wide page, eye travel is cut in half by placing the particulars in the middle, rather than the orthodox left, with figures on both sides.

7. *Use guidelines* *. When more than six lines of columnar data are shown, a fine guideline aids the eye in moving across the sheet.

8. *Use boxes and gutters* *. A box is a segment of a report enclosed within a heavy boundary line; a gutter is the area between boxes. The box-and-gutter technique divides the reported data on a single sheet into a number of logical segments, each of which can be assimilated piecemeal. At the same time, the reader can still appreciate the overall relationship of each segment to the whole.

9. *Indent to the left.* This technique adds clarity and emphasis. With particulars moved to the left, the reader goes from the detail to the subtotals and grand total in this manner, rather than the orthodox. This procedure provides two advantages: major totals stand out clearly and are easily caught by the eye at a glance, and relationships are sharpened so that it is clear which amounts foot to which totals.

10. *Use capitals as well as small letters* *. The resulting variety provides differentiation, and thus emphasis and de-emphasis.

11. *Emphasize with lines and spaces.* This arrangement offers still another means of emphasis and differentiation, and thus clarity.

12. *Use red and black figures logically.* Where a leadoff caption is used, all amounts that contribute to the item should appear black; all amounts that reduce it, red. Where comparisons are made, "better" differences should appear black; "worse" differences,

red. The total of a column equals the total of the black amounts less the total of the red amounts. (In Figure 1, the red amounts are shown in parentheses.)

13. *Make it easy to add down.* Reports will add down more readily if by applying suggestions 9, 10, 11, and 12.

14. *Eliminate dollar signs and commas* *. Every reader knows the report is in dollars; commas serve no better than the empty spaces. Eliminating them leaves the reports uncluttered and saves countless keystrokes.

15. *Report in round numbers when practicable* *. Most accounting reports can be prepared in even dollars. (The only notable exception is unit reports covering unit selling price, unit cost, unit gross profit, and the like.) Rounding to the nearest thousand dollars is best confined to summary "flash" reports, designed to give a quick view of operations.

16. *Drop meaningless percentage points* *. There is no reason to carry calculations out to several places after the decimal when the original data may not be wholly accurate. It is generally sufficient to carry percentages to just one place after the decimal.

17. *Use uniform paper in a uniform way.* Place sheets always with the long side vertical, or always with the short side vertical.

18. *Use uniform page sequence.* This is a timesaver in reading and preparing reports.

19. *Use uniform binders.* They make for easy storage and use of reports.

20. *Use tabs and dividers.* They aid quick look-ups and invite more frequent use of reports.

CHARTS ENABLE QUICK UNDERSTANDING

Charts are becoming more widely used to point out salient aspects of financial reports to those who are not as figure-oriented as accountants. Charts offer several advantages. They enable vast quantities of data to be presented in an easily understood manner. They show movement, change, relationships, and the results of events. They are especially useful for emphasizing important points in either written or oral reports. And they are adaptable; there is a chart for every purpose.

Line Charts

Line charts are used to show the movements of one or more quantities over a stated period. Time units are usually shown horizontally on the chart, while the units of quantities are measured vertically. Points are then plotted on the chart by measuring from the time and unit scale. In Figure 19-2, for example, 20,000 units are related to September, 25,000 units to October, and so on. Connecting these points by lines shows the variability over the period of production, sales, earnings, or whatever the chart is describing.

Bar Chart

A bar chart is a form of graph that presents an analysis of data by means of heavy lines or bars drawn to base line. The area covered by the bar represents the relative

PARTICULARS	Amount	%
Mail opening	64 271	6.4
Entry	30 021	3.0
Index	74 786	7.5
Pricing	81 041	8.1
ORDER CLERICAL	250 119	25.0
Adjustment	41 700	4.2
Credit	12 796	1.3
ADJUSTMENT CLERICAL	54 496	5.5
CLERICAL TOTAL	**304 615**	**30.5**

Department 1	2 764	.3
Department 2	12 444	1.2
Department 3	80 691	8.0
Department 4	80 001	8.0
Department 5	24 786	2.5
Department 6	9 742	1.0
Department 7	8 743	.9
Department 8	9 901	1.0
DEPARTMENT EXPENSE	229 072	22.9
Packing	74 201	7.4
Billing	39 434	3.9
PACKING AND BILLING	113 635	11.3
OPERATING TOTAL	**342 707**	**34.2**

CLERICAL AND OPERATING TOTAL	**647 322**	**64.7**
GENERAL EXPENSES	300 100	30.0
MISCELLANEOUS	14 245	1.4
OTHER INCOME	(2 758)	(.2)
OTHER DEDUCTIONS	41 091	4.1
EXPENSES TOTAL	**1 000 000**	**100.0**

Figure 19-1
Model Expense Statement

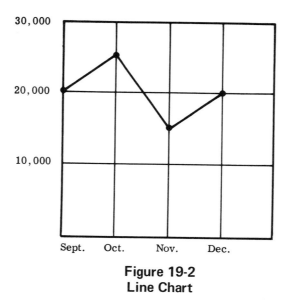

Figure 19-2
Line Chart

magnitude of the quantity being measured. For example, the area covered by a bar representing 40,000 units sold in one month would be 50 percent larger than the area of the bar representing 20,000 units in another month.

Figure 19-3 uses a bar chart to portray the overall profit contribution structure of all items in a given product line. It can also be used to display the profit contribution structure for all products. The same basic format can be adopted to display sales performance by regions or by salesmen.

With this chart, including the summary listings at the bottom, management can see at a glance the relative profit contribution of all items in a product line. The classification of products by range of profit contribution assists in pinpointing those items which represent a drag on overall profitability. The periodic preparation of this chart will also provide a clear picture of the effect of product mix on overall profitability.

The summary listings at the bottom should, of course, be supplemented by detailed listings that identify each product within each group, together with their individual sales and profit contributions.

Scatter Chart

A scatter chart is a graphic plotting of the magnitude of one factor against the magnitude of another. Time is not a factor in the scatter chart. Rather, the scatter chart determines whether a correlation exists between two variables.

If a financial manager wants to know if the sales of his company are directly affected by shifts in the gross national product, he could use a scatter chart shown in Figure 19-4. The horizontal scale represents gross national product in billions of dollars. The vertical scale represents company sales in millions of dollars.

The points are plotted and a line is drawn to bisect the path of the points. A straight

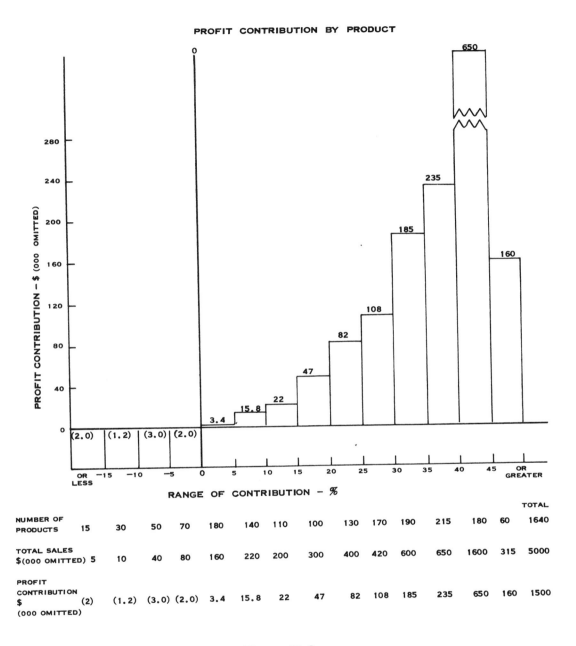

Figure 19-3
Bar Chart Showing the Overall Profit Contribution of
All Items in a Product Line

line close to all the points indicates a correlation between company sales and gross national product. If the plotted points are widely scattered from the line, little or no correlation exists.

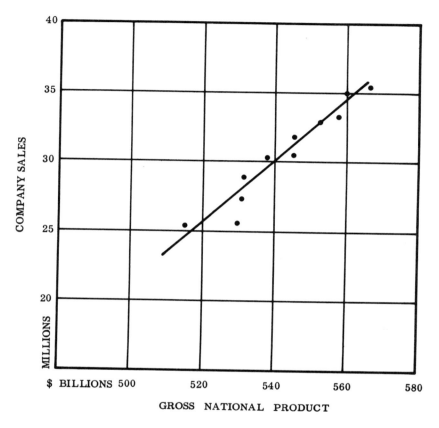

Figure 19-4
Scatter Chart

Semi-Logarithmic Chart

This chart has one scale that is logarithmic and the other that is arithmetic. If the horizontal scale is arithmetic, and years are the time units involved, these units would appear in equally spaced intervals along the base of the chart. But the vertical logarithmic scale would be unequally spaced. In Figure 19-5, the distance between $100,000 and $200,000 is the same as the distance between $200,000 and $400,000. Thus, the semi-logarithmic chart can be used to compare percentage changes, in this case, between sales and earnings.

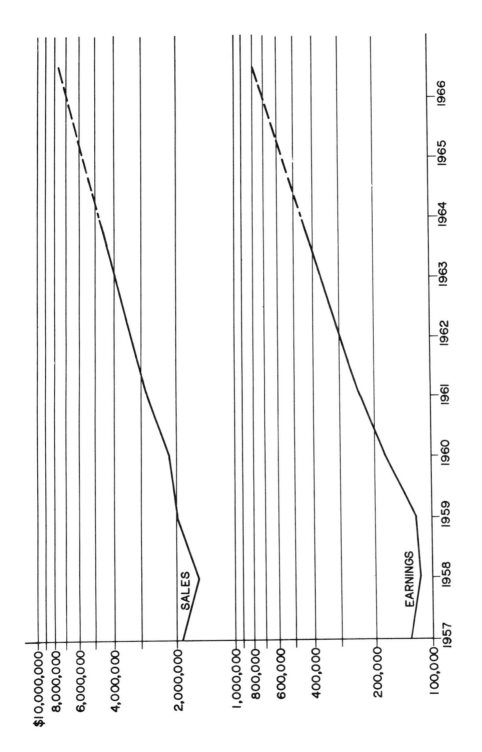

Figure 19-5
Semi-Logarithmic Chart Comparing Percentage Changes
Between Sales and Earnings

REPORTS THAT AID IN MANAGEMENT BY EXCEPTION [1]

Management by exception is what people do when they (1) set goals for themselves and for others, (2) assign responsibility for achieving these goals, and (3) put intensive effort only on those goals that are *not* being achieved. The following section examines what this description of management by exception means to the financial report writer.

1. *Set goals for others.* All but the smallest business organization require the assignment of numerous goals to numerous executives. In compiling reports that aid in management by exception, the writer must know what these goals are.

2. *Assign responsibility to achieve goals.* Personnel who are assigned goals are also given responsibility for achieving them. The writer must know who has been assigned what responsibility.

3. *Intensive effort on goals not being achieved.* When an exception report indicates that certain goals are not being achieved, management must initiate remedial measures. Exception reports should not include every performance that falls short of its goal.

What Is an Exception?

There is no universal rule for designating a performance as an exception. One approach is to experiment with several degrees of variation in deciding what range of exception should be used. Too small a variation will flood people with "exceptions" to the point where they will not act on any exception.

A useful way to avoid this is to discuss the matter with the persons who will be receiving the reports. A president may want to consider only negative deviations of more than 30 percent in the profit of each product, whereas the sales manager may want to examine both positive and negative deviations of five percent or more. The president may want to know when the cost of a product exceeds 10 percent of the goal, whereas the production manager may want to know when costs get out of line by as little as two percent.

High and Low Exceptions

The report should show high exceptions as well as low ones. A high exception with respect to a profit-type goal should be reported so that management will understand the exceptionally good performance, and apply this knowledge to other phases of the company's operations. And of course a low exception should be reported so that corrective action may be taken.

Figure 19-6 illustrates a schedule of exception ranges for monthly sales volume by product for the president, sales manager, and salesman.

[1] Adapted from Jim D. Savas "Reports to Aid in Management by Exception", in *Encyclopedia of Accounting Forms and Reports,* Vol. II, prepared by the Prentice-Hall Editorial Staff, 1964.

THE XYZ COMPANY

Exception Ranges for Monthly Sales Volume

(Exception Ranges are Stated as a Percentage of the
Monthly Sales Volume Goal)

Product	For the President		For the Sales Manager		For the Salesman	
	High Exception	Low Exception	High Exception	Low Exception	High Exception	Low Exception
A	+20%	−20%	+10%	−10%	+5%	−5%
B	+20	−20	+10	−10	+5	−5
C	+20	−15	+10	− 7	+5	−5
D	+20	−20	+10	−10	+5	−5
E	+15	−10	+ 7	− 5	+4	−4
F	+10	− 5	+ 5	− 3	+2	−2
G	+15	−10	+ 7	− 5	+4	−4
H	+15	−10	+ 7	− 5	+4	−4
I	+10	− 5	+ 5	− 3	+2	−2
J	+10	− 5	+ 5	− 3	+2	−2

Notes: The plus (+) figures indicate the trigger points for reporting
"high exceptions". A deviation which is equal to, or
larger than, the positive figures shall be considered a
"high exception"
The minus (−) figures indicate the trigger points for reporting
"low exceptions". A deviation which is equal to, or of
larger negative value than, the negative figures shall be
considered a "low exception"
A deviation which is smaller than the positive figures and
larger than the negative figures shall be considered a
"no exception"

Figure 19-6
Schedule of Exception Ranges

How Reporting by Exception Makes Management's Job Easier

There are three methods of reporting business results: (1) full reporting without comments, (2) full reporting with comments, (3) exception reporting.

1. *Full reporting without comments.* This type of reporting shows all goals and results achieved against these goals. This leaves it up to the person receiving the reports to decide which of his goals need special attention. Though this is not reporting by exception, this type of report can be used in management by exception. The person receiving the reports can check them to see whether the reported items fall within certain predetermined exception ranges for his action. However, there is a major disadvantage inherent in this type of reporting. It gives the executive too much detail, making it difficult for him to identify the significantly "off" items. He has to wade through every item to find those that warrant his concentrated effort.

2. *Full reporting with comments.* This type of reporting sets up a full report as above and, in addition, identifies items falling into an exception range. An exception item is noted with an asterisk if it falls in the low exception range for profit-type goals, or if it falls in a high exception range for cost-type goals. Two asterisks denote an item if it falls in the high exception range for profit-type goals, or if it falls in a low exception range for cost-type goals. Items with no asterisk fall in the no exception range.

3. *Exception reporting.* This type of report shows only those items that fall in an exception range. These items are noted with asterisks as in full reporting with comments. In effect, the analytical task of evaluating performance against goals using exception range yardsticks is transferred from the reader to the writer of the report, as is the case in reporting in full with comments. In exception reporting, however, the report is reduced to include only those items within an exception range requiring special attention. Figure 19-7 illustrates these three types of reports.

REPORTING TO STOCKHOLDERS

In addition to internal managerial reports, the finance officer is also responsible for making increasing amounts of information available to growing numbers of stockholders.

Brevity and Organization—Two Key Features

A short summary at the start and a clear organization of the material are what most readers want. The annual report writer must remember that his firm's report is a minor event in the busy lives of most of those who receive it. He must decide what there is about his company—besides its dividend rate—that will interest the stockholders, the majority of whom are women.

A skillfully written summary will arouse the reader's interest and lead him to special narrative sections with provocative headings, and perhaps even to the financial statements, if they are written so that the layman can understand them. And a well organized report with a complete table of contents will enable the reader to grasp the essentials quickly. Content and style, then, determine the suitability of an annual report.

WHAT SHOULD GO IN THE ANNUAL REPORT?

Every annual report should reflect the character of the specific company. Whether a company manufactures producer or consumer goods, is large or small, has conservative or aggressive stockholders, has poor or good earnings—these and many more factors determine the type of information and the elaborateness or simplicity of the report.

Nevertheless, all good reports provide certain basic information. The following are typical contents of informative reports: [2]

---

[2] J. Brooks Heckert and James D. Willson, *Controllership* (New York: The Ronald Press Company, 1963), pp. 578–579.

Full Reporting Without Comments

To: The President

THE XYZ COMPANY
MONTHLY SALES VOLUME REPORT (August 19   )

Product Name	Goal	Actual
A	$4,175	$3,838
B	12,000	10,982
C	25,000	31,337
D	8,350	9,984
E	100,000	93,678
F	125,000	122,369
G	41,700	67,311
H	75,000	32,675
I	200,000	188,639
J	200,000	208,619

Full Reporting With Comments

To: The President

THE XYZ COMPANY
MONTHLY SALES VOLUME REPORT (August 19   )

Product Name	Goal	Actual	% Achieved
A	$4,175	$3,838	91.9
B	12,000	10,982	87.8
C	25,000	31,337	125.7**
D	8,350	9,984	119.7
E	100,000	93,678	93.7
F	125,000	122,369	97.8
G	41,700	67,311	161.5**
H	75,000	32,675	43.5*
I	200,000	188,639	94.2*
J	200,000	208,619	104.2

Exception Reporting

To: The President

THE XYZ COMPANY
MONTHLY SALES VOLUME REPORT (August 19   )

Product Name	Goal	Actual	% Achieved
C	$25,000	$31,337	125.7**
G	41,700	67,311	161.5**
H	75,000	32,675	43.5*
I	200,000	188,639	94.2*

Figure 19-7
Examples of Management Reports

1. BASIC
    a. *Highlights or summary page.* This presents fundamental and comparative data on financial results and conditions as well as operating information. Particularly important are:
    Per-share earnings
    Per-share dividends
    Book value
    b. *President's comments.* Such a section, under the signature of either the chairman of the board or president, or both, is most effective as a one or two page bird's-eye view stressing the overall outlook and problems likely to affect the company's future. It generally avoids facts and figures presented elsewhere.
    c. *Narrative section.* This segment of the annual report provides the explanation and detailed story of the business. Through the use of commentary, charts, and photographs, it describes the activities of the various departments and/or areas of significance to the company.
    d. *Financial statements.* Comparative financial statements, including appropriate footnotes and the opinion of independent auditors, provide the basic information on the results of stewardship.
    e. *Historical statistical summary.* Such a section provides a long-term—usually ten or more years—picture of relevant operating and financial statistics.
2. SUPPLEMENTAL—BUT DESIRABLE. By experience, other features found helpful in best presenting the corporate story include:
    a. *Table of Contents.* Permits quick reference in a multi-page booklet.
    b. *Attractive cover design.* An appropriate photograph or drawing implying the nature of the business, or products, or industry has been found a helpful communication device.
    c. *Directory.* This portion indicates the names of officers and directors, and perhaps other key management personnel, as well as counsel, independent auditors, transfer agents, registrars, etc. At present, also, the tendency is to show the affiliation of directors who are not corporate officers.

WHAT ABOUT THE STYLE OF THE ANNUAL REPORT?

Almost as important as *what* is said in an annual report is *how* it is said. The narrative part of the report should use a simple, conversational style. The report should contain distinctive headings and subtitles. Photographs or illustrations help speed the reader along, and charts and graphs instantly depict performance trends.

Financial Statements Need Special Attention

The principle of using simple English applies directly to the description of a firm's financial condition. Many companies are wary of changing conservative and accepted

How We Stood on December 31, 19___

Cash (Cash on hand is sufficient for about one month's operation) . . . . $

Our customers and others owe us (Accounts Receivables) . . . .

Finished goods, goods in process, raw materials and supplies in
  plants and warehouses (Inventories) . . . .

Current expenses paid for in advance (Taxes, Insurance, etc.) . . . . _____

Out of this comes:

  What we owe our employees for wages . . . . $

  What we owe for raw materials, supplies, expenses, and

  taxes . . . . _____

  This difference is the money used to run the business
  (Working Capital) . . . . $

Besides Working Capital we own:

  Buildings, machinery and equipment (after subtracting the
  allowance for accumulated wear and tear) . . . . $

  Other assets, including investments, and good will . . . . _____

The balance is the interest of the 6,500 stockholders . . . . $

Figure 19-8
Simplified Balance Sheet

Income and Expenses in 19___

Income

Products sold to customers (after allowing for freight, trade discounts, etc.) . . . $

  We received income from foreign and domestic investments, etc.,

  amounting to . . . . _____

  Which gave us a total income of . . . . $

Expenses:

  For raw materials, fuel, supplies, etc. . . . . $

  For wages, selling and general expenses . . . . $

  We figure the wear and tear of buildings and machinery, to be . . . . $

  We paid out or set aside for tax payments . . . . _____

  Which made our total expenses . . . . $

Net earnings:

  This left a profit of . . . . $

  Out of which the 6,500 owners of our business received as dividends . . . . $

  The balance, added to the stockholders' investment in the

  Company, was . . . . $

Figure 19-9
Simplified Statement of Income

methods of presenting financial information. The simplified statements in Figures 19-8 and 19-9 are not intended to change the system of accounting. They do suggest that simplicity will help make the statements generally understood to the untrained.

In these statements assets and liabilities become what the company "owns" and what it "owes"; depreciation is expressed as "wear and tear"; "allowance for" replaces the unfamiliar (to the reader) "reserves"; and "surplus" is expressed as "profits employed in the business."

KEEP THE REPORT HONEST

The annual report is recognized as a valuable public relations tool. Since the report is read not only by stockholders but also by employees, security analysts, and general investors, it offers an ideal opportunity for telling the company story in a way that generates good will, secures venture capital, and stimulates sales.

But what should a company do if things didn't go so well last year? Should it candidly admit that it had a tough year? Or should it use vague generalizations and glowing double-talk to disguise the fact?

A Plea for Less Floss, More Fact

Mr. William H. Dinsmore, who has edited seven award-winning annual reports, describes corporation reports as representing "one of the flossiest and least informative art forms of our times." [3] Dinsmore says that most reports go unread. "I know enough about annual reports to know I can't understand them. Anyway, everything is always going to be rosy is the comment of a typical investor who owns shares in fifteen corporations."

Euphemistic double-talk, says Dinsmore, has led to an alienation of the stockholder. In reviewing thousands of annual reports, he found that "a year of declining profits is generally described as 'a year of transition'." Most corporate reports end up "freighted with vague generalizations, cliches, half-truths, total omissions, unsubstantiated claims, and downright distortions."

> 'Our aggressive and imaginative management team, whose competence is equal to the best, has given unstinting service,' was the humble expression of one chairman. Another chief executive, still struggling to restore per-share earnings to the level of 1955 reported: 'The devoted performance of all our employees was a source of strength throughout the year.' But later on the same report comments that 'vigilant expense control' was required to minimize constantly rising costs of labor. There is no breakdown anywhere in the report of such costs or explanations of how they came into being.
>
> Sales or earnings may be up or down, but progress is always 'encouraging.' Competition is 'strenuous,' cost-cutting efforts are being 'intensified,' research

---

[3] William H. Dinsmore, "Dear Stockholders: Everything Looks Rosy. . . ," *Harper's Magazine,* March 1965, pp. 133–138.

and new product development 'expanded.' Employees are 'loyal' and their efforts are 'appreciated' and may be 'counted upon to continue.'

A Refreshing Approach

Instead of reading with a peculiar sameness, a corporation's annual report should bear the personal stamp of the chief executive officer. As an example of an earthy style with a refreshing frankness, Dinsmore cites the report of the S. D. Warren Paper Company. President George Olmstead, Jr., writes that " 'most of our shrinkage in profits was due to things of our own making—and so the Big Bellyache and the Bleeding Ulcers are essentially our own responsibility.' " Olmstead then explains where management guessed wrong and what they proposed to do about it.

A company's annual report is unquestionably the single most important document that it publishes. The report also is a major expense. To serve its purpose, the annual report must be readable and it must be believable. As stockholders become more sophisticated, they resent finding bombast when seeking facts. A company does itself a disservice as well as its readers if it fails to meet this need.

DISTRIBUTING THE REPORT

In addition to shareholders, annual reports usually go to four other groups: employees, security analysts, customers, and the general public. The nature and size of a firm's business determine the extent to which it will want to distribute the report. The trend is to make the report widely available, since one of its purposes is to promote good public relations by telling the company story.

Advertising the Report

Many companies advertise their reports in the financial sections of newspapers or in financial journals. Sometimes they participate in collective advertisements. Under this arrangement, each company sponsoring the advertisement usually shows the cover of its annual report and gives a brief description of its operations.

The advertisement may run for several full pages. To get a report, readers simply circle the identifying numbers of the companies in which they are interested. The reports come to them directly from the companies, not from the newspaper or journal.

Mailing the Report to Local and National Groups

In addition to advertising, or in place of advertising, some companies mail their reports to certain groups in the local community. Large companies maintain nationwide mailing lists. Figure 19-10 suggests local readers who may be interested in your report, and Figure 19-11 suggests a wider range of recipients.

Associated Groups
    Stockholders
    Employees
    Suppliers of raw materials, etc.
    Union leaders
    Employment agencies
    Chamber of Commerce members
    Service club members
    (Rotary, Kiwanis, Lions, etc.)
Press, Radio, and Television
    Editors of local newspapers
    Editors of county weeklies
    Suburban or community magazines
    Chamber of Commerce paper
    Local radio and television stations
Financial
    Local banks
    Savings and loan associations

    Brokerage offices
    Trustees of estates
Opinion Leaders
    Consumer groups
    Heads of local business firms
    Professional men
    Clergymen
    Officers of fraternal societies
    Women's clubs
    Principals and teachers of high schools
    Business schools
    Colleges and universities
    Leaders of youth groups
    Local librarian
Local Officials
    Mayor or city manager
    Members of board of supervisors

Figure 19-10
Community Distribution Points

Associated Groups
    Agent and representatives
    Dealers and jobbers
    Distributors (wholesale and retail chain
        stores)
    Trade associations
    Business magazines
    Trade magazines
    Advertising publications
    Public relations publications
Financial
    Commercial banks & trust companies
    Investment bankers
    Stock exchange members
    Security Analysts
    Investment Counselors
    Insurance companies
Government Officials
    SEC, ICC, FTC, FCC (as appropriate)

    Depts. of Commerce and Labor
    Library of Congress
    Appropriate Senators & Congressmen
    Governor & Secretary of State where
        incorporated
    Governor and Secretary of State where
        plants are located
Press
    Financial editors
    Business news editors
    Financial writers and colleges.
    Editorial writers
    Press services
Other
    Big city public libraries
    Leading universities and colleges
    Schools of Business Administration
    Schools of Commerce and Finance
    Law Schools

Figure 19-11
National Distribution Points

20

Managing People in the Financial Division

20

Managing People in the Financial Division

‑‑‑

ORGANIZE TO MANAGE

An expert in personnel administration was visiting a client's plant recently. While entering the building, he witnessed an accident in the street. Several employees were also entering the plant and went to aid. He later discovered that of the seven people on the scene two were managers and five were employees from different departments. The predominant action of the rescuers was standing by and watching. Three ambulances were eventually called and none were needed. There was, however, a serious danger of fire but no fire engine was called. Few orders or instructions were given within the group. Those that were given seemed to have no effect on the other six people. Later while working in the plant he noticed several of the same people on the job. Each was performing his job calmly and efficiently. The managers seemed in control of their areas and gave instructions to subordinates frequently and easily. The outsider was struck by the marked difference in the same people outside and inside the plant. The important distinction was that inside the plant the people were organized and outside they were totally disorganized. The difference in performance was spectacular.

What It Means to Organize

On his first day on the job, the new employee knows the importance of organizing. He knows that every other employee except him knows when he should arrive at his work station, what he should do first, how much he should produce, who can help him with problems, and whom to notify in case of unusual situations. The new man's problem is that he doesn't know these things. He is not part of the organization yet. By contrast the worst organizational problems are found in new organizations where all the people are "first day on the job."

371

How to Organize

Since new groupings of people are poorly organized, it seems plausible that the passage of time will solve the problem of newness. Time may improve the organization. Far *more* important than time are the conscious efforts of a manager to do the following:

1. Assign job tasks.
2. Train workers in job tasks.
3. Clarify inter-relationships between job tasks.
4. Explain procedures for exceptional conditions.
5. Set up lines of communication.

Once these basic problems are solved, the organization begins to develop its own personality. From that point on lack of organization ceases to be a problem. A new problem soon replaces it—how to make the organization respond to changes in mission, workload, and other job related factors. Listed below are most frequent causes of organizational strain and how to handle them:

1. *Increase in workload*—The financial organization is called upon to make monthly closings, annual reports, special reports, tax audits, etc. To handle these problems all employees must be well-trained, aware of their responsibility, aware of the need to complete the work, and convinced that the workload is equitably distributed.

2. *Change in procedure or organization.* In contrast to #1 (above), what is required to overcome resistance to change is a flexibility. The discipline called for in #1 is not conducive to flexibility. In fact, it generally produces rigidity. The path to a flexible organization is through constantly informing subordinates about the 'big picture,' building employees' self-confidence and self-awareness, and solving the problems employers bring to their supervisors.

3. *Change in supervisor.* The new financial manager will hear 'But we don't do it *that* way' many times before he is truly in control. His actions, his attitudes, the changes he makes will effect the organization from the moment he takes charge. Before acting he should make a *careful, detailed* survey of the good and bad points of the organization as he finds it before attempting to get things done his way. The most common failing among new supervisors is to complain about the failures of previous supervisors and pay little heed to what positive accomplishments have preceded his arrival. The "savior complex" is to be avoided. The overall financial manager should squelch such talk before it becomes a habit.

4. *Change in personnel.* The loss of trained people often causes shifts in workload, changes in responsibilities, and need for retraining. The most important way to prevent trouble is to cross-train. With adequate back-up in trained personnel, no one employee can cause a hole in the organization. Cross-training also reduces boredom, and gives junior employees a sense of growth within the organization.

LINE AND STAFF IN FINANCE

Applying the concept of line managers and staff is often difficult in the financial group. According to management theory line managers form the skeleton of the organization. They are the people in the chain of command, the people who get the job done. The staff man reports to a line manager and aids him in accomplishing his mission. The staff man is generally a specialist who advises, plans, and coordinates. Within the financial organization the following job titles are generally line managers:

1. Treasurer
2. Controller
3. Chief Accountant
4. Office Manager
5. Payroll Supervisor
6. Payables Supervisor
7. Credit Manager

The following are generally staff:

1. Tax accountant
2. Systems analyst
3. Assistant controller
4. Property accountant
5. Financial analyst
6. Budget analyst
7. Cost accountant

The difficulty with clear definitions of staff positions is that many accounting positions have line responsibilities attached to them. For example, cost accountants turn out regular reports, and direct the cost clerks' activities. The financial manager must be careful to avoid too many hybrid positions in his organization. Instead of combining the best features of line and staff, hybrid positions combine the worst as the following list shows:

1. The managerial burden becomes diffused among several individuals.
2. The specialist becomes entangled in administrative problems.
3. Not enough planning is done.
4. No one individual has time to advise the manager on solutions to problems.

What is Staff?

Described below is the type of work normally produced by a line manager's staff. This is often called Complete Staff Reports.

The line manager or his staff sets priorities and decides which problem will be attacked. A given problem is then analyzed and described. Possible solutions are listed. The resources or costs required for each possible solution are spelled out. The risks of each course of action are set forth. The influence of environment and uncontrollable factors is assayed. Finally, a recommended course of action is set forth. From the first step to the last the presentation is built upon relevant facts. Conclusions point back to the hard facts which were their basis. The analysis does not hedge, does not leave openings for alternate opinions, does not assume that the boss has superior prior knowledge of the facts. It is a logical advocacy of a course of action. It is left for the manager to agree or disagree with the conclusion.

WAGE AND SALARIES IN THE FINANCIAL AREA

Salary Review Must Be Scheduled

The most common management failure in salary administration is lack of consistency. The periodic pre-scheduled conference between the employee and his supervisor is essential. The next step towards consistency comes from insisting that certain subjects be covered in that conference. Companies that install and enforce meaningful salary review programs have less turnover. The program pays off in the following ways:

1. It lets the employee know when and how his performance will be appraised.
2. It reduces confusion in manager-subordinate relations.
3. It keeps open lines of communication (downwards and upwards) in the organization.

With these advantages, the program would seem to be easy to operate. It is not, however, because people fail to follow the rules. In a typical example, a manager will interview an applicant and the applicant will ask when the first salary review will occur. The manager says "Oh, in six months or a year" and drops the subject. At the sixth month point, the employee waits for the manager to make a move. If nothing happens the employee does one or more of the following:

1. Assumes he has performed poorly and thinks he has chosen the wrong job.
2. Assumes that the manager purposely tricked him and that in the future he will trick the manager.
3. Leaves the job.
4. Tells all the other employees about how deceitful "the company" is.

When the problem is brought to a manager's attention, he says one of the following:

1. That he never promised a raise in six months.
2. That he said six months *or* a year and he is taking the other option.
3. That he thought he indicated that raises were given in six months only under exceptional conditions.
4. That the employee is doing poorly and that reviewing the problem with the employee would only aggravate the problem.

The confusion about the promise plus a manager hesitant to take positive action lead to trouble. The burden is upon higher management to see that uniform commitments are made at time of hire and salary reviews take place whether the immediate superior wants them or not.

The close relationship between a superior and subordinate often makes the superior defer conferring with the subordinate about his progress. When conferences do take place, it is common to find that no real communication has taken place. The manager has failed to tell the whole story. To prevent this companies have installed pre-printed forms which the manager fills out and the employee reads and signs. The personnel manager should know the conference schedule and follow up to see that the forms are made out. Figure 20-1 shows a sample Master Salary Review Schedule which the Personnel Manager should keep. An alternative would be to have the schedule under

Dept. No.	Emp. No.	Name	Grade	Date Hired	Date of Last Review	Date of Next Review
47	783	J. Brown	11	11/24/63	12/07/67	12/07/68
47	567	J. Jones	8	04/28/56	04/15/68	10/15/68
47	356	K. Smith	14	05/05/57	07/18/67	07/18/68
47	222	E. Alex	10	09/28/65	10/17/67	10/14/68
49	678	L. Hill	7	06/16/67	06/16/67	06/16/68

Figure 20-1
Master Salary Review Schedule

control of the financial manager or his secretary. Figure 20-2 shows a Performance Review form after completion. Figure 20-3 shows a worksheet to be used in filling out the Performance Review. The Performance Review should be filled out by the manager in advance of the conference. At the time of the conference the manager should read the form to the employee, allowing opportunities for comments and questions. Before concluding the conference the employee should be given the form to read and sign.

THE POWER TO MANAGE

Power is an important cornerstone to managing in an organization. The financial manager can appoint a senior accountant to the position of "Chief Accountant." Does the new appointee then have the power to manage? The answer is no. The man has only been given the *authority* to manage. The authority flows downward in the organization by means of job titles, organization charts, etc. Another ingredient must be added to authority before managerial power is present. This ingredient is influence. Influence is the privilege granted a manager from below—the willingness of subordinates to follow their leader. Influence is intangible and difficult to define. It is that person-to-person feeling which a manager establishes so that the followers will obey him. Different managers establish their influence over subordinates in different ways. The financial manager should be aware of the four cornerstones of influence. These are prerequisites to the power which leads to effective management.

1. Technical competence and knowledge of the managers' and subordinates' jobs.
2. Awareness of what is going on within each manager's area of responsibility.
3. Good lines of communication with the organization. Important messages should flow upwards and downwards in the organization smoothly.
4. Rapport and understanding between superiors and subordinates. The manager must convey to the subordinates a sense of purpose. The subordinate must be able to tell the manager about the problems arising in accomplishing the organization's mission.

Employee **JANE SMITH** Position **COST CLERK**

Date Employed **12/20/67** Date in Position **12/20/67**

A. PERFORMANCE APPRAISAL (Rate the individual by placing a mark in the box which best describes his performance.)

	OUTSTANDING	GOOD	ADEQUATE	INADEQUATE	COMMENTS (Any change in the last 12 mos.)
1. KNOWLEDGE OF JOB—Familiar with the various procedures of the position.	☐	☒	☐	☐	
2. ABILITY TO GET THINGS DONE—Able to complete assigned tasks on time.	☐	☐	☒	☐	AIM FOR BETTER FOLLOW THROUGH
3. JUDGEMENT—Able to grasp facts, interpret and reach correct conclusions.	☐	☐	☒	☐	
4. HANDLING PEOPLE—Able to obtain maximum results from subordinates.	☐	☐	☒	☐	SHOULD RELAX A LITTLE
5. COOPERATION—Responds positively to and works effectively with others.	☐	☐	☒	☐	
6. DEVELOPING SUBORDINATES—Effectively delegates assignments and trains subordinates.	☐	☐	☐	☐	NOT APPLICABLE
7. ACCEPTANCE OF RESPONSIBILITY—Seeks responsibility; willing to assume new duties.	☐	☒	☐	☐	
8. COMPANY LOYALTY—Exhibits positive attitude toward Squibb policies.	☐	☐	☒	☐	
9. CONDITION OF DEPARTMENT—Maintains assigned work area in an orderly manner.	☐	☐	☒	☐	

Figure 20-2
Performance Review Page 1

B. COMPARATIVE RATING (Rate the individual by placing a mark in the box which best describes his performance in comparison with other employees with similar service and experience with Squibb.)   ☐ Outstanding   ☐ Above Average
                       ☒ Average   ☐ Below Average

C. SPECIAL CONTRIBUTIONS (Describe special contributions made during the period. What has he actually done to reduce costs, etc.?) _____

SUGGESTED SEVERAL IMPROVEMENTS

D. PLAN FOR IMPROVEMENT
    1. What are the qualities that are used to the best advantage?_____

DEVELOPED QUICKLY WITH NO PRIOR JOB

EXPERIENCE

    2. What are the qualities that need development or improvement?_____

FOLLOW THROUGH ON UNSOLVED PROBLEMS

E. POSITION STATUS (check one)
    ☐ Employee is immediately promotable_____
                                   (to what position)
    ☐ Employee is eventually promotable_____
                                   (to what position)   (when)
    ☐ Employee is not promotable
    ☒ Decision deferred because employee too new on job

F. REPLACEMENT STATUS
    Who is best qualified to succeed this employee?_____ _NOT APPLICABLE_ _____
    Now?_____ If not, how soon?_____

G. SALARY ADMINISTRATION DATA
    1. Increase recommended: $_____   Type_____   Effective _____
    2. Approved in Manpower Profit Plan $_____   Type _____   Effective_____

H. APPROVALS
    1. Appraisal by_____   Date _____
    2. Reviewed and approved by_____   Date _____
    3. Approved by_____   Date _____
    4. Approved by_____   Date _____
    5. Personnel Department reviewed by_____   Date _____

Performance Review Page 2

Factors for Measuring Performance:

1. Knowledge of Job—Is employee familiar with the procedures required? Does he have the technical know-how and background to be self-sufficient? Are there areas of expertise he has not yet mastered?

2. Ability to Get Things Done—Are assignments completed in a professional manner? Are they completed on time? Are there too many loose ends left hanging?

3. Judgment—Does the employee seek out relevant facts? Do they lead him to proper conclusions? Is the employee decisive.

4. Handling People—Does the employee elicit cooperation from his fellow employees? Does he show proper amounts of courtesy and tact when required? Can he stand up for his rights when he has to?

5. Developing Subordinates—Does he train those people under him properly? Does he delegate responsibility so as to develop stronger subordinates?

6. Accepting Responsibility—Do added duties cause a problem? Will he stand behind his decisions and promises? Will he seek additional responsibility?

7. Company Loyalty—Does the employee have a positive attitude towards the company, its policies, and its management?

8. Condition of Department—Are the work stations under his control kept in a neat and orderly manner?

Figure 20-3
Performance Review Worksheet

INTERVIEWS THAT ACCOMPLISH THEIR GOALS

The manager is called upon to spend considerable time in various types of interviews. The time is well spent if the interview accomplishes its purpose. An employment interview seeks to find out about the applicant, explain the job to him, and help decide if the applicant should be hired. A counseling interview with an existing employee seeks to root out problems, explain policy, and prevent emotional roadblocks from hampering the organization.

The Employment Interview

The employment interview can follow several formats. The more common types are:

Type 1. Patterned based on applicant
Type 2. Patterned with preset questions
Type 3. Non-directive
Type 4. Analytical (in depth)

Type 1. The patterned interview can be done with the aid of an employment application. A filled out sample is shown in Figure 20-4 with circled numbers representing points to be verified. The corresponding numbered questions are shown in Figure 20-5. Some questions may be omitted if no pertinent data appears on the application.

Sample Employment Application

Figure 20-4

NAME (Last, first, middle)
SMITH, JOHN R.

STREET ADDRESS (Under remarks list address(es) for last ten years, if not the same as shown here)
12 GREEN ST.

CITY DAYTON,   STATE N.J.   ZIP CODE

TYPE OF POSITION APPLIED FOR
ACCOUNTING CLERK

WHAT SALARY WOULD YOU ACCEPT

REFERRED TO THIS COMPANY BY (Name of person or employment agency)
STATE UNEMPLOYMENT OFFICE

HEIGHT	WEIGHT				SEX
☐ MARRIED	☐ SINGLE	☐ WIDOWED	☐ DIVORCED	☐ SEPARATED	☐ REMARRIED
					☐ MALE ☐ FEMALE

NO. OF CHILDREN
2

AGES

IF MARRIED, GIVE MAIDEN NAME			
RELATIONSHIP	FULL NAME	BY WHOM EMPLOYED IN U.S.A.	EMPLOYER'S ADDRESS IN U.S.A.
HUSBAND OR WIFE	HELEN K. SMITH	H & H BUTTON CO.	DAYTON, N.J.

1. How long have you lived on Green St.?
2. How do you like Dayton?
   Where did you live before you moved to Dayton?
3. a. Is there a particular part of accounting you are most interested in?
   b. Is there any type of accounting you would not be interested in? Why?
   c. What type of work would you hope to be doing in five years?
   d. If a chance comes up for you to manage other people, would you be interested?
   e. If we found a position in_____ which you seem very interested in but the job was hectic, would you rather try for something else?

Note: The intention is to get the interviewee to express himself, to find out what type of person he is. On the first questions (1 & 2) the interviewee is "cold" and tends to give very guarded replies. As the interviewee warms up, the interviewer should expect his answers to be more open and honest.

4. What did_____ tell you about opportunities here?
5. Where do your children go to school? What grades are they in?
6. How long has your husband/wife worked at_____?

Note: The easiest questions for an interviewee to answer are questions of fact. The more difficult and revealing questions ask for his opinion. When the interviewer senses that the interviewee is hesitating, withholding information, or confused, he should switch back to questions of fact. After the situation is stabilized, he can return to the opinion questions.

Figure 20-5
Sample Questions from Patterned Interview with Application

The interview starts with the top of the application, and ends when the interviewer has reached the end of the application.

Type 2. An interview could be based on a preset series of questions. Most of the questions would be asked irrespective of the answers to previous questions. A sample of such an interview format is shown in Figure 20-6. The interviewer can digress from the prearranged format at any point. He may decide to return to the preset questions later in the interview. Thus the preset interview need not be inflexible. It offers the financial manager the following advantages:

1. Since a manager does not conduct interviews every day, the preset format is a valuable aid to men whose technique may be rusty.
2. Following the format prevents the omission of important questions.
3. With the knowledge of what he will ask next, the manager can concentrate on the answer being given.

Type 3. The non-directive interview has gained in popularity recently. The basic principle is that an interviewee will tell the important facts about himself if simply given the chance. To give him a chance, the interviewer allows the interviewee to choose the topic of conversation. The guidelines for the interviewer are:

1. Do not disagree
2. Do not interrupt

1. Introduction
2. Basic facts
   a. What type of position are you interested in?
   b. Why did you apply here?
3. Personal Data
   a. Are you married?
      How long have you been married?
   b. Where do you live?
   c. How many people do you support?
   d. Who are they?
   e. What do you do with your spare time?
4. Work History
   a. Are you currently employed?
      If yes, why do you want to leave?
      If yes, what kind of work are you currently doing?
   b. With reference to last job
      What was your job when hired?
      What was your job when you left?
      Why did you leave?
      What was your supervisor's title?
      How many people did he supervise?
      Did you like that type of work?
   c. What other jobs have you held in the same line of work?
5. a. Describe Openings Available
   b. Are there any questions about what I have described?
6. Adaptability to Position Opening
   a. Does the position sound like something you would like? Why?
   b. If you had your way, what would you want to be doing five years from now?
   c. Do you mind working under pressure?

Figure 20-6
Preset Interview Format

3. Do not change the subject
4. Listen carefully
5. Empathize with the interviewee
6. Use questions only to clarify what has been said or when the interviewee stops talking.
7. All comments, voice tones, and gestures should invite the interviewee to continue talking.
8. Talk at the interviewee's level and from his point of view.

Since all of the interviewer's attention should be on the applicant, there is no chance to make notes. The interviewer must train himself to retain a comprehensive outline of what transpired and write it down later if possible. The unskilled interviewer is often thrown off by one phrase or statement and misses important facts. In summary, the non-directive interview is deceptively simple. The talker seems to be the performer playing the difficult role. In fact, the listener has the harder task—to absorb and retain what is being said to him. The busy financial manager will find this technique hard to master on a part-time basis. It is recommended that the manager use the non-directive interview only for counseling as discussed below. Uniformity of results can be assured by using standard Interview Rating Records as shown in Figure 20-7. An Interview Rating Record can be used effectively with Type 1 and Type 2 interviews. The interviewer would complete the form in private immediately after the interview. The form has the advantage of standardizing the appraisal of applicants.

Type 4. The probing analytical interview is a professional technique used by psychologists and counselors. If psychological tests are administered, it takes the form of the one hour "chat" with the professional psychologist. It treats the interviewee as a quasi-medical subject and evaluates his mental strength. Its value to the financial manager is only as part of a broader total psychological fitness rating which a consultant provides. Questions such as "Do many people like you?" are not recommended for a line manager talking to an applicant for the following reasons:

1. The answers are too ambiguous and diverse.
2. The interpretation of the answers is difficult, if not impossible for the amateur.
3. The possibility of mishandling such a sensitive interview and irritating the applicant should not be overlooked.
4. The superior-subordinate relationship is distorted during the first meeting.

For these and other reasons the analytical interview should be left to professionals.

The Counselling Interview

The financial manager's position requires that he maintain solid person-to-person relationships with those under him. Lack of time, pressure of events, and changing conditions often cause these bonds to weaken or decay. Eventually the subordinate or superior will sense the need to sit down for a serious talk. The manager's task is to make such sessions productive. Productive does not mean that all differences will be smoothed over. These problems which persist should, at least, be recognized by all parties for what they are. They will, thereby, be kept in a proper proportion. A manager should think of a counselling interview in three phases—the build-up, the transactions, the resolution.

The Building-Up

The subordinate called into the boss's office is wary, alert, and watching for clues. Through his mind run such questions as:

1. Why me?
2. What's happening?
3. What's he got up his sleeve?

Figure 20-7

Interview Rating Record

INSTRUCTIONS: Rate applicant by placing a check in appropriate box for each category.

NAME	DATE
ADDRESS	DATE AVAILABLE
INTERVIEWED BY	POSITION SOUGHT	SALARY EXPECTED

Personal Appearance	☐ EXCELLENT	☐ NEAT	☐ AVERAGE	☐ POOR	☐ UNTIDY
Personality	☐ EXTREMELY PLEASING	☐ LIKEABLE	☐ AVERAGE	☐ POOR	☐ OFFENSIVE
Poise	☐ VERY SELF CONFIDENT	☐ AT EASE	☐ AVERAGE	☐ ILL AT EASE	☐ FIDGETY, EMBARRASSED
Conversation	☐ TALKS VERY EASILY	☐ RESPONSIVE	☐ ORDINARY	☐ NEEDS QUESTIONING	☐ UNABLE TO CONVERSE
Leadership	☐ DEFINITELY A LEADER	☐ GOOD EVIDENCE OF LEADERSHIP	☐ AVERAGE	☐ LIMITED	☐ A FOLLOWER, NO ADMINISTRATIVE CAPABILITIES
Compared to Present Employees in Similar Positions	☐ EXCELLENT	☐ ABOVE AVERAGE	☐ AVERAGE	☐ POOR MATERIAL	☐ NOT NEARLY AS GOOD
Experience and Education for Position Sought	☐ HIGHLY QUALIFIED	☐ VERY WELL QUALIFIED	☐ BASICALLY QUALIFIED	☐ MUCH TO LEARN	☐ ENTIRELY LACKING
Over-All Evaluation	☐ EXCELLENT PROSPECT	☐ GOOD PROSPECT	☐ AVERAGE PROSPECT	☐ FAIR PROSPECT	☐ NOT SUITABLE

GENERAL COMMENTS *(Use reverse side if necessary)*

RECOMMENDATIONS

	SIGNED

ACTION TAKEN

DIAGRAM OF THE STRUCTURE OF AN INFORMAL GROUP

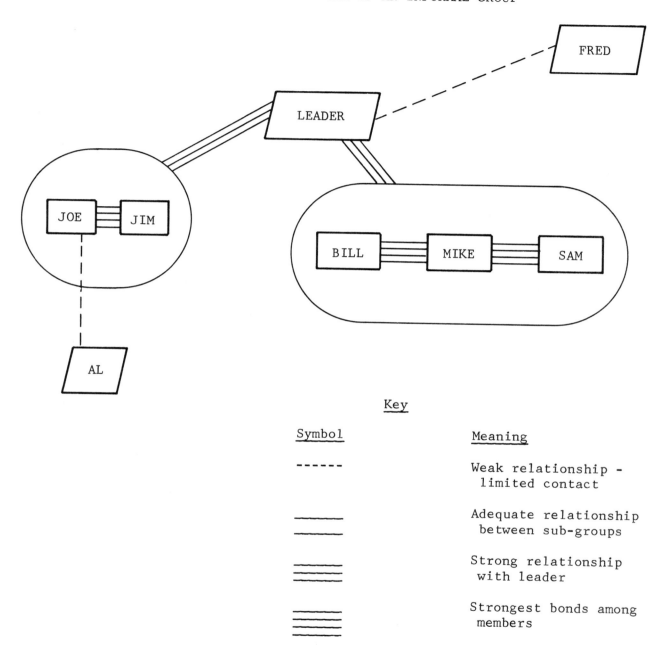

Key

Symbol	Meaning
------	Weak relationship - limited contact
————	Adequate relationship between sub-groups
═══	Strong relationship with leader
≡≡	Strongest bonds among members

Figure 20-8
Diagram of the Structure of an Informal Group

In this state of mind no communication can take place. The build-up must accomplish two things:

1. Define a purpose for the meeting which the interviewee understands.
2. Establish rapport with the interviewee. The interviewee's curiosity and anxiety must be dealt with first. The manager should explain the purpose of the talk. The real purpose might upset the interviewee. Shown below are typical choices which leave room for covering the specific issues later in the interview:
   A. The annual budget is coming up and it would be a good idea to review our problems and progress.
   B. We are reviewing the work flow in the whole plant. I thought we'd talk it over and see if we can come up with some ideas.

Establishing rapport can be a difficult task. Rapport is a state of emotional equilibrium. Two individuals are emotionally in tune, when rapport exists. In some cases it can be established with a brief exchange, a joke, a laugh, a smile or a complaint. Other individuals can never establish more than the weakest relationships. The financial manager in a counselling interview is faced with a dilemma. One hour or more of general conversation may be required to establish contact with a truculent accountant. Spending the time must be weighed against the loss of valuable executive time. If the time is not spent the interview will not bear fruit. The manager doesn't want to waste time, but how should he avoid it?

Often the first stage of the interview turns into a protracted ventilation as the employee explains all his frustrations, desires, fears, preferences, etc. The manager must listen carefully and respond to it in an understanding manner. When interrupted or cut off while explaining what is important to *him,* the employee knows the manager isn't interested. Establishing rapport takes effort. The manager must work at it. He should listen carefully and ask relative questions.

Transactions

After considerable effort the interview will reach the stage where the business at hand can be transacted. To the manager it often seems an uphill battle, listening to a worker's fantasies, frustrations, fears, and boasts. However, the time and effort are well-spent if a serious exchange can then take place. Exchange is the important concept. The manager should bring the conversation to a specific topic. By presenting the manager's viewpoint, listening carefully to reactions, and responding honestly, the interviewer can communicate with the interviewee. Up to this point the interview has been non-directive. At this point the manager injects his personality and opinions— not to override the subordinate, but to express his honest opinion.

In explaining himself the manager may find it advantageous to avoid strong authoritarian statements. The subordinate may interpret these as orders and limit his responses to simple yeses.

Resolutions

The conclusion of the interview is a crucial phase. These problems brought up in the first two phases must be resolved. Possible resolutions are:

1. A course of action chosen.
2. A need for further information noted.
3. Agreement made to discuss it again.

The decisions on how to resolve the problems discussed should be joint decisions. The interviewer may sense that the interviewee shys away from involving himself in these decisions. The interviewer can resolve the problem himself or defer action by agreeing to continue discussion later. The danger of deferring too many questions is that no timely action may be taken on any of them.

The salient features of counselling interviews should be kept in mind.

1. They start out non-directive but change to directive when real issues are discussed.
2. They are time-consuming and should not be attempted if the time is not available.
3. They require at least one good listener—the superior.
4. They must result in purposeful conclusions agreed to by both parties.

GAINING INSIGHT INTO HUMAN RELATIONS

Apart from the formal structure which shows up on the organization charts a manager is faced with a labyrinth of informal structures with which he must deal. To deal with human problems a manager relies on his knowledge of people as emotional creatures. Two important tools are presented in this section—the needs hierarchy and the informal groups.

Needs Hierarchy in the Modern Office

Psychologists and researchers have pointed to a phenomenon called "The Needs Hierarchy" or "The Ladder of Needs" to explain some human behavior. A worker is viewed as having the following five levels of desires which he as a human being wants to satisfy:

1. Security of life and limb
2. Security of food and shelter
3. Social acceptance by other people
4. Social recognition of superiority by other people
5. Fulfillment of his inner dreams

Once he satisfies his requirements for a lower need (Number 2, for example) he concentrates all his energy on the next need (Number 3). If that need is eventually satisfied, he moves up to the next level (Number 4). However, if a lower level (Number 3) were later threatened, he would forget about striving upwards (Number 4) and spend all his efforts on the lower.

Applying this to current problems leads to some interesting conclusions such as:

1. Everyone is now relatively free from the threat of violence.
2. Most productive people in business have come to take for granted the availability of food and shelter.
3. Because of 1 & 2 (above) there is no way to threaten a worker with withdrawal of the first two basic needs.
4. Therefore, concepts of authoritarianism are outmoded since workers won't respond to such primitive threats.
5. The worker in the typical office environment of today seeks the gratification of friendship and rewards of superior achievement (Needs # 3 & 4).
6. Since he is still the emotional creature he was when he spent his time protecting his life and food supply, he is trying just as hard to gain Needs # 3 & 4 as he did to gain Needs # 1 & 2.

These conclusions help explain the strong emotional forces at work in an office today. Managers are often amazed at irrational acts, jealousies, outbursts, etc. which result from seemingly minor events in an office. People are capable of very strong responses when they sense that their needs are not being satisfied. In the past, some supervisors thought that "a good bawling out in front of everybody will teach them all a lesson." Few managers today will attempt such a confrontation since most workers will give up a job rather than have their social standing undermined.

Another important change is found in workers seeking higher levels of satisfaction. A man seeking food, shelter, or physical security is dealing with tangible things. A man dealing in friendship, esteem of his fellow workers, or dream fulfillment is dealing in intangibles. Thus, the man himself is much more apt to become confused about whether he is achieving his goals. The manager must be careful to understand what the worker sees as his problems. Taking the worker's point of view, no matter how irrational it may seem to the manager, is the only way to understand what is going on.

Applying Needs Hierarchy to Specific Problems

The following example is designed to illustrate the insight gain from the Needs Hierarchy.

Mr. Jones, the office manager, was having trouble with two cost clerks, Smith and Brown. Smith was amiable and easy to talk with, but had lower output than the other workers. He was inclined to be careless and made more than his share of errors. Although Jones would not want to dismiss Smith, he wished he could motivate him to try harder. Jones knew that Smith was an amateur mountain climber and had attained fame for his achievements in mountain climbing and rescue work. Jones also noticed that Smith seemed to have strong friendships outside the company but was not closely allied with anyone in the office.

Brown was a very hard worker and took the job quite seriously. When things went wrong in other parts of the company which affected the cost department, Brown became quite frustrated. He often took work home with him. Brown tried very hard to maintain friendships with fellow workers. His fierce attitude about the job, however, scared most people away. Jones found himself constantly trying to soothe Brown and prevent him from stirring up arguments with other workers and departments. Brown was a fast and accurate worker but needed a lot of close attention.

Analysis of Smith. The 'underinvolved' worker is a common problem. Smith's needs hierarchy was stable and easily satisfied. Smith derived his social satisfaction from off-the-job situations. Furthermore, he had achieved notoriety and self-fulfillment in his outside activities. If Jones could have watched Smith mountain climbing on weekends, he would have seen an involved motivated man. Jones' problem is to find ways for Smith to achieve social rewards on the job. Those friendships which Smith has should be encouraged by change in work assignments, etc. Once Smith is involved he will be easier to handle.

Analysis of Brown. Brown is the exact opposite of Smith. Brown is too dependent on his job for needs satisfaction. Brown probably views himself as a superior worker. When job-related problems come up, he is willing to risk alienating friends and co-workers to protect his concept of superior job performance. Typically, Jones would find that Brown's life off the job was a dull and uninteresting routine. This, of course, was causing him to strive even harder to fulfill his needs on the job.

INFORMAL GROUPS ON THE JOB

People are very adept at organizing themselves into groups. Without any instructions or commands, human beings can group together into informal groups. Informal groups are self-sufficient entities. They have their own leader, their own group values, and code of behavior. They also assign "problem" members to special roles of isolant and deviant. To understand the informal group, a manager must first accept the following definitions:

1. *The Informal Group.* Any group of three or more people who have a patterned social relationship among themselves.
2. *The Informal Leader.* The member of the group who makes the group's decisions, sets group goals, and generally handles the leadership role.
3. *The Group's Values.* Those beliefs which are commonly held by all members of a group. Common examples in an office would be "We never volunteer for overtime," "People who voluntarily chat with bosses are apple polishers," "We all think the fringe benefits are pretty cheap."
4. *Isolant.* A group member who keeps his contact with the group to a minimum without completely breaking away. This may be a self-imposed role or the group members may avoid contact with the isolant.
5. *Deviant.* A group member who chooses to violate the group's values or code of behavior. Examples would be as follows:

    A. A member who constantly engaged the boss in small talk and is overly friendly towards him.

    B. A member who openly criticizes the actions of the group leader.

Groups react to deviants by punishing them in any of the following ways:

1. Avoiding contact (forcing the deviant to become an isolant)
2. Insulting him
3. Attempting to lower his status in the group
4. Disagreeing with everything he says

Appraising Groups in the Office

The best way to discover a group's structure, values, leader, etc. is to observe members interacting with one another. In the social context each time one person talks to another, asks a question, or tells a joke he reinforces the group structure. Therefore, the person talked to the most is the group leader. A closer look will show that the leader is most often asked questions, sought for advice, or complimented in some way. Knowing the leader makes it easier to name all the other group members. Isolants are generally easy to recognize because of their very limited social role. Deviants can be identified by their non-typical actions or by the disciplinary measures imposed on them by the groups.

A diagram of the group is often useful in analyzing group structure. Such a diagram is shown in Figure 20-8. Al is shown as a low-status member of the group and has limited contact with other members. Most of his contact is with one member—Joe. Joe and Jim are shown as a sub-group which simply means that these two have a particularly close relationship. Another sub-group of three people is shown. Typically, sub-groups compete with each other for the attention, time, and preferential treatment of the leader. Fred is shown as an isolant and probably a deviant also. What contact he has with the group is limited to contact with the leader. Since he is causing the groups problems as a deviant the strongest member, the leader, has been given the job of dealing with him. Another possible situation would be for a sub-group to become deviant and isolated. When this happens, there is a danger that the group will break apart. The leader's job is to reconcile differences between sub-groups and prevent further difficulty.

Practical Problems Stemming from Group Problems

The effect of human problems on the organization can be quite profound. For example a manager may find that one clerk has not told another about a group of invoices that were supposed to be processed several weeks earlier. By viewing the people as an informal group, the manager would find that the uninformed clerk is an isolant-deviant. The discipline imposed by the group could have gone so far as to stop all communications with the isolant-deviant—even important job information!

Another example would be the new manager who can't seem to get control of his work group. From the informal group point of view a manager would realize that he had passed over the information leader of the group to appoint a man the group considered a stranger. The group will show its loyalty to *their* leader by resisting the new leader. If the informal leader leads the group in undermining the new supervisor, the resistance will be even more difficult to overcome.

The manager has many options available to him to overcome problems caused by the informal group. Some possibilities are:

1. Alternate work assignments to change the structure of the group.
2. Selectively apply rewards and punishments to alter the group's values.
3. Attempt to disband the group by transferring or dismissing the leader (However, the group will quickly choose a new leader).
4. Try to promote the leadership jobs only to the informal leaders of the groups.

In summary, the manager must deal with people as he finds them—individuals with needs, aspirations, likes, and dislikes.

Index